THIRD EDITION

Scenic Routes & Byways

OREGON

TOM BARR

gpp®

travel

Guilford, Connecticut

All the information in this guidebook is subject to change. We recommend that you call ahead to obtain current information before traveling. Globe Pequot Press assumes no liability for accidents happening to, or injuries sustained by, readers who engage in activities described in this book.

To buy books in quantity for corporate use or incentives, call **(800) 962-0973** or e-mail **premiums@GlobePequot.com**.

All photos by Tom Barr unless otherwise noted.

Editor: Kevin Sirois
Project Editor: Lynn Zelem
Layout: Casey Shain
Maps: Trailhead Graphics © Morris Book Publishing, LLC

ISSN 1549-540X
ISBN 978-0-7627-7956-7

Printed in the United States of America
10 9 8 7 6 5 4 3 2 1

CONTENTS

The Scenic Routes & Byways

ABOUT THE AUTHOR

Tom Barr is the author of *Unique Arizona, Unique Georgia,* and *Unique Washington: A Guide to the State's Quirks, Charisma, and Character* and has written the text for two photo books, *Portrait of Oregon* and *Portrait of Washington.* He lives in Marysville, Washington.

ACKNOWLEDGMENTS

Scenic Routes & Byways Oregon is the work not of a single person but of many. My thanks to Globe Pequot for giving me the opportunity to update it and to Kevin Sirois for guiding it through the production process. Many organizations listed in Appendix A: For More Information played important roles in helping me update this book by providing information, answering my e-mails, and, in some instances, reviewing chapters and referring questions to others who they felt had more direct knowledge of the routes, communities, and attractions that were being updated. I thank them for their time and for going beyond my expectations.

INTRODUCTION

On travel posters Oregon is often depicted as an isolated image of towering mountains surrounded by lush forests and rushing streams. That is but one image, for in Oregon you will find a coastline with some of the earth's most spectacular scenery, the magnificent Columbia River Gorge, deserts filled with sagebrush, unspoiled wilderness, fertile farmlands, vineyards, and orchards.

This is land created by uplifting and volcanism, sculptured by ice, and refined by water and wind. The Cascade Mountains extend north to south, forming a giant natural wall that divides the state and dictates its climate by trapping moisture-laden clouds from the Pacific Ocean. West of the mountains lie verdant valleys, lush forests, and rich farmlands.

East of the Cascades the landscape turns to high desert, scattered forests of ponderosa pine, grasslands and cattle ranches, and deep canyons. The Blue Mountains stand isolated and soar into the sky from flat plains. In the northeast corner the Wallowa Mountains contain some of the state's most magnificent scenery and are often compared to the Swiss Alps.

In Oregon nature has created a diverse landscape and climate ranging from rain forests to arid desert. Nature's violence has moved and uplifted mountain ranges; cut deep gorges; created Fort Rock, Crater Lake, and Newberry Crater; and left as reminders of its awesome power unusual geologic formations like Hole-in-the-Ground, Crack-in-the-Ground, Abert Rim, and Winter Ridge.

Crisscrossing the land are rivers celebrated in history and legend. The Columbia, which forms the northern border, was the river of exploration. Oregon Trail immigrants farmed the rich lands along the Willamette and made it the river of settlement. Others, such as the Snake, Rogue, Umpqua, and Deschutes, have acquired reputations for their breathtaking scenery, fishing, and whitewater rafting.

The land and water provide habitats for a vast array of wildlife. Forests and mountains are home to deer, elk, bears, cougars, and raccoons. Beavers and otters inhabit riverbanks, and along marshes and the shore you'll see thousands of ducks and geese, plus great blue herons, several species of cranes, woodpeckers, and bald and golden eagles. Forests of Douglas fir, ponderosa, and lodgepole pine blanket mountain ranges and tower over oaks, alders, and vine and big-leaf maples. Myrtlewoods stand in clusters near the coastline. In the Columbia River Gorge, the

Overview

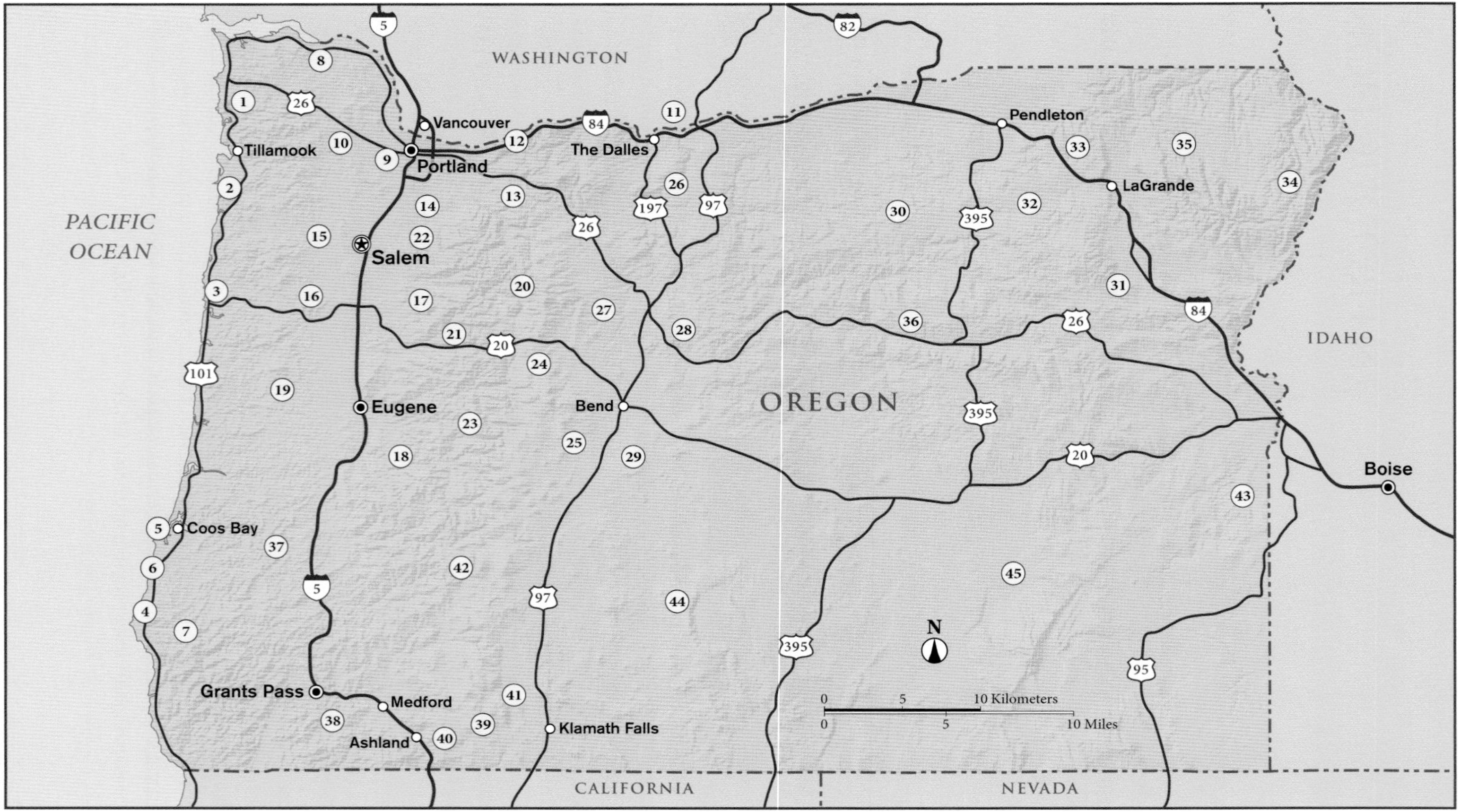

WASHINGTON
IDAHO
PACIFIC OCEAN
OREGON
CALIFORNIA
NEVADA
Vancouver
Portland
Tillamook
Salem
Eugene
Coos Bay
Grants Pass
Medford
Ashland
Klamath Falls
Bend
The Dalles
Pendleton
LaGrande
Boise
N
0 5 10 Kilometers
0 5 10 Miles

Among the ships you can see at the Columbia River Maritime Museum are historic craft on permanent display, sternwheeler sightseeing vessels, and a passing parade of Columbia River traffic.

Kalmiopsis Wilderness, and southern Oregon's Table Rocks are plants that grow only in these protected spots.

Oregon's shoreline was explored by Sir Francis Drake, Captain James Cook, and other seafarers. Lewis and Clark, trappers, and mountain men followed the Columbia River to the sea. In the 1840s pioneers by the thousands endured the hardships of the Oregon Trail to claim the rich lands of the Willamette Valley. They were followed by miners, merchants, ranchers, and timber men. Their legacy lives on in tales of lost gold mines and lost wagon trains and in sprawling ranches, historic districts, towns, and cities.

Scenic Routes & Byways Oregon invites you to explore Oregon's magnificent scenery. The 45 drives take you from the rockbound coast to the high desert, into the Columbia River Gorge, through rugged canyons, and to mountain lakes. The drives cover the Oregon coast from the Washington to California borders. You can discover the Columbia River Gorge on a historic highway that is considered an engineering masterpiece, travel by several waterfalls, or see views from the gorge's rim.

Flowers at Shore Acres State Park were brought by ship's captains from around the world.

Several drives cross portions of the Oregon Trail. Others take you to gold rush towns, museums, and historic sites. You can also select drives into the high Cascades, through lava beds, around mountain peaks, by wildlife refuges, and into national forests, parks, and monuments. En route you'll find roadside waterfalls, cascading streams, scenic overlooks, botanical gardens, mountain lakes, and desert reservoirs.

Along these drives you'll find attractions for children, outstanding camp-grounds, fishing streams, and spots for sailboarding, hang gliding, and whale watching. With *Scenic Routes & Byways Oregon,* you can take a romantic stroll on a black sand beach by a chalky white cliff or watch blazing sunsets and winter storms in the shadow of a historic lighthouse. Other drives will guide you to trail-heads leading into the Three Sisters Wilderness, to the rim of Crater Lake, inside Newberry Crater, and to the beautiful headwaters of the Metolius River. If you're adventurous, you can take a jet boat ride on the Wild and Scenic Rogue River or ride a cliff-hugging dirt road into the heart of Hells Canyon to the rim of the deepest gorge in the continental US.

The depth of 1,932 feet and the clarity of its water create Crater Lake's sapphire blue color.

Most of these drives were created by local chambers of commerce and regional tourism divisions. With two exceptions, all are paved: The Bandon-Powers-Gold Beach Loop contains approximately 10 miles of gravel and is normally passable with a family car; the 24 miles from Imnaha to Hat Point is often rough and should not be attempted with a low-clearance vehicle. Since unpaved surfaces change with the season and some paved roads are closed in winter, check road conditions before you depart for these areas.

While *Scenic Routes & Byways Oregon* provides a comprehensive introduction to the state's scenery, it is by no means all-inclusive. To cover all of Oregon's scenic roads would fill another book.

The drives included here range from 5 to 325 miles in length. Some are perfect for an afternoon getaway or a weekend side trip, or you may wish to include several as part of an extended vacation. Regardless of which drives you select, you'll find them a rewarding experience.

Rocky south coast shoreline offers fascinating sea life in tide pools, along with foaming surf, crashing waves, and interesting geologic formations.

How to Use this Book

Scenic Routes & Byways Oregon describes 45 highway and back-road drives throughout the state. Each drive description is complemented with a map showing the route, campgrounds, special features such as historic sites, recreation areas, connecting roads, and nearby towns.

The descriptions are divided into the following categories.

General Description provides a quick summary of the length, location, and scenic features of the route.

Special Attractions are prominent, interesting activities and features found along the route. Additional attractions are included in the description. Some activities, such as fishing and hunting, require permits or licenses that must be obtained locally.

Location gives the area of the state in which the route is located.

Drive Route Number includes the specific highway names and numbers on which the drive travels.

Travel Season notes whether the specific route is open all year or closed seasonally. Some highways are closed to automobiles in winter due to snow but are open for snowshoeing, cross-country skiing, and snowmobiling. Opening and closing dates are approximate and subject to regional weather variations. Always check local conditions.

Camping includes listings of all state park, state forest, national forest, national park, and Bureau of Land Management campgrounds along the route.

Services list communities with at least a restaurant, groceries, lodging, phone, and gasoline.

Nearby Attractions are major attractions or activities found within 50 miles of the scenic drive.

Appendix A: For More Information lists names and contact information of organizations that provide detailed information on the drive and its attractions.

The Route provides detailed traveler information, along with interesting regional history, geology, and natural history. Attractions are presented in the order a traveler encounters them when driving the route in the described direction. If you travel the route from the opposite direction, simply refer to the end of the route descriptions first.

Interstate Highway/ Featured Interstate Highway	——⑨⓪—— / ——⑨⓪——	
US Highway/ Featured US Highway	——〈89〉—— / ——〈89〉——	
State Highway/ Featured State Highway	——〈22〉—— / ——〈22〉——	
County Road/ Featured County Road	——[42]—— / ——[42]——	
Local Road/ Featured Local Road	——————— / ———————	
Trail	- - - - - - - - - - - - - -	

Bridge	⁀	Museum	🏛
Building/Structure	■	Pass	) (
Campground	▲	Point of Interest	▫
Capital	✪	Route Number	⑩
City	◉	Small State Park, Wilderness or Natural Area	♠
Dam	—		
Lighthouse	⛄	Town	○
Lodge	⛏		
Mountain, Peak, or Butte		▲ *Black Butte*	
River, Creek		~~~~~~~~~~	
Body of Water		⬭	
State Line		- · · - · · - · · - · · - · · - · · - ·	
State Forest		▭	
National Forest		▭	
Wilderness Area		▭	
Other Designated Area		▭	

Northern Oregon Coast

General Description: A 115-mile drive on a paved highway along the northern coast through resorts, picturesque oceanside communities, and forests.

Special Attractions: Historic sites, spectacular scenery, outstanding seafood, Lewis and Clark National Historical Park, Seaside, Cannon Beach, Haystack Rock, 15 state parks and waysides, lighthouses, whale and storm watching in season, camping, fishing.

Location: From Astoria to Lincoln City.

Drive Route Number: US 101.

Travel Season: All year. Frost and snow are rare. Winter mornings bring heavy fog.

Camping: 5 state park campgrounds, 3 USDA Forest Service campgrounds, plus numerous private RV parks.

Services: Full services are available at major cities along the route.

Nearby Attractions: Washington's Long Beach Peninsula, Lower Columbia River, Lewis and Clark National Wildlife Refuge, Camp 18 Logging Museum.

For More Information: Astoria/Warrenton Area Chamber of Commerce, (503) 325-6311, (800) 875-6807, www.oldoregon.com; Seaside Visitors Bureau, (503) 738-3097, (888) 306-2376 (USA), www.seasideor.com; Cannon Beach Chamber of Commerce, (503) 436-2623, www.cannonbeach.org; Nehalem Bay Area Chamber of Commerce, (503) 368-5100, (877) 368-5100, www.nehalembaychamber.com; Rockaway Beach Chamber of Commerce, (503) 355-8108, (800) 331-5928 (USA), www.rockawaybeach.net; Tillamook Chamber of Commerce, (503) 842-7525, www.gotillamook.com; Lincoln City Visitor and Convention Bureau, (541) 996-1274, (800) 452-2151 (USA), www.oregoncoast.org.

The Route

The 363 miles of US 101 from the Astoria Bridge to the Oregon-California border have been designated the **Pacific Coast Scenic Byway** by the US secretary of transportation. Because it contains multiple qualities that exist nowhere else and is considered a destination unto itself, it has also been designated an All-American Road. On the northern Oregon coast, US 101 starts as a joint highway with US 26 in downtown Astoria at the **Megler-Astoria Bridge.** This is also the departure point for visits to **Lewis and Clark National Historical Park,** which is spread in 12 sites along approximately 40 miles of southwest Washington's **Long Beach Peninsula** and south along the northern Oregon shoreline to **Ecola State Park.** Washington sites include the **Cape Disappointment State Park Interpretive Center, Fort Columbia State Park, Station Camp,** and **Dismal Nitch.** Continuing south, US 101 is framed by forest on the east while offering intermittent views of coastline and small communities on the west. South of Seaside the highways divide as US 26 extends east to Portland. US 101 continues south, skirts

Northern Oregon Coast

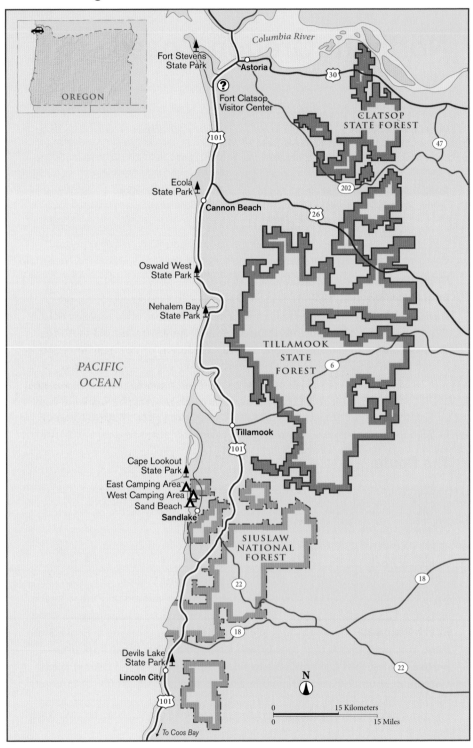

Tillamook Head, weaves by **Arch Cape** and **Cape Falcon,** and curves along the shores of Nehalem and Tillamook Bays. After turning inland for 24 miles, it returns to the coast near **Neskowin,** then travels through forest on the final few miles to **Lincoln City.**

Allow more time than you think you'll need; leisurely travel is virtually a necessity. The scenery is spectacular. Traffic is usually heavy, even on weekdays, and the narrow two-lane road has an abundance of curves.

Travelers will find mild temperatures throughout the year. Summer days are usually in the 60- to 70-degree range. While winter days also reach into the 60s, sun is limited. December and January bring heavy rains and morning fog. The calmest weather usually comes in autumn.

Astoria

Astoria is the oldest American settlement west of the Rocky Mountains. Established in 1811 by John Jacob Astor as a fur trading post, it has evolved into a bustling seaport of 10,000 people. At Coxcomb Hill overlooking the city, coast, Columbia River, and mountains, the area's history spirals around 128-foot-high **Astoria Column** in a pictorial frieze. You can see dozens of Victorian homes on residential drives and step into an 1890s parlor at the restored **Flavel House,** built by a sea captain and converted into a museum. The **Columbia Maritime Museum,** 6 blocks east of the bridge on US 30, interprets a rich seafaring history with ship models, fishing equipment, interactive exhibits, the bridge from a Fletcher-class destroyer, and the **Lightship *Columbia,*** which is a National Historic Landmark.

Although the coast appears ageless, the section between the Columbia River and Tillamook Head is an infant in terms of geologic time. Astoria's sandstone base was deposited about 20 million years ago. Sand dunes extended to near Tillamook head until the 1930s, when European bunch grass and shrubs were planted to halt their progress.

Crossing **Young's Bay,** 3 miles south of town, US 101 leads west to **Warrenton, Fort Stevens State Park,** and east to **Fort Clatsop National Memorial.** Warrenton is a center for deep-sea fishing and charter boats and also has moorage and other facilities for private crafts.

Fort Stevens

Clatsop Indians inhabited this area for thousands of years before befriending and trading with Lewis and Clark. **Fort Stevens** dates to the Civil War. It was the only fortification in the continental US fired on by the Japanese in World War II. The spot where the shells landed is marked near the access road. Restored Civil War earthworks, original World War II gun batteries, a memorial rose garden, a replica of a Clatsop Indian longhouse, and a museum can be toured. Near the shoreline parking area and campground, surf washes against the rusting ribs of the **Peter Iredale**—Oregon's most visible shipwreck. From the campground, with its 174 full-hookup, 302 electrical, and 6 tent sites, and 11 deluxe cabins, you can explore the beach, hike to a small lake, and fish the surf.

Lewis and Clark on the Coast

Fort Clatsop is the historical park's main Oregon visitor center. Children enjoy exploring a replica of the log fort that served as the 1805–1806 winter quarters for Lewis and Clark's Corps of Discovery. A marked nature trail leads through a rain forest to a landing on the **Lewis and Clark River,** where several replicas of Indian canoes are displayed. A 6.5-mile **Fort to Sea Trail** begins here and ends at **Sunset Beach,** where the explorers hunted and gathered seafood.

Seaside, at mile 17, has been a popular resort for more than 100 years. You can learn about Pacific Ocean sea life at an aquarium, see a replica of the salt cairn where Lewis and Clark's expedition boiled sea water to make salt, and take a 2-mile stroll along its famous beachfront promenade.

Ecola State Park, 4 miles south, marks the southernmost point explored by Lewis and Clark. There is a good chance of seeing deer roaming the grounds and sea lions and birds on offshore rookeries. The scenery can be enjoyed from 6 miles of sandy beaches surrounded by steep cliffs and offshore rocks and on trails through a forest and atop **Tillamook Head.** Hikers have a choice of several treks, including an 8-mile segment of the Oregon Coast Trail that is also part of the Lewis and Clark National Historic Trail. A 2-mile loop trail winds through large Sitka spruce en route to a hike-in camp situated on Indian Creek. A 1.5-mile hike to the beach is a favorite for birders and tide-pool exploration.

As you approach **Cannon Beach,** watch for a replica of a ship's cannon west of the highway. From the roadside you'll also see **Haystack Rock** rising from the shore as a black bullet-shaped dome. At 235 feet, it is the world's third-largest freestanding monolith, a protected bird sanctuary, and among the coast's most photographed sites. The beach connecting the rock to the south part of town is often filled with kite flyers, sunbathers, beach tricycles, and sand castle builders.

During the next 30 miles, US 101 passes nine parks and waysides, crosses four rivers, and meanders through five beachfront towns. You can view the spectacular rocks, headlands, and open beaches from atop roadside viewpoints or at park shorelines. Depending on the site, you can explore sea caves, search for agates, stroll a secluded beach, hike into forested mountains, launch your boat, or ride a horse. Anglers have a choice of casting into surf or stream from a jetty, beach, or boat. The

The Wreck of Peter Iredale *at Ft. Stevens State Park is Oregon's most famous and most photographed shipwreck.*

rewards are usually superb catches of silver and chinook salmon, cutthroat trout, and steelhead. At low tide you also can gather clams and catch crabs. Several roadside villages feature an abundance of antiques and crafts shops, galleries, and restaurants.

Continuing South

Oswald West State Park is situated 4 miles south of Cannon Beach in a rain forest of massive spruce and cedar trees. In the park you can hike part of the Oregon Coast Trail and take a short walk to the tip of **Cape Falcon.**

Continuing south, a series of jagged mountain peaks dominate the eastern horizon. Many are former volcanoes that erupted under the ocean. The most prominent, **Neahkahnie Mountain,** erupted about 20,000 years ago and may have been an offshore island.

At **Nehalem** the route jogs inland around the secluded bay. **Nehalem Bay State Park,** on the south shore, caters to horseback riders and bikers with equestrian trails, camps, and corrals; a 1.5-mile bike trail; and a 60-site hiker/biker camp. Along with 265 electrical hookup sites, there is a meeting hall and a fly-in camp.

Rockaway Beach, 10 miles south, stretches along the highway in a string of weathered but well-maintained hotels. It is a popular weekend retreat for those

who wish to kick back and look out at vast expanses of waist-high beach grass, sandy shorelines, and arched offshore rocks.

From **Garibaldi,** 5 miles south, the road skirts the eastern shore of Tillamook Bay and touches the western tip of the **Tillamook State Forest.** A huge cement smokestack serves as sole reminder of Garibaldi's past as a bustling mill town. The **Garibaldi Museum,** across the highway by the smokestack, is devoted to Captain Robert Gray, who discovered the Columbia River and named it after his ship.

Tillamook

Cheese has made **Tillamook** world-famous. The Tillamook Cheese Factory on US 101 features historical exhibits, a gift shop, and a cafe. A full-scale replica of the commercial sailing ship *Morning Star*—the first chartered vessel in the Oregon Territory—is displayed at the cheese factory. The chamber of commerce shares the factory parking lot and has detailed information on local sightseeing, camping, and outdoor recreation. Downtown the **Pioneer Museum,** housed in a former courthouse, is known for its natural history displays.

At Tillamook you have a choice of either staying on US 101, which jogs inland for 24 miles before continuing along the ocean at Pacific City, or enjoying the magnificent scenery of the 38-mile **Three Capes Scenic Loop** through Capes Meares, Lookout, and Kiwanda. One state park campground with 38 hookups and 173 tent sites and 3 forest service campgrounds featuring 141 sites are situated along the loop.

On US 101 you'll pass a blimp hangar built during World War II. At 1,038 feet wide and 190 feet high, it is the world's largest wooden structure and home of the **Tillamook Air Museum,** which displays over two dozen vintage aircraft from World Wars I and II and a Russian Mig from the Korean conflict. This section also provides access to Trask River salmon, steelhead, and trout fishing. Two short trails take you from the roadside to 266-foot-high **Munson Falls,** the highest falls in the Coast Range.

A paved forest service road near the community of **Hebo** winds up the forested slopes and past a scenic lake to the summit of 3,154-foot **Mount Hebo.** The area is known for its outstanding views of forest and ocean, plus hiking, fishing, and nature study of rare silver-spot butterflies and wildflowers. You can also camp in 15 forest service sites in **Hebo Lake Campground,** which has toilets and drinking water.

From **Pacific City,** US 101 crosses the small inlet of **Nestucca Bay,** then opens onto vistas of serene beaches and headlands as it continues through the

Haystack Rock, Route 1, draws beachcombers, sand castle builders, photographers, wildlife watchers, and tide pool explorers.

US 101 hugs the cliff sides of the northern coast's Cape Falcon, offering panoramic views of the Pacific Ocean coastline.

family resort area of **Neskowin.** Near Neskowin you enter the western edge of the **Siuslaw National Forest.** Short roads branch from the highway to Cascade summit, Nature Conservancy, and Harts Cove Trail.

Cascade Head Experimental Forest, 1 mile south of Neskowin, is situated in a scenic rain forest. At 1,770 feet, Cascade Head is the coast's highest headland. More than 230 bird and 56 mammal species have been sighted in the 10 square miles of Sitka spruce and cliff-top meadow.

North of Lincoln City, US 101 intersects OR 18, which crosses the Coast Range to McMinnville, Newberg, and Salem. A short scenic side trip begins at East Devil's Lake Road, skirts the 5-mile-long lake, and ends in Lincoln City. **Devil's Lake State Park** offers fishing, boating, and picnicking. Twenty-eight full-hookup sites and 54 tent sites, plus a hiker/biker camp, are on a shoreline surrounded by thick pine forest.

Lincoln City sits about a mile south of the 45th parallel, equidistant between the equator and the North Pole. Entering town, you'll cross the D River. At less than 1 mile long, it is the world's shortest river. Easy access to surf fishing, championship kite flying competitions, and a variety of antiques, crafts, and art galleries make Lincoln City a favorite vacation and weekend getaway destination all year.

2

Three Capes Scenic Loop

General Description: A 38-mile signed drive on a paved highway along bays, wildlife refuges, and 3 scenic capes.

Special Attractions: Historic sites, spectacular coastal scenery, 3 state parks, Sand Dunes Recreation Area, lighthouses, wildlife, Octopus Tree, Oregon Islands National Wildlife Refuge, Three Arch Rocks National Bird and Sea Lion Refuge, hang gliding, sailboarding, fishing, hiking, camping.

Location: Oregon coast between Tillamook and Pacific City.

Drive Route Name: Three Capes Scenic Loop Highway.

Travel Season: All year. Winter storms can cause hazards from falling trees and blinding rain. If the day is foggy, delay your trip or you'll miss the most spectacular scenery.

Camping: 1 state park campground, 3 forest service campgrounds, plus several private RV parks.

Services: Full services at Tillamook. Limited services at Oceanside, Netarts, Sandlake, and Pacific City.

Nearby Attractions: Munson Creek Falls, Mount Hebo Recreation Area, Trask River, Oregon North Coast and Central Coast Scenic Drives, Depoe Bay, Newport.

For More Information: Tillamook Chamber of Commerce, (503) 842-7525, www .gotillamook.com; Cape Lookout State Park, (503) 842-4981, (800) 551-6949, www .oregonstateparks.org.

The Route

The drive starts in downtown **Tillamook** at the junction of US 101 and Third Street. Following **Three Capes Scenic Loop** signs west, travelers skirt scenic **Tillamook Bay** and **Bayocean Spit,** then take **Cape Meares Loop Road** through a mixed forest to the cape summit. Descending to near sea level at **Oceanside,** the route curves around **Netarts Bay** and through old-growth forest to **Cape Lookout.** Taking Cape Lookout Road south through Sandlake's dunes, it passes the entrance to the varicolored sandstone cliffs of **Cape Kiwanda State Park,** then finishes with ocean views as it passes through **Pacific City.**

During summer travelers will enjoy balmy, pleasant days in the 60s and 70s. Although winter days also reach into the 60s, fog and rain often obscure the scenery. Most of the 100 inches of rain the area receives falls between November and March.

Three Capes Scenic Loop

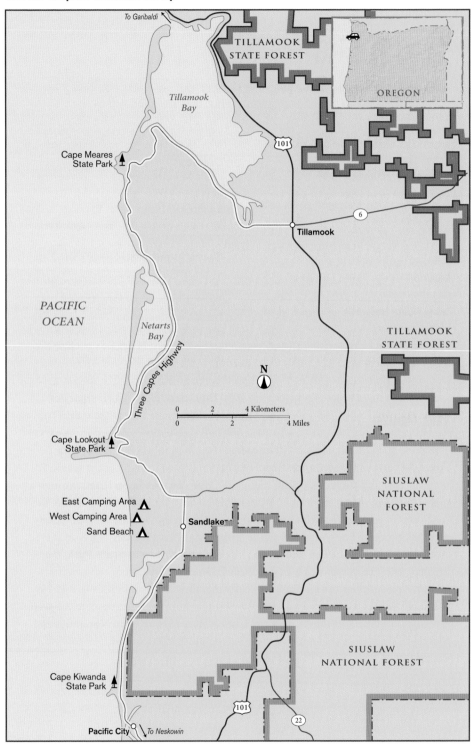

Land of Many Waters

The name Tillamook was derived from an Indian word meaning "land of many waters." Several rivers meander through Tillamook County and empty into the ocean near the city. They offer good clamming, crabbing, and fishing. Bird watching, hunting, sailboarding, and hang gliding are also popular.

Tillamook County Pioneer Museum, on Second Street 1 block east of US 101 and Third Street, occupies the former courthouse. It contains one of the state's best exhibits of natural history. Gun collections, Native American artifacts, a stagecoach, a pioneer home, antique toys, and a full-size forest fire lookout station are also displayed.

The cheese that has made the county world famous can be sampled at the **Tillamook County Creamery Association factory,** 2 miles north on US 101. The creamery shares a parking lot with the Tillamook Chamber of Commerce and a full-size replica of the first chartered ship in the Oregon Territory.

Leaving Tillamook, the route passes a marina, RV park, and public boat launch. Staying at water level, the highway winds around oak-covered cliffs and **Tillamook Bay,** where morning haze often evokes serenity as it cloaks land and water in various shades of blue. Low scrub brush–covered headlands enclose the bay on the north, and small islands protect the entrance.

Watch for birds as you turn south on **Bayocean Road,** for 250 species have been sighted in this area. From 1920 to 1950 **Bayocean Spit,** which separates Tillamook Bay from the Pacific Ocean, was the site of a resort community. Over the years it was washed into the sea by shifting sands, water, and winds. The spit offers a wide sandy beach and a jumble of driftwood washed ashore by tides. It also has a boat launch and good jetty fishing.

Cape Meares

After 2 miles the route turns inland and begins a short climb through a thick forest to **Cape Meares State Park.** The park extends from the summit to the shoreline several hundred feet below. It includes 138 acres of old-growth Sitka spruce and western hemlock, sandy beaches, and vertical sea cliffs. The cliffs and forest provide nesting areas for tufted puffins, pelagic cormorants, and pigeon guillemots. The area is protected as Cape Meares National Wildlife Refuge. Both Cape Meares and Cape Lookout are composed of basalt from volcanoes that erupted about 15 million to 20 million years ago.

You may see some of the wildlife on a short section of the Oregon Coast Hiking Trail that cuts through the woods near the parking lot and runs along the cliff's edge. It also winds by the **Octopus Tree,** which is an easy 100-yard

The Octopus Tree (depicted), a lighthouse, offshore islands, and ocean views are among the highlights at Cape Meares State Scenic Viewpoint.

walk from the parking area. This giant Sitka spruce was once featured on *Ripley's Believe It or Not.* The tree has a base circumference of about 50 feet.

Six candelabra limbs about 12 feet around extend 30 feet horizontally from the main trunk and then turn upward. The candelabra branching and unusual size were formed by strong coastal winds and abundant rain. Hikes into the cool, moist rain forest are often rewarded with displays of sunlight filtered through fog.

Walk west from the parking lot on a paved path, and you'll see the giant lens of **Cape Meares Lighthouse** seemingly suspended in space. The path extends to the base of the lighthouse on a ledge below. At 38 feet high it is the West Coast's shortest lighthouse. Built in the 1880s, it is inactive but open to visitors from May to September. The one-ton hand-ground lens was manufactured in Paris, shipped around Cape Horn, and lowered onto the 200-foot cliff with a special hand-operated crane made of local spruce trees. Despite all the planning and preparations, a legend persisted for a number of years that the lighthouse had been built on the wrong cliff.

The 38-foot tower of the Cape Meares Lighthouse is the shortest on the Oregon Coast.

Oregon Islands National Wildlife Refuge

From the lighthouse cliff you have a spectacular view of the Pacific Ocean below: crashing waves, sheer cliffs, sandy beaches, and the offshore rocks and reefs of the **Oregon Islands National Wildlife Refuge.** The refuge is part of a network of 1,400 offshore promontories along 300 miles of the Oregon coast that provide breeding and resting areas for seabirds and marine mammals. Because the wildlife is easily disturbed, the refuge is closed to public use.

A trail, protected by cyclone fencing, stays within inches of the cliff's edge as it leads east from the lighthouse into the forest along a small lake and down to the shore lined with sea caves filled with driftwood. The lake attracts boaters and water-skiers. Surf anglers, sailboarders, picnickers, and agate hunters congregate on the shoreline.

A few miles south of the park, the highway descends to superb near-sea-level scenery at Oceanside, which offers excellent beachcombing, hang gliding, and surf fishing. The coast's largest concentration of **tufted puffins** gathers offshore on the **Three Arch Rocks National Bird and Sea Lion Refuge.** About 75,000 common murres, pigeon guillemots, storm petrels, cormorants, and gulls nest on virtually every available ledge. Look for sea lions on the lower rocks.

About 3 miles south, the route winds around **Netarts Bay,** affording magnificent views of rugged black offshore rocks. **Netarts,** a prime clamming, crabbing, and surf-fishing area, provides ocean access with the only boat ramp along this section. The nearby **Whiskey Creek Fish Hatchery** is operated by a Tillamook anglers club to help maintain fish populations. Facilities, leased from Oregon State University, include a picnic area, hiking trails, and a viewing area where you can watch returning chum salmon.

Cape Lookout

From Netarts the highway traverses through 5 miles of mixed forest to **Cape Lookout State Park,** where rugged cliffs, sandy beaches, and unspoiled Netarts estuary come together. The 1,974-acre park, set in a coastal rain forest of Douglas fir, western hemlock, red alder, and Sitka spruce, serves swimmers, sand castle builders, and anglers who cast into the surf for perch and other bottom fish. More than 150 species of birds have been sighted, and thousands of California murres nest here. Seventeen miles of trails meander through the forest and along the shore. A brochure identifies plants and trees on the 2.5-mile **Cape Trail,** which takes you through the woodlands to the tip of the basaltic cape.

Geologists have concluded that the cape is a remnant of several ancient lava flows. Some parts are solid rock and appear to have cooled on dry land. Other sections contain rounded or billowing rocks called pillow basalts, which were formed underwater.

The promontory is pocked with small coves on its north flank, while the south face rises as a sheer precipice from the sea. From the tip you can see Tillamook Head 42 miles north and Cape Foulweather 39 miles south, with the Falcon, Meares, and Cascade Head Capes in between. Some of the 38 full-hookup and 173 tent sites offer beachfront views. Other facilities include a hiker/biker area, a group camp, 6 deluxe cabins with bathrooms, kitchens, and TV, and day-use and picnic grounds.

Five miles south of Cape Lookout, the route enters a tip of the Siuslaw National Forest, then quickly leaves the tree-lined corridor. Dunes flank the highway, and sand drifts across the road. Dune buggy and all-terrain vehicle tracks crisscross the 5-square-mile **Sand Dunes Recreation Area.** You're likely to see kites and hang gliders soaring above and brightly colored sailboards in Sand Lake and eight other recommended sailboarding sites. The lake is frequented by trout, salmon, and steelhead anglers. Near the beach, the East and West Camping Areas are open all year and contain a total of 140 sites. **Sand Beach** is near the highway and has 101 sites and a dump station; the campground closes in winter. The campgrounds are operated by the forest service.

A few miles south, the **Clay Myers Natural Area** on **Whalen Island** is bordered by the **Sand Creek estuary** and has over a mile of beach, acres of wooded uplands, grassland, and tidal marsh. You can see the estuary from a 1.5-mile Island Loop Trail while watching for possible sightings of otter, deer, and birds.

Cape Kiwanda

The highway briefly turns inland and back to forest as it winds south to **Cape Kiwanda.** Photographers from around the world have been challenged to capture on film the brilliant red-and-yellow sandstone cliffs and spectacular wave action. Hang glider enthusiasts launch from the huge dunes, which extend from its eastern slope into the pine forest. On the south side, short trails lead around the summit and down to tide pools at the base of steep wave-washed cliffs. Like Cannon Beach, Cape Kiwanda has a **Haystack Rock,** which rises dramatically out of the surf a few hundred yards offshore. Without the rock to protect it from the pounding of the ocean, Cape Kiwanda's soft cliffs would already have been ground into sand.

Cape Kiwanda has been the local dory-launching site since the 1920s. It is the only spot on the Pacific coast where these picturesque fishing boats launch into the surf. The open-topped, double-ended boats can usually be seen on any calm day between Memorial Day and Labor Day, trolling for chinook and silver salmon or working the reefs around Haystack Rock for bottom fish. Cape Kiwanda's waters and shorelines also yield clams and crabs.

At **Bob Straub Wayside,** walk over it and see picturesque **Nestucca Spit** separating the bay from the ocean where the route reaches Pacific City. You can park in front of a sand dune. In this fishing village without wharfs, docks, or piers, virtually everyone owns a dory. Some are available for charters. On one-day trips you may land chinook and silver salmon or ling cod, bass, red snapper, and other bottom fish. The town also offers good opportunities for whale watching, clamming, crabbing, sailboarding, and seeing wintering geese.

A mile east of Pacific City, the route concludes as it reaches a junction with US 101.

3

Central Oregon Coast

General Description: A 123-mile drive along the central Oregon coast shoreline and sand dunes, affording spectacular views from water level and ridgetops.

Special Attractions: Depoe Bay, Cape Foulweather, lighthouses, Newport, Darlingtonia State Wayside, Sea Lion Caves, Oregon Dunes National Recreation Area.

Location: Central Oregon coast between Lincoln City and Coos Bay.

Drive Route Number: US 101.

Travel season: All year.

Camping: 4 state park campgrounds with full hookups and 2 with electricity. 19 forest service campgrounds with fire pits, picnic tables, and either flush or vault toilets; some with water. Numerous private RV parks.

Services: Full services at Lincoln City, Newport, Waldport, Florence, Reedsport, North Bend, and Coos Bay. Limited services at Depoe Bay, Yachats, Winchester Bay, and Gardiner.

Nearby Attractions: Oregon North Coast and South Coast Scenic Drives, Three Capes Scenic Loop.

For More Information: Lincoln City Visitor and Convention Bureau, (541) 996-1274, (800) 452-2151 (USA), www.oregoncoast .org; Depoe Bay Chamber of Commerce, (541) 765-2889, (877) 485-8348, www .depotebaychamber; Greater Newport Chamber of Commerce, (541) 265-8801, (800) 262-7844 (USA), www.newport chamber.org; Waldport Chamber of Commerce, (541) 563-2133, www.waldport chamber.com; Yachats Area Chamber of Commerce, (541) 547-3530, (800) 929-0477, www.yachats.org; Florence Area Chamber of Commerce, (541) 997-3128, www.florence chamber.com; North Bend Information Center, (541) 756-4613, www .northbendcity.org/north_bend_oregon_ information-center.htm.

The Route

US 101 stays close to the ocean on the 123 miles between Lincoln City and Coos Bay. It begins with water-level rocky coves and bays, then ascends **Cape Foul-weather** and descends to scenic beaches and thick brushy hills. South of Waldport it follows the base of hills, makes a steep ascent over **Cape Perpetua,** sweeps down to rugged shorelines, and runs through the heart of the **Oregon Dunes National Recreation Area.**

Weather is usually mild, with spring days in the 50s and summer days averaging 60 to 70 degrees. Though winter days can also reach the 60s, temperatures average in the low 50s. Fall is the most dependable season for calm, warm weather.

At **Lincoln City** you'll find 7 miles of beach, the greatest number of hotel rooms between San Francisco and Portland, and numerous shops specializing in coastal crafts and recreation equipment. **D River Wayside,** downtown, overlooks

Central Oregon Coast

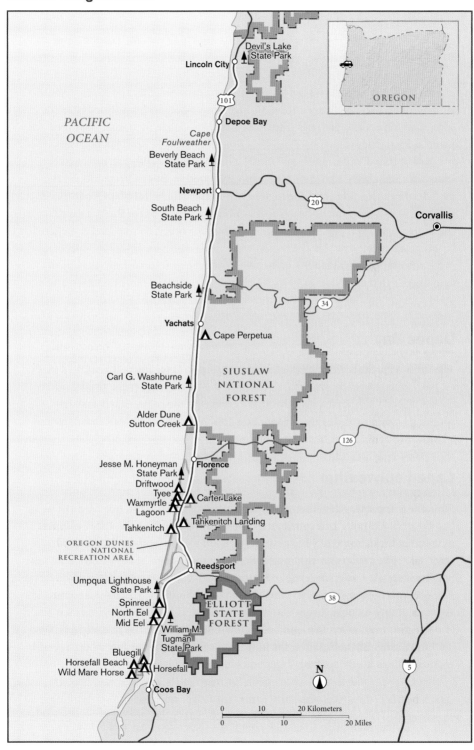

PACIFIC OCEAN

OREGON

Lincoln City

Devil's Lake State Park

101

Depoe Bay

Cape Foulweather

Beverly Beach State Park

Newport

20

Corvallis

South Beach State Park

Beachside State Park

34

Yachats

Cape Perpetua

SIUSLAW NATIONAL FOREST

Carl G. Washburne State Park

Alder Dune Sutton Creek

126

Jesse M. Honeyman State Park

Florence

Driftwood
Tyee
Waxmyrtle
Lagoon

Carter Lake

Tahkenitch Landing

Tahkenitch

OREGON DUNES NATIONAL RECREATION AREA

Reedsport

Umpqua Lighthouse State Park

38

Spinreel
North Eel
Mid Eel

ELLIOTT STATE FOREST

William M. Tugman State Park

Bluegill
Horsefall Beach
Wild Mare Horse

Horsefall

Coos Bay

5

N

0   10   20 Kilometers

0   10   20 Miles

the world's shortest river, which is less than a mile long. **Scenic Devil's Lake State Park,** nearby, includes campgrounds with 28 full hookups and 55 tent sites.

Lincoln City is becoming a center for glass-art lovers. With help from an experienced glass artist, you can blow your own paperweights and vases at some studios. Others teach glass painting, fusing, mosaics, and other techniques and several boutiques and galleries display, sell, and specialize in unique glass products made at local studios.

Siletz Bay, 7 miles south on US 101, contains high-yield crab beds and is known for its salmon and steelhead fishing. **Gleneden Beach Wayside,** on the bay's south shore and across the highway from the deluxe **Salishan Resort** and golf course, is a convenient beach access. **Fogarty Creek State Park,** a mile farther, offers a sandy creek for wading, shorelines for ocean fishing, and a sheltered beach picnic area.

At **Boiler Bay Wayside,** 3 miles south, you can see the rusting remains of a ship's boiler that exploded in 1910. The bay is a designated marine garden and a good spot for watching migrating whales and winter storms.

Depoe Bay

You cross a classic concrete arched bridge at **Depoe Bay,** where the world's smallest harbor encompasses six square acres and shelters a picturesque fishing and charter fleet. When waves rush through a crevice in the rocky basalt coastline, a spouting horn near the bridge produces spectacular geysers of seawater. Migrating whales are often sighted near the shoreline.

Cape Foulweather

For a short and exceptionally scenic side trip along Otter Crest, leave US 101 at Rocky Creek Wayside and continue to **Cape Foulweather.** The cape is a jumble of volcanic rocks, some of which erupted underwater and others on dry land. It emerged above sea level with the rising of the Coast Range island—around 20 million years ago. It was discovered and named by Captain James Cook in 1778.

From the visitor center, 453 feet above the rocky shore, you have a commanding view of tiny hilltop villages and miles of coastline. With binoculars you may also see cormorants, sea lions, and other wildlife on offshore rocks and reefs. **Devil's Punchbowl State Park,** on the loop, features a marine garden, a beach, and a rock formation where seawater boils and churns at high tide.

Yaquina Head Lighthouse, on the central Oregon coast, was built in 1873 and is the last example in Oregon of a combined keeper's quarters and lighthouse tower.

The portion of US 101 that bypasses Otter Crest meanders through forested highlands to **Beverly Beach State Park.** The park has a sandy shoreline and marine fossils impregnated in rocks. A campground with 128 tent, 75 electrical, and 53 full-service hookups, plus primitive and group camps, is situated in a forest of Douglas fir overlooking the beach.

About 5 miles south is **Yaquina Head Lighthouse,** built in 1873 and still operating. From its headland, which is the last remnant of a volcano, you can see a variety of shorebirds on the cliffs and rocks, and during migrations glimpse whales in the waters below.

Newport

At **Newport,** 4 miles south, US 101 passes a junction with US 20, which links the coast to Toledo, Philomath, Corvallis, and Albany. Wide shorelines have made Newport a year-round playground for surfers, scuba divers, anglers, and clam and Dungeness crab gatherers. Agate collectors comb beaches for the semiprecious stones uncovered by waves.

Several attractions are situated on or near US 101 in Newport. **Yaquina Bay State Recreation Area's lighthouse,** built in 1891, is Oregon's last example of a combined keeper's quarters and lighthouse tower. It exhibits 1800s furnishings, is open daily except holidays, and is available for private tours by prior arrangement. **Old Town** bayfront encompasses commercial and charter-fishing docks, an undersea garden, and a wax museum. South of the bay, the **Mark O. Hatfield Marine Science Center** showcases a variety of marine life and has special handling pools for children. At the **Oregon Coast Aquarium** next door, visitors can view sea life and demonstrations on the 29-acre site landscaped with native flora. The nearby **South Beach State Park** provides 227 electrical campsites and contains a variety of coastal plant species.

Ona Beach State Park, 8 miles south of Newport, is a departure point for kayakers, canoeists, and birders who paddle upstream to the **Beaver Creek Natural Area** to spot bald eagles, blue and green herons, and various other birds. The seven miles between Ona Beach and Waldport offer access to sandy beaches, rocky shorelines, and fishing from trails at **Seal Rock State Park** and **Driftwood Beach Wayside.** North of Waldport, US 101 crosses Alsea Bay and a junction with Highway 34, which extends east through the coast range to Philomath.

The bay and **Waldport** area are favorites of surf and freshwater anglers, as trout, salmon, and bay and razor clams are caught here. On the bay's south end, exhibits at **Alsea Bay Historic Interpretive Center** depict the history of transportation and the coastal highway system. At **Beachside State Recreation Site,**

3 miles south of Waldport, 32 electrical and 42 tent sites, as well as a hiker/biker camp, are scattered along the shoreline.

On the 35-mile section south to Florence, the highway cuts through some of the central coast's best scenery. It enters the Siuslaw National Forest, passes 13 state parks and waysides and 5 forest service campgrounds with a total of 243 sites.

Yachats

The picturesque village of **Yachats,** 8 miles south of Waldport, sits on an ancient beach line and is a favorite weekend retreat, renowned for spring-summer smelt runs, beaches for rockhounding, and rocky promontories offering dramatic views of churning surf. The name is a Native American word meaning "at the foot of the mountain" and refers to nearby **Cape Perpetua.** Atop the 803-foot cape, also named by Captain Cook, you'll find a visitor center and several trails. They lead through some of Oregon's largest spruce trees to a 37-site forest service camp-ground and **Devil's Churn,** where tides rush through a shoreline channel, offering outstanding views of the rocky coastline.

Neptune State Park is about a mile south of the cape and displays a forest of windswept trees. Elk often wander into **Carl G. Washburne Memorial State Park,** a few miles farther south, where 58 full hookup and 7 walk-in tent sites are situated close to tide pools.

Sea Lion Caves

Sea Lion Caves, a mile south, is one of the world's largest sea caves and the only mainland home of the **Stellar sea lion.** For a small admission, you can watch them sunning themselves on the rocky bluffs and take an elevator 208 feet down to their cavern, which is 12 stories high and as long as a football field. From the cavern's natural window, you have an outstanding view of **Heceta Head Light-house,** sitting on a bluff across a forested bay.

Darlingtonia State Wayside, 5 miles north of Florence, is named after a car-nivorous plant. A 0.5-mile trail meanders through bogs of the insect-eating plants, which are also called **cobra lilies.**

In north **Florence** US 101 junctions with OR 126, a two-lane highly scenic route to Eugene. A turn west at the junction takes you to the 1-mile **Siletz River Estuary Scenic Drive** and to the ocean beach or south to Florence's Old Town waterfront. Its former factories and commercial businesses house many small arts and crafts shops and a variety of restaurants.

Oregon Dunes National Recreation Area

Florence is the northern gateway to the **Oregon Dunes National Recreation Area,** which stretches south 47 miles along the coast. The dunes were once sedimentary rock, which was eroded away by waves. Some are moving north from 6 to 18 feet per year, burying trees and filling small lakes that were created when the sand dammed small streambeds. About half of the 14,000 acres of dunes—some over 500 feet high—are open to off-road vehicles. While dune buggy driving, hiking, and horseback riding are popular, the area is also a favorite of sailboarders, flower lovers, anglers, and shellfish collectors. Cutthroat trout, salmon, and steelhead inhabit rivers; trout, bass, catfish, bluegill, and perch are found in local lakes.

Jessie M. Honeyman Memorial State Park, 3 miles south of Florence, is known for its wild rhododendrons and magnificent white dunes that slope down to several freshwater lakes. Facilities include an outdoor theater, boat ramps, bathhouses, 47 full hookup, 121 electrical, and 187 tent sites.

At **Oregon Dunes Overlook,** midway between Florence and Reedsport, your view encompasses miles of pine forest, dunes, and the ocean. For a closer look at the landscape, take the hiking trail through the wildlife habitats: forest, grassland, beach, marsh, and dunes. Seven forest service campgrounds provide 264 sites. Trails from the campgrounds meander through the dunes to beaches and scenic viewpoints and border small lakes that are open for fishing.

Reedsport & Continuing South

At **Reedsport** US 101 meets OR 38. It parallels the Umpqua River east to the historic community of Scottsburg, then joins I-5 near Drain. **Dean Creek Elk Viewing Area,** about 7 miles east of the junction, contains a resident herd of **Roosevelt elk,** which can be seen from the roadside. The **Oregon Dunes National Recreation Area headquarters** is located on US 101 in Reedsport and offers a 20-minute film on the dunes, plus information on various recreational opportunities including dune buggy rides, tours, hikes, beachcombing, camping, and fishing.

Winchester Bay, 4 miles south, houses one of Oregon's largest sport-fishing charter fleets at **Salmon Harbor.** The Umpqua and Smith Rivers, which form the bay, are reliable springtime bass fisheries. From mid-February through mid-May, operators also offer whale-watching trips.

Umpqua Lighthouse State Park, near an operating lighthouse, has 20 full hookup and 24 tent sites by a forest, small lake, and sand dunes.

Three forest service campgrounds south of the park offer 115 sites. **William A. Tugman State Park,** near Lakeside, contains 94 electrical sites, 16 yurts, and a hiker/biker camp.

From **Lakeside,** on the shores of Ten Mile Lake, the route continues south through 6 miles of forest and dunes. Four forest service campgrounds at the southern dune area boundary provide 135 sites surrounded by sand dunes.

The drive concludes by crossing **Coos Bay** over the **McCullough Memorial Bridge** and entering **North Bend.** At 5,305 feet long, it is the longest coastal bridge. Its distinctive architectural and decorative features include a 1,709-foot cantilever truss main span flanked by a series of 170- to 265-foot concrete arches.

4

Southern Oregon Coast

General Description: A 115-mile drive along the southern Oregon coast, with its magnificent beaches and forested hills.

Special Attractions: Bandon waterfront, Cape Blanco, Prehistoric Gardens, Battle Rock, Cape Sebastian, Rogue River, rugged coastline parks, storm and whale watching.

Location: Southern Oregon coast between Coos Bay and the California border.

Drive Route Number: US 101.

Travel Season: All year. Winter storms are major attractions. January and March are prime months for watching migrating whales.

Camping: 4 state park campgrounds with full hookups and 2 with electricity, plus private RV parks.

Services: Full services at Coos Bay, Bandon, Gold Beach, and Brookings. Limited services at Langlois, Port Orford, Wedderburn, and Pistol River.

Nearby Attractions: Oregon Dunes National Recreation Area, Golden and Silver Falls State Park, Oregon Central Coast Scenic Drive, Charleston Harbor/Seven Devils Loop Drive, Bandon Scenic Ocean Views Drive, Bandon/Rogue River/Gold Beach Scenic Loop, California Redwoods, Smith River Scenic Byway.

For More Information: Bay Area Chamber of Commerce, (541) 226-0868, (800) 824-8486 (USA), www.oregonsadventurecoast .com; Bandon Chamber of Commerce, (541) 347-9616, www.bandon.com; Greater Port Orford and North Curry Chamber of Commerce, (541) 332-8055, www.discover portorford.com; Gold Beach Visitors Center, (541) 247-7526, (800) 525-2334 (USA), www.goldbeach.org; Brookings Harbor Chamber of Commerce, (541) 469-3181, (800) 535-9469, www.brookingsor.com.

The Route

South of Coos Bay, US 101 parallels **Isthmus Slough** for a few miles, then cuts southwest over wooded hills to **Bandon.** Traversing flat and rolling hills, it moves inland through thick forest, flanks mountains, and descends along magnificent shorelines to **Gold Beach.** Climbing **Cape Sebastian**'s western slopes, the scenery reaches its zenith in a series of state parks with spectacular views of deep ravines, offshore rocks, and inlets. The south coast is the heart of myrtlewood country. At roadside shops and factories, you can watch craftsmen shape the distinctive hardwood, carving out dishes, jewelry, and figurines.

The south coast enjoys Oregon's mildest climate. Near the California border, summerlike weather is common early in the year as winter days rise into the 70s and 80s. Summer temperatures climb to over 90 degrees. Most of the annual 70 to 90 inches of rain falls between November and April. Frost is rare, and snow is virtually unknown. The mild weather produces Christmas camellias, flowering

Southern Oregon Coast

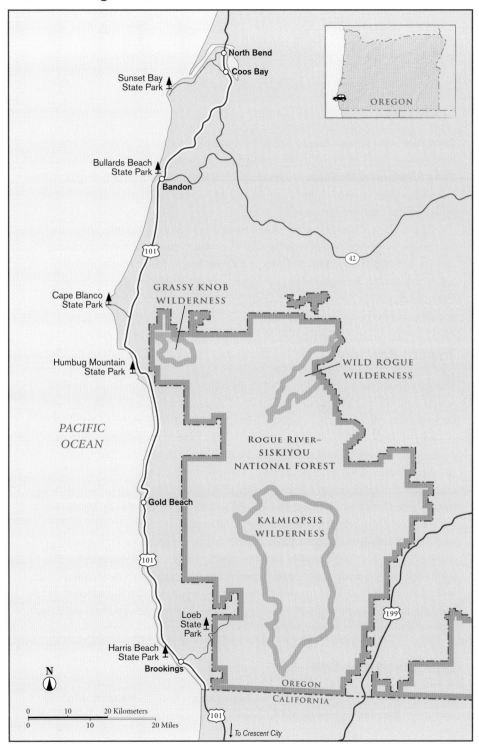

OREGON

North Bend

Coos Bay

Sunset Bay
State Park

Bullards Beach
State Park

Bandon

101

42

GRASSY KNOB
WILDERNESS

Cape Blanco
State Park

WILD ROGUE
WILDERNESS

Humbug Mountain
State Park

ROGUE RIVER–
SISKIYOU
NATIONAL FOREST

PACIFIC
OCEAN

Gold Beach

KALMIOPSIS
WILDERNESS

101

199

Loeb
State
Park

Harris Beach
State Park

Brookings

N

OREGON

CALIFORNIA

0   10   20 Kilometers

0   10   20 Miles

101

To Crescent City

plums, and daffodils in January and magnolia, azalea, and rhododendron displays in late winter. Look for palm trees, eucalyptus, and towering redwoods near the California border.

Coos Bay

Coos Bay is the world's largest lumber shipping port and the largest natural harbor between San Francisco and Puget Sound. On or near US 101, you can visit the **Coos Historical & Maritime Museum** and the **Marshfield Sun printing museum** and tour a Coast Guard cutter at a roadside dock. Local industries offer tours of mills and myrtlewood factories.

The 40-mile **Charleston Harbor/Seven Devils Scenic Loop** is accessible by traveling west from either North Bend or Coos Bay. It offers the superb coastal scenery of **Sunset Bay, Shore Acres** and **Cape Arago State Parks,** and the 4,400-acre **South Slough Estuarine Sanctuary. Bastendorff Beach County Park** features 74 water and electric and 25 tent campsites. Sunset Bay has 29 full-hookup, 34 electrical, and 66 tent sites.

Toward Bandon

Between Coos Bay and Bandon, US 101 meanders through a series of low hills, which were formed 40 million to 50 million years ago when sand and mud were deposited near the shore. They contain coal that was mined in the early 1900s. Although all traces of mining have virtually disappeared, coal seams still remain, possibly along with oil and natural gas. Five miles south of Coos Bay, US 101 intersects with **OR 42,** a scenic but slow route through Coquille, Myrtle Point, and Coast Range forests to I-5 near Roseburg. After 2 miles of angling southwest through the Coos County Forest on US 101, a turn west onto **Seven Devils Road** takes you to a sandy beach at **Seven Devils Wayside.**

At **Bullards Beach State Park,** 4 miles south, photo and informational displays in the restored **Coquille Lighthouse** highlight coastal shipwrecks. The 1,266-acre park spreads over several miles of shoreline and impressive sand dunes and contains 104 full-hookup and 81 electrical campsites and a horse camp. A 1.5-mile hiking path and 7 miles of horse trails invite exploration of several expansive beaches and impressive sand dunes.

Bandon-by-the-Sea

Cheese, cranberries, and winter storms have brought fame to **Bandon,** which is also called **Bandon-by-the-Sea.** Old Town, at the waterfront, is the departure point for boating and fishing and for the 5-mile **Bandon Ocean Scenic Views Drive** that heads west past the Coquille River Museum to spectacular natural rock pillars.

Between Bandon and Port Orford, 26 miles south, you will travel inland by **Ocean Spray's cranberry bogs** past dairy and sheep farms, over rolling plains, and through fir forests. The coast, seen in glimpses, lies 2 to 6 miles west. Diversified recreation includes a wild-game park where children can pet and feed some of its 400 exotic animals, sailboarding at **Floras Lake,** and quiet walks along secluded beaches at **Paradise Point State Park.** From July through October rare **brown pelicans** feed along the **Elk River.** The nearby Sixes River and the Elk are both productive trout, salmon, and steelhead streams.

Cape Blanco Lighthouse & Port Orford

At the community of **Sixes,** take a side road west to **Cape Blanco Lighthouse** and **Hughes House.** Built in 1898, the two-story, 11-room Victorian home was part of a 2,000-acre ranch. The 1878 lighthouse still operates and is the most westerly lighthouse in the contiguous 48 states. From adjacent **Cape Blanco State Park,** you have sweeping views of rocks and beaches, a 7-mile horse trail, and 150 acres of open riding range. The campground has 53 electrical sites, 4 cabins, a horse camp, and a 3-mile trail winding down to chalky white cliffs and a black sand beach.

At **Port Orford,** 4 miles south, you are in the nation's westernmost incorporated city. In 1851 it became the south coast's first settlement when a blockhouse was built to protect homesteaders from hostile Native Americans following a skirmish at the oceanfront monolith of Battle Rock. Today **Battle Rock City Park** is a short stroll from the highway and a picture-perfect setting for picnics, sunbathing, and swimming. Sweeping views of the southern coastline await visitors who walk to the top of the often-photographed rock.

The Port Orford area also attracts ocean scuba divers, Floras Lake sailboarders, and Elk River and Sixes Rivers fly fishers.

The geologic history of the south coast is dramatically different from that of the northern and central shoreline. Rocks on the south coast are much older, having been laid down as sediments about 100 million to 200 million years ago. Afterward, the oceanic crust shifted and they were twisted, crystallized, and thrust up against the Coast Range.

South of Port Orford the highway climbs through a lush Douglas fir rain forest and follows a thin stream along the north base and eastern edge of **Humbug Mountain,** a gravel conglomerate deposited over 100 million years ago. A steep 3-mile path to the 1,756-foot peak starts at the highway near **Humbug Mountain**

State Park and rewards the hardy with a panoramic view that extends into California. At the state park your options include picnicking and camping in a virgin forest, strolling a sandy beach, and spending the night in one of 32 electrical and 62 tent campsites. Short trails take you to nearby trout streams and an unusual black sand beach.

The rain forest aura continues through **Prehistoric Gardens,** 12 miles south of the park, near Humbug Mountain's base. Life-size dinosaur replicas peeking through lush vegetation delight children, and there's a gift shop and restaurant for the adults.

Rogue River

Near Gold Beach the highway crosses the mouth of the **Rogue River.** The river has a legendary reputation for outstanding salmon and steelhead fishing. Its headwaters begin about 200 miles east in the Cascade Mountains near Crater Lake. Jet boat excursions into the Rogue's Coast Range canyons are available from several operators. Most feature either a 32-mile run east to **Agness** or a 104-mile round-trip that takes you into the Wild and Scenic section and through whitewater rapids. Some trips deliver the mail to families and businesses along the shore, and all feature narratives covering history and wildlife. North and south riverbank roads offer a scenic side trip to Agness with views of the river from ridgetops.

Gold Beach, 1 mile south, takes its name from placer gold deposits found at the Rogue's mouth during the 1880s. Today the county seat attracts whale, sea lion, bird, and storm watchers. Look for palm trees along the highway and agates. There is also a variety of salt- and freshwater fishing.

South of Gold Beach the drive climaxes in a thick rain forest and a series of spectacular capes and parks that have been called the earth's finest shoreline scenery. At **Cape Sebastian,** 700 feet above sea level, wild azaleas and rhododendrons brighten spring landscapes along a 2-mile segment of the Oregon Coast Trail. **Pistol River State Park** is a sailboarder's and sightseer's delight, with a sandy beach where you can hike over sand dunes while enjoying magnificent cliffs and offshore rocks.

At **Boardman State Park** 10 miles of the Oregon Coast Trail extend along remote beaches and cliff sides overlooking magnificent arches, sea stacks, and offshore monoliths. **Rainbow Rock,** south of the park, displays colorful bands of chert, which formed in deep water on the ocean floor. **Harris Beach State Park**

Battle Rock, on the Southern Oregon coast, was named for a confrontation that took place between Native Americans and settlers in 1851.

features 35 full-hookup, 50 electrical, and 63 tent campsites above a spacious beach with trails winding down to shorelines and tide pools. The panoramic view extends into California and encompasses huge offshore monoliths, beach rock formations, and **Goat Island,** Oregon's largest coastal island. Goat Island is a bird refuge, and most of the offshore rocks and reefs are part of the **Oregon Islands National Wildlife Refuge.** During this segment you'll also cross **Thomas Creek Bridge.** At 300 feet above water level, it is the highest coastal span north of San Francisco.

Brookings & Southward

Brookings, 5 miles north of the California border, is a fresh- and saltwater fishing hot spot. At **Azalea State Park,** on the highway, in late spring and fall several varieties of azaleas bloom on 36 acres. The community of **Harbor,** separated from Brookings by the Chetco River, has the only **lily research station** in the US. Ninety-five percent of the world's commercial Easter lilies are grown in the 13 miles between Brookings and Smith River, California, to the south.

The **Chetco River** is an outstanding trout, steelhead, and cutthroat fishing stream. **Alfred A. Loeb State Park** is 10 miles northeast of Brookings on the river's north bank and features outstanding wildflower displays and 48 electrical sites and 3 cabins near a myrtlewood grove. A 1-mile nature trail winds through a virgin stand of coastal redwoods, some of which are more than 500 years old.

About 4 miles south of Brookings, the **nation's largest Monterey cypress** sits along US 101 in front of the **Chetco Valley Museum.** A mile south, **Winchuck Wayside** offers access to the **Winchuck River** and one last spot to watch birds and beachcomb the Oregon shoreline. Nearby **Crissey Field State Recreation Site** is a spacious welcome center exhibiting cutting-edge environmentally friendly features, countertops made of local myrtlewood, brochures, and staff to assist visitors in planning Oregon sightseeing. A short interpretive trail meanders through driftwood, dunes with unique plants, and old-growth Sitka spruce.

From the border US 101 continues south 21 miles to Crescent City. You can reenter Oregon by taking US 199 north to Jedediah Smith Redwoods State Park, Oregon Caves National Monument, and on to Grants Pass.

Crashing waves along the southern Oregon coast have made this a favorite destination for winter storm watchers.

5

Charleston Harbor, Seven Devils Loop

General Description: A 40-mile drive through Charleston Harbor, into 3 magnificent coastal parks and an estuary.

Special Attractions: Charleston Harbor, Sunset Bay, Shore Acres, and Cape Arago State Parks; South Slough National Estuarine Reserve; formal gardens; storm, whale, and wildlife watching.

Location: Southern Oregon coast west of Coos Bay and north of Bandon.

Drive Route Names: Cape Arago Highway, Seven Devils Road.

Travel Season: All year. Prime whale-watching periods are mid-December through mid-January and mid-March through mid-April. February is usually the best month for crashing surf and magnificent waves.

Camping: 1 county park with full hookups and 1 state park campground with full hookup and electrical sites. 2 small hiker/biker camps, plus private RV parks.

Services: Full services at Coos Bay and Charleston.

Nearby Attractions: Golden and Silver Falls State Park, Oregon Dunes National Recreation Area, Oregon Central Coast Scenic Drive, Bandon Scenic Ocean Views Drive, Bandon/Rogue River/Gold Beach Scenic Loop.

For More Information: Bay Area Chamber of Commerce, (541) 269-0215, (800) 824-8486 (USA) www.oregonsadventurecoast.com; Charleston Information Center, (541) 888-2311, (800) 824-8486

The Route

The route can be driven by taking either the ocean beach exits at **North Bend** and **Coos Bay** and traveling west to Cape Arago Highway or by turning onto Seven Devils Road 13 miles north of Bandon and reversing the itinerary.

From North Bend/Coos Bay, the route travels south along the bay to **Charleston Harbor,** descends to the shoreline at **Bastindorff Beach** and **Sunset Bay,** then climbs a bluff for sweeping overlooks at **Shore Acres** and **Cape Arago State Parks.** Backtracking 4 miles, it heads south to **South Slough Estuary** and two state park waysides, then ends at a junction with US 101, about 13 miles north of Bandon.

Travelers can expect warm summer days in the 70s and 80s and winters in the 60s and 70s. November through February brings heavy rains and gale-force winter storms with spectacular waves.

From the **Coos County Museum and Information Center** in North Bend, the drive heads west for several blocks on Virginia Street. Turning south, it enters Coos Bay and proceeds west through the Empire District. At the waterfront the highway stays along the shoreline for the 6 miles south to Charleston. This section is a local favorite for clamming, crabbing, and perch and salmon fishing.

Charleston Harbor, Seven Devils Loop

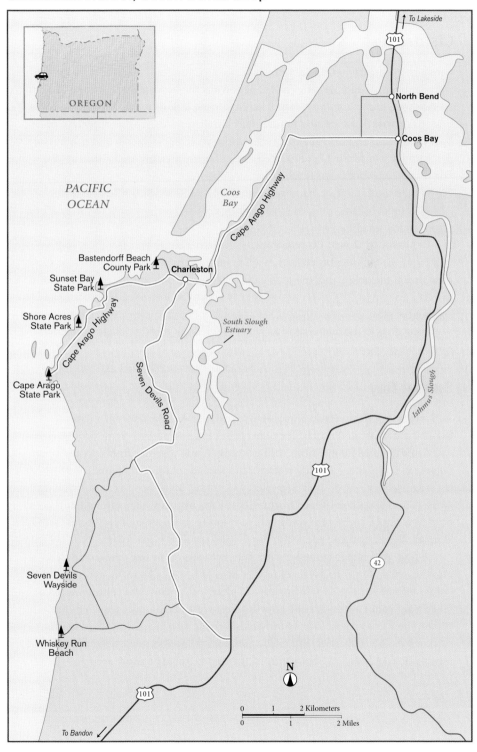

OREGON

PACIFIC
OCEAN

*Coos
Bay*

To Lakeside

101

North Bend

Coos Bay

Cape Arago Highway

Bastendorff Beach
County Park

Charleston

Sunset Bay
State Park

*South Slough
Estuary*

Shore Acres
State Park

Cape Arago Highway

Seven Devils Road

Isthmus Slough

Cape Arago
State Park

101

42

Seven Devils
Wayside

Whiskey Run
Beach

101

N

0   1   2 Kilometers
0   1   2 Miles

To Bandon

Charleston

Crossing the bridge to **Charleston,** you'll see a picturesque small-boat basin filled with commercial and pleasure craft. The town is the heart of local commercial and sportfishing, and you may wish to take time to explore its oyster farms, tide pools, fresh fish markets, shops, and boutiques. Charter services, marine suppliers, and boat ramp facilities are available. At the docks you can catch crab and fish for surf perch and smelt, herring, and tomcod or dig for razor clams on the flats at low tide.

A mile south of town, turn west onto Coos Ed Road. **South Jetty** is at the base of a small hill and offers a large parking area and a short walk to the base of a wave-eroded sea cliff.

Bastendorff Beach County Park, at the jetty's south end, is a great spot for walking dogs, building beach fires, playing in the surf, and watching sunsets. Cast your line in the ocean and you may land kelp greenling, ling cod, and starry flounder. The 25 tent and 74 water and electrical sites overlook rugged headlands and lush marsh grass.

Returning to the main highway, you enter a thick forest of coastal pine, spruce, alder, maple, and hemlock.

Sunset Bay

At **Sunset Bay State Park,** 1 mile south, two high headlands form a natural frame for a white sand beach. They also protect the camp and picnic grounds, situated in a forested ravine, from strong winds. While you may find kelp and other flotsam in the parking lot after a storm, the absence of undertows and currents make Sunset Bay one of Oregon's safest swimming, small boating, and kayaking areas. A 3-mile section of the Oregon Coast Trail begins at the parking lot. It goes over cliffs near a cormorant rookery, down to the shore, up to Shore Acres, across Simpson Beach, and ends on a cliff top 3 miles south at Cape Arago.

A huge picnic area provides a magnificent view of the bay. Short trails lead into the dense forest, across three foot bridges over a small stream, and to a promontory viewpoint. The 29 full-hookup, 35 electrical, and 66 tent campsites and a hiker/biker camp border an old-growth forest with a lush undergrowth of ferns and lupine. Deer and raccoons sometimes wander into the park, and, in season, blackberries, huckleberries, thimbleberries, and salmonberries are free for the picking. Porcupines and bobcats prowl the woods but are seldom seen.

Shore Acres

The highway is part of the Oregon Coast bicycle route, and you'll need to watch for cyclists on the narrow section to **Shore Acres.** Midway between the two parks, a viewpoint overlooks a meadow of sea grasses, spectacular headlands, and Cape Arago Lighthouse to the north. Built in 1866, it sits on an island 3 miles west of Charleston. It is still active and not open to the public. A barrier-free trail starts at the viewpoint, passes through the meadow near the cormorant rookery, and ends at **Shore Acres State Park.**

In the early 1900s Shore Acres was the centerpiece of an estate that included Sunset Bay and Cape Arago. It was owned by timber magnate Louis Simpson, whose pride and joy was his formal garden. Ship captains often brought him exotic flowers from around the world. New varieties of rhododendrons, azaleas, and other flowering shrubs were planted at Shore Acres years before they appeared in American nurseries.

Today Shore Acres draws visitors in equal numbers to see the restored gardens and to watch waves crash against the sandstone cliffs.

A tall spruce and pine forest forms a natural amphitheater for the 7.5-acre garden and an original caretaker's cottage. As an **American Rose Society test site,** the garden features a variety of roses, plus several species of hydrangeas, fuchsias, and wisterias. Snowball bushes, several kinds of roses, and other flowers bloom during winter.

An adjacent oriental garden and some of Simpson's original pampas grass, bamboo, cypress, and palm trees surround a circular pond. The pond is fed by a stream from nearby coastal hills and flows over a cliff to empty into the ocean. Plaques identify water hawthorne, floating heart, oriental cherry, and other plants.

The gardens are used as an open-air theater for concerts, receptions, and other events. Each month several marriages take place at the caretaker's cottage. Protected from westerly winds by tall hedges, the gardens also offer the best picnic spots. Paved paths descend to a sandy, secluded cove at Simpson's Beach and wind along cliffs to a glass observation building.

Nature's Spectaculars

From late November through February, the shoreline is the setting for some of nature's most spectacular shows. Breakers surge into sandstone cliffs, spread in giant 100-foot fans, collapse, and are pulled out to the ocean as churning waves of creamy, milk-white water. On calm days the shoreline is an endless succession of curves, coves, headlands, and beaches that appears to extend to the Cape Arago Lighthouse. Rocks north of the glassed storm-watching shelter exhibit distinctive

layers of sediment and stand broken and tilted like ships bows poised before sinking. Deposited some 40 million to 50 million years ago as a series of thick sands and muds, they are prime examples of the power of nature and the relentless pounding of the sea.

At **Simpson Reef Viewpoint,** near the entrance to Cape Arago, 30 to 40 sea lions or seals are often seen on the offshore rocks of Oregon Islands National Wildlife Refuge. Since the wildlife is easily disturbed, the refuge is closed to public use.

Cape Arago

Cape Arago's parking lot is one of the coast's best whale-watching sites. Each year thousands of gray whales migrate by here on a 6,000-mile journey from Alaska to Mexico and back.

The cape was recorded by early explorers. A plaque in the south cove commemorates a possible anchoring in 1579 by Sir Francis Drake. Captain James Cook sighted it in 1778 and named it Cape Gregory. Later it was renamed to honor a 19-century French physicist and geographer.

From the parking lot a serpentine trail winds down the triangular headland to two beaches. With the natural amphitheater of tall cliffs as a backdrop, you can enjoy a beach bonfire, beachcombing, sunbathing, and wading in the water. You'll need a license to surf fish and a permit if you plan to collect sea urchins, crabs, abalone, clams, mussels, and other invertebrates. Picnic tables and benches are situated on ledges along the trail, and a small hiker/biker camp is nestled in the forest near the park entrance.

Seven Devils Road

Leaving Cape Arago, the route backtracks 5 miles, then turns south on **Seven Devils Road.** The highway curves through 4 miles of thick pine forest and clear cuts to **South Slough Estuary**'s visitor center.

During the last ice age, sea level in this area dropped about 300 feet, as water froze into thick sheets. About 10,000 years ago, when the ice melted, it flooded the Millicoma River's mouth and created Coos Bay. South Slough is a southern extension of the bay, which is Oregon's second-largest estuary. Here fresh and salt water meet, and the plants and wildlife of both intermingle. Uplands provide

Exotic plants, formal gardens, and a pond at Shore Acres State Park were part of a timber baron's estate in the early 1900s.

shelter for raccoons, bobcats, and bald eagles, and beavers build dams along the wetlands. The estuary provides a nursery for sole, flounder, salmon, and crab and a stopover for vultures, great blue herons, and mergansers. As the home of the nation's first estuarine reserve, South Slough preserves more than 4,400 acres of salt marsh, tide flats, open water, and upland forest.

From the hilltop visitor center, the panorama encompasses the various habitats between forest and water. Several trails offer splendid views as they meander through majestic Sitka spruce stands and wildflower meadows to the water's edge for closer looks at old logging railroad pilings, beaver dams, and islands.

Bring your canoe and you can spend the day paddling through the scenic Winchester and Sengstacken arms. Before departing, check the weather and tides, make sure you have at least one approved floatation device for each passenger, and obtain a free route map from the visitor center. The canoe launch is situated off a side road, 1 mile south of the visitor center.

A mile beyond the canoe launch, Seven Devils Road bends east. South of the curve a short side road branches west to **Whiskey Run Beach** and **Seven Devils Wayside.** Nearby, 25 wind turbines provide energy for a wind-powered farm.

Jedediah Smith camped at Whiskey Run in 1828. A gold rush in 1851 led to the establishment of a camp that lasted about two years. Its seemingly endless sandy shoreline is perfect for beachcombing, clam digging, and agate hunting.

The drive concludes 1.5 miles south of the Whiskey Run turnoff, where Seven Devils Road reaches a junction with US 101.

6

Bandon,
Ocean Scenic Loop

General Description: A 5-mile drive along the Bandon waterfront and a coastline of spectacular seascapes and monoliths.

Special Attractions: Bandon waterfront, Bandon/Coquille River Historical Museum, South Jetty, Elephant Rock, Face Rock, Devil's Kitchen, Bradley Lake, views of lighthouse, sailboarding, fishing, beachcombing, wildlife, storm watching, whale watching.

Location: Southern Oregon coast west and south of Bandon.

Drive Route Names: 1st Street, Jetty Road, Ocean Drive, 11th Street, Beach Loop Drive, Seabird Drive.

Travel Season: All year. Winter storms are major attractions in January and February.

Camping: 1 state park campground 1 mile north of drive with full hookup and electrical sites, plus commercial RV parks.

Services: All services at Bandon.

Nearby Attractions: Charleston Harbor, 7 Devils Loop Drive, Oregon Dunes National Recreation Area, Oregon Central Coast Scenic Drive, Bandon/Rogue River/Gold Beach Scenic Loop.

For More Information: Bandon Chamber of Commerce, (541) 347-9616, www .bandon.com.

The Route

From **Bandon**'s Old Town waterfront, the drive travels southwest to the multiuse **South Jetty,** offering good views of the Coquille River, Bandon Bar, and a lighthouse across the river. Climbing a small hill, it passes several cliff-top viewing areas that provide beach access and spectacular offshore rock formations. A freshwater lake enclosed by a sand dune can be reached on a short walk near the southern end of the drive. The shoreline and favorable winds have made **Coquille River Bay** and the beaches favorite sailboarding areas.

Summer temperatures climb to the 70s and low 80s, and summerlike days in early spring are not uncommon. Early autumn is the most dependable season for warm, calm weather. Temperatures average in the mid-50s and low 60s during winter. Storm watching has become such a major winter activity that Bandon has proclaimed itself the storm-watching capital of the world. The **Bandon Storm Watchers Society** offers informational programs on weather, shipwrecks, oceanography, and other subjects.

At the turn of the 20th century, Bandon was a bustling seaport serving sailing ships, riverboats, and sternwheelers. In September 1936 the town was virtually destroyed in seven hours as a devastating fire leveled all but 15 of the estimated 500 buildings.

Bandon, Ocean Scenic Loop

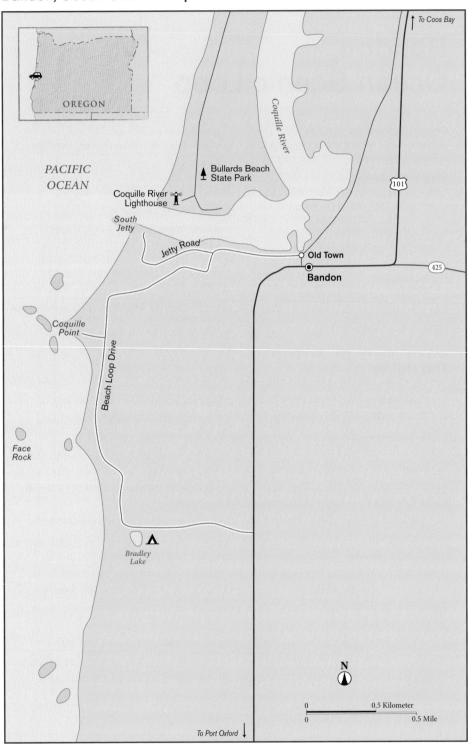

To Coos Bay

OREGON

PACIFIC
OCEAN

Coquille River

Bullards Beach
State Park

Coquille River
Lighthouse

101

South
Jetty

Jetty Road

Old Town

425

Bandon

Coquille
Point

Beach Loop Drive

Face
Rock

Bradley
Lake

N

| 0 | 0.5 Kilometer |
| 0 | 0.5 Mile |

To Port Oxford

At the waterfront, in addition to departing on guided cruises of the Coquille River, you can also fish and throw a crab net from the docks at the small picturesque boat basin and stroll the short boardwalk. If you're looking for local arts and crafts, you may wish to plan a couple of extra hours browsing Old Town's many shops. They feature local paintings, weaving, leather, silversmithing, stained glass, woodworking, and pottery. The area is also notable for its antiques shops, restaurants, and stores specializing in local candies and cranberry and cheese products.

Coquille River Lighthouse & Along the Shore

From the waterfront you'll see the **Coquille River Lighthouse,** perched on the north jetty across the river. Built in 1896, it was the last of eight lighthouses constructed on the coast and one of the few ever hit by a ship. Decommissioned in 1939, it displays historic photos.

To visit the lighthouse and its historic photo displays, travel north 1 mile and turn west on Bullards Beach State Park Road. The park offers 104 full-hookup and 81 electrical sites and hiker/biker and horse camps. A 1.5-mile hiking and 7-mile horse trail will take you along the ocean beach and riverbanks. **Bandon Marsh National Wildlife Refuge,** across the Coquille River, is a prime place to see thousands of migrating birds including shorebirds, peregrine falcons, and other raptors.

From Old Town begin the scenic drive by traveling west on 1st Street by canneries and waterfront buildings. About 2 blocks west of Old Town, a US Coast Guard station building, constructed in 1939 and decommissioned in 1946, houses the **Bandon/Coquille River Historical Museum.** Exhibits cover local maritime operations and shipwrecks and include a natural history room and several thousand Native American artifacts.

As the route turns west onto Jetty Road, it passes a pond that attracts pelicans, egrets, herons, and shorebirds. The Coquille River meets the sea at the usually treacherous **Bandon Bar** off the South Jetty, affording one of the best spots for watching breakers crash against rocks. Be careful where you park. During winter storms waves toss driftwood like matchsticks and cover the parking lot with snow-white foam.

The jetty area has some of the best local clam beds and fine surf fishing for perch, kelp greenling, ling cod, starry flounder, and smelt. You're also likely to see kites fluttering from the beach. The wide sandy shoreline, which continues south 0.5 mile to Elephant Rock, is one of the coast's most scenic beaches. Walkers may be rewarded with a variety of agates, jasper, and serpentine. At low tide look for shells, sand dollars, petrified wood, and fossilized scallops. Whales are often sighted from the jetty, where the view also includes the lighthouse and **Tupper Rock,** a traditional Native American sacred site.

Oregon Islands National Wildlife Refuge

Back on the main loop, the route climbs a small hill and turns west onto Beach Loop Drive. **Coquille Point,** 0.8 mile south, overlooks **Elephant Rock.** Like all of the offshore reefs and sea stacks, Elephant Rock was once part of the shoreline. As the ocean eroded away soft sands and soil, the rocks became separated from the mainland.

They are part of the **Oregon Islands National Wildlife Refuge** and closed to public access. In summer you'll see murres, puffins, and pelicans. Winter brings migrating whales and the spectacle of waves crashing through the elephant's eye. Stairs connect the viewpoint to the beach, where harbor and elephant seals congregate, and there are also tide pools and caves to explore. In this section it's against the law to touch the seals and collect tide pool life.

From Elephant Rock you can hike south along the beach to Face Rock. If you go, watch for sneaker waves, which come unexpectedly and are capable of moving large logs.

Face Rock & Devil's Kitchen

Face Rock and **Bandon Ocean State Park,** 0.7 mile south, overlook one of the largest and strangest displays of offshore rocks to be seen anywhere along the Oregon coast. According to a local legend, Face Rock is a Native American maiden who was turned to stone by an evil spirit. Surrounding rocks are her dog, cat, and kittens. Nearby, magnificent stone pillars rise out of the ocean. You can descend to the beach by stairs and hike south about 14 miles on a wide sandy beach. Several small streams empty into the ocean along the way. The shoreline is pocked with tide pools and often yields semiprecious agates, petrified wood, and driftwood.

The route continues south, providing good views of the ocean, and passes a stable that rents horses for beach and lake rides. Despite its name, **Devil's Kitchen** offers a safe beach for children to play in the water and a picnic area protected from wind by huge headlands. A small stream runs near the picnic area, which is framed both north and south by magnificent offshore sea stacks. The rock formations are particularly striking when silhouetted by a flaming sunset. While waiting for the sun to work its magic, you can keep warm with a beach fire made from the usually plentiful supply of driftwood.

The short drive along the Pacific at Bandon overlooks some of the southern Oregon coast's most impressive offshore monoliths.

During the next mile the route traverses forest and scrub brush and passes three entrances to Bandon State Park. The day-use areas feature numerous picnic tables looking out at offshore monoliths. Beaches are popular with sunbathers and horseback riders. Motorized vehicles are allowed south of the third exit. Though you can hike several miles south along the shoreline, the scenery does not offer the spectacular rocks seen along the coast near town.

Bradley Lake

At a curve where the route turns east, a large parking area signals access to unsigned **Bradley Lake.** From the parking area a short walk on a wooded trail and up and down a large sand dune will take you to its shores. The freshwater pond, enclosed by dunes, is a favorite local swimming, sunbathing, and stocked rainbow trout fishing hole. There are no facilities at the site, but a nearby commercial campground in a refreshing pine grove contains 40 sites, 20 of which have electricity.

The drive concludes 0.6 mile east at a junction with US 101. You can return to Bandon city center and Old Town by traveling 3 miles north on US 101.

7

Bandon, Rogue River, Gold Beach Scenic Loop

General Description: A 114-mile drive, including 11 miles of gravel through southern Oregon's Coquille River Valley, over the spine of the Coast Range mountains, and along the Rogue River.

Special Attractions: Bandon, Victorian homes, Coos County Logging Museum, Rogue River–Siskiyou National Forest, Wagner House Pioneer Museum, Wild and Scenic Illinois and Rogue Rivers, wildlife observation, waterfalls, camping, hunting, outstanding mountain and river views.

Location: Southern Oregon between Bandon, Coquille, Agness, and Gold Beach.

Drive Route Numbers: OR 42 South, OR 42, CR 242, FR 33.

Travel Season: Though the route is open all year, travel is best between June and September.

Camping: 1 state park campground with full-hookup and electrical sites. 6 forest service campgrounds with picnic tables, fire pits, and vault or flush toilets; some with water. Several county and private RV parks.

Services: Full services at Bandon, Coquille, Myrtle Point, and Gold Beach. Limited services at Powers and Agness.

Nearby Attractions: Rogue River Wilderness, Wild and Scenic Rogue River, Oregon Dunes National Recreation Area, Oregon Central Coast Scenic Drive, Charleston Harbor/7 Devils Loop Drive, Bandon Scenic Ocean Views Drive, California redwoods, Smith River Scenic Byway.

For More Information: Bandon Chamber of Commerce, (541) 347-9616, www .bandon.com; Coquille Chamber of Commerce, (541) 396-3414, www.coquille chamber.net; Gold Beach Visitors Center, (541) 247- 7526, (800) 525-2334, www .goldbeach.org; Myrtle Point Chamber of Commerce, (541) 572-5200 (no website); Powers Chamber of Commerce, (541) 439-2167 (no website); Rogue River– Siskiyou National Forest, Powers Ranger District, (541) 439-6200, www.fs.fed.us/r6/ rogue-siskiyou.

The Route

At Bandon and Gold Beach, the drive begins at sea level and reaches an elevation of about 2,290 feet north of Agness. From Bandon it proceeds east on OR 42 South along the Coquille River 18 miles to Coquille, then follows OR 42 through Myrtle Point. Turning south on CR 242, it traverses a wide, flat, wooded valley. Near Powers the Coquille River meanders in and away from the route, offering a spectacular deep roadside canyon. Climbing into the Coast Range, it follows FR 33 to Agness and along the Rogue River canyon's rim to Gold Beach.

Winter days with temperatures in the 70s and 80s are common on the south coast. Summer temperatures climb to over 90 degrees. Inland, at Agness and Powers, the weather is slightly warmer. Frost is rare and snow is virtually unknown on the coast. Snow in the Coast Range usually melts quickly.

Bandon, Rogue River, Gold Beach Scenic Loop

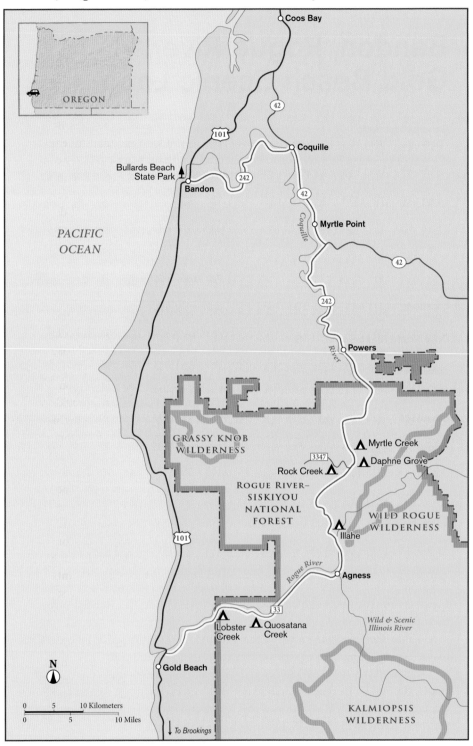

OR 42 South begins in north Bandon at a junction with US 101. Bullards Beach State Park, west of the junction, has 104 full-hookup and 81 electrical campsites overlooking the beach. At Bandon Fish Hatchery, 1 mile east, you can picnic on lawns along Geiger Creek and see large schools of fingerling and adult salmon, steelhead, and rainbow trout.

From the hatchery OR 42 South crosses the southern end of the Coos Basin. Underneath the ravinelike fold are thousands of feet of sand and mudstone that may have been deposited in a shallow bay some 45 million years ago. They contain thick deposits of coal, some of which were mined early in the 20th century.

The mines have disappeared and been replaced by flocks of sheep and cattle, rustic barns and farmhouses, and stands of isolated oaks that share the landscape with rolling hills and the narrow, placid Coquille River. During July wild sweet peas add splashes of purple and white along the roadside.

Coquille & Myrtle Point

Boat ramps at **Riverton and Sturdivant Riverfront Park** near Coquille offer access to the river for boating, canoeing, and fishing for fall chinook and coho salmon, striped bass, American shad, winter steelhead, and sea-run cutthroat. Sturdivant also has moorage docks.

About 4 miles east, you'll enter the first of the route's several myrtlewood groves. The trees, which grow to 100 feet tall and can live for 300 years, provide raw materials for a thriving cottage industry that produces an assortment of souvenirs.

Coquille, 3 miles east, features some of the area's best-preserved Victorian homes. At the **Coquille Valley Museum,** you can learn more local history as you see collections of tools, photographs, antiques, and a local newspaper's turn-of-the-20th-century printing press. As OR 42 follows the flood plain of the Coquille River 9 miles southeast to **Myrtle Point,** you'll pass more myrtlewood groves and crumpled lava and sandstone that were once part of the Pacific Ocean floor.

As you enter town, 1 block west of the highway you'll see a dark gray onion-domed building. It was modeled after Utah's Mormon Tabernacle and built in 1910 by the Church of Jesus Christ of Latter-Day Saints. As the **Coos County Logging Museum,** it now displays collections of blacksmith tools, various saws, and high-climbing gear. Several of Myrtle Point's Queen Anne–style homes and commercial buildings date from the 1860s to 1910.

Three miles east of Myrtle Point, the route turns south on **CR 242.** The pastoral landscape is rimmed by thick forest east and south of the highway and the lazy Coquille River and fields of cattle on the west. A sawmill burner shaped like a coffeepot evokes a bit of nostalgia and hints at the area's once-booming timber economy.

After a few miles mountain slopes come down to the roadway, and the highway becomes a series of curves and starts a gentle climb. At **Coquille Myrtle Grove State Natural Area,** 10 miles south of the junction, thick oak, maple, and myrtle trees close off sunlight for a dense ground cover of ferns and provide a cool respite for picnickers on the Coquille River banks. In dry summers the river is only a few feet wide, shallow enough to wade across, and so still that shoreline trees are reflected in its waters. On the 6 miles to Powers, the river becomes a thin blue ribbon in a deep roadside canyon as the highway passes under a canopy of trees, by a jumble of meadows, and through a dense fir forest.

Powers

If you're planning on hiking, camping, and observing wildlife, stop at the **Powers Ranger Station** for trail maps, campground locations, and information on road conditions. The station also issues bird and animal checklists as well as fact sheets on black bears and other wildlife.

The **Wagner House** in Powers is a one-and-a-half-story hand-hewn cabin built in 1872. It is Coos County's oldest preserved building, and inside you can see original family furnishings and historic artifacts. At **Powers County Park** you'll find tennis courts, basketball hoops, a baseball field, and a large pond for swimming, canoeing, boating, and stocked rainbow trout fishing. The campground features 30 tent sites, 40 RV sites with hookups, and 3 cabins that can be rented from the county parks department.

From Powers the route follows the South Fork Coquille River into the jumbled and twisted mountains. Some 200 million years ago, these mountains were sediment on the Pacific Ocean floor. When the oceanic crust slid out from under them, they were scraped off the ocean floor, jammed against the land mass, heated, crystallized, bent, and uplifted.

Rogue River–Siskiyou National Forest

In 2004 the **Rogue River** and **Siskiyou National Forests** merged, creating a 1.8 million–acre national forest that extends from almost the Pacific Ocean through the Siskiyou Mountains east to the crest of the Cascades. About 4 miles south of Powers, the road enters a section of the forest that is a mixture of predominantly Douglas fir, with myrtlewoods, alders, maples, and oaks in valleys and a lush undergrowth of ferns, blackberries, willows, and manzanitas. You may see blacktailed deer and Roosevelt elk along the highway. Black bears, river otters, and raccoons inhabit the area along with great blue herons and red-tailed hawks. The forest is also a habitat for cougars, bobcats, and great horned owls.

South of Powers, the Rogue River–Siskiyou National Forest stretches to the far horizon as it fills valleys and mountainsides in wave after wave of trees.

Elk Creek Falls, 2 miles south of the boundary, drops from a cliff near the highway. A 1-mile trail winds past the falls and through a stand of old-growth timber to the **Big Tree picnic area,** which contains the **world's largest Port Orford cedar tree.**

During the next 10 miles, the road winds through a rugged narrow canyon, around ridges, and by two forest service campgrounds. **Myrtle Grove** has 4 tent sites and 1 for RVs, and Daphne Grove has 13 tent sites and 1 for RVs.

At Eden Valley and Glendale Junction, you leave FR 219 and continue southwest on FR 33. FR 3347, near the junction, heads southwest about a mile to 7 tent and 3 trailer sites at **Rock Creek Campground.** Nearby, **Azalea Lake Trail** offers a moderate to steep 1.4-mile hike to the lake and several unimproved campsites along the shore.

The pavement ends at a summit overlooking a seemingly endless ocean of fir trees that fill valleys, hills, and mountains in every direction. Logging truck traffic comes from several side roads, and you will want to proceed carefully on the somewhat narrow 10.7 miles of gravel downgrade. **Foster Bar Campground,** about 4 miles south, has 6 campsites that serve primarily Rogue River hikers and rafters. It has restrooms but no drinking water. **Illahe Campground** is near the

Jet boats and mail boats can be seen plying the Wild and Scenic Rogue River from overlooks near Agness.

gravel's southern end and features 1 group and 14 tent spaces. Near the campground, the 40-mile **Rogue River Trail** begins and extends east 42 miles through the Rogue River Wilderness to Graves Creek.

Back on pavement, you'll pass a small resort and continue south 2.5 miles to **Agness** on the banks of the Rogue River. The resort has a campground and cabin rentals, a restaurant and lounge, gas and oil, fishing supplies, groceries, a liquor store, and a post office.

Wild & Scenic Rogue River

As you cross the bridge, look east and you'll see the Wild and Scenic section of the Rogue River and the western edge of the 36,000-acre **Rogue River Wilderness.** A 40-mile stretch of the river bisects the wilderness, which is accessible only by boat and two trails.

This section is one of the few where mail is delivered by boat. The route, which took days when deliveries started in 1895, now takes only a few hours. Anglers and vacationers have been passengers since 1926.

A lodge on the south bank is a Rogue River mail-boat lunch stop. Established in 1903, it offers a main lodge with the atmosphere of an inn, plus several rustic cabins and a store stocked with groceries, gas, propane, bait, and tackle. Next door, **Agness RV Park** features 90 full-hookup sites on 1,000 feet of river frontage.

Cougar Lake Resort is a mile west and caters to hunters and anglers. The Rogue has a legendary reputation as a premier salmon, steelhead, and trout stream, and the area is also known for its deer, elk, bear, and grouse hunting.

Wild & Scenic Illinois River

A mile west of the resort, the **Wild and Scenic Illinois River** empties into the Rogue. From a viewpoint on the west end of the bridge, you can photograph the streams as they come together. Continuing west on the edge of a ridge, several pullouts offer spectacular views of the sheer cliffs, deep blue river, forested banks, and sandbars. Occasionally mail and jet boats filled with sightseers streak up the river, go around curves, and disappear into the wilderness.

Intermittent views of the canyon are broken by stands of maple, oak, Douglas fir, alder, and cedar. After 12.5 miles the road descends to river level at **Quosatana Creek Campground.** A favorite of anglers, it provides fish-cleaning and trailer dump stations, a boat ramp, and 43 tent sites near the riverbank. Walking the short barrier-free trail through the myrtlewood grove is a great way to loosen up while enjoying the cool pine-scented forest and shaded river.

The route exits the Rogue River-Siskiyou National Forest under a tunnel of tree limbs, then continues through a wooded corridor to US 101. **Lobster Campground** is about 4 miles west of Quosatana Creek and has seven tent trailer sites, a boat ramp, and restrooms.

The **Rogue River Bridge,** on US 101 at the exit, has been designated a National Historic Civil Engineering Landmark. Built in 1931 and designed by Oregon's premier bridge builder, Conde B. McCullough, it has decorative features that include Egyptian obelisks, gothic arches, and repeated use of supporting arches.

8

Portland, Columbia River, Astoria

General Description: A 198-mile drive through northwestern Oregon along the Columbia River, along the northern Oregon coast, and through the Tillamook State Forest.

Special Attractions: Willamette River, Sauvie Island, Columbia River, Astoria, Fort Stevens, Lewis and Clark National Historical Park, Clatsop and Tillamook State Forests, wildlife, sailboarding.

Location: Northwestern Oregon between Portland and Astoria.

Drive Route Numbers: US 30, US 101/26, US 26.

Travel Season: All year. Winter can bring extremely icy conditions but rarely closes the highways.

Camping: 1 state park with full-hookup and electrical sites; 1 state park with primitive sites. Several city and county campgrounds and RV parks.

Services: All services at Portland, St. Helens, Rainier, Astoria, and Seaside. Limited services at Scappoose, Columbia City, and Clatskanie.

Nearby Attractions: Columbia River Gorge, Oregon City, Fort Vancouver National Historic Site, Mount St. Helens, Cannon Beach, Northern Oregon Coast Drive, Washington County Scenic Loop.

For More Information: Travel Portland, (503) 275-8355, (877) 678-5263, www.travelportland.com; South Columbia County Chamber of Commerce, (503) 397-0685, www.SCChamber.org; Clatskanie Chamber of Commerce, (503) 728-2502, www.clatskanie.com/chamber; Astoria Warrenton Area Chamber of Commerce, (503) 325-6311, (800) 875-6807, www.oldoregon.com; Seaside Visitors Bureau, (503) 738-3097, (888) 306-2326 (USA), www.seasideor.com.

The Route

Leaving Portland, the route follows the trail of Lewis and Clark north along the Willamette and Columbia Rivers to Rainier. En route it passes through several small towns, 2 to 12 miles apart, and scenery that varies from intermittent views of the Columbia, its river traffic, tiny islands, and the verdant Washington shoreline to patches of marshland and mixed forests of Douglas fir, western hemlock, and willow. Fossils found in rocks along this section indicate that 30 million to 35 million years ago this was part of the continental shelf. At **Rainier** the Columbia bends around a promontory and US 30 cuts inland and through the forested **Coast Range.** After returning to the Columbia near Astoria, the drive takes US 101/26 south along the Oregon coast for 19 miles. It returns to Portland by following US 26 through **Tillamook State Forest** and Washington County farmlands.

Summer temperatures range from the upper 50s to mid-80s and drop to the 40s and mid-50s in winter. Spring brings warm sunny days in the 60s and 70s. Autumn is the most dependable season for warm, calm weather. While these

Portland, Columbia River, Astoria

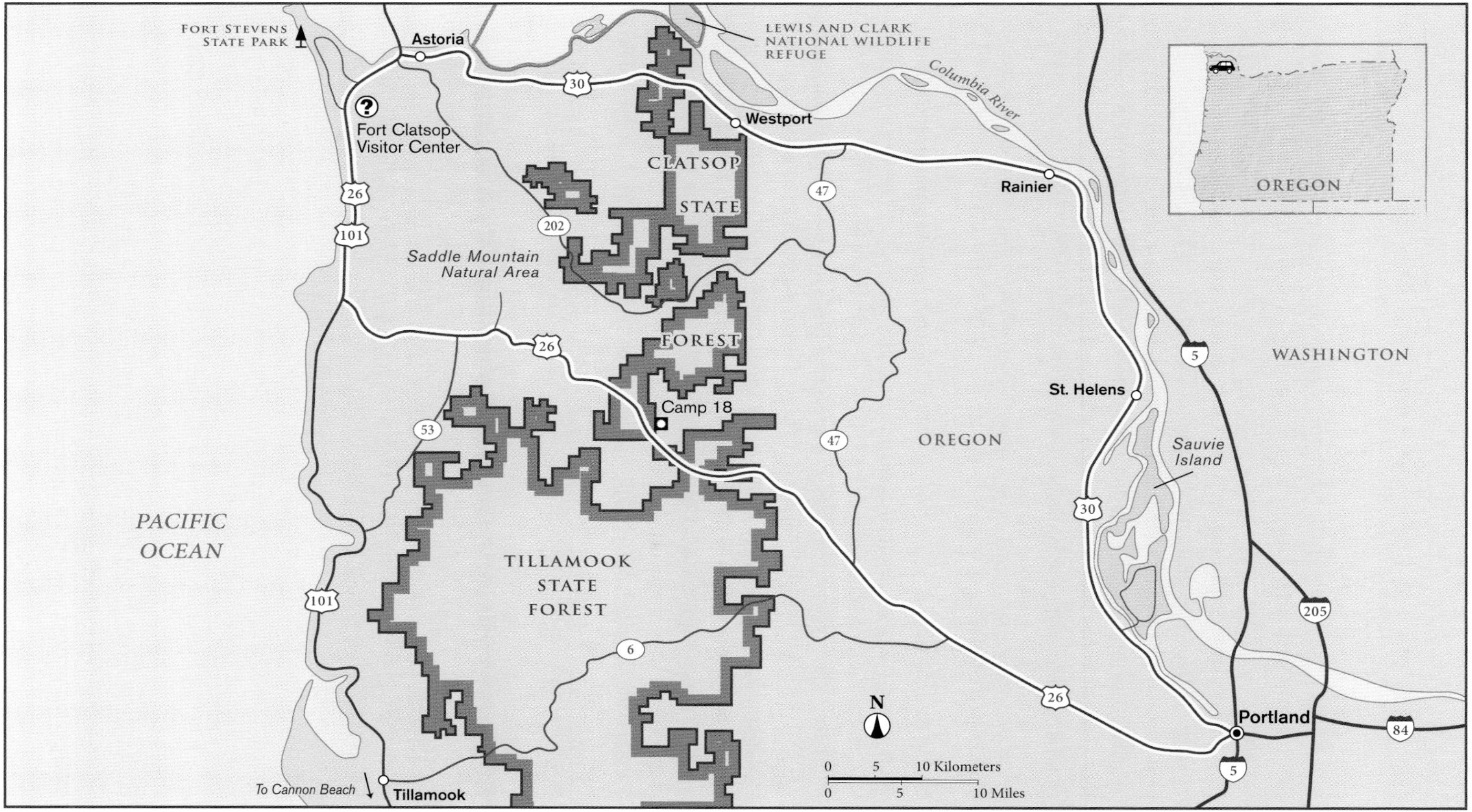

routes seldom close, fog and surface or "black" ice are hazards in winter.

As the drive leaves Portland, it offers good views of the **Willamette River** and the **Port of Portland**'s docks filled with loading equipment and products awaiting export.

The Willamette empties into the Columbia a few miles north at Sauvie Island. Both rivers figured prominently in the settlement of the Pacific Northwest. The Columbia, which begins in British Columbia and flows about 2,000 miles through Washington and Oregon to Astoria, attracted fur trappers and explorers seeking the "Great River of the West." Oregon Trail emigrants came west, attracted by the rich farmlands along the Willamette's banks.

Sauvie Island

Idyllic **Sauvie Island,** accessible by a short bridge across **Multnomah Channel,** is the world's largest freshwater island and a favorite spot to buy fresh fruits and vegetables from roadside stands and to fish sloughs and ponds for catfish, crappie, and perch. Each year more than 250 species of birds live on or pass through the island. At **Bybee Howell Territorial Park,** 2 miles north of the bridge, split-rail fences enclose a pioneer orchard and an 1880s home.

At **Scappoose,** 8 miles north, a two-story candle stands out among buildings lining the highway. **J.J. Collins Marine Park,** accessible by boat, is a wildlife area for bird watching with a 1.5mile nature trail and a few tent campsites. **Airport Park,** inside the city limits, has RV sites and electrical hookups. North of town a two-lane county road links Scappoose with the settlements of Pittsburg and Vernonia, 20 and 26 miles west.

St. Helens Historic District, Columbia City & Rainier

St. Helens, at 28 miles, offers 3 marinas and 10 blocks of 1800s buildings in the **Riverfront National Historic District.** The Georgian revival–style **Columbia County Courthouse,** built of black basalt, is the district's centerpiece and one of the best places to see Washington's **Mount St. Helens.** Departures for **Sand Island,** Oregon's only designated marine park, leave from a boat dock behind the courthouse. On the island you'll find 37 campsites with picnic tables, nature trails to waterfowl areas, and a beach.

The Columbia River is almost a mile wide as it flows past **Columbia City,** where you can watch large freighters mingle with pleasure boats at **Ruth Rose Richardson River Front Park** and take a path down to the water's edge. The **Caples House Museum,** across the street, was built in 1870 and is divided into period parlors, doctor's offices, kitchens, and family rooms furnished with antiques, and a children's attic with a country store is also on the grounds.

As the route continues north it passes the site of the demolished **Trojan Nuclear Power Plant,** crosses **Deer Island,** named by Lewis and Clark, and traverses open fields, a mixed forest, and rocky bluffs. They were formed between 11 million and 25 million years ago when lava from northeastern Oregon volcanos flowed into the area.

The scenery changes to marshlands, open fields, and a corridor of Douglas fir, then overlooks the Columbia River as the drive approaches **Rainier.** During summer you can expect to see a variety of watercraft ranging from row and power boats filled with fishers to sailboats and pleasure craft to large cargo ships. In the port city **Riverfront Park** and **Prescott Beach** afford free access to the Columbia shoreline and great views of river traffic. **Lewis and Clark Bridge** provides a giant arched frame behind the town and links Oregon with Longview, Washington.

Beyond Rainier, US 30 cuts across a plain, away from the river, through rock cliffs, and by two Mount St. Helens viewpoints. At **Clatskanie** deer and elk sometimes venture out of the forest and into town. You can fish for trout, salmon, and steelhead within the city limits and sailboard at nearby **Jones Beach.** The **Flippin House,** a few blocks south of the highway, is a National Historic Site, built by a logger in the 1880s and patterned after a castle. It is furnished with antiques.

Leaving the Clatskanie Valley, the highway bisects meadows filled with sheep, Christmas tree farms, and stands of cottonwoods that are harvested and used in paper making.

At **Westport,** for a change of pace and a small toll, you can take a ferry on a 25-minute round-trip to Washington's **Puget Island,** where you may see deer, seals, and eagles.

The road climbs into the thick woodlands of **Clatsop State Forest** and the **Coast Range,** where posted speeds slow to 30 and 40 miles per hour before reaching a high point of 656 feet. **Bradley State Park,** on the eastern slopes, is a day-use area with picnic tables and scenic views of mountains and river. Deer and elk frequent the area.

West of the mountains, the Columbia River sandbars and islands reappear and are visible for the rest of the way into Astoria. 20 of the islands compose the 35,000-acre **Lewis and Clark National Wildlife Refuge,** which is accessible only by boat. The refuge is a resting area for swans, geese, and ducks.

Astoria

During the 25 miles to **Astoria,** you pass **Gnat Campground and Fish Hatchery,** which raises summer and winter steelhead. The forest service campground has 12 sites. The Big Creek hatchery, 3 miles west, offers group tours and interpretive signs explaining its autumn chinook and winter steelhead program. The creek is a popular salmon and steelhead fishing spot.

*The view from Coxcomb Hill includes the Astoria-Megler Bridge, which spans the
Columbia River and connects Astoria, Oregon, to southwestern Washington.*

Watch for eagles, as you'll also pass a sanctuary for them on a side road near
milepost 87. A Lewis and Clark Trail site and John Day County day-use park signal the approach to Astoria.

As you near Astoria, you'll see the **Astoria-Megler Bridge** spanning the
Columbia. At 4.1 miles long, it is the world's longest continuous truss span bridge.
On foggy days it's easy to understand why early seafarers missed the mouth of the
river, which was finally discovered by Captain Robert Gray on May 11, 1792, and
named after his ship.

The **Columbia River Maritime Museum,** on US 30, interprets various
aspects of the area's colorful history. The mouth of the Columbia River, behind
the museum, is one of the world's most dangerous sandbars and has claimed over
2,000 ships and over 700 lives. From atop Coxcomb Hill the 125-foot **Astoria
Column**'s observation tower provides a superb view of the city, Pacific Ocean,
Columbia River, and Washington and Oregon forests.

*At Astoria Column, atop Coxcomb Hill, the area's history spirals
to the top of the 128-foot high structure in a pictorial frieze.*

Ships of all shapes and sizes ply the Columbia River in front of the Columbia River Maritime Museum.

US 30 ends at **Astoria Bridge.** The bridge marks the start of US 101 and the approximate midpoint for 12 sites that compose the **Lewis and Clark National Historical Park,** stretching along the southwest Washington and northern Oregon coasts. Washington sites include **Cape Disappointment State Park Interpretive Center, Fort Columbia State Park,** and **Station Camp.** In Oregon the sites you'll pass that are included in the historical park are Fort Stevens with a replica of a Clatsop Indian longhouse; Fort Clatsop, the main Oregon visitor center, which has a reconstructed fort and trails leading to a river and the ocean; and Seaside's salt works.

The drive proceeds south on US 101/26, passing a junction with OR 202, a scenic mountain route leading east to Jewell and Mist. Crossing Youngs Bay, it enters the Warrenton/Hammond Recreation Area, the north coast's major center for deep-sea fishing charters.

Fort Clatsop & Fort Stevens

Two miles farther, signs direct you 3 miles east to **Fort Clatsop,** the site of Lewis and Clark's 1805–1806 winter encampment. It rests in a dense forest of Douglas fir and hemlock and contains a reconstructed log fort, a marked nature trail, and a canoe landing on the Lewis and Clark River.

Fort Stevens, 7 miles west of US 101/26, guarded the Pacific coast from the Civil War through World War II, when it became the only US mainland installation fired upon by the Japanese. At the 3,700-acre state park, you can fish two lakes and the ocean for bass, perch, and stocked trout, and tour concrete batteries, guns, and a memorial garden with 170 species of roses. Nine miles of hiking and biking trails meander through a forest of shore pine to the beach and a campground with 117 full-hookup, 303 electrical, and 6 tent sites, and 11 deluxe cabins.

Continuing south, the main highway passes fields of European bunchgrass— planted during the 1930s to arrest spreading sand dunes—woodlands, Del Rey Beach, and the resort communities of Gearhart and Seaside.

US 26–The Sunset Highway

South of Seaside the highways divide, and the drive takes US 26 to Portland. The land grows older as you continue east. Sandstones near the ocean were formed about 15 million to 20 million years ago, while interior sands and basalts were laid down about 40 million to 50 million years ago. Along US 26, called the **Sunset Highway,** attractions are few and services are limited. The highway honors the Oregon National Guard's 41st Infantry Division, which is known as the Sunset Division.

The **world's largest Sitka spruce tree** stands 2 miles east of the junction at a roadside rest area. It is 52 feet, 6 inches in circumference, 216 feet high, and has a crown spread of 93 feet.

The **Necanicum River** parallels the highway as you travel through a spruce corridor and at mile 10 pass a junction with OR 53, which leads 14 miles south to Wheeler.

Saddle Mountain

Saddle Mountain Natural Area, 1 mile beyond the junction, has restrooms, picnic grounds, and 10 primitive campsites. A 7-mile steep, narrow waved road twists through a thick forest to a trailhead parking lot, where there are 10 walk-in primitive sites. The 6-mile round-trip hike to the top is strenuous. On clear days from the 3,283-foot summit—the highest point in Oregon's northern Coast Range—the view can extend from Nehalem Bay to Mount Hood and north to Washington's Mount St. Helens, Mount Adams, and Mount Rainier. Saddle Mountain, known for its spring wildflower displays, also exhibits prime examples of pillow basalts, which were formed underwater some 55 million years ago.

Camp 18, at 18 miles, is a beautiful lodge-style restaurant made from local stone and logs that were hand peeled with draw knives. An outdoor logging museum exhibits early-20th-century steam donkeys and locomotives.

A continuous sea of Douglas and noble fir, Sitka spruce, and western red cedar frames the highway as it climbs into the Coast Range and through Clatsop and Tillamook State Forests. Between 1933 and 1945 several fires burned a total of 355,000 acres of the Tillamook forest, and the event is now known as the Tillamook Burn. The area has been replanted through aerial seeding. Cresting at 1,642 feet, it affords horizon-wide views of valleys, hillsides, and mountain slopes covered with waves of fir trees. A county road at 22 miles extends north to Jewel, where elk, deer, and waterfowl congregate near the highway.

Sunset Springs Rest Area, a few miles east, includes a history of the Tillamook Burn, picnic tables, and restrooms. Dairy farms, meadows, and apple and nut orchards provide the scenery from the Washington County line to Beaverton's industrial parks and shopping malls. Portland's west hills, a string of small volcanos 3 miles east of Beaverton, were active as recently as three million to five million years ago. Hilly Washington Park borders US 26 and brings the drive to a perfect end by offering a magnificent view of the city, with Mount Hood serving as a dramatic backdrop. The beautiful park's attractions include the Portland Zoo, the World Forestry Center, an arboretum, rose test gardens, and a Japanese garden.

9

Washington County Vineyard & Valley Scenic Tour

General Description: A 50-mile signed loop on paved highways through northwestern Oregon's Washington County farmlands, orchards, and wine country.

Special Attractions: Vineyards, museums, historic sites, orchards, farmlands, scenic vistas, Hagg Lake.

Location: Northwestern Oregon 9 miles west of Portland.

Drive Route Numbers: OR 99 West, Beef Bend Road, Roy Rodgers Road, OR 210 and OR 217, US 26, Old Scotch Church and Glencoe Roads, OR 6 and OR 8, Helvetia Road, OR 47, Gaston, Laurelwood, Laurel, Bald Peak, and Scholls Ferry Roads.

Travel Season: All year.

Camping: There are no campgrounds along the route or in Washington County.

Services: All services in Tigard, Beaverton, and Forest Grove.

Nearby Attractions: Columbia River Gorge, Oregon City historic sites, Champoeg State Park, Fort Vancouver National Historic Site, Washington Park Zoo, World Forestry Center, Portland/Columbia River/Astoria Scenic Drive, 99 West Scenic Drive.

For More Information: Washington County Visitors Association, (503) 644-5555, (800) 537-3149 (USA), www.visit washingtoncountyoregon.com; Tigard Area Chamber of Commerce, (503) 639-1656, www.tigardchamber.org; Sherwood Chamber of Commerce, (503) 625-7800, www.sherwoodchamber.org

The Route

The loop starts in the business and residential areas of **Sherwood,** then heads north to US 26, which is a good place to start the drive if you wish to avoid the congestion of the first few miles. Turning west, it bisects business parks and farmlands, briefly touches the edge of a forest, then moves south through vineyards to **Forest Grove.** After circling scenic **Hagg Lake,** it concludes by traveling east through farms and fruit and nut orchards.

Washington County lies on a bed of basalt lava, representing the westernmost end of the **Columbia Plateau.** The lava flowed out of eastern Oregon and down the Columbia River about 20 million years ago. After the last ice age, the area was buried in floodwaters that deposited sand, gravel, and topsoil.

The rich land and six months of frost-free weather are conducive to growing a variety of fruits, vegetables, and commercial crops. Farms, roadside stands, and vineyards along the drive offer seasonal produce and wine tastings.

Summer days in the high 70s to mid-80s are ideal for driving. Spring and fall days average in the high 60s. While temperatures dip to an average of 33 degrees in January, they climb into the 50s during February and March.

Washington County Vineyard & Valley Scenic Tour

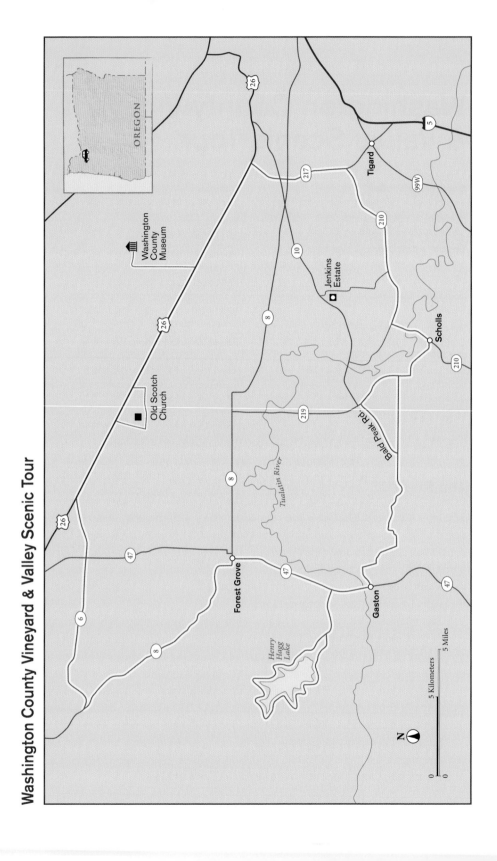

The Washington County Visitors Association has a downloadable video that highlights experiences that can be enjoyed along the Vineyard and Valley Scenic Tour Route. The drive can be started either in Sherwood or at Helvetia Road and is signed in both directions. Because of narrow roads and low bridges, it is not recommended for tour buses or bicyclists.

In Sherwood the drive starts by following OR 99 West north to Tigard, then turns west on Beef Bend Road, then north on Roy Rodgers Road, passing through 2 miles of a residential area, apple orchards, and Christmas tree farms, and ends at OR 210. A turn west on OR 210 takes you to **Ponzi Vineyards**—1 mile from the junction—where you can sample award-winning pinots, chardonnays, and dry white Rieslings.

The route turns east on OR 210, bisecting pastoral farms with cement-block barns and pastures enclosed with white wooden fences. At Washington Square, the area's largest shopping center, the drive turns north on OR 217, passing business parks, commercial centers, motels, and Beaverton Town Square Mall before entering a greenway. Four miles north, it turns west at the Astoria/Tillamook exit onto US 26.

US 26–The Sunset Highway

US 26 is also called the **Sunset Highway.** The name honors Oregon's 41st Infantry Division, which saw extensive combat in both world wars. To reach Portland Community College's Rock Creek campus, turn north on 185th Street, then east on Springville Road. The **Washington County Museum** on campus displays an extensive collection of photographic equipment, thematic exhibits on the history of Washington County from Indians to high technology, and 25,000 historic photographs. An 1853 jail building is also on the site.

Helvetia Vineyards and Winery, on Helvetia Road off US 26, produces pinot noir, chardonnay, and pinot gris and welcomes visitors on most major holidays or by appointment. **Rice NW Museum of Rocks and Minerals,** also accessible via Helvetia Road, is listed on the National Register of Historic Places and is known for its unique architectural style. It displays emeralds, large cluster crystals, petrified wood, dinosaur eggs, fossils, and other rocks and minerals.

Rejoining US 26, the drive continues west through grass and grain fields to Jackson School Road. A turn south and then west puts you on Old Scotch Road, where the **Tualatin Plains Presbyterian Church,** also known as the **Old Scotch Church,** has served local residents since 1876. The white wooden building with an unusual eight-sided steeple is the county's most photographed site. **Joe Meek,** mountain man and first US marshal of the Oregon Territory, is buried in the church cemetery along with his family and other pioneers.

Fruit & Wine Country

Peterson Farm Apple Country, about 1 mile west and south on Glencoe Road, raises 50 varieties of apples, pears, and cherries. You can picnic in the farm's orchard and sample cider from July through December.

Following Glencoe Road north to US 26, the drive continues west to OR 6. After 7 miles of brushy rolling hills, broken by wheat fields, it passes a junction with OR 8 and winds northwest through thick stands of Douglas fir. **Gales Creek,** known for its large steelhead, cascades over moss-covered rocks along the roadside.

From the junction the drive follows OR 8 south through berry fields, oak-covered hillsides, and picturesque farms with aging barns and herds of dairy cattle. Several wineries along this segment offer public tastings and feature pinot noirs, gewürztraminer, Rieslings, and specialties.

At **Tualatin Estate Vineyards** you can sample and purchase chardonnay and other wines in a tasting room or picnic area overlooking a magnificent 85-acre vineyard and the **Tualatin Valley.**

Shafer Vineyard Cellars offers pinot gris, Riesling, and others in a tasting room or large oak-shaded picnic area with a gazebo. The **Gales Creek Valley** spreads below, and on Sundays during July and August you can listen to jazz concerts.

David Hill Winery and Vineyard, 3 miles southeast of Shafer Vineyards, produces pinot noir, pinot gris, and Riesling. The tasting room is open 11 a.m. to 5 p.m. daily.

Forest Grove

Forest Grove, 10 miles south of the junction, was named for its white oak and fir forests that shade virtually every street. **Old College Hall,** on the Pacific University campus in downtown, is the oldest educational building in use west of the Rocky Mountains. Inside you'll find a magnificent reception room and a museum with oriental and pioneer relics. The **Valley Art Association,** close to campus, exhibits and sells Northwest pottery, jewelry, and paintings. **SakeOne,** on Elm Street, is the first American-owned producer of sake rice wine. It offers tastings.

South of Forest Grove, OR 47 becomes Scoggins Valley Road. After 2 miles a turn west on Dilly Road will take you to **Montinore Estate.** A Victorian mansion, a drive lined with oak trees, and rolling hills covered with grapes create a relaxing setting for sampling Müller-Thurgau, pinot gris, and gewürztraminer.

Henry Hagg Lake

The loop's scenic highlight lies 2.5 miles south when you turn west on Scoggins Valley Road into **Scoggins Valley Park** and **Henry Hagg Lake.** An 11-mile scenic drive circles the 1,113-acre man-made lake, situated in a dense forest at the base of the Coast Range. In summer the water is covered with boaters, water-skiers, and anglers fishing for rainbow trout, perch, and largemouth and small-mouth bass. You can also enjoy numerous picnic sites; 15 miles of hiking trails to shorelines and surrounding forest; observation decks for viewing elk, deer, eagles and ospreys; and an elevator-equipped fishing dock that floats on the lake. Special-use and group picnic sites require reservations.

Wineries & Farms

To see one of Oregon's oldest wineries, Elk Cove, go south 2 to 3 miles from the lake entrance on OR 47 to Gaston. **Elk Cove Winery** offers sweeping views of the vineyards and tastings of pinot noir and gris and dessert wines.

Backtrack on OR 47 to join the loop heading east on Gaston, Laurelwood, and Laurel Roads. In this 6-mile stretch you'll pass farmlands and fruit and nut orchards, cross the Yamhill County line, and turn north onto Bald Peak Road. At the summit of the small hill, which is the county's highest point, **Bald Peak State Park**'s picnic tables and lawns offer a panorama of the Cascades, Coast Range, and Willamette Valley.

This region produces 90 percent of the nation's filberts. You'll see some of the groves, along with stands of walnut, and apple and cherry orchards, as the remaining 5 miles of the loop returns to OR 210 (Southwest Scholls Ferry Road) and another crossing of the Tualatin River.

At **Smith Berry Barn and Boutique** in the crossroads of Scholls, you can pick raspberries and purchase jams, nuts, and hand-crafted gifts. A few miles east, **Oregon Heritage Farm** offers samplings of fresh cider, plus apples, vegetables, and nuts in season.

Jenkins Estate & Cooper Mountain Vineyards

Turning onto Tile Flat Road, the drive heads north 3 miles over a series of roller-coaster, grass-covered hills to **Jenkins Estate.** The hunting lodge–style main house is a National Historic Site. Paths wind through the 68 acres of forest, lawns, and flower and rock gardens. Wild rhododendrons start the displays in spring, and formal gardens bloom throughout the summer. Though the home is only open by appointment, you can stroll through the gardens during the hours that the gates are open. To and from the estate, you'll pass **Cooper Mountain Vineyards.** The 105-acre vineyard was homesteaded in 1865 and is situated on an extinct volcano. Tastings of pinot noir, chardonnay, and pinot gris are offered daily.

Returning to OR 210, you head east and then south on Vandermost Road. At **Ponzi Vineyards,** on Winery Lane, you can top off your trip with award-winning pinots and chardonnays.

The last stop on the drive is **Hoffman Farms Store,** where you can buy Oregon-grown products. The drive concludes at Roy Rodgers Road.

10

Wilson River, Oregon Coast, Willamette Valley

General Description: A 194-mile loop on paved roads through northwestern Oregon's Tillamook State Forest, Coast Range, northern coast, and Willamette Valley.

Special Attractions: Historic Tillamook Burn, scenic Wilson River, vineyards, mountain and ocean scenery, dairy lands, historic sites.

Location: Northwestern Oregon between Forest Grove, the Oregon Coast, and Tigard.

Drive Route Numbers: OR 8, OR 6 (Wilson River Highway), Three Capes Scenic Loop Road, US Highway 101, OR 18, OR 99 West.

Travel Season: All year. During summer dry periods smoking is prohibited on Tillamook State Forest trail hikes.

Camping: 6 state forest and 4 forest service campgrounds with picnic tables, fire rings, and flush or vault toilets; some have drinking water. 2 state parks, 1 with full hookups and standard and hiker/biker campsites, 1 with hiker/biker sites.

Services: All services in Forest Grove, Tillamook, Lincoln City, McMinnville, and Tigard. Limited services in Pacific City and Sheridan.

Nearby Attractions: Columbia River Gorge, Washington Park Zoo, World Forestry Center, Portland/Columbia River/Astoria Scenic Drive, Depoe Bay, Cannon Beach, Newport, Washington County Scenic Loop, 99 East and West Scenic Drives.

For More Information: Forest Grove Chamber of Commerce, (503) 357-3006, www.FGChamber.org; Washington County Visitors Association, (503) 644-5555, (800) 537-3149 (USA), www.visitwashington countyoregon.com; Oregon Department of Forestry, Forest Grove District, (503) 357-2191, www.oregon.gov/ODF; Tillamook Area Chamber of Commerce, (503) 842-7525, www.gotillamook.com; Lincoln City Visitors and Convention Bureau, (541) 996-1274, (800) 452-2151 (USA), www.oregoncoast.org; Sheridan-West Valley Chamber of Commerce, (503) 843-2347; McMinnville Chamber of Commerce, (503) 472-6196, www.mcminnville.org; Newberg: Chehalem Valley Chamber of Commerce, (503) 538-2014, www.chehalemvalley.org; Tigard Area Chamber of Commerce, (503) 639-1656, www.tigardchamber.org.

The Route

Portland travelers can join the loop by taking the **Sunset Highway (US 26)** west about 25 miles to a junction with OR 6. From Forest Grove the drive follows OR 8 northwest for 10 miles to OR 6, then travels through the **Tillamook National Forest** and over the peaks of the **Coast Range.** Although the area was devastated by a series of fires between 1933 and 1950, it has been replanted and exhibits a mature forest of noble fir, Sitka spruce, and western red cedar, dominated by 75-foot Douglas firs. After following the Wilson River to **Tillamook,** sightseers can choose between traveling south on US 101, which jogs inland through a

Wilson River, Oregon Coast, Willamette Valley

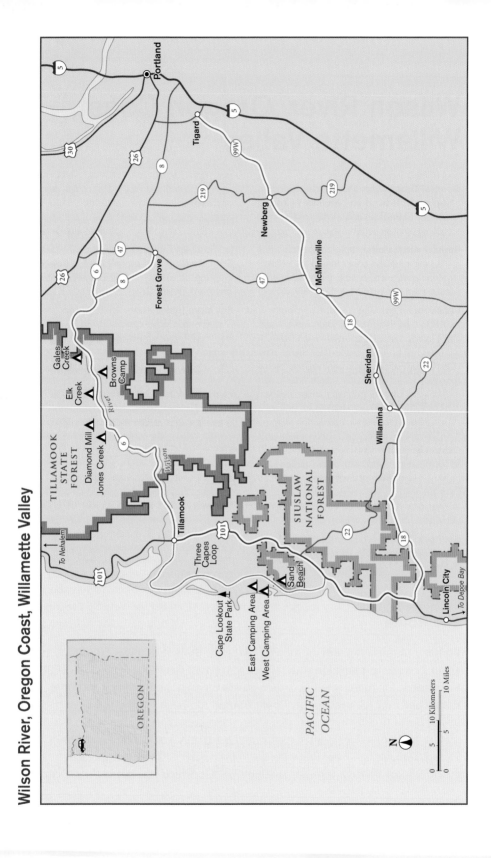

Many of the offshore rocks along the Oregon Coast are wildlife refuges that attract birds, seals, and other wildlife.

forested corridor, or taking the Three Capes Scenic Loop. The return on OR 18 and OR 99 stays on relatively low, flat land as it mixes forest at the beginning with Willamette Valley farmlands near the end. Traffic is generally light on OR 6. OR 18 and 99 West are major connecting routes to the coast. Traffic is moderate during weekdays and heavy on weekends.

Inland summer days range in the high 70s to mid-80s. Spring and fall average in the high 60s. Though temperatures average in the low 30s in January, they range in the 50s during February and March. On the coast summer days are usually in the 60- to 70-degree range, and winter days fall in the mid-50s. The calmest weather comes in autumn.

From **Forest Grove** the drive follows OR 8 northwest through stands of oak trees, picturesque farms, and several vineyards that offer tastings at selected hours. Turning west onto OR 6, **Gales Creek** riffles along the roadway lined with giant Douglas firs. **John W. Blodgett Arboretum,** 2 miles west of the junction, is owned by Pacific University. It is used primarily for botanical research, and several environmental studies and forestry classes are taught here. There are no visitor facilities.

The Oregon coast shoreline is a spectacular mixture of sandy beaches, thick fir forests, and rugged headlands.

Tillamook State Forest

Less than a mile beyond the arboretum, you enter the eastern boundary of the 364,000-acre **Tillamook State Forest** and begin a 5-mile ascent to the **Coast Range** summit of 1,556 feet. **Gales Creek Forest Park,** north of the highway, offers 21 shaded sites. **Rogers Camp Trailhead** at the summit is a day-use parking facility used by hikers, off-road vehicle enthusiasts, mountain bikers, and horseback riders. An easy 2-mile trail along a wooded stream with a beaver colony, an old railroad grade, and logging roads links it with **Gales Creek Park.** Another easy hike takes an elk trail 2 miles south to **Browns Camp,** which has 30 RV campsites and is a staging area for horseback riders and motorcyclists.

Climb the 72 steps to the top of the lookout tower at Tillamook Forest Center and you'll be rewarded with sweeping views of the forest from the center below and up the slopes to the top of the Coast Range mountains.

The forest fire of 1933, the infamous **Tillamook Burn,** started 4 miles north of the summit and raged through the Coast Range with a force that uprooted and twisted off trees and cracked cliffs with the intense heat. Ash and cinders fell on Tillamook, 40 miles away, and had to be shoveled off the streets. Later fires brought the total burned to 355,000 acres.

The **Wilson River,** a rushing torrent in springtime and a lazy, sluggish stream during summer, begins near the summit and meanders in and away from the roadside for the rest of the drive to Tillamook. The layers of sedimentary rock interspersed with basalt lava, which you'll see in the river canyon's rugged cliffs, are part of an ancient ocean floor. About 35 million years ago, a tectonic plate shifted, slid under another plate, and jacked it up, raising the ocean floor above sea level and creating the Coast Range mountains.

Campgrounds & Staging Areas, Traveling West

The endless waves of hills, valleys, and peaks covered with dark blue-green trees are havens for deer, elk, and the seldom-seen black bear and mountain lion. All are fair game for hunters.

A few miles west of the summit, a side road leads north about a mile to 14 campsites situated near the base of **Kings Mountain** and at the confluence of Elk Creek and the Wilson River. Several hikes start at **Elk Creek Campground** and wind around the mountain, by waterfalls and wildflower displays, and to the 3,226-foot summit. The hikes range from easy to difficult and cover from 2 to 9 miles.

Continuing west, the highway passes side roads extending 1 to 2 miles north to a large undeveloped staging area for off-road vehicles at **Diamond Mill Campground,** and 44 vehicle and walk-in tent sites at Jones Creek. Two area stores offer bait, gas, and groceries, serving not only picnickers but also whitewater rafters and steelhead and sea-run cutthroat trout anglers.

South Fork Prison Camp, off the highway, is a minimum-security correctional institution with a capacity for 160 inmates. Many of them are assigned to the Department of Forestry and State Parks to perform reforestation and maintenance.

A few miles west, **Tillamook Forest Center,** managed by the Oregon Department of Forestry, interprets the Tillamook Burn, reforestation, and sustainable forest management with exhibits, maps, and stories. Walk the 72 steps to the top

Tillamook State Forest extends more than 364,000 acres in Northwestern Oregon.

of the center's 40-foot lookout tower and you'll see a replica of the tower's interior with mapping equipment, bed, and desk and enjoy sweeping views of hills and mountains filled with trees from the valley floor to the summit. A nature trail leads through the forest to a suspension bridge straddling the Wilson River.

Foothills of moss-covered oaks signal the beginning of Tillamook County's dairy lands. The road's final 15 miles pass several boat ramps as it follows the shallow river channel through farmlands into Tillamook.

Tillamook & US 101

Tillamook County Pioneer Museum, on the corner of OR 6 and Second Street, occupies a former courthouse and contains one of the state's best natural history exhibits. OR 6 ends 1 block west of the museum at an intersection with US 101. Two miles north of the junction at the **Tillamook County Creamery Association factory,** you can sample the cheese that has made the town internationally famous.

The 38-mile **Three Capes Scenic Loop** starts at the intersection of OR 6 and US 101. It features magnificent coastal scenery, several offshore wildlife refuges, a sand dune area, and full-hookup camping at Cape Lookout State Park. Three forest service campgrounds offer a total of 241 sites.

At Tillamook US 101 jogs inland and away from the ocean for 21 miles before continuing along the shoreline at **Pacific City.** Along this section is a **World War II blimp hangar.** It is one of the world's largest wooden structures and houses the **Tillamook Air Museum.** Over 30 rare aircraft range from World War I Spads and Boeing Stearmans to World War II Messerschmitts, B-25 Mitchell bombers, and P-38 Lightning and Mustang fighters to a Russian Mig jet fighter.

The area is also the gateway to the Trask River's salmon, steelhead, and trout fishing, plus back roads and trails to the **Hebo Mountain summit** (elevation 3,154 feet), which offers lake fishing and a 15-site forest service campground. Two short trails start at the highway and end at 266-foot Munson Creek Falls, the highest of the Coast Range waterfalls.

From Pacific City, where the Three Capes Loop ends, US 101 heads south through the family resort area of Neskowin and over Cascade Head. Three miles north of Lincoln City, the drive turns east onto OR 18.

The Wilson River is a raging torrent in springtime, but dwindles to a shallow stream in late summer.

OR 18

For the first 9 miles, the drive traverses ancient basalts and mudstones formed about 50 million years ago. Some of them are visible in the banks of the **Salmon River,** which parallels the highway. **H.B. Van Duzer Forest State Scenic Corridor,** with picnicking and fishing, signals the beginning of a magnificent 9-mile corridor of stately Douglas fir, Oregon oak, and alder. At the lumbering community of Grand Ronde, OR 18 merges with OR 22, which extends northwest to US 101.

At **Willamina** a scenic side road loops north of town through the Coast Range foothills, then rejoins the main highway near Sheridan. The loop takes you past **Willamina Falls** and a large rock known as an erratic, which was moved here by an ice age glacier. A nearby park and arboretum feature more than 120 trees and native and exotic wildlife.

Willamette Valley

Near Sheridan the merged highways split, and OR 22 angles 30 miles southeast to Salem. OR 18 leaves the forest and bisects low rolling hills of open farmland as it heads 9.5 miles east to enter the northwestern corner of the **Willamette Valley.** The Yamhill River, weaving in and out of the roadside east to Dundee, is fished for trout, steelhead, salmon, bass, crappie, and bluegill.

The Willamette Valley's rich soil was the main attraction and prime motivation for the thousands of emigrants who endured the hardships of the Oregon Trail. En route to Tigard you'll cross valley farms and orchards that grow cherries, plums, wheat, nursery stock, grass seed, and 90 percent of the nation's filberts. Several communities along the highway reflect the pioneer heritage.

As you approach McMinnville you'll see the **Evergreen Aviation and Space Museum.** A Boeing 747 perched on its roof makes it easy to spot. In addition to **Howard Hughes's "Spruce Goose,"** the museum houses over 90 aircraft and 30 original or replica spacecraft including a Titan II missile, Mercury, and Gemini spacecraft. Other attractions include 4 waterslides that start in the airplane and empty into a large inside pool, a children's museum, a wading pool for smaller children, and a solar system rendition that you can walk across.

McMinnville, 6 miles east of Amity, exhibits the traditional main street of small-town America by preserving 52 commercial buildings spanning the 1880s to the 1930s.

Taking OR 99 from McMinnville, you'll pass **Linfield College,** a comprehensive liberal arts school established in 1849. **Lafayette,** 4 miles east, straddles the highway with a few blocks of historic buildings and a large antiques mall. At

Yamhill Locks Park you can picnic and fish on the Willamette River bank overlooking the crumbling cement walls of locks that aided navigation from 1900 to 1954.

Argyle Winery on OR 99 makes chardonnay, sparkling wine, and several varieties of pinot noir. The Argyle tasting room is open 7 days a week from 11 a.m. to 5 p.m. Argyle's 15-minute tour takes you through the sparkling wine process from chilling and pressing grapes to bottling.

Newberg & Tigard

At **Newberg,** a mile east, you can take a self-guided walking tour of more than 50 homes and buildings built from 1880 to 1928. They include a variety of architectural styles and portions of two Donation Land Claims. **Hoover-Minthorn Museum House,** 1 block south of OR 99 at Second and River Streets, was the boyhood home of Herbert Hoover from 1885 to 1889. It exhibits many original bedroom furnishings, photographs, and souvenirs. **Hoover Park,** across the street, offers a pleasant picnic spot with a variety of trees, a rhododendron garden, and stone creek-bank retaining walls built during the 1930s by the Works Progress Administration.

On the concluding 20 miles to **Tigard,** OR 99 cuts across the low hills of the westernmost edge of the **Columbia Plateau** basalt lava flows while passing clusters of businesses and open fields.

11

Mosier, Rowena Dell, Maryhill Loop

General Description: A 50-mile drive on the eastern portion of the Historic Columbia River Highway and into Washington state.

Special Attractions: Columbia River Gorge National Scenic Area and Historic Highway, Tom McCall Preserve, The Dalles Dam, Horsethief Lake State Park, Maryhill Museum of Art, Stonehenge replica, fishing, boating, sailboarding.

Location: Columbia River Gorge between Mosier and Biggs.

Drive Route Numbers: US 30, US 197, WA 14, US 97.

Travel Season: All year. Some roads become extremely icy in winter.

Camping: In Washington 3 US Army Corps of Engineer sites offer primitive camping; 2 state parks, 1 with standard sites and 1 with hookups. In Oregon there are no campgrounds on the loop, but several with hookups are in the immediate area on I-84.

Services: All services at The Dalles and Biggs. Limited services at Mosier and Rowena.

Nearby Attractions: Hood River Valley Scenic Drive, Mount Hood Loop, Columbia River Gorge Scenic Drive, Sherman County Loop Tour, Goldendale Observatory.

For More Information: The Dalles Area Chamber of Commerce, (541) 296-2231, (800) 255-3385 (USA), www.thedalles chamber.com.

The Route

US 30 from The Dalles to Mosier and west from exit 35 to Troutdale has been designated the **Historic Columbia River Highway Scenic Byway.** Containing unique characteristics and having become a destination unto itself, it also met the qualifications for an All-American Road. When it was completed in 1922, the Historic Columbia River Highway extended from The Dalles to the Pacific Ocean and was considered an engineering masterpiece. One newspaper said it "possesses the best of all the great highways in the world, glorified."

Starting at **Mosier,** the drive incorporates the first 14 miles of the historic highway as it travels east atop the ridges of the **Columbia River Gorge National Scenic Area,** affording magnificent views of the river and Washington countryside. Descending into **The Dalles,** it crosses the Columbia River and follows WA 14 east to **Maryhill** and the **Stonehenge replica** while offering continuous views of Oregon's Columbia Gorge. The drive concludes by returning to Oregon at **Biggs.** Travelers can join the drive at Biggs, The Dalles, and several I-84 exits west to Mosier. For the most direct access to **Mosier,** take exit 69 and travel 0.5 mile south into town. Traffic is usually light on the historic highway and moderate on WA 14.

Mosier, Rowena Dell, Maryhill Loop

Temperatures from the mid-90 to over 100 degrees are common during summer. Travelers will find spring and fall days between the upper 40s and the low 60s. Winter days range from below freezing to the low 40s, and gorge winds often create extremely icy conditions between November and February.

The drive begins by crossing the picturesque **Mosier Creek Bridge.** At 120 feet long, it is the second-longest single arch on the highway. It was built in 1920 and was the first bridge designed by Conde B. McCullough. Later he became world famous for his bridges on the Oregon coast and Central America's Inter-American Highway. A trail from a small parking area by the bridge is an easy 0.5-mile hike over a hillside to a pioneer cemetery that contains some of Mosier's founders and then takes you along the gorge rim to **Mosier Falls overlook.**

After the bridge the road climbs abruptly and curves around hills of scrub oak and pine and by apple and cherry orchards protected by rows of Lombardy poplars. Looking north you will see the Columbia River below and Washington across the water. Two miles east of Mosier, the road passes a large Georgian home with a two-story portico nestled on a north hillside. It was built in 1913 by wealthy Bostonian Mark Mayer, who donated the land for Mayer State Park.

Unmarked **Memaloose Overlook,** 1 mile east of the home, was established as a memorial to the Indian burial grounds on the Columbia's **Memaloose Island,** which is visible below. Memaloose State Park is near the island and accessible only to westbound travelers on I-84; it contains 47 full-hookup, 63 tent, and 20 primitive camping sites.

Rowena Dell

US 30 continues east for several miles along the flat-topped ridges and terraced lava outcroppings of **Rowena Dell.** With its sparse vegetation, the terrain is somewhat reminiscent of the southwestern US and known locally as the "Grand Canyon" of the gorge. Formed about 15 million years ago and refined by ice age glaciers and floods 12,000 years ago, the Dell is a protected nature preserve. From February through May it presents Oregon's premier wildflower displays. One of the gorge's most picturesque bridges spans **Dry Canyon Creek.**

At **Rowena Crest Viewpoint** the drive reaches its highest level, about 1,000 feet above the river. From the viewpoint the Columbia River and its canyon seem to stretch east to infinity, and US 30 serpentines around bluffs below. On clear days your 360-degree view encompasses 11,235-foot Mount Hood, plus Washington's 12,276-foot Mount Adams and the Klickitat River Canyon.

Rowena Crest Viewpoint in the Columbia River Gorge affords panoramic views of rugged cliffs and sweeping curves called the Rowena Loops.

Tom McCall Preserve

The Dell and **Governor Tom McCall Preserve,** across the highway, lie in a transition zone between the moist west side and the dry prairie east of the mountains. The 230-acre Nature Conservatory site supports 300 species of plants. Thompson's broadleaf lupine, waterleaf, Columbia desert parsley, and Hood River vetch are unique to the gorge. Mule deer, golden eagles, ospreys, Lewis woodpeckers, and numerous other birds inhabit the area. Watch for rattlesnakes, ticks, and poison oak if you decide to take the short walk through the meadows to the steep cliff edge. Tom McCall Preserve and the Rowena Loops overlook are at their most colorful between late April and mid-summer, when photographers rush to these areas to capture paintbrush, balsamroot, Columbia desert parsley, broadleaf lupine, and a host of other wildflowers.

Rowena Loops & Mayer State Park

The highway gradually descends from the steep viewpoint for several miles in a series of sweeping curves. Called the **Rowena Loops,** they were built to fulfill the stipulation of the highway's engineer, Samuel Lancaster, that "the maximum grade of any ascent/descent should not exceed five percent." The decorative stonework along the loops were made by Italian stonemasons and extend several miles east to a turnoff to **Mayer State Park.**

The park, accessible from a 1-mile side road over I-84, is a favorite Columbia River picnicking, swimming, and boating site. From the shoreline you have outstanding views of the gorge's steep cliffs and Washington's terraced hills. Pier fishing usually lands smallmouth bass, chub, and carp. In the main channel you may be rewarded with catfish, salmon, sturgeon, and steelhead.

The Dalles

From the park you can travel to **The Dalles** via I-84 or return to the historic highway through the community of **Rowena.** Until 1845, when the Barlow Road provided an alternate route to Oregon City, the Rowena area was a staging point for Oregon Trail emigrants who made the final leg of their journey by floating down the Columbia.

As US 30 nears The Dalles, it traverses some of the area's best-preserved **scablands.** The barren slopes were created 13,000 years ago when ice age floods washed away topsoil and loose bedrock.

The **Columbia Gorge Discovery Center and Museum** is a great place to learn more about the gorge's natural and cultural history, Lewis and Clark, and the

Oregon Trail. The center offers maps, visitor information, and a 33-foot-long water model of the Columbia River before it was dammed. You can ride a windsurfing simulator, or walk or bike through 50 acres of interpretive and multipurpose paved trails. The center also has scenic overlooks, orchards, gardens, and ponds.

Entering The Dalles, the drive crosses **Mill Creek Bridge,** which was built in 1920 as part of the original highway. Many of the 19th-century Italianate and gothic homes in **Trevitt Addition,** 1 block east of the bridge, are on the National Register of Historic Places. One block north of US 30, which becomes Third Street downtown, the original **Wasco County Courthouse** contains local artifacts and photos. In 1854 the small frame building became the seat of government for the largest county ever created in the US. Wasco County covered 130,000 square miles and extended from the Cascades to the Rockies.

Old St. Peter's Church, on Third Street, was built in 1897. A 6-foot-high rooster caps the spire of this beautiful redbrick gothic revival structure. At The Dalles waterfront, Google's modern campus occupies the former site of an aluminum smelter.

About 2 miles east of town, you turn north on US 197, pass the entrance to **The Dalles Dam and Visitor Center,** and cross the Columbia River into Washington. At the visitor center you can see Native American petroglyphs, explore history and environmental exhibits, and take a free train ride to the dam's fish ladder and powerhouse.

In Washington State

On the Washington side, roads lead from the main highway to the dam, the Port of Klickatat Industrial Area, and two Army Corps of Engineers–operated parks near the shores of 24-mile-long **Lake Celilo Reservoir.** High bluffs protect the lake from strong winds, making it an ideal spot for beginning and intermediate sailboarders and a popular spot for boating, waterskiing, and fishing. The shoreline is a habitat for bald eagles, nesting Canada geese, and mule deer. You'll find beaches and boat ramps at Spearfish and Hess Parks, and nearby Avery Boat Ramp. .

Turning east on WA 14, you follow the lake's shore to **Horsethief Lake State Park.** Through the centuries Native Americans came from throughout the Northwest to Horsethief Lake and Celilo Falls to trade and catch annual supplies of salmon. Artifacts found here indicate that the trade network extended as far east as Michigan.

While most Native campsites have been covered by water, you can still see original petroglyphs on a 5-minute walk from the parking lot. The many recreational opportunities range from fishing and sailboarding to hiking, rock climbing, and overnighting in 8 tent, 8 utility sites with power and water, and 2 primitive hiker/biker sites that are available on a first come, first served basis.

From Horsethief Lake the highway starts 4 miles of climbing and curving through dry grass hills. Several turnouts afford magnificent views of Oregon's Columbia Gorge and the river's traffic of boaters, water-skiers, sailboarders, and large barges filled with lumber, gravel, grain, and other commodities. The highway peaks at a summit overlooking the site of **Celilo Falls** and the community of **Wishram.** Until it was inundated by dam backwaters in 1957, Celilo Falls was the major obstacle to water travel on the Columbia.

St. James Mission Church in Wishram retains reminders of the town's past as a major Burlington Northern Railroad switching point by displaying relics from a mobile railroad chapel car. The mission's bell came from a train engine.

The drive exits the Columbia River Gorge National Scenic Area by descending through a winding canyon with rustic barns and homes made of black Columbia River basalt.

Maryhill Museum & Stonehenge

A few miles beyond, **Maryhill Museum of Art** sits on a flat plain, literally in the middle of nowhere. Built in 1907 as a mansion by businessman and world traveler Samuel Hill, it houses original bronzes, plasters, watercolors, and sketches by Auguste Rodin. Many include his fingerprints and signature. Maryhill's *The Thinker* is the only plaster cast of the reduced version in existence. Other exhibits include extensive collections of Native American artifacts; chess sets; 19th-century American, Dutch, and French paintings; weaponry; and the queen of Rumania's gold-leafed furniture.

A steam locomotive is a centerpiece at **Maryhill State Park,** 3 miles east near the junction of WA 14 and US 97. It offers swimming, boating, picnicking, and a 50-hookup trailer campground.

The **Stonehenge replica,** a mile east of the junction, was also built by Samuel Hill. The full-size reproduction of England's Stonehenge was started in 1918 and completed in 1929 as America's first World War I memorial. A diagram at the replica suggests how the original, built around 1350 BC, may have been used by ancient astronomers to measure time and mark seasons of the year through observing positions of the sun and moon.

The drive concludes by returning to US 97 and crossing the bridge to Biggs, Oregon. From Biggs you can return to The Dalles through the gorge on I-84.

12

Columbia River Gorge Historic Highway

General Description: A 65-mile drive on paved roads through the most scenic section of the Columbia River Gorge from river level to 893 feet.

Special Attractions: Spectacular gorge scenery, 7 roadside waterfalls, Oregon Trail terminus and water route, Bonneville Dam, Hood River Marina Sailpark, sailboarding, hiking, rain forest.

Location: Northern Oregon border between The Dalles and Troutdale.

Drive Route Numbers: I-84 and US 30.

Travel Season: All year.

Camping: 3 state park campgrounds, 2 with full hookups and 1 with electricity. 4 forest service campgrounds with picnic tables, fire rings, flush or vault toilets, and drinking water.

Services: All services in The Dalles, Hood River, Cascade Locks, and Troutdale.

Nearby Attractions: Mount Hood Scenic Loop, Sherman County Loop, Washington State's Maryhill Museum and Stonehenge Replica, Fort Vancouver National Historic Site.

For More Information: The Dalles Area Chamber of Commerce, (541) 296-2231, (800) 255-3385 (USA), www.thedalles chamber.com; Hood River County Chamber of Commerce, (541) 386-2000, (800) 366-3530 (USA), www.hoodriver.org; Columbia River Gorge Visitors Association, (800) 98-GORGE (984-6743), www.crgva.org.

The Route

The most scenic section of the Columbia River Gorge lies on the 43 miles between The Dalles and Troutdale. It has been designated as a National Scenic Byway and an All-American Road. From The Dalles to exit 35 and the Historic Columbia River Highway (US 30), it follows I-84 on a water-level roadbed with the serene Columbia River ever present on the north and towering cliffs on the south. The final 22 miles climb a southern ridge lined with 7 major waterfalls and viewpoints overlooking the gorge, the Columbia River, and Washington State. Mileposts begin with zero at Portland, and exit numbers on I-84 roughly correspond to the number of miles from Portland.

Columbia River Gorge

When it reaches Oregon, the Columbia has flowed 1,000 miles through British Columbia and Washington. The gorge you travel through today is the aftermath of 40 million years of ashfalls, mud slides, lava flows, and erosion. During the last ice age, about 13,000 years ago, the gorge was refined by a series of 600- to 1,000-foot-deep floods that swept away hillsides, leaving streams to drop over

Columbia River Gorge Historic Highway

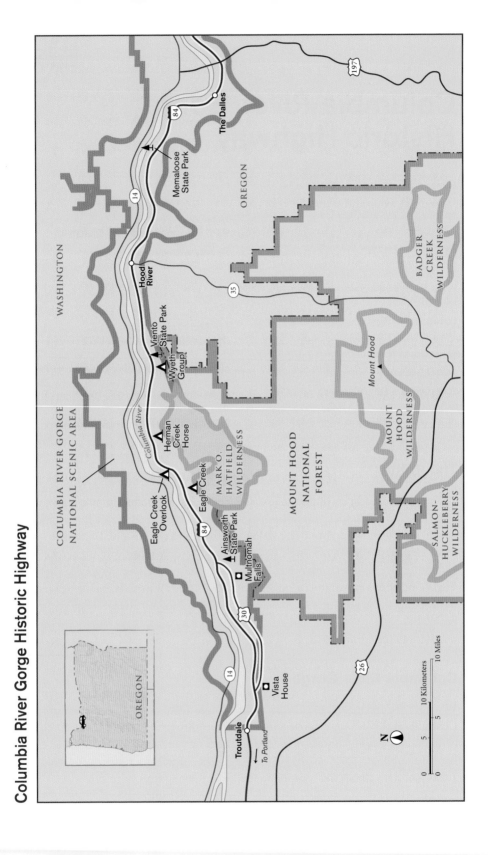

cliffs as waterfalls and exposing tilted rocks and ancient lava flows. Evidence of virtually every type of geologic violence can be seen, including tablelands uplifted and tilted at 45-degree angles; giant slides of mud, rock, and sand; outcroppings from lava flows; columnar basalt; and erosion caused by wind, water, and ice age floods.

Summer travelers will find temperatures in the 90s and 100s in The Dalles and about 5 to 10 degrees cooler from Hood River westward. Spring and fall days range from the upper 40s to the low 60s. The gorge is usually colder in winter than surrounding areas as temperatures dip to the low 30s and 40s. Icy roads are common, and occasionally I-84 may be closed briefly because of snow.

The diversity of climate, ranging from cool and wet in the western gorge to dry in the eastern section, coupled with rich volcanic soil, has proven to be an ideal combination for growing over 30 varieties of grapes. Since the 1990s over 50 vineyards and 30 wineries have supported the local wine industry. In 2004 191,000 acres spanning both sides of the Columbia River were designated an American Viticulture Area.

The Dalles

The Dalles has been a meeting place for Native Americans for more than 12,000 years, a Lewis and Clark campsite, and a Hudson's Bay Company post. Prior to the opening of the Barlow Road around Mount Hood in 1845, The Dalles marked the end of the overland portion of the Oregon Trail. From The Dalles and Rowena, travelers, with their wagons, livestock, and belongings, were rafted and portaged down the Columbia to the Willamette River and Oregon City.

A National Historic District exhibits Italianate, gothic, Queen Anne, and other 19th-century homes. Other historic sites include the original 1859 courthouse and **Fort Dalles Surgeon's Quarters,** established in 1856. **The Dalles Dam** includes a Lewis and Clark exhibit and a petroglyph collection and offers free train rides to viewpoints of the dam and spillway. You can learn more about Lewis and Clark at the **Columbia Gorge Discovery Center and Museum.** It also gives live raptor presentations, has paved hiking and biking trails and a native plant walk, and interprets the natural and cultural history of the gorge from the ice age through the Oregon Trail to modern times.

West of The Dalles

From The Dalles the drive heads west, with I-84 sandwiched between high tiers of stone benches, table rocks, and columnar basalt that all compete for attention with the placid Columbia River and the moss-colored rolling hills of Washington.

Rowena, at exit 76, and Mosier, at exit 69, are gateways to a 9-mile segment of the **Historic Columbia River Highway (US 30)** that can be driven as an alternative to I-84 or incorporated as a loop. The US 30 segment features several points of interest: a picturesque bridge; **Tom McCall Preserve,** which contains diverse plants and animals; **Rowena Dell,** a protected botanical area known for its spring wildflowers; and **Mayer State Park,** which offers a sweeping vista of the eastern area.

Memaloose State Park Rest Area, a few miles west on I-84, overlooks an Indian burial ground on a Columbia River island. The campground includes 47 full-hookup, 63 tent, and 20 primitive sites on the river's edge.

Hood River

From Mosier past Hood River, I-84 hugs the banks of the Columbia River. The gorge opens into a giant mountain-rimmed bowl covered with Christmas tree–size Douglas firs. **Hood River Marina Sailpark,** at exit 63, was built to accommodate the thousands of sailboarders who have made Hood River world famous as a sailboarding hot spot. The facility incorporates the Port of Hood River, a boat basin, swimming and sailboard launching beaches, and a county museum. This exit is also the starting point for the Mount Hood Loop drive on OR 35. White Salmon Bridge, which spans the Columbia River, connects to WA 14 west to Vancouver and east to the Maryhill Museum.

Hood River has been famous for apples and other fruit since at least 1900. The main business district retains several brick and stone buildings from the 1920s. The **Hood River Hotel,** built in 1910 and renovated in the late 1980s, and the **Hood River Railroad Depot** are listed on the National Register of Historic Places. During spring and summer **Mount Hood Railroad** operates scheduled sightseeing excursions through orchards and Cascade Mountain foothills.

Tours of local wineries are available from several operators, and if you take a scenic side trip through the Hood River Valley, you'll find them nestled among apple, pear, and other fruit orchards. Many offer tastings. Hood River is also the place to sample a variety of beers and ales made in brewpubs, such as **Double Mountain Brewery** and **Big Horse Brewing. Full Sail Brewing Company** started in Hood River in 1987 when it began catering to sailboarders and has become virtually a national brand.

The **Columbia Gorge Hotel,** at exit 62, is situated on a section of the historic highway on a high bluff overlooking the river. At this Spanish mission–style hotel built in 1921, you can stay in rooms with antique-style furnishings and four-poster and brass beds. Stone bridges and guard rails are indicative of the stonework on the historic highway and overlook a 200-foot waterfall behind the hotel that plunges from the bluff to the river below.

Bridge of the Gods. Licensed by Shutterstock.com.

West of Hood River the gorge varies from the moss-colored hues of Douglas fir to the yellowish greens of cottonwood and alder. **Viento State Park,** at exit 56, has 55 electrical and 18 tent sites. **Wyeth Group Campground,** at exit 51, with 14 sites, and **Herman Creek Horse Camp,** at exit 47, with 7 sites, are operated by the forest service.

Bridge of the Gods

Exit 44 provides access to Cascade Locks, commercial RV parks, and **Bridge of the Gods Historic Site.** According to an Indian legend, this was the site of a natural stone arch that spanned the Columbia. When two "warrior god" volcanos—Oregon's Mount Hood and Washington's Mount Adams—fought over the "goddess" volcano, Mount St. Helens, the bridge collapsed, causing the Cascades of the Columbia.

The cascades, actually caused by rock slides, were considered the most treacherous part of the 2,000-mile Oregon Trail. After locks were built in 1896, river traffic was able to bypass the dangerous rapids. Rendered obsolete with the construction of Bonneville Dam, they are part of a park that contains the first Northwest steam locomotive and two museums, one of which is the home of a former

Bonneville Dam is one of several massive dams that have tamed the once turbulent Columbia River. LICENSED BY SHUTTERSTOCK.COM.

lock tender. Sternwheeler cruises through Columbia River Gorge also originate at the park. The steel-trussed Bridge of the Gods connects Oregon with WA 14. Cascade Locks is also a trailhead for the Pacific Crest Trail, which extends from Canada to Mexico.

West of Cascade Locks are two forest service campgrounds, **Eagle Creek** and **Eagle Creek Overlook.** The campground was built in 1915 and was the nation's first forest service campground. It has 17 sites. Eagle Creek Overlook was a Civilian Conservation Corps project developed in the 1930s as a viewpoint to construction of Bonneville Dam. It can accommodate 90 people and 40 cars and is often used for family gatherings and group events. Although there are no hookups, it also takes trailers.

Bonneville Dam, at exit 40, features a multilevel visitor center with fish ladders and an underwater viewing room. At a shaded pond area you can see trout, salmon, sturgeon, and other local species.

Historic Columbia River Highway

Exit 35 is the eastern access to the Historic Columbia River Highway. Built between 1913 and 1920, it is still considered an engineering marvel. Samuel

Lancaster, the highway's chief engineer, saw the project as a unique opportunity to reconcile nature and civilization. His purpose, he said, was "to find the beauty spots, or those points where the most beautiful things along the line might be seen to the best advantage, and if possible, to locate the road in such a way as to reach them."

Lancaster's road incorporated the era's most up-to-date standards. Graceful bridges complement natural settings and blend with the environment. Stone guardrails, dry masonry, and rock walls, which appear intermittently throughout the drive, are characteristic of the stonemason's artistry and training in old-world road-building traditions. Lancaster succeeded so well in attaining his objectives that the drive is sometimes referred to as a mystical experience.

Waterfalls

The historic highway begins by winding through a typical Cascade rain forest of fir, maple, and alder, enhanced by moss and thick ground cover of ferns and wildflowers. **Ainsworth State Park,** 1 mile west of exit 35, offers 45 full-hookup campsites in an idyllic setting along with a 1.25-mile hiking trail. Nearby **Horsetail Falls** drops in a rushing torrent. A 1.3-mile trail takes you to an upper cascade called **Pony Tail Falls.** Horsetail is one of seven major waterfalls along the highway. Each has space for parking.

Oneonta Gorge, 2 miles west, is a forest service botanical area with more than 50 species of wildflowers, flowering trees, and shrubs. If you want to see the falls, wait until summer, when the stream is low. Bring rubber boots; you'll need to hike up 900 feet of the creek bed.

The gorge's centerpiece, **Multnomah Falls,** drops from a ledge 2 miles west. At 620 feet, it is the fourth-highest waterfall in the US. You can take a trail to a bridge at the 69-foot lower falls, then zigzag your way to the top.

Multnomah Falls Lodge was built in 1925 as a travelers' way station. The stone Cascadian-style structure includes a lounge, restaurant, patio dining, and coffee and gift shop.

Waterfalls & Vista House

Westward from Multnomah Falls the highway climbs 600 feet in 8 miles. In keeping with Lancaster's decree that the road have a maximum grade of 5 percent and curve radii of not less than 100 feet, much of the route is a series of figure-eight curves. You'll see four waterfalls in this section: **Wahkeena,** mile 31; **Bridal Veil,** mile 29; **Shepperd's Dell,** mile 27; and **Latourell,** mile 26; plus several historic private residences, bridges, and barns.

Vista House and Crown Point are among the most famous and most photographed sites in the Columbia River Gorge. LICENSED BY SHUTTERSTOCK.COM.

Like virtually everything on the highway, **Vista House,** at mile 24, was part of Lancaster's vision. **Crown Point State Park,** where it sits, was, according to Lancaster, the ideal site for "an observatory from which the view both up and down the Columbia could be viewed in silent communion with the infinite." Although the igloo-shaped Vista House is open only in summer, the parking lot and circular lower promenade are accessible all year. The view from 733-foot Crown Point encompasses extinct volcanos in Washington, the Columbia River, Beacon Rock—an 800-foot-high volcanic plug—and the spectacular eastern rim of the gorge.

Portland Women's Forum State Park, at mile 10, offers a magnificent view of the entire gorge amphitheater. This is the place to photograph Vista House, perched on Crown Point, with the Columbia below and the gorge wall in the background, just as you've seen it in thousands of pictures.

The remaining 10 miles to **Troutdale** pass through thick forest by Dabney and Lewis and Clark State Parks and the Sandy River, which is known for its spring smelt runs. Both parks are day-use facilities.

From Troutdale travelers have the option of continuing west to Portland via I-84 or traveling 3 miles south to US 26 and taking the Mount Hood Loop drive.

13

Mount Hood National Scenic Byway

General Description: A 105-mile paved and signed loop around the southern slopes of Mount Hood and through the Hood River Valley to the Columbia River Gorge Scenic Area. When the Columbia River Gorge drive is added from Hood River to Troutdale, the total mileage is 130 miles.

Special Attractions: Spectacular mountain scenery, 6 ski areas, rivers, Mount Hood National Forest, Oregon Trail historic sites, Hood River Valley.

Location: Southern slope of Mount Hood between Gresham and Hood River.

Drive Route Numbers: US 26, OR 35.

Travel Season: All year.

Camping: 13 forest service campgrounds with picnic tables, fire pits, and flush or vault toilets. Some have drinking water. 2 county parks, 1 with hookups and 1 with tent sites.

Services: All services at Gresham, Sandy, Government Camp, and Hood River. Limited services at Rhododendron and Zigzag.

Nearby Attractions: Mount Hood Wilderness, Warm Springs Indian Reservation, Badger Creek Wilderness, Salmon-Huckleberry Wilderness, Fort Vancouver National Historic Site, Columbia River Gorge Scenic Drive, Mosier-Maryhill Scenic Drive, Sherman County Scenic Drive, Biggs–The Dalles Oregon Trail Route.

For More Information: Travel Portland (503) 275-9750, (877) 678-5263, www.travelportland.com; Gresham Area Chamber of Commerce Visitor Center, (503) 665-1131, www.greshamchamber .org; Sandy Area Chamber of Commerce, (503) 668-4006, www.sandyoregon chamber.org; Hood River County Chamber of Commerce, (541) 386-2000, (800) 366-3530 (USA), www.hoodriver.org; Mount Hood Area Chamber of Commerce, (503) 622-3017, www.mthood.org; Mount Hood National Forest, (503) 668-1700, www .fs.usda.gov/mthood; Hood River Ranger Station, (541) 352-6002; Troutdale: West Columbia Gorge Chamber of Commerce, (503) 669-7473, www. westcolumbia gorgechamber.com; Columbia River Gorge Visitors Association, (800) 98-GORGE (984-6743), www.crgva.org

The Route

Mount Hood dominates the Oregon skyline as a giant cylindrical white-topped cone. At 11,235 feet elevation, it is Oregon's tallest mountain and a recreational area for all seasons. It offers spring wildflower meadows; camping, hiking, and climbing during summer; fall foliage; and skiing year-round.

Native Americans called it Wy'East, and according to their legends, it was a great chief who had been turned into a mountain as punishment and retaliated by spouting fire and boulders. In 1792 it was renamed Hood to honor an English navy admiral.

The mountain was formed between 1 million and 10 million years ago in a series of eruptions that extended over thousands of years, the latest in 1907.

Mount Hood National Scenic Byway

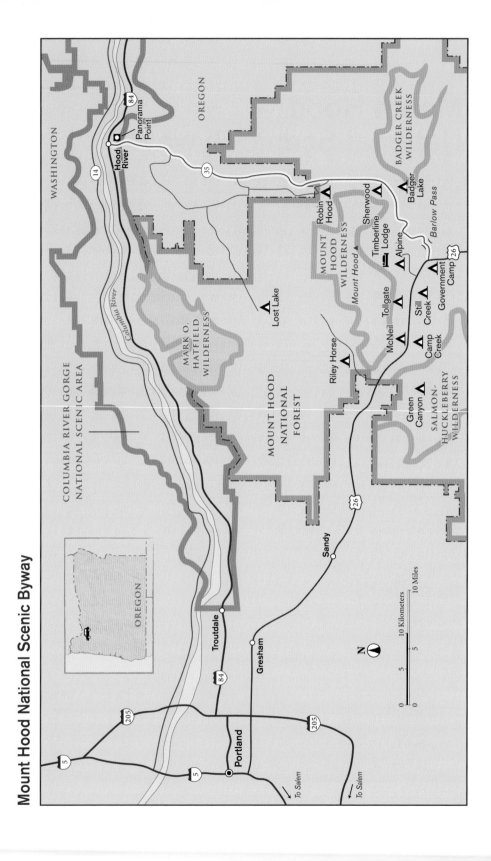

US 26

This route was declared a National Scenic Byway in 2005. US 26 follows the general route of the historic Barlow Road, which was established in 1845 and offered Oregon Trail travelers an alternative to reaching western Oregon without fording the treacherous rapids of the Columbia River. The drive circles Mount Hood's southern slope and runs along ridges affording magnificent views of thick forest covering a sea of canyons, cliffs, hills, and mountains. After reaching a maximum elevation of 6,000 feet at Timberline Lodge, it concludes by taking OR 35 through the picturesque orchards of the Hood River Valley. The **Mount Hood Loop** is often combined with the Columbia River Gorge drive. For the best progression of scenery, begin at the western end in **Troutdale** and **Gresham** and end in **Hood River** or continue with the Columbia River Gorge drive to Troutdale. Traffic is usually moderate during the week and heavy on weekends.

Temperatures in the Hood River Valley average in the mid-60s in summer. Winters range from 33 to 43 degrees. Spring days are usually between 49 and 56 degrees. Autumn temperatures average in the high 50s. Temperatures at Mount Hood are unpredictable but average 5 to 10 degrees less than in the valley. Snow flurries can fall at Timberline Lodge in late spring and early summer.

Sandy

If you are starting the drive from Portland, follow I-84 east and take exits 13 to 16A at Troutdale, which is often called the gateway to the Columbia River Gorge. Take 242nd Street and travel south to Gresham. En route you'll pass the historic **McMenamins Edgefield** estate's winery, brewery, and golf course. Turning east at Gresham you can follow the tour route on Burnside Street, which becomes Dodge Park Boulevard to **Dodge Park.** It provides access to the old-growth forest and rugged **Sandy River Canyon.** If you elect to follow US 26 from Gresham east 9 miles to the community of **Sandy,** you'll pass open meadowlands and climb the Cascade foothills. **Jonsrud Viewpoint** near Sandy provides a spectacular view of the Sandy River.

Sandy is the western gateway to the Mount Hood area and a service center with outdoor recreation equipment retailers and rental companies, wineries, breweries, and shops. Five miles east of Sandy the farmlands end abruptly. Dark green forest closes in and remains virtually unbroken until the Hood River Valley. The stately 150-foot evergreens are primarily Douglas fir, with a rich mixture of western red cedar and western hemlock. Oregon oaks, cottonwoods, and alders add burnt-yellow accents to the dark evergreens. Wild rhododendrons add splashes of red, white, and purple during springtime, and the vivid reds and yellows of oaks and vine maples brighten autumn. On the eastern horizon a mountain ridge forms an amphitheater for tree-covered hills.

Mount Hood

On the 15 miles to **Mount Hood Ranger Station** at Brightwood, the drive parallels the Salmon River as it passes a candy factory and trout-fishing farm in 30 acres of meadows with free fishing in 10 ponds. If you're planning to camp, cross-country ski, or climb Mount Hood, you need to stop at the ranger station for maps and permits. Although there is no hiking trail to the summit, Mount Hood is the most frequently climbed glaciated peak in North America. Lists of minimum equipment necessary for a safe ascent are available at ranger stations, along with fact sheets on day hikes from forest service roads and trailheads along the highway.

Mount Hood RV Park, across the street, is a multipurpose full-service resort with space for 550 recreational vehicles, river frontage, an indoor pool and sauna, and a 350-acre recreational park. **Wildwood Recreation Area,** east of the station, is the departure point for several roadside hiking trails into the cool, inviting forest. The **Resort at the Mountain,** east of the recreation area in Welches, is a 157-room complex with golf, tennis courts, and a pool. Condominiums, a Swiss restaurant, and shops featuring hand-crafted gifts and antiques are nearby.

Zig Zag Ranger Station, a mile east of Welches, has been an administrative office since 1907. The 18 buildings were constructed by the Civilian Conservation Corps between 1933 and 1942. The Wy'East Rhododendron Gardens, which surround the offices, contain more than 50 varieties of rhododendrons that bloom during May and June.

From Zigzag a road leads north to **McNeil Campground,** with 34 sites, and **Riley Horse Camp,** with 14 sites. **Green Canyon Campground,** a couple miles south of Zigzag, has 15 sites.

Mount Hood National Forest

East of the station the highway enters the 1.06-million-acre **Mount Hood National Forest,** which extends east past Hood River. On the 12 miles to Government Camp, it is easy to envision the hardships pioneers faced in crossing the mountains as the road climbs dramatically and serpentines along the ridge of a valley filled with trees from roadside to horizon. As it clings to the mountainside, virtually every inch is a viewpoint.

Tollgate Campground, with 9 tent or RV and 4 campsites, features a replica of the Barlow Road's western tollgate. Nearby **Camp Creek Campground** has 24 sites. Several forest service roads start at the highway and lead to scenic viewpoints or trailheads. This is a winter recreation area, and signs warn of the need to carry traction tires or chains. From November through April permits are required to use snow parks.

Laurel Hill, at milepost 46, was the most difficult section of the Barlow Road. Wagons were lowered down the steep slopes by makeshift winches made with ropes lashed to trees. The hill provides eastbound travelers with the first view of Mount Hood's snowcapped peak.

Government Camp & the Ski Bowl

Government Camp, a few miles farther east, was named for an army detachment that camped here in 1849. Today the resort community is a winter sports center serving six ski areas that stretch east for about 20 miles. Numerous cross-country ski trails also start from Government Camp. **Alpine Campground,** north of town, has 16 sites, and **Still Creek,** near the highway, contains 26 sites.

Mount Hood Ski Bowl, across the highway from Government Camp, is America's largest night skiing area, with 34 lighted runs. Its facilities include a lodge, 4 double chairlifts, and 5 surface tows. In summer you can enjoy the mountain scenery from an alpine slide, ride in go-karts, or rent horses to explore the backcountry. There are activities to entertain the children. You can jump from the bungee tower, climb a rock wall mountain, and play disc golf.

Summit Ski Area, 2 miles east, dates to 1926 and is the oldest ski area in the Pacific Northwest and the second oldest in the nation. It rents tubes and discs for non-skiers. The 3 miles of trails are excellent for beginners.

Timberline, Trillium Lake & Snowbunny

Two miles east, a steep 6-mile side road leads to **Timberline,** at the 6,600-foot level, passing seasonal waterfalls and vistas of seemingly endless forests, peaks, and valleys. While most come to enjoy year-round day and night skiing, Timberline is also a major stop for sightseers. **Timberline Lodge,** constructed during the 1930s as a Works Progress Administration project, is a National Historic Landmark and an impressive monument to the skill of its builders. It contains 71 rooms, a lounge, and an outdoor pool.

Easy access to **Trillium Lake,** 2 miles south of US 26, has made it a favorite rest and picturesque picnicking spot. Some of the 61 campsites can accommodate oversize trailers. Nearby **Still Creek Campground** has 26 sites.

Snowbunny is 3 miles east of Timberline's road and is a snow-play area with a sliding hill and snack bar. The area was the site of a Barlow Road tollhouse and pioneer campground. A small cemetery near Snowbunny contains graves of several children and adults who perished on the Barlow Trail.

Mount Hood provides a spectacular background for sightseers and photographers at Trillium Lake. Licensed by Shutterstock.com.

OR 35

A few miles farther, the drive turns onto OR 35 and US 26 continues southeast to Vale. A gravesite near the junction marks the final resting place of a pioneer woman. Shortly after the junction, OR 35 crosses the Pacific Crest Trail at 4,157-foot-high Barlow Pass.

The loop road reaches its highest point at 4,647-foot **Bennett Pass. Mount Hood Meadows,** near the summit, encompasses the mountain's largest ski area.

It covers 2,000 acres, contains 60 slopes and trails, and can move 12,000 skiers per hour on 11 chairlifts. From the lounge, with its 120-foot glass wall, you have a magnificent close-up view of the mountain's snowcapped peak.

The 9 miles to **Cooper Spur Ski Area** feature some of the best highway scenery as the road winds through canyons, by cliffs, and along the Hood River. En route it passes several campgrounds, hiking trails, and forest service roads. Sherwood, Badger Lake, and Robin Hood campgrounds have a total of 42 sites.

The Cooper Spur access road is a historic district. **Cloud Cap Inn,** built in 1889, was the first structure constructed on Mount Hood. It offers a superb view of the snowcapped peak. Other sites include an 1889 wagon road, an early-20th-century log clubhouse, cookstoves constructed of native rock, and a public shelter built in 1939 by the Civilian Conservation Corps. **Tilly Jane Campground,** built in 1926, and **Cloud Cap Saddle** contain a total of 17 tent sites that are open only during summer. The panoramic view of Washington's Mount Adams, Mount Rainier, and Mount St. Helens from **Inspiration Point** has graced numerous postcards and calendars. **Cooper Spur Ski Area** caters to families and includes a restaurant, rope tows for tubing, a Nordic center, and a T-bar lift.

As OR 35 leaves the Mount Hood National Forest, it passes through stands of alder and cottonwood, brilliant green in spring and bright yellow in autumn. **Routson County Park,** on the banks of the Hood River near the boundary, offers river fishing for trout and steelhead. Because of the steep climb, the 20 campsites are not recommended for trailers.

Fruit orchards have been the center of the Hood River Valley economy since 1900 and come into view near the ranger station by the community of **Mount Hood.** Toll Bridge Park, at Mount Hood, features 20 full-service, 45 partial-hookup, and 20 tent sites.

The remaining 15 miles continue north through the fragrant orchards and vistas of the valley's fields and forests. **Panorama Point,** 3 miles east of the highway near Hood River, offers a sweeping view of the valley capped by Mount Hood in the background. The drive concludes by entering the Columbia River Gorge National Scenic Area and Hood River, where OR 35 crosses I-84.

14

French Prairie Loop

General Description: A 60-mile drive through northwestern Oregon's Willamette Valley and French Prairie's agricultural lands and historic areas.

Special Attractions: Oregon Trail terminus, Willamette Falls, Aurora Historic District, French Prairie historic churches, Champoeg State Heritage Area, Willamette River, camping, museums.

Location: Northwestern Oregon between Oregon City and Newberg.

Drive Route Numbers: OR 99 East, OR 219, Champoeg Park Road.

Travel season: All year.

Camping: 1 state park campground with 12 full-hookup, 67 electrical, and 3 group sites.

Services: All services in Oregon City, Canby, Woodburn, and Newberg. Limited Services in Aurora and St. Paul.

Nearby Attractions: Portland, Columbia River Gorge, Multnomah Falls, Salem, Silver Falls Loop, Mount Hood National Scenic Byway, 99 West Scenic Drive, Washington County Vineyard and Valley Scenic Tour.

For more information: Oregon City Chamber of Commerce, (503) 656-1619, (800) 424-3002, www.oregoncity.org; Travel Portland, (503) 275-9750, (877) 678-5263, www.travelportland.com; Canby Area Chamber of Commerce, (503) 266-4600, www.canbyareachamber.org; Woodburn Area Chamber of Commerce, (503) 982-8221, www.woodburnchamber.org; Newberg: Chehalem Valley Chamber of Commerce, (503) 538-2014, www.chehalemvalley.org; Champoeg State Heritage Area, (503) 678-1251, www.oregonstateparks.org.

The Route

Several versions of this drive exist, including separate itineraries for the **OR 99 East** and **French Prairie** segments. This drive, which combines the two, can be taken from Portland by traveling 13 miles southeast to Oregon City. It can also be joined from I-5 at exit 263 at Brooks, exit 271 at Woodburn, or exit 278 at Aurora/Donald.

History and architecture take precedence over natural scenery that includes the **Willamette River,** hop and berry fields, and open farmland. It was this rich soil and abundant wildlife along the Willamette that attracted the first fur trappers and later Oregon Trail emigrants to the area. The drive is at its most colorful in early spring when several commercial flower farms burst into riots of color and their owners open their display gardens to visitors.

From **Oregon City** the drive moves south along the banks of the Willamette River to the **Aurora Historic District,** then passes through hop yards and berry fields en route to Brooks. After retracing about 5 miles, it turns northwest, passing

French Prairie Loop

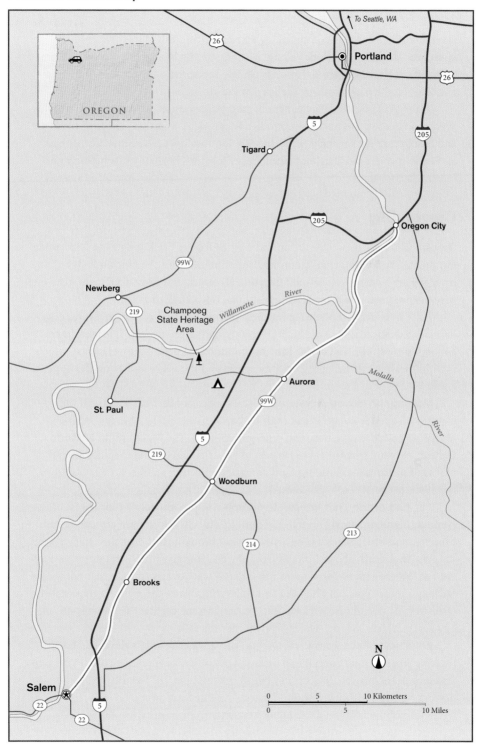

several small crossroads communities that are distinguished by their unique churches. The drive concludes along the banks of the Willamette River at **Champoeg State Heritage Area.** Traffic is usually moderate to heavy on OR 99 East and light on the back roads in the French Prairie section.

In the Willamette Valley generally mild temperatures prevail all year. Winters average in the low 50s and drop into the 40s at night. Summers range in the 70s and 80s. Spring days usually fall in the 60s, autumn days in the low 70s. Winter and early spring mornings may bring heavy fog, which usually lifts before noon but can last for days.

Oregon City

Oregon City was the western terminus of the Oregon Trail. It dates to 1829 when Dr. John McLoughlin, chief factor and superintendent of the Hudson's Bay Company at Fort Vancouver, claimed the land. Oregon's first provincial legislature met here in 1843, and it was the territorial capital from 1845 to 1852.

The city is divided, with the business section situated at river level and residential areas sprawling along a cliff overlooking the waterfront. The areas are connected by streets and a **130-foot-high municipal passenger elevator,** which is within walking distance of both city center and the historic sites on the upper levels.

McLoughlin House, a National Historic Site, stands 2 blocks east of the elevator on Center Street. It was built by Dr. McLoughlin in 1846 and contains his gaming table, china, bed, and other possessions. The **McLoughlin Historic District,** surrounding the home, is part of his original plat and includes several blocks of picturesque dwellings and churches reflecting architectural styles from the 1840s to the 1930s.

The **End of the Trail Interpretive Center,** approximately 5 blocks east of the elevator, highlights travel on the trail with exhibits of covered wagons, river rafts, firearms, and other relics. Some artifacts were brought west over the Oregon Trail.

Walking south about 4 blocks from the elevator gives you a magnificent overview of **Willamette Falls,** which spills about 40 feet over a rocky basalt horseshoe. During summer you can also take an exhilarating cruise through the rock-walled waterway. A second scenic viewpoint, situated on the highway 0.6 mile south of city center, offers a closer, water-level view of the falls.

Willamette Falls Locks was Oregon's first water resource development project. You can tour the original lockmaster's office by appointment and see photographs of the historic locks. They began operating in 1873 and have been designated a National Historic Site and Historic Engineering Site.

South of the falls the drive follows the wide Willamette River as it weaves

The Willamette Valley's climate and fertile soil are ideal for vineyards and wineries.
LICENSED BY SHUTTERSTOCK.COM.

through mixed stands of oak and cottonwood. The river begins more than 100 miles south in the Cascade foothills near Eugene and is one of the few that flow north. Turning onto Northeast Territorial Road at **Canby,** you follow the directional signs west and north to **Molalla River State Park.** The **Canby Ferry,** near the park, transports cars and passengers across the Willamette River to a west side connecting road.

The day-use park, near the mouth of the Molalla River, is known for its large rookery of great blue herons. A 1.5-mile trail will take you through a lush undergrowth along the Willamette's shoreline to a boat ramp.

Canby is a service center for the flower, berry, and dairy farms along the highway south of town. The Canby Depot Museum on OR 99 interprets the town's history.

Turning east on Barlow Road, the drive cuts through a landscape reminiscent of the European countryside on the 4.4-mile side trip to **St. Josef's Wine Cellars.** The winery produces pinot noir and pinot gris. A rustic German tasting room and picnic grounds are open all year and the vineyard also hosts concerts, grape stomps, and other events.

FRENCH PRAIRIE LOOP   **103**

Aurora National Historic District

The **Aurora National Historic District,** 2 miles south on OR 99 East, was started as a commune in 1856 by William Keil, a Prussian tailor, self-proclaimed physician, and fundamentalist preacher. At its peak the colony numbered 600 people and covered 15,000 acres.

Although the commune was disbanded after Keil's death in 1877, the town has retained several blocks of historic buildings. Most of them are large, reflecting the communal ownership and German architectural influence. The **Old Aurora Colony Museum** complex includes an ox barn, two homes, a communal wash house, and a farm machinery building. On a short walking tour, you can see 35 buildings from the 1865–1933 period, 20 of which are on the National Register of Historic Places. **Aurora**'s 21 antiques, collectible, and specialty shops have made the Travel Channel's and MSN.com's lists of the best antiquing towns in America.

Near Aurora the Willamette River veers west. OR 99 East cuts through Christmas tree farms, hop yards, and berry fields en route to Woodburn and Brooks. The **Wooden Shoe Tulip Farm** in Woodburn brightens the spring landscape with 40 acres of flowers and celebrates the annual blooming with a spring tulip festival.

Western Antique Powerland Museum

At Brooks you turn west onto Brookdale Road and cross I-5 to the **Western Antique Powerland Museum.** Some 15 museums and associations dedicated to preserving antique farm machinery, steam-driven vehicles, and antique implements are housed on the Western Powerland grounds. The on-site **Oregon Electric Railway Museum** is the largest trolley museum in the Pacific Northwest. It has over a mile of track with overhead wire and yard leads, a car barn with four tracks, a powerhouse, and a depot. Other museums preserve blacksmith and machine shops, trucks, tractors, and model railroads. The **Great Oregon Steam Up,** held the last weekend of July and first weekend in August, attracts over 10,000 people who come to watch tractor pulls and steam-driven vehicle parades and to ride trolleys of various sizes. Hours vary with the season and individual museums. Closed November through February.

You can see more flowers on both sides of Brooks. **Adelman Peony Gardens,** east of town, displays and sells hundreds of varieties of the colorful flower on 8 acres that it opens to the public during May and June. With 200 acres, **Schreiner's Gardens,** a few miles west of Brooks, is the nation's largest retail iris grower. Their 10-acre display garden opens in early May and stays open from dawn to dusk during the blooming season. The riot of colors ranges from black to pure white with reds, blues, copper, purple, and many hues in between.

After returning to OR 99 East and traveling north a couple of miles, the drive turns west at Gervais and enters the southern edge of **French Prairie.** The community has a unique square-steepled church and a historic cemetery that contains a section for Old Russian Believers.

From Gervais to the conclusion of the drive, you'll pass through the heart of the Willamette Valley's French Prairie farmlands. Cattle, sheep, and poultry farms mingle with a patchwork of fruit orchards and field crops. Among them are sugar beets, grass for grass seed, corn, hops, apples, peaches, cherries, berries, and vegetables. The valley was formed about 35 million years ago when a section of the Pacific shoreline was uplifted and also created the Coast Range mountains. Floods following the last ice age deposited the rich silt that forms the basis of the productive croplands.

Four miles west at St. Louis, a picturesque white country church, built in 1889, sits at the intersection of OR 219. Turning north on OR 219, which is also signed as **French Prairie Road,** you cut through the center of the prairie, passing oak and cottonwood thickets, pasturelands, and picturesque farmhouses and barns.

St. Paul

After 7 miles you turn onto Blanchet Road and, on the mile west to **St. Paul,** travel by hop-yard trellises and farmlands and a stately colonial home built in 1882. Look north as you approach town and you'll see a beautiful French cross towering above large elaborate headstones in **St. Paul Cemetery.** Many of the graves date to the 1800s.

Today the town is better known for its **annual rodeo,** which is among the 20 largest in the US and attracts national performers. St. Paul was the core of French Prairie and second only to Astoria in the order of white settlement in Oregon. French Canadians began settling here as early as 1828, attracted by the water transportation and the brigade trail that connected the area to Fort Vancouver.

A brick in the chimney of an old cabin west of town is dated 1832, and 10 other sites and buildings are linked to the French-Canadian era. They range from churches, missions, and cemeteries to boardinghouses. The Catholic church, which dominates the skyline, was built in 1846 as a cathedral for the archdiocese.

In St. Paul **Heirloom Roses** opens its 5 acres of rose gardens year-round at no charge. You can also see and buy more flowers, plus seasonal fresh fruit and vegetables, at **French Prairie Gardens.**

Champoeg

Continuing north on OR 219, you travel through 7 miles of grasslands and nursery stock gardens to the Willamette River and Champoeg Road. A marker 0.25 mile north of the intersection commemorates the site of the Willamette Valley's first trading post. It was established in 1811 by the Astor Company and subsequently was operated for 10 years by the Northwest Company. The post was instrumental in bringing the first trappers, adventurers, and settlers to the French Prairie region.

Turning east on Champoeg Road, you travel 2.5 miles through a wooded corridor to the **Robert Newell House,** a reconstruction of an 1850s pioneer home. It contains governors' wives' inaugural gowns, antique guns, Native American artifacts, a vintage quilt collection, and basketry. A one-room schoolhouse, with 1850s furnishings, and an original wooden jail are also on the grounds.

A quarter mile east, **Champoeg State Heritage Area's visitor center** sits on a ridge overlooking lawns and forests on the riverbank below. Displays interpret the natural setting, the fur trade, French-Canadian settlers, and the struggle for the Oregon country.

Champoeg was an early hub for river travel and contained a settlement of 30 buildings and 200 people. Until the 1840s the Oregon country was shared by the US and Great Britain under a "joint occupancy agreement." On May 2, 1843, settlers met at Champoeg and voted to establish a provisional government. It was the first organized American government in the Pacific Northwest.

Group picnic areas; 12 full-hookup, 67 electrical, and 6 walk-in tent sites; a group RV camp; and hiker/biker camps are tucked away in a forest of black cottonwood, Douglas fir, western red cedar, Oregon white oak, and big-leaf maple. Deer, coyotes, beavers, and mink are sometimes seen along hiking trails, and sheep graze in adjacent fields. A boat ramp provides access to Willamette River salmon and steelhead fishing.

Although floods destroyed the town, several historic sites are marked, including a pioneer grave and cemetery. A pioneer mother's cabin museum overlooks the Willamette River. Its antiquities include a mastodon tooth found in the park and relics brought over the Oregon Trail.

From Champoeg you can conclude by traveling 13 miles east to Aurora and I-5 or west 5 miles to Newberg.

15

Eugene to Tigard

General Description: A 122-mile signed scenic drive through Willamette Valley cities, farms, vineyards, and historic areas.

Special Attractions: Historic sites, wildlife refuges, wineries, McDonald Experimental Forest, Peavy Arboretum, valley scenery, Willamette River.

Location: Western Willamette Valley between Eugene and Tigard.

Drive Route Numbers: OR 99, OR 99 West.

Travel Season: All year.

Camping: No campgrounds on the route. Champoeg State Park Campground, with 12 full-hookup, 67 electrical, and 3 group tent sites, is situated about 8 miles south of Newberg. A Bureau of Land Management campground at Alsea Falls has 16 tent sites and is approximately 14 miles west of the route.

Services: All services in Eugene, Junction City, Corvallis, Monmouth, McMinnville, Newberg, and Tigard.

Nearby Attractions: Albany historic districts, Dorena Lake, covered bridges, Salem, Alsea River Back Country Byway, Columbia River Gorge, Silver Falls Loop, 99 East–French Prairie Loop Scenic Drive, Eugene–Willamette Pass Scenic Drive, Washington County Vineyard and Valley Scenic Tour.

For More Information: Eugene, Cascades & Oregon Coast–Travel Lane County, (541) 484-5307, (800) 547-5445, www.travel lanecounty.org; Junction City–Harrisburg Area Chamber of Commerce, (541) 998-6154, www.jch-chamber.org; Corvallis Tourism, (541) 757-1544, (800) 334-8118 (USA), www.visitcorvallis.com; Monmouth-Independence Area Chamber of Commerce, (503) 838-4268, (800) 772-2806, www .micc-or.org; McMinnville Chamber of Commerce, (503) 472- 6196, www.McMinnville .org; Newberg: Chehalem Valley Chamber of Commerce, (503) 538-2014, www .chehalemvalley.org; Tigard Area Chamber of Commerce, (503) 639-1656, www .tigardchamber.org; Albany Visitors Association, (541) 928-0911, (800) 526-2256 (USA), www.albanyvisitors.com; Champoeg State Heritage Area, (503) 678-1251, www.oregonstateparks.org.

The Route

OR 99 was the main north–south avenue through the fertile Willamette Valley for over 30 years. Today it offers travelers an opportunity to bypass the hustle and bustle of I-5, a few miles east, and take a leisurely trip through the valley's rich farmlands, small historic communities, and quiet college towns. Along the way visitors travel through a variety of croplands producing Christmas trees, grass for grass seed, wheat, nursery stock, cherries, prunes, grapes, and nuts. Numerous wineries along the route offer tours and tastings.

The valley is a series of basalt ridges and basins filled with rich silt and gravel transported to western Oregon from as far away as Montana. They were deposited

Eugene To Tigard

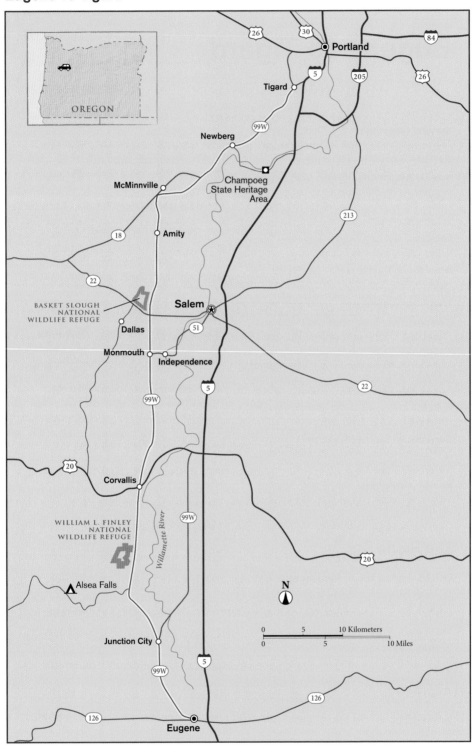

some 12,000 years ago by huge floods following the last ice age. The valley was raised above sea level about 35,000 years ago at the same time the Coast Range mountains were lifted by shifting of tectonic plates. Gradually, through faulting and shifting, the valley was lowered and widened.

The loop begins on OR 99 West in downtown Eugene and continues in a straight line, north through Corvallis to McMinnville. Turning east, it passes through several historic communities before concluding at Tigard. Most of the route is flat farmland, broken by thickets of Oregon oak, ash, and maple. On clear days you can see the lofty peaks of the Cascades to the east and the forested slopes of the Coast Range to the west. From I-5 the drive can be joined at connecting highways at exit 249 in Salem, exit 233 in Albany, and exit 194 in Eugene.

Usually travelers will find winter temperatures ranging from the low 30s to 40s. Summer highs are usually in the low 80s. Spring and autumn days average in the low 70s.

Eugene to Junction City

Eugene, Oregon's second-largest city, is the home of the **University of Oregon** and is a major cultural center with an economy based in wood products and outdoor recreational vehicle manufacturing. National entertainers appear at the **Hult Center for the Performing Arts,** which is recognized for its architectural design and acoustics. **Hendricks Park Rhododendron Garden** displays over 6,000 rhododendrons. The Willamette and McKenzie Rivers are productive trout fisheries where visitors can experience the serenity of tranquil streams and lush forest along a network of parks, bike paths, trails, and picnic areas.

From Eugene OR 99 extends 17 miles north to **Junction City,** where it divides into two roads. OR 99 East continues to Harrisburg and Albany, while OR 99 West leads north to Monroe and on to Corvallis and Tigard.

Blue Star Wayside, midway between Eugene and Junction City, is a popular stocked trout fishing hole about three car lengths from the road. At **Washburn Wayside,** between Junction City and Monroe, you can picnic in the shade of an oak grove and take a short trail through the woods and meadows. **Broadley Vineyards Winery and Cafe,** housed in an old brick building on the banks of the Long Tom River in Monroe, is open by appointment, offering tastings of its pinot noirs.

William L. Finley National Wildlife Refuge

About 12 miles north a short, well-maintained gravel road leads through the **William L. Finley National Wildlife Refuge.** At the 5,325 acres of marshland and forest, you may see Canada geese, deer, a resident herd of elk, and five species of woodpeckers. The **Fiechter House,** adjacent to the park headquarters, was built in the 1850s and is a prime example of classical revival architecture.

A few miles north of the refuge, **Tyee Wine Cellars,** on Greenberry Road, produces pinots, chardonnays, and gewürztraminers. It opens for tastings, vineyard hikes, and picnicking on weekend afternoons from May through October.

Willamette Park and Natural Area, at Corvallis's southern city limits, provides a pleasant spot to relax while enjoying the lazy river and its passing parade of water-skiers, boaters, and barges. The boat launch's unique concrete plank floats on the water. North of the park, OR 99 crosses US 20, which extends 11 miles east to Albany and west to Newport. **Albany**'s collection of more than 150 homes and buildings represent several 19th-century architectural styles and are preserved in four historic districts.

Corvallis & Adair Village

In Latin **Corvallis** means "heart of the valley." The name is appropriate, for Corvallis is the county seat, a major commercial and industrial center, and the home of **Oregon State University.** The Victorian Italianate-style **Benton County Courthouse** is the oldest in Oregon still used for its original purpose. With a visitor's bureau walking brochure, you can see 25 buildings dating from the 1850s to the 1920s. **Chip Ross Park, Jackson-Frazier Wetland,** and several other parks near the city limits are popular bird-watching spots.

At **Peavy Arboretum,** 5.5 miles north on OR 99, more than 160 trees and shrubs are maintained by Oregon State University's **College of Forestry.** You can feed ducks, hike two trails, and take several treks, horseback rides, and drives into adjacent **McDonald Experimental Forest.** The 7,000 acres of old- and new-growth timber surround two lakes. You can explore the forest on hiking, biking, and horse trails. A short scenic drive on Barry Creek and Tampico Roads passes 11 historic sites.

Adair Village, a few miles north, is a small community of about 840 people; the town is bordered by forest and low rolling hills. During World War II it was the second-largest city in Oregon; more than 100,000 men from all 48 states were trained here for overseas combat. A sign north of the village commemorates the divisions that trained here. **E.E. Wilson Wildlife Area,** north of town, provides opportunities to hunt, fish, and observe wildlife. The grounds of the Oregon Department of Fish and Wildlife's regional office at Adair Village include a small lake for fishing and swimming.

During the next 10 miles, the highway bisects flat meadows and rolling hills. **Helmick State Park**'s grove of trees serves as a day-use area for picnickers. It was established in 1922 and was the first plot of land donated to the state for use as a park.

Monmouth & Independence

At **Monmouth** a side trip of a few blocks takes you west to the beautiful campus of **Western Oregon State University.** The **Jensen Arctic Museum,** on campus, is the only West Coast museum dedicated exclusively to the Arctic culture. It contains over 3,000 artifacts, including collections of art, tools, and clothing.

Independence, 2 miles east of Monmouth on OR 51, offers a quick step into the past. The city park amphitheater, on the banks of the Willamette River, hosts free movie nights and concerts in summer. At the annual **Hop and Heritage Festival** you can sample local brews and watch a vintage auto parade, tractor pulls, and other antique entertainments. Look across the street and you'll see a business district with charming early-1900s buildings, several of which house antiques and collectibles shops. The nearby **Heritage Museum** is filled with Native American artifacts, an 1888 covered wagon, and re-creations of a schoolroom and parlor. Its scenic overlook is often used by birders.

Basket Slough & Dallas City Park

At the junction of OR 99 and OR 22, a turn west will lead 5 miles to **Dallas.** The downtown square includes a courthouse and other Italianate, colonial, and gothic revival buildings dating to the 1800s. **Dallas City Park** covers 35 acres with an arboretum, Japanese garden, 18-hole disc golf course, tennis courts, and two playgrounds.

Basket Slough National Wildlife Refuge, north of Dallas on OR 22, was established to protect wintering Canada geese, but about 200 other species of wildlife also use it. You can see them from several viewpoints and roads that meander through the habitats.

Wine Country

Rejoining OR 99 West, 5 wineries in the 9 miles to **Amity** signal the first of 17 vineyards in Yamhill County. Most offer public tastings of pinot noir and chardonnay, plus specialties such as chenin blanc, Riesling, vintage brut, and cabernet sauvignon.

In addition, the area is a breeding ground for thoroughbred horses, and you're likely to see fields with grazing Morgans, Tennessee walkers, Arabians, and Clydesdales. The area between Amity and Tigard also grows 90 percent of the nation's filberts.

The historic **Amity Church of Christ,** on OR 99 West, was founded in 1846. It is the oldest Christian church west of the Rockies.

By taking an 8-mile side trip northeast on OR 223, you can see an original 1856 blockhouse from Fort Yamhill in Dayton's **Courthouse Square Park.** A picturesque brick Baptist church across the street was built in 1886.

OR 99 continues north to **McMinnville,** which preserves 52 commercial buildings spanning the 1880s to the 1930s. **Linfield College,** on OR 99, was established in 1849 and is a comprehensive liberal arts school.

Evergreen Aviation and Space Museum is a must-see, and with an actual Boeing 747 perched atop the building, it's hard to miss. While **Howard Hughes's "Spruce Goose"**—the world's largest wooden airplane—is the centerpiece, you'll also find 90 aircraft, a Titan II missile, 30 original or replica landing modules, lunar rovers, and Mercury and Gemini spacecraft. An IMAX theater and a water park with 4 slides that begin in the Boeing 747 offer their own special pleasures.

A UFO costume parade, a pet costume contest, and experts on UFO-related topics have helped make McMinnville's **UFO Festival,** held in May, the nation's second-largest UFO celebration.

Lafayette is a few miles west and contains an interesting museum with 20 showcases of pioneer memorabilia housed in an 1892 church. **Yamhill Locks Park,** filled with tall shade trees, offers a refreshing picnic spot with a playground, nature walks, and access to canoeing and fishing on the Willamette River bank. It overlooks the broken cement walls of locks that served navigation from 1900 to 1954.

En route to Dundee you'll pass several orchards and wineries. **Argyle Winery** is located on OR 99 in Dundee. A 15-minute tour takes you through the sparkling-wine process from chilling and pressing grapes to aging wine. The Argyle tasting room is open daily from 11 a.m. to 5 p.m. A filbert orchard is across the street.

Newberg & the Hoover Home

Newberg is the home of **George Fox College,** started by Quakers in 1885 and named after the founder of the Friends Church. The college's most famous alumnus, Herbert Hoover, is memorialized in the **Hoover Academic Building,** which contains his bedroom furnishings and antiques. From 1885 to 1889 he lived at the **Hoover-Minthorn Museum House,** 1 block south of OR 99 at Second and River Streets.

Rodgers Boat Landing, 1.7 miles south of the home, provides access to the Willamette River. From the landing you may see a variety of Willamette River traffic, including jet boaters, anglers, and large commercial barges along with blue herons, kingfishers, and migrating geese.

The OR 99 West drive concludes by passing clusters of businesses, stands of trees, and open fields on the 20 miles east to Tigard.

16

Benton County Loop

General Description: A 109-mile signed scenic loop through Willamette Valley farms, vineyards, and foothills of the Coast Range mountains.

Special Attractions: Waterfalls, South Fork of the Alsea River, Willamette River, William L. Finley National Wildlife Refuge, McDonald Experimental Forest, Peavy Arboretum, mountain and valley scenery, historic sites, wineries.

Location: Western Willamette Valley between Corvallis and Alpine.

Drive Route Numbers: Alpine Road, CR C-03-45120, Bellfountain Road, US 20, OR 223, Airlie Road, OR 99 West.

Travel Season: All year, though CR C-03-45120 to Alsea Falls and the access road to Marys Peak may close temporarily due to snow.

Camping: 1 Bureau of Land Management campground with picnic tables, fire rings, vault toilets, and drinking water.

Services: All services in Corvallis. Limited services in Philomath and Alpine.

Nearby Attractions: Albany historic districts, Linn County Covered Bridges Scenic Drive, 99 West–Eugene–Tigard Scenic Drive.

For More Information: Corvallis Tourism, (541) 757-1544, (800) 334-8118 (USA), www.visitcorvallis.com; Philomath Area Chamber of Commerce, (541) 929-2454, www.philomathchamber.org; Albany Visitors Association, (541) 928-0911, (800) 526-2256 (USA), www.albanyvisitors.com.

The Route

This route begins at the southern end of Benton County and travels west through the heavy forests of the Coast Range. From **Alpine** it heads north through forest, Christmas tree farms, and wineries to Philomath. Returning to forests, it makes a brief swing west on US 20 before turning north through woodlands and wineries. It concludes by taking OR 99 south to **Corvallis.** Traffic is usually light on the back roads and moderate to heavy on OR 99 West. Most of the route traverses pillow basalts that formed underwater and were part of the Pacific Ocean floor 50 million to 60 million years ago. The area was raised above sea level about 35 million years ago.

Usually travelers will find winter temperatures ranging from the low 30s to 40s. Summer highs are generally in the low 80s. Spring and fall days average about 70 degrees. Most of the 40 inches of rain per year falls in winter.

The drive begins 14 miles south of Corvallis at the junction of OR 99 West and Alpine Road. Taking Alpine Road west, you travel along a ridge covered with oak trees that overlooks rolling hills and meadows. The road ends 3.5 miles west at Alpine, where a general store and a few homes are clustered around an intersection.

Benton County Loop

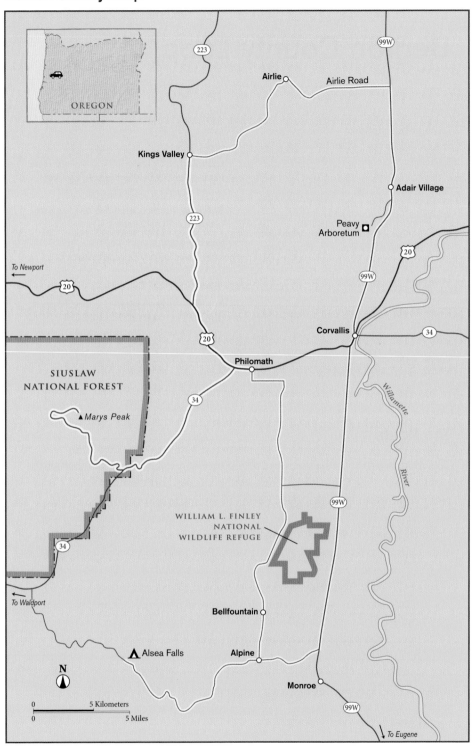

Alsea Falls, southwest of Alpine, is one of the highlights on a scenic side trip into the Coast Range mountains. Licensed by Shutterstock.com.

From Alpine you can take a scenic side trip to Alsea Falls by traveling west on Foster Road and turning onto CR C-03-45120.

Into the Coast Range

After a short stretch of pastoral valley farms, the paved county road climbs into the Coast Range foothills and becomes a Bureau of Land Management National Back Country Byway. The rewards for negotiating hairpin turns and frequent logging trucks are lush Douglas fir forests; an abundance of columbines, foxgloves, and other wildflowers; and flaming vine maples in autumn. From pullouts you'll see an endless dark green forest filling hills, valleys, peaks, and ravines.

Deer and elk are prevalent, and the scenic Alsea River's South Fork, which parallels much of the route, is a good stream to try your luck at catching coho and chinook salmon, steelhead, and trout. **Alsea Falls** is a rushing whitewater cascade just a short walk from the roadside parking lot or a 1-mile riverside hike from the 16-unit BLM campground.

The 10.6 miles from Alpine to the falls are generally usable all year without special equipment. From the falls the pavement continues west, then turns to gravel east of Alsea where it joins OR 34.

Bellfountain

Returning to Alpine, the drive traverses 2 miles of oak-covered hills as it takes Bellfountain Road north. Look east at Bellfountain and Dawson Roads, and you'll see **Bellfountain Community Church,** an excellent example of 19th-century Queen Anne church-style architecture. By turning west at Dawson Road, you can picnic in the shade of huge Douglas firs at **Bellfountain Park.** Established in 1851, it is the county's oldest park and contains the **longest picnic table in the US** cut from a single piece of wood. **Hull-Oakes Lumber Company** (23837 Dawson Rd., Monroe), west of the park, operates one of the nation's last steam-driven sawmills. It is on the National Register of Historic Places and makes long timbers used in trestles, ship masts, spars, and beams. You can tour it by calling (541) 424-3112 in advance.

Two miles north of the intersection, a well-maintained gravel road meanders through the 5,325 acres of **William L. Finley National Wildlife Refuge** to an eastern entrance on OR 99 West. Its marshes, creeks, and meadows attract virtually every species of bird found in the Willamette Valley. While it was established to protect Canada geese, you may see wood ducks and hooded mergansers nesting in summer. Ruffed grouse, ring-necked pheasants, and mourning doves are also seen along with deer and a resident herd of elk. The **Woodpecker Loop Trail** meanders through a mixed forest of Douglas fir, maple, Oregon ash, and oak that is a habitat for five species of woodpeckers. Several historic buildings near the headquarters include a barn and an 1850s classical revival–style home.

Two miles north, Bellfountain and Tyee Wine Cellars offer tastings, vineyard hikes, and picnicking. Both bottle pinots, chardonnays, and gewürztraminers.

Bellfountain Road cuts across rolling hills dappled with Christmas tree farms, hay fields, and dairy farms as it continues 5 miles north to Philomath.

Philomath

Philomath is a combination of Greek words meaning "lover of learning" and was named after a local college, which closed in 1929. The imposing college building houses the **Benton County Historical Museum.** The museum is on the National Register of Historic Places and contains Calipooia Indian artifacts, Camp Adair photographs, logging equipment, and other collections. A second-floor gallery features changing exhibits of local arts, crafts, and photography.

OR 34 starts at Philomath and ends at Newport on the Oregon coast. This highway provides an opportunity for a scenic side trip. About 10 miles south of Philomath, a side road spirals off OR 34 to the summit of **Marys Peak,** where sweeping views of mountain and valley forests, streams, and meadows stretch to the far horizons. At 4,097 feet elevation, it is the highest peak in the Coast Range, often has snow during winter, and is a hiker's favorite during the rest of the year.

Covered Bridges

A few miles south, you can visit **Alsea River Trout Hatchery,** which raises rainbow trout and steelhead. The hatchery has stream, sturgeon, and trophy trout ponds, and the nearby **Alsea River** yields good catches of winter steelhead and cutthroat trout. At the community of **Alsea,** your options include taking the graveled and paved county road to Alsea Falls and Alpine or continuing on OR 34 to Waldport. West of Alsea the highway passes by several county parks with boat launches. **Hayden Covered Bridge** (World Guide Number 37-02-05), 1.5 miles west of Alsea, was built in 1918 and is still in use.

From Philomath the drive follows US 20 west for 5 miles through a forested corridor. At Wren it passes **Harris Covered Bridge** (World Guide Number 37-02-04) and turns north onto OR 223. The bridge was built in 1936 and is still used. Motor-home crossings are not recommended due to limited clearance.

To Kings Valley

Deer are so plentiful along the 9 miles to **Kings Valley** that signs ask you to watch for them. You'll also see sheep farms, magnificently dilapidated barns, thickets of Douglas fir forest, and the last Christmas tree farms.

Kings Valley Community Chapel, at the junction of Maxwell Creek Road and OR 223, is an excellent example of the gothic church style that was prevalent here during the 19th century. **Paul M. Dunn Forest,** nearby, is an Oregon State Research Project where you can study and photograph plants.

Turning east onto Maxwell Creek and Airlie Roads, you'll pass low rolling hills covered with Airlie vineyards. **Airlie Winery** specializes in pinot noir, chardonnay, marechal foch, Müller-Thurgau, Riesling, and gewürztraminer.

Adair Village

After 3 miles turn south onto OR 99 West, and you will pass through **Adair Village.** During World War II the army training center covered 50,000 acres. The area east of the highway was a base camp, and hills to the west were used for maneuvers. To simulate actual conditions, full-scale models of European towns were built. Few of the buildings remain.

Tall fir trees line the highway as it continues south to Corvallis. **Peavy Arboretum,** 2 miles south of Adair Village, is maintained by OSU's college of forestry and exhibits more than 160 trees and shrubs from the US and several other nations. In the adjacent **McDonald Experimental Forest,** you can hike through 7,000 acres of new- and old-growth timber, by lakes, and to historic sites.

Corvallis

The drive concludes 5.5 miles south in **Corvallis.** The town's attractions include 25 historic buildings displaying a variety of architectural styles from the 1850s to the 1920s, Oregon State University, and Avery Park's rose garden, with over 250 species of roses, a rhododendron garden, an historic locomotive, picnic areas, and playgrounds. Benton County Courthouse, the oldest working county courthouse west of the Mississippi, is a prime example of Victorian Italianate architecture and contains local history displays.

17

Linn County
Covered Bridges Loop

General Description: A 51-mile drive on paved 2-lane county roads through farmlands and crossroads communities to 5 covered bridges.

Special Attractions: 5 covered bridges, fish hatchery, historic church, Santiam River.

Location: Eastern Willamette Valley between Albany and Lyons.

Drive Route Numbers: US 20, OR 226, Gilkey Bridge Road, Shamanek Bridge Drive, Richardson Gap Road, Fish Hatchery Road.

Travel Season: All year.

Camping: There are no campgrounds along the route.

Services: All services in Albany. Limited services in Crabtree and Scio.

Nearby Attractions: Albany historic districts, North Santiam Canyon Scenic Drive, Santiam Scenic Loop Drive, Silver Falls Scenic Loop Drive.

For More Information: Albany Visitors Association, (541) 928-0911, (800) 526-2256 (USA), www.albanyvisitors.com.

The Route

Five of Oregon's 53 covered bridges are included on the drive, which forms a rectangle as it extends through a small valley framed by the Cascade foothills and western ridges. The route can be driven from I-5 by traveling east from exit 238 on Jefferson/Scio Road, then turning south on Robinson Road and starting at Gilkey Bridge, or by taking exit 233 at Albany to US 20. OR 22 travelers can join by exiting at Lyons and following OR 226 southwest 8 miles to Hannah Bridge. While traffic is usually light, allow time for leisurely driving, as posted speeds sometimes drop to between 15 and 20 miles per hour.

Background on Bridges

All of the bridges are identified by name and cataloged in the **World Guide Number System,** which is a national indexing system used to identify covered bridges. The six-digit number identifies the state, county, and bridge location. Since Oregon is number 37 when states are listed alphabetically, the first number for each Oregon bridge is 37.

While they are wistful reminders of a horse-and-buggy past, covered bridges served a multitude of purposes beyond providing access across streams. During Prohibition illegal liquor was often stored in them, and outlaws used them for cover while awaiting their victims. Political rallies, dances, and church meetings were sometimes held in them.

Linn County Covered Bridges Loop

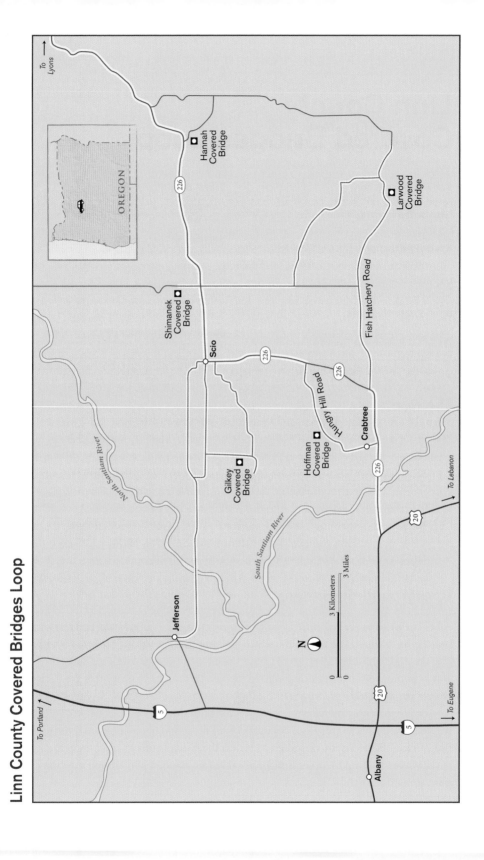

One-lane Gilkey Bridge spans Thomas Creek.

Because timber was abundant, covered bridges were economical to build. By covering them, they were protected from Oregon's rainy weather, and their life span was doubled.

Travelers will find moderate temperatures in the Willamette Valley. Summer highs rarely rise above the mid-80s. Spring and fall days average in the low 70s. Winter days hover between the low 30s and low 40s. Temperatures in the mid to high 60s are common in spring and fall. Mornings can bring heavy fog that obliterates the surrounding countryside.

From Albany you begin by traveling 9 miles east through open farmland on US 20. Turning onto OR 226, which is signed as Crabtree Road, you cross the Santiam River, lined with flat fields and clumps of oak trees. A turn north onto Cold Springs Road takes you 0.25 mile into Crabtree, where you join Hungry Hill Road 1 block east of the first cross street.

Hoffman & Gilkey Bridges

During the 1.5 miles to Hoffman Bridge, there is a wistfulness of times gone by as you pass classic weather-beaten barns with diamond-shaped windows, austere two-story houses, and grazing cattle. A bed of volcanic ash, deposited 30 million to 35 million years ago, when this area had a subtropical climate, provides the fertile base for the dairy farms and fields of hay, wheat, and vegetables, which you'll pass along the route.

Ninety-foot-long **Hoffman Bridge** (World Guide Number 37-22-08), built in 1936, is surrounded by woods and rests on original hand-hewn timbers, which were cut at Hungry Hill and hauled down by teams of horses. Instead of the exposed trusses common to most covered bridges, it displays unique gothic-style windows. Crabtree Creek meanders out of the hills, under the bridge, and into an open field.

Old barns and modern ranches with brick homes and white board fences stand on rolling hillsides and grasslands as Hungry Hill Road and OR 226 stretch north toward Scio. One mile south of Scio, the drive turns west at Gilkey Road and follows it 4 miles to Goar Road and **Gilkey Bridge** (World Guide Number 37-22-04). The 120-foot-long one-lane bridge, built in 1939, spans Thomas Creek and once stood next to a covered railroad bridge. Gilkey was once a nearby town but has virtually disappeared.

Hannah, Shimanek & Larwood Bridges

From Gilkey Bridge you can travel east to Scio on either Jefferson/Scio Road or by backtracking on Gilkey Road. **Scio Depot Museum** displays a caboose and contains an interesting collection of Willamette Valley artifacts. You can enjoy a picnic lunch on a shaded creek bank next to the century-old railroad station.

OR 226 cuts through potato and hay fields on the 7 miles to Camp Morrison Road. **Hannah Bridge** (World Guide Number 37-22-02) crosses Thomas Creek about 100 feet south of the intersection. It has been there since 1936 and is among the most picturesque. The 120-foot-long bridge is situated at the mouth of a forested canyon and was designed with rounded portals and exposed trusses. It has appeared in several television commercials and is a popular summer swimming and diving spot.

After backtracking through 2 miles of wooded countryside and pastoral farmlands, you turn west onto Shimanek Bridge Drive. It ends at **Shimanek Bridge** (World Guide Number 37-22-03), situated at the intersection of Richardson Gap Road.

Since 1861 five bridges have occupied this site. The present structure was built in 1966 and is the county's newest, and at 130 feet, it is also its longest. Its louvered windows, red paint, and old-style portal design with squared rather than rounded corners are unique.

After following Richardson Gap Road 4.5 miles south through flat hay fields and rolling oak- and alder-covered hills, you turn east on Fish Hatchery Road and travel 3.6 miles to **Larwood Bridge** (World Guide Number 37-22-06).

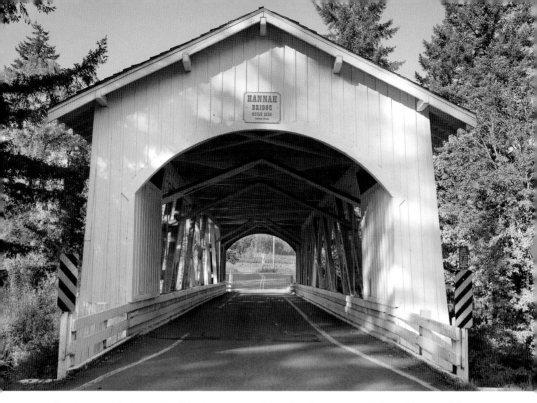

Scenic Hannah Covered Bridge has appeared in television commercials and is one of the area's most photographed sites. LICENSED BY SHUTTERSTOCK.COM.

The bridge dates to 1939 and is near the confluence of the **Roaring River** and Crabtree Creek. A small creek-bank park next to the bridge is a delightful picnic and swimming spot and provides a good angle for photographing the bridge. A restored waterwheel across the stream adds a bit of nostalgia. The TV show *Ripley's Believe It or Not* said the Roaring River was the only river in the US that empties into a creek.

Roaring River Fish Hatchery

Roaring River Park and **Roaring River Fish Hatchery** are about 1 mile east of the bridge. At the park you can fish the Roaring River, enjoy a large day-use area with picnic shelters and playground equipment, walk a plant identification trail, and take short hikes from the parking lot through the dense forest to the river's edge.

The Oregon State Department of Fish and Wildlife operates Roaring River Fish Hatchery. It produces about one million rainbow trout per year, along with some 225,000 winter and summer steelhead. Each pond holds about 20,000 fish. You'll also see the settling basins and a display pond with sturgeon and albino cutthroat, brook, and brown trout.

After returning to Richardson Gap Road, the drive concludes 1 mile south at **Providence Pioneer Church.** The picturesque church was founded in 1853 by Oregon's first circuit rider. The church that stands today was built in 1893 and is still in use. The cemetery on the church grounds contains many pioneer graves. From its hilltop you have a commanding view of the valley below.

To rejoin US 20, take Fish Hatchery Road west. By turning south to Sweet Home, you can see three more covered bridges on the Santiam Loop Scenic Drive to Brownsville.

18

Eugene, Willamette Pass, US 97 Junction

General Description: A 91-mile drive from the Willamette Valley through the Central Oregon Cascades and over Willamette Pass.

Special Attractions: Outstanding mountain scenery, Willamette Valley, mountain and reservoir lakes, waterfalls, covered bridges, Willamette and Deschutes National Forests, camping, hiking, waterskiing, canoeing, boating, snowmobiling, cross-country and downhill skiing.

Location: West-central Oregon between Eugene and Willamette Pass.

Drive Route Number: OR 58.

Travel Season: All year.

Camping: 2 Army Corps of Engineers campgrounds; 23 forest service campgrounds with tables, fire pits, and flush or vault toilets. Some have water.

Services: All services at Eugene and Oakridge. Limited services at Westfir.

Nearby Attractions: Lane County covered bridges, Dorena Lake, Diamond Peak Wilderness, Newberry Crater National Monument, Cascade Lakes Highway, Waldo Lake Wilderness, Crater Lake National Park, Robert Aufderheide Scenic Byway.

For More Information: Eugene, Cascades & Oregon Coast–Travel Lane County, (541) 484-5307, (800) 547-5445 (USA), www .travellanecounty.org; Oakridge-Westfir Chamber of Commerce, (541) 782-4146, www.oakridgechamber.com.

The Route

This busy corridor connects **Eugene,** the state's second-largest city, with central Oregon. It is also one of Oregon's most magnificent drives, affording the eastbound traveler roadside views of the Willamette River, the valley floor, and Lookout Point Reservoir, framed by a continuous panorama of thick forested mountain slopes and peaks. The westbound traveler begins on the Cascade's eastern slopes, surrounded by steep cinder cones and several glacier-carved lakes, which are accessible from short side roads. Crossing **Willamette Pass** at 5,128 feet, the road descends amid towering fir-covered mountains. The final 44 miles west of Oakridge offer roadside views of the reservoir and river. In addition to a diversity of man-made and natural scenery, the route includes fascinating geology and virtually unlimited opportunities for outdoor recreation.

Traffic is usually fairly heavy. You will want to stay within the 55-mile-per-hour speed limit and use the frequent turnouts to let semis and logging trucks pass before descending the 6 percent downgrades with runaway-truck ramps. The route is heavily patrolled by the state police.

Eugene, Willamette Pass, US 97 Junction

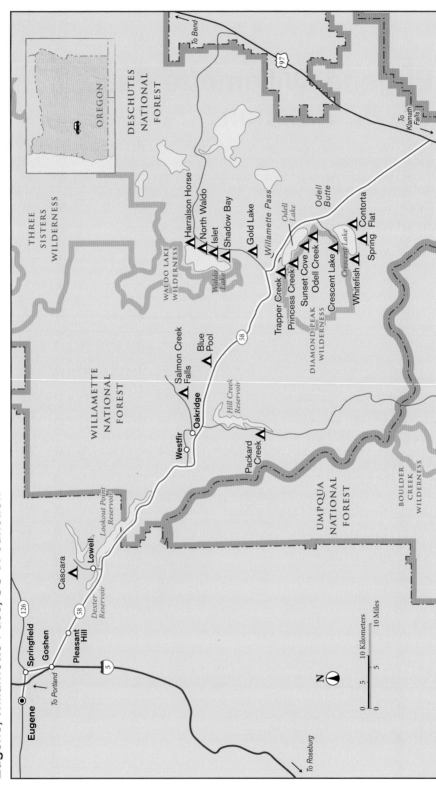

During the summer you can expect temperatures in the high 70s and low 80s. Winters average in the high 40s and low 50s. Spring days are usually in the mid-60s, while autumn temperatures range from the mid-60s to mid-70s.

In the Eugene-Springfield area, the drive starts at I-5, exit 188. **Howard Buford Recreation Area,** 2 miles east of the exit, is situated on the banks of the Coast Fork of the Willamette River. At 2,363 acres it is Lane County's largest park and has 16 miles of trails that attract hikers, horseback riders, and birders. It includes **Mount Pisgah Arboretum**, where you can walk 5 miles of trails by wildflower and rhododendron species gardens and through groves of incense cedar, redwood, Douglas fir, and Oregon white oak. At the visitor center you can participate in a "touch me" nature exhibit.

After passing 5 miles of picturesque barns and farmland, you'll enter the community of Pleasant Hill and cross a side road leading 3 miles north to Jasper. Within 7 miles of Jasper, you can see five of Lane County's covered bridges as you follow the north bank of the Willamette to rejoin OR 58 at Lowell.

At Pleasant Hill OR 58 starts the gradual climb that continues through Willamette Pass. This section was formed between 15 million and 30 million years ago during a period of intense volcanic activity. The dark roadside rocks are basalts mixed with lighter colored andesites.

Elijah Bristow State Park, 3.7 miles east, offers 10 miles of hiking, biking, and equestrian trails and the opportunity to fish the Willamette for trout, salmon, steelhead, walleye, and small- and largemouth bass. A connecting trail links it to **Dexter State Recreation Site,** 2.5 miles east, which provides a large picnic area, 18-hole golf course, boat launch, and a sweeping water-level view of Dexter Reservoir and Dam. **Dexter Reservoir** and **Lookout Point Reservoir,** a few miles east, are Army Corps of Engineers earth-and-gravel-fill dams that operate as a single unit to provide flood control, irrigation, improved navigation, and power generation. At both you can fish all year and enjoy seasonal waterskiing, sailing, swimming, picnicking, and hunting.

Note: Occasionally public health advisories about blue-green algae are issued at Dexter State Recreation Area. Blue-green algae can produce toxins that are harmful to humans. According to the Oregon Parks and Recreation Department, the algae appears from time to time in various lakes and streams throughout the state. When the alerts are in effect, people and animals should avoid going in these waters, including all forms of boating, and fish should not be taken from these areas, as the fish may carry the algae.

Dexter Reservoir, between Eugene and the Cascade Mountains, offers a variety of attractions and activities for outdoor enthusiasts.

Covered Bridges, Reservoirs & National Forest

Lowell Covered Bridge (World Guide Number 37-20-18), built in 1945, stands near an intersection 2.3 miles east. It is Oregon's widest covered bridge. An interpretive center details Lane County's covered bridges—four of which are within a 10-minute drive of the center. The side road connects to the north shore's Wimberly County Park, Lowell Ranger Station, a marina, and a viewpoint of 14,360-acre Lookout Point Reservoir stretching through a narrow fir-forested canyon. A paved side road near the Corps of Engineers' 92-site **Pine Meadow Campground** angles northeast along 22 miles of **Fall Creek Reservoir.** Three forest service campgrounds, with a total of 42 sites, are situated along the timbered shoreline of the 1,852-acre reservoir. The nearby **Fall Creek Trail** has been designated a National Recreation Trail.

Two miles east, the route passes **Lookout Point Dam**. Across the highway you'll see a granite cliff. It is a **magma plug,** about 1 mile in diameter, formed from molten lava that pushed into solid rock and cooled slowly without reaching the surface.

After following the reservoir for several miles, the highway enters the 1.68-million-acre **Willamette National Forest,** which encompasses 8 wilderness areas, 7 major Cascade mountain peaks, and 1,400 miles of trails. Cutting through a Douglas fir and oak corridor, you pass public boat ramps, small county park camping areas, private RV parks, and the forest service's 66-site **Black Canyon Campground.**

Seventeen miles east, the route reaches Westfir Junction. By traveling 2 miles north, you can see **Office Covered Bridge** (World Guide Number 37-20-39) in the community of **Westfir.** The 180-foot-long bridge is the town's dominant landmark. The junction is also the southern access to the Robert Aufderheide National Forest Service Scenic Byway, which extends 70 miles north along the Wild and Scenic North Fork of the Middle Fork of the Willamette River and the South Fork of the McKenzie River.

The Middle Fork of the Willamette River runs through Oakridge, a mile east of the junction. At **Green Waters Park,** on the riverbank, you can swim, fish, and walk a nature trail. **Salmon Creek Falls**' 15-unit campground offers an overnight on a mountain slope north of town.

Hills Creek Reservoir, 3 miles southeast of Oakridge, fills 2,735 acres of a narrow forested canyon surrounded by rugged mountains. You may see waterfowl, black-tailed deer, wintering elk, bald eagles, and ospreys along the 44 miles of shoreline. The lake is a popular waterskiing and sailboarding spot, and anglers are rewarded with catches of kokanee, rainbow trout, crappie, largemouth bass, and catfish. **Larison Cove,** on the northwest end, is reserved for canoes and non-motorized boats. It offers a beautiful forested shoreline, tranquility, and picnic sites that are accessible only by trail or canoe. The 57 sites at **Packard Creek** and **Sand Prairie Campgrounds** on the western shore overlook the scenic lake in a mixed forest of western hemlock, fir, cedar, and hazelnut. **Sacandaga Campground,** several miles south on the Willamette River banks, has 16 sites. Packard Creek fills up fast on Fridays; Sacandaga Campground is usually lightly used and is the place to be if you're seeking solitude.

East of Oakridge the highway enters the high Cascades by passing **McCredie Springs** and **Blue Pool Campgrounds**' 25 sites. Ahead of you, waves of trees fill mountainsides as the road disappears into a canopy of mixed Douglas fir, maple, oak, poplar, western red cedar, and hemlock. Many are so tall, you won't be able to see their tops from inside your vehicle. Soon you begin a 5-mile, 6 percent climb, pass through a tunnel, dip into a ravine, and start another 6 percent climb. Many of the deep crevasses and basins that became mountain lakes were gouged out by glaciers in the last ice age.

Salt Creek Falls, Waldo Lake & Willamette Pass

At the top of the second climb, **Salt Creek Falls,** Oregon's second-highest water-fall, drops 286 feet over a basalt ledge. Looking west from the viewpoint, Salt Creek weaves a thin line through a narrow forested ravine. By following a 2.5-mile trail along the canyon rim, you'll see several more cascades en route to Diamond Creek Falls.

Two miles east, a side road leads northeast along 13 miles of **Waldo Lake.** Carved out of the Cascades at an elevation of 5,414 feet, it is Oregon's second-largest natural non-alkali lake. The water is so clear that on calm days you can see to a depth of 100 feet. A 21-mile loop trail around the lake will take you by isolated beaches, coves, and meadows and into the adjacent **Waldo Lake Wilderness.** It is used by hikers, equestrians, and mountain bikers. The lake is also a popular spot for sailboarding and canoeing. Five forest service campgrounds along the access road provide a total of 232 sites.

After passing two viewpoints overlooking the 35,400-acre **Diamond Peak Wilderness,** the highway reaches the Willamette Pass summit. Watch for side road that leads north to tiny **Gold Lake,** which is open to fly fishing. The pass is a favorite ski area and capable of moving 11,100 skiers per hour on 6 lifts, including a high-speed lift accommodating 6 people, 4 triple chairs, and 1 double chairlift. It covers 555 acres of skiable terrain, 225 acres of groomed terrain, with 5 beginner, 11 intermediate, and 13 advanced/expert runs, plus more than 12 miles of Nordic trails. Facilities include a lodge, day-care and children's learning center, and snow-making system.

East of the pass the trees are smaller and the undergrowth thins because the mountains, acting as a shield, cut off rain and snow. Much of the soil is covered with yellow pumice that erupted from Mount Mazama about 7,000 years ago.

Deschutes National Forest & Crescent Lake

About 4 miles east of the summit, the Willamette National Forest ends and the 1.8 million–acre **Deschutes National Forest** begins. The highway crosses the Pacific Crest Trail, which winds south by Odell Lake, through the Diamond Peaks Wilderness, and on to California. Through the trees on the south side of the highway,

The thick forests of the Diamond Peak Wilderness stretch to the horizon and can be seen traveling west on OR 58.

you can see beautiful **Odell Lake** ringed by a thick forest of dark blue-green trees and framed by the Diamond Peaks. Short side roads lead to its tranquil shore and boat ramps that are usually busy as anglers launch in search of trout. Its easy access makes it one of Oregon's busiest lakes and supports a year-round resort at the east end, a trailer park on the west end, and 3 forest service campgrounds nestled in the trees around its shoreline. They contain a total of 85 sites.

Two miles east, a short side road leads south to its sister, **Crescent Lake.** A small service community with a minimart, marina, motel, and gas station surrounds the lake. Like Odell, it is a year-round favorite of trout anglers and cross-country skiers. The 9 forest service campgrounds ringing the lake offer 205 sites, including several group camps and a horse camp.

East of Crescent Lake, the highway passes a side road leading 4 miles north to **Davis Lake** and 5 forest service campgrounds with 70 sites. Continuing east, you'll see the tall, perfectly cylindrical cone of 7,037-foot **Odell Butte** punctuating the horizon. **Crescent Creek Campground,** north of the butte, has 9 sites. A few miles further, the highway passes dead trees killed by pine beetles, crosses the Little Deschutes River, and ends at a junction with US 97. From the junction you can travel north 24 miles to La Pine or south 8 miles to Chemult.

19

Eugene, Florence, Junction City

General Description: A 139-mile drive along 2-lane paved highways through Willamette Valley farmlands and Coast Range mountains.

Special Attractions: Beautiful forests, low mountains, reservoir park, river valley, scenic lake, covered bridges, sand dunes, ocean beach scenic drive.

Location: West-central Oregon between Eugene and Florence.

Drive Route Numbers: OR 126 and OR 36.

Travel Season: All year.

Camping: 3 Bureau of Land Management and 3 forest service campgrounds with tables, fire pits, flush or vault toilets. 1 state park campground with full-hookup, electrical, and tent sites. 1 Lane County Park campground with electricity and 1 Siuslaw Port Commission RV park with hookups.

Services: All services at Eugene and Florence. Limited services at Noti.

Nearby Attractions: McKenzie River, 99 West Scenic Drive, Highway 58–Eugene–Willamette Pass Scenic Drive, William L. Finley National Wildlife Refuge, Lane County covered bridges, Dorena Lake.

For More Information: Eugene, Cascades & Oregon Coast–Travel Lane County Oregon, (541) 484-5307, (800) 547-5445 (USA), www.travellanecounty.org; Siuslaw National Forest, (541) 750-7000; Fern Ridge Chamber of Commerce, (541) 935-8843, www.fernridgechamber.com; Florence Area Chamber of Commerce, (541) 997-3128, (800) 524-4864, www.florence chamber.com.

The Route

From Eugene, **OR 126** takes travelers through the western Willamette Valley and over the crumpled ridges of the Coast Range to Mapleton, then follows the Siuslaw River into Florence. En route it passes century-old farms, covered bridges, small roadside communities, tiny ponds, creeks, and rivers. The return on **OR 36** stays in the rugged **Siuslaw River Canyon,** offering a roadside of rocky cliffs, narrow ravines, and a river that changes from slow and meandering to rushing cascades as the road climbs a basalt ridge to serene **Triangle Lake.** It concludes with the Willamette Valley farmlands. During the week traffic is usually light to moderate on both highways and moderate to heavy on weekends. The rural countryside, a narrow road, and some sharp turns dictate a slow pace.

Summer travelers can expect temperatures in the high 70s and low 80s. Winters average in the high 40s and low 50s. Spring days are usually in the mid-60s, while autumn temperatures range from the mid-60s to mid-70s. Rainfall averages 90 inches per year on the coast and 120 inches in the mountains.

Eugene, Florence, Junction City

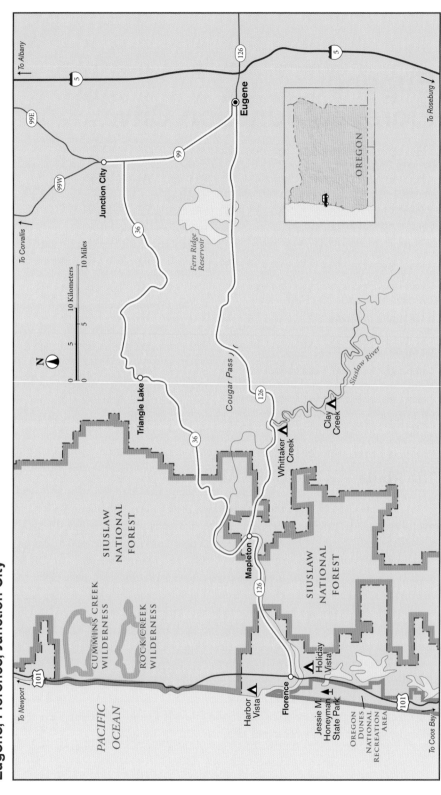

Fern Ridge Reservoir

OR 126 starts as a business loop in downtown Eugene and winds its way west on Garfield and 11th Streets. Shedding the city's congestion, it cuts through grasslands and oak-covered ridges. After about 7 miles it passes **Fern Ridge Reservoir,** which extends north 4.5 miles as it fills a shallow lowland. Although you're likely to have only moderate success at catching crappies, bass, and cutthroat and stocked rainbow trout, you'll find it an excellent lake for sailboarding, power boating, and waterskiing.

Six parks on the graceful curve of the western shore overlook the reservoir and draw heavy use from picnickers, swimmers, and wildlife watchers. The southwest shore has been designated a wildlife refuge. The marshlands are nesting and stopover habitats for gulls, ducks, geese, herons, egrets, and raptors. You may see nesting ospreys in the large oaks, willows, pines, and apple trees in **Perkins Peninsula Park** along OR 126. A pullout, 0.6 mile west, overlooks a breeding ground for yellow-headed blackbirds and purple martins. Bird checklists and viewing area guides are available at Fern Ridge's headquarters. In fall the surrounding lands are open to shotgun and archery hunting for waterfowl and deer. The reservoir was created by damming the Long Tom River and is drained in the winter to control flooding. A private concession near the park operates 37 tent/trailer campsites and **Lane County's Richardson Park** has 88 nonelectric sites.

To the Coast Range

West of Fern Ridge the highway continues for a few miles through the valley's flat grasslands and low oak-covered hills as it passes several farms that have been here more than 100 years. A mile west of Venita, you can purchase gas, groceries, and liquor at roadside stores. A few miles beyond, you'll cross the Long Tom River and pass three vineyards, which offer tastings of chardonnay, pinot noir, and Rieslings. Each May the area celebrates both bird and wine with its annual **Wings and Wine Festival.**

After the highway passes several ponds frequented by ducks and geese, the ascent into the **Coast Range** starts in stands of alders. Two miles west, you're into a continuous forest of Douglas fir, western hemlock, and western red cedar. Except for small valley meadows, squeezed in the flatlands of wooded hills and mountains, the forest will be your constant companion during the 32 miles to Mapleton. When the highway dips down into Noti, you'll see log decks and lumberyards extending from one end of the community to the other.

Passing clear-cuts, Christmas tree farms, and roadside meadows with a few head of grazing cattle and horses, the quintessential Oregon forest begins with gorgeous huge Douglas firs enclosing the highway. A series of curves and patched highway signal the ascent to the 769-foot summit of **Cougar Pass.** A few miles east of Walton, which has a gas station and store, **Wildcat Creek** starts meandering along the roadside. A couple miles west, **Walton Wildcat Covered Bridge** (World Guide Number 37-20-04) straddles Turner Creek. The bridge was built in 1925 and is located at the Austa Wayside boat ramp. By turning south on CR 4390 at the bridge, you can use **Whittaker Creek Campground** as your base for salmon and steelhead fishing in the Siuslaw River. The Bureau of Land Management campground has 31 tent and trailer sites, a boat ramp, a playground, and swimming areas. **Kentucky Falls Recreation Trail,** about 12 miles south of the campground, is a 4-mile round-trip hike to 89-foot twin waterfalls. BLM's **Clay Creek Campground,** nearby, offers 21 sites, 2 group picnic shelters, and softball field surrounded by rugged mountains and a forest of Douglas fir, western hemlock, red cedar, and big-leaf maples.

The descent from the mountains is exceptionally scenic. Stands of alders and moss-draped trees create a natural tunnel, and sandstone and igneous rock outcroppings frame a small canyon. The mountains were created about 35 million years ago, when they were uplifted from the ocean floor. Prior to the lifting, volcanism covered existing sandstone and molten lava. The rocks you see along the highway are actually part of the ancient sea floor, which has been exposed layer by layer as streams eroded down through the rock.

Turner Creek is a good trout stream and meanders alongside OR 126 for about 4 miles. A small BLM campground with 7 sites is situated south of the highway near the west end of the creek.

Mapleton

At **Mapleton** OR 126 meets OR 36 then follows the Siuslaw River westward. If you're planning to hike or camp in the Oregon Dunes Recreation Area or other parts of the forest, the Siuslaw National Forest's Mapleton office, on OR 126, can assist you with trail maps, camping permits, and hiking, hunting, and fishing information.

Between Mapleton and Florence the river spreads into two channels separated by small islands and mudflats and is lined with lumberyards, boat basins, and a golf course. The Siuslaw Port Commission's **Holiday Harbor Campground,** in historic Old Town along the Siuslaw River, includes 67 full-hookup, 25 water and electric, and 13 dry campsites. All hookup sites have basic cable TV.

Florence

OR 126 ends at a junction with US 101. By continuing straight ahead, you can take the 2.4-mile **Siuslaw Estuary Scenic Drive,** which cuts through stands of dwarfed lodgepole pines and ends at the Pacific Ocean on a sandy beach and grass jetty. At the jetty you can sailboard and kayak; cast a line in the surf for salmon, perch, and ling cod; dig clams and crabs; fly kites; and comb the beach for shells, driftwood, and other treasures washed ashore by the tides.

Harbor Vista Park offers a sweeping view of whitecaps, sandy beaches, and the shoreline forest. The park, at the end of the estuary drive, has 38 RV and tent campsites. Most have electricity and water.

By turning south at the end of the access road, you'll follow the picturesque shoreline to **Florence**'s waterfront district. The district is a combination of specialty shops, restaurants, theaters, a boat basin, converted warehouses, and picturesque commercial buildings.

Several attractions along US 101 are within a few miles of Florence. Heceta Lighthouse, Sea Lion Caves, Darlingtonia Botanical Gardens, and the Sutton Recreation Area are 5 to 12 miles north of town. Sutton Creek and Lake Campgrounds, situated in a sand dune area, feature a total of 79 tent trailer sites.

Some 75 creeks and rivers empty into the ocean along 30 miles of beach in and around Florence. Twenty-two lakes surround it, with 17 of them stocked with rainbow trout. You can also get your limit of crabs and clams, and avid anglers can enjoy landing largemouth bass, catfish, king salmon, steelhead, fresh- and saltwater perch, white and green sturgeon, and shad.

The **Oregon Dunes National Recreation Area** begins north of Florence and stretches for 47 miles along the coast. **Jesse M. Honeyman State Park,** 2 miles south of town, contains magnificent 500-foot-high sand dunes, 3 freshwater lakes, and 47 full-hookup, 121 electrical, and 187 tent sites.

North Fork Siuslaw Road, 1 mile east on OR 126, leads 17 miles to **North Fork Campground,** where you'll find 7 group sites and a boat launch. You can use the campground as a base for salmon, steelhead, and cutthroat trout fishing, as well as hikes to an old homestead on a riverbank and along a 4,000-foot nature trail.

As the Coast Range mountains fill the horizon and picturesque homes and boat basins frame the highway, the return to Mapleton seems more scenic than it did on arrival.

Siuslaw River Canyon

From Mapleton OR 36 stays in the narrow **Siuslaw River Canyon.** En route to Deadwood you can photograph the slow-moving stream against a background of mountains filled with magnificent trees from several waysides offering boat ramps, swimming, and access to fishing holes. Around Swisshome the highway stretches along a ridge, with whitewater cascading below, then cuts through dairy farms as it passes **Deadwood Covered Bridge** (World Guide Number 37-20-38). The bridge was built in 1932 and stands about 100 feet south of the highway; it also is known as Lost Creek and Nelson Creek Bridge. At **Lake Creek Wayside,** the river boils and churns in a series of whitewater cascades that twist, turn, and rush over basalt slabs and boulders.

Triangle Lake

About 1 mile east the drive reaches its highest point as it climbs out of the canyon at **Triangle Lake.** The lake is at 1,000 feet elevation and is stocked with rainbow trout. Wild cutthroat, kokanee, catfish, bluegill, and bass make it an angler's dream come true. It also sees heavy use by water-skiers, boaters, and swimmers. A quaint church, at the southern end, was built in the 1950s but looks as if it has been here for centuries.

After Triangle Lake the highway leaves the lush green mountains and descends into the wide-open meadows of the Willamette Valley. On the remaining 20 miles, it passes aged barns—including a round one—isolated stores, Christmas tree farms, and the Long Tom River. Reaching US 99 West, you can conclude the drive by either traveling north 2 miles to Junction City or south 15 miles to Eugene.

20

North Santiam Canyon

General Description: A 90-mile drive on paved roads starting near sea level in Salem and rising to 4,500 feet at Hoodoo Ski Bowl.

Special Attractions: Detroit Lake, Willamette National Forest, fishing, hiking, hot springs, alpine and cross-country skiing.

Location: West-central Oregon between Salem and the Cascade Mountains.

Drive Route Numbers: OR 22, OR 126/US 20

Travel Season: All year.

Camping: 11 forest service and 2 Bureau of Land Management campgrounds with tables, fire pits, and vault or flush toilets; some with drinking water. 1 state park campground with full-hookup, electrical, and tent sites.

Services: All services in Salem. Limited services at Stayton, Lyons, Mill City, and Detroit.

Nearby Attractions: McKenzie–Santiam Pass Scenic Byway, Silver Falls Loop Drive, Covered Bridges Drive, Mount Jefferson and Middle Santiam Wildernesses, headwaters of the Metolius River.

For More Information: Travel Salem, (503) 581-4325, (800) 874-7012, www.travelsalem.com; Stayton/Sublimity Chamber of Commerce, (503) 769-3464, www.staytonsublimitychamber.org; North Santiam Chamber of Commerce, (503) 897-5000, www.NSChamber.org; Willamette National Forest, Supervisor's Office, (541) 225-6300, www.fs.usda.gov/willamette; Detroit Ranger Station, (503) 854-3366.

The Route

Starting at exit 253 off I-5 in southeast **Salem,** the drive climbs gradually from an elevation of 154 feet to 4,500 feet at **Hoodoo Ski Bowl.** The first 15 miles are straight and flat as the route crosses eastern Willamette Valley farmlands and clumps of trees underlaid by basalts. On the section to **Detroit Lake State Park,** tree-lined corridors alternate with canyon bluffs, the riffling **North Santiam River,** and the **Big Chief** and **Detroit Lake Reservoirs.** The remaining 40 miles are virtually a continuous corridor of Douglas fir, with occasional views of surrounding snowcapped peaks. Weekday traffic is usually moderate but includes large trucks. Since 90 percent of the recreational users come from the surrounding area, traffic is heavy on weekends and holidays.

Weather is conducive to recreation all year. An average rainfall of 39 inches supports a luxuriant mixed forest of Douglas fir, maple, oak, and alder, together with wild rhododendron and scotch broom displays in the spring. Summer temperatures are usually in the low 80s. Five- to 20-mile-per-hour breezes help cool evenings. Winters range from daytime highs in the low 50s to below freezing in

North Santiam Canyon

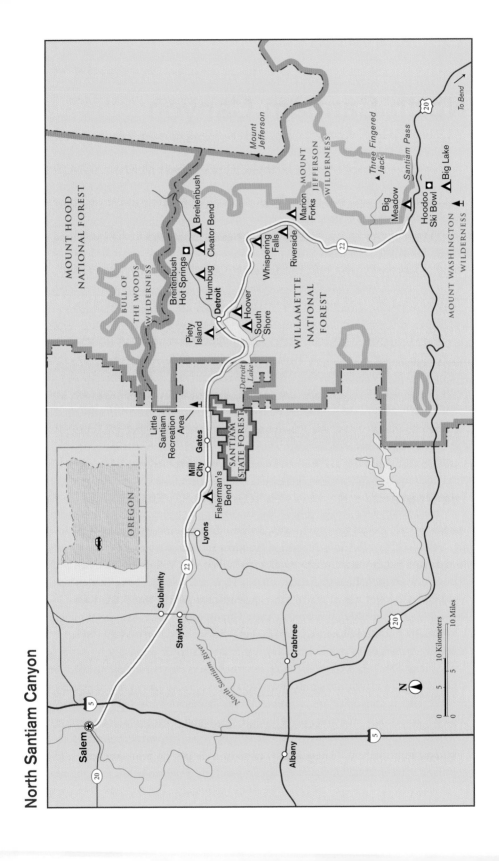

the mountains. Spring days are usually in the mid-60s, while autumn temperatures range from the mid-60s to mid-70s.

From exit 253 at I-5, the North Santiam Highway (OR 22) starts as four lanes and stretches east through dairy farms, grasslands, and field crops, punctuated by isolated stands of willow, alder, and oak. The Cascade foothills are a constant hazy blue on the horizon ahead. During the first 5 miles, the road passes the Oregon State Reformatory and the exit to OR 214, which is the southern access to the Silver Falls Scenic Loop Drive.

Sublimity, Stayton & the Santiam River

At mile 11.5 **Sublimity** and **Stayton** lie about a mile north and south of the highway, respectively. Both are small service communities. You'll find two city parks in Sublimity and two streams running through Stayton, which is situated on the banks of the Santiam River. **Jordan Covered Bridge** (World Guide Number 37-24-02), built in 1937 and moved to Stayton in 1988, is used to connect two parks. The original structure burned in 1994 and local citizens rebuilt it on the same site in Stayton Pioneer Park. You can rent the bridge for weddings, receptions, and family reunions.

East of Stayton the highway narrows to two lanes until the end of the drive. The farmlands and floodplain are replaced by the western Cascade foothills, which were formed through repeated volcanic eruptions. As the road continues to climb, the rocks become younger, for flows from each succeeding volcano covered older rock.

As the road parallels the **Santiam River,** it appears to divide the foliage. Alders and oaks line the riverbank south of the highway, while Douglas firs and pines cover north-side hills and ridges. You can expect to see anglers fishing off banks and boats, for the Santiam is renowned as a prime steelhead, rainbow trout, and salmon stream. The forests also support deer and elk, which are often seen along the road and in a narrow canyon en route to Mehama.

OR 22 and OR 226 meet at Mehama. OR 226 continues 1 mile south to Lyons and then angles southwest to Scio. The northern segment of the Linn County Covered Bridges Loop starts 7 miles east of Scio on OR 226.

Little Santiam Recreation Area

Old Mehama Road loops northeast on 10 miles of pavement and about 8 miles of gravel to the Elkhorn region and the **Little Santiam Recreation Area** before rejoining OR 22 at Gates. The Elkhorn region balances summer homes and a golf course with ranching, logging, and copper, lead, and zinc mining.

At the recreation area you can picnic in a thick forest, take extended wilderness hikes, and swim in natural pools along the pristine **Little Santiam River.** The Bureau of Land Management provides 23 tent sites in its **Elkhorn Valley Campground.**

Between Lyons and Mill City, 7 miles east, you can camp along the roadside on the banks of the North Fork of the Santiam River at the BLM's **Fisherman's Bend Campground.** It has 39 sites. Nearby **North Santiam State Park** provides a good view of the riffling river that is partially hidden by trees along the roadside. The park offers a shaded picnic area, fishing, and short trails for walks along the riverbank.

In keeping with its name, lumber mills line the highway through **Mill City,** at mile 28. A travel information center has brochures and fact sheets on local recreation. At **Gates,** 3 miles east, you'll find a small airport, motel, RV park, and restaurants.

You may wish to take a break from driving with a stop at **Maple Rest Area** and walk a nature trail where you might see deer and other wildlife. **Niagara County Park** attracts more visitors than any local park due to its natural scenic beauty, location, and history, which dates to the 1890s, when a dam was built near here. It has picnic tables and a trail that leads to the river.

East of Gates the highway enters a canyon, which is particularly striking in autumn when maples turn to russets and yellows and are highlighted by evergreens and columnar basalt cliffs. Roadside stops include Maples Rest Area; Paddlesaddle Park, with a boat ramp, trails, picnic tables, and fire pits; and Niagara County Park, where you can walk a trail down to the river.

Detroit Lake

Big Cliff Dam, at mile 38.5, is an Army Corps of Engineers project and part of the Detroit Lake system. As a reregulating dam and small reservoir, it smooths power generation water release from Detroit Dam and controls the downstream river level fluctuation. Reregulations at Big Cliff may cause the lake level to fluctuate as much as 24 feet daily. The dam offers good views of the Santiam River and classic cement highway barriers.

Three miles east the road enters the Willamette National Forest and Detroit Lake State Recreation Area. At 1.6 million acres, the national forest is approximately the size of New Jersey. It ranks first among 156 national forests in producing lumber and is used by campers, boaters, swimmers, hikers, anglers, skiers, and snowmobilers.

Detroit Lake, situated in the Cascade Mountains, attracts hikers, nature lovers, fishers, and boaters. Licensed by Shutterstock.com.

Rocks surrounding the dam have been bleached greenish gray by hot water and steam. Some absorbed water while they were underground molten lava and cooled to become granite.

Detroit Dam rises 463 feet from its foundation in the narrow, steep, rocky slopes of **North Santiam Canyon** to create a lake with 32 miles of shoreline. The concrete gravity structure has public restrooms and barriers that protect anglers and sightseers from traffic. From May to September the lake is kept at the highest possible levels for the enjoyment of water-skiers, swimmers, and other visitors who fill shoreline day-use areas, trailer campgrounds, and boat launches.

At **Marigold Day Use Area,** 4 miles east of the dam, you can camp in a fragrant Douglas fir and Engelmann spruce forest at Piety Island's 22 sites. It was named for a former highway construction camp (covered by the lake) and serves water recreation needs with a swimming area, a bathhouse, a wide paved boat launch, and a separate launching area for water-skiers.

Two miles east, **Detroit Lake State Recreation Area** and the **Detroit Ranger Station** straddle the highway. At the ranger station you can get trail maps, campground information, and snow-park permits.

The recreation area offers a magnificent roadside viewpoint with snowcapped Mount Jefferson on the southern horizon and Detroit Lake in the foreground. On the lake's north shore, the campground contains 8 loops with 133 tent, 72 electrical, and 106 full-hookup sites scattered through a Douglas fir forest. Conveniences range from hot showers, boat ramps, and docks to evening amphitheater programs.

Detroit, a few miles east, is a roadside community with seasonal accommodations, RV parks, 2 boat docks, and boat rentals. Check your fuel gauge before continuing east, for Detroit has the last gas station for 55 miles. Nearby, **Hoover South Shore Campground** includes 35 sites, plus a group camp capable of accommodating up to 70 people. A short distance west, South Shore Campground's 32 sites overlook the lake.

Breitenbush Side Trip

Breitenbush Hot Springs, 10 miles north of Detroit, is a retreat and conference center open to the public for overnight stays and day use. Reservations are required for all visits. The center is set in the forest along the **Breitenbush River.** Guests enjoy natural hot spring pools, tiled tubs, and a wet sauna. Bathing in the springs is clothing optional. Several trails start at the center and meander through an ancient forest. The **Breitenbush Gorge Trail** has been designated a National Recreation Trail. Four forest service campgrounds with a total of 65 sites are located on or near the road between Detroit and Breitenbush.

West Cascades National Scenic Byway

The section of OR 22 from Detroit to the junction with US 20 and on to McKenzie Bridge composes the McKenzie–Santiam segment of the **West Cascades National Scenic Byway.** The West Cascades Byway begins 75 miles north at Estacada and extends 220 miles south, with the last leg including the Robert Aufderheide Memorial Drive. The Estacada-Breitenbush portion begins with several miles of outstanding views of the Clackamas River and Canyon and includes several campgrounds and Breitenbush Hot Springs. Other highlights along this segment include the **Riverside National Recreation Trail,** which winds through 4 miles of old-growth forest and rewards you with more outstanding views of the Clackamas River. **Bagby Hot Springs Trail,** north of Breitenbush, meanders through Douglas fir and cedar forest and by a 1913 cabin to the hot springs where clothing is also optional for bathing. A Northwest forest service pass is required to park at the trailhead.

The middle section of the West Cascades Scenic Byway is described from here to the junction with US 20 and in the Santiam Loop Drive from the OR 242 portion from US 20 to McKenzie Bridge (Route 24). Route 23 contains a complete description of the Aufderheide segment.

After Detroit the highway enters a forested corridor, which continues virtually unbroken for the 27 miles to the junction with US 20. The beauty is in the trees, which cluster tightly together and display a smattering of oaks and light green vine maples among the thick Douglas and white firs. Wild rhododendrons add splashes of reds and pinks in late May and early June. At periodic turnouts you have ample opportunities to photograph the Santiam's riffles, Mount Jefferson, and occasional roadside cascades.

Every few miles a campground lies tucked away in the woods and close to the river. They start with **Whispering Falls**' 16 sites, at elevation 2,000 feet. Then comes **Riverside** with 37 sites, **Marion Forks** with 15 sites, and **Big Meadows** with 9 camp spots, plus corrals, a loading ramp, and troughs for horses.

Marion Forks Restaurant, at milepost 68, is open 7 days a week and has the only food along this stretch. Migrating salmon and steelhead intercepted at the Minto Station egg collection facility, 4 miles west of Big Cliff Dam, are fertilized and transported to nearby **Marion Forks Salmon Hatchery.** When they reach fingerling size, they are released to continue their normal migratory cycle. You can see adult steelhead and salmon and feed rainbow trout at the hatchery's ponds.

At elevation 3,000 feet you enter a snow zone and winter recreation area. In winter traction tires and devices are mandatory. You need a permit, available at forest service ranger stations, to park at **Big Springs Sno-Park.** The park is a staging area for cross-country skiing and snowmobile runs.

Hoodoo Ski Bowl

OR 22 meets US 20 at mile 83, and the route overlaps the McKenzie–Santiam Pass Scenic Byway on the remaining 8 miles to **Hoodoo Ski Bowl.** As you spiral east up the steep grade, Three Fingered Jack is a continuous presence on the northeastern horizon.

Hoodoo Ski Bowl, west of the Santiam Pass summit, is a family-oriented ski area with a triple chair, 1 double chair, and 2 rope tows. The top elevation is 5,703 feet, with 30 percent of the terrain geared to beginners, 40 percent to intermediate, and 30 percent for advanced skiers. It has 32 runs, an 800-foot tubing run, and approximately 12 miles of Nordic trails, plus 2 day lodges and a day-care center. **Big Lake Campground,** nearby, offers 49 tent, auto, and trailer sites on a scenic lake surrounded by thick forest and towering mountain peaks.

From Hoodoo you have the option of continuing east over the 4,617-foot Santiam Pass summit and driving about 17 miles to Sisters or following US 20 55 miles west to Albany.

21

Santiam Loop

General Description: A 67-mile arc on 2-lane paved highways through open farmland, thick forests, and historic communities.

Special Attractions: Willamette National Forest, Foster Reservoir, Green Peter Lake, covered bridges, fish hatchery, museums, Menagerie Wilderness, historic districts, Santiam Canyon, fishing, hiking, recreational gold panning, rockhounding.

Location: West-central Oregon between Albany and Brownsville.

Drive Route Numbers: US 20, OR 228.

Travel Season: All year.

Camping: 4 forest service and 1 Bureau of Land Management campgrounds with tables, fire pits, and vault or flush toilets; some with drinking water. 1 state park campground with primitive sites. Several commercial RV parks are also situated on the route.

Services: All services in Albany, Lebanon, and Sweet Home. Limited services at Brownsville.

Nearby Attractions: Salem, Eugene, McKenzie–Santiam Pass Scenic Byway, North Santiam Canyon Scenic Drive, Linn County Covered Bridges Scenic Drive.

For More Information: Albany Visitors Association, (541) 928-0911, (800) 526-2256 (USA), www.albanyvisitors.com; Lebanon Chamber of Commerce, (541) 258-7164, www.lebanon-chamber.org; Sweet Home Chamber of Commerce, (541) 367-6186, www.sweethomechamber.org; Willamette National Forest, Supervisor's Office, (541) 225-6300, www.fs.usda.gov/willamette; Sweet Home Ranger District, (541) 367-5168.

The Route

From Albany the drive extends southeast through the farmlands of the Willamette Valley to Sweet Home. Foster Lake, the Santiam River, and the dense Willamette National Forest offer striking scenery as the route heads east into the Cascade foothills. Returning to Sweet Home, it concludes by traveling west to the Brownsville Historic District. Traffic is usually moderate to heavy. The tour can be joined at I-5 by driving east from exit 216 to Brownsville or by taking exit 233 at Albany onto US 20.

Travelers will find summer temperatures in the low 80s. Winters range from daytime highs in the low 40s to the low 50s and below freezing on the slopes of the mountains. Spring days in the mid-60s are common. Autumn temperatures range from the mid-60s to mid-70s.

Santiam Loop

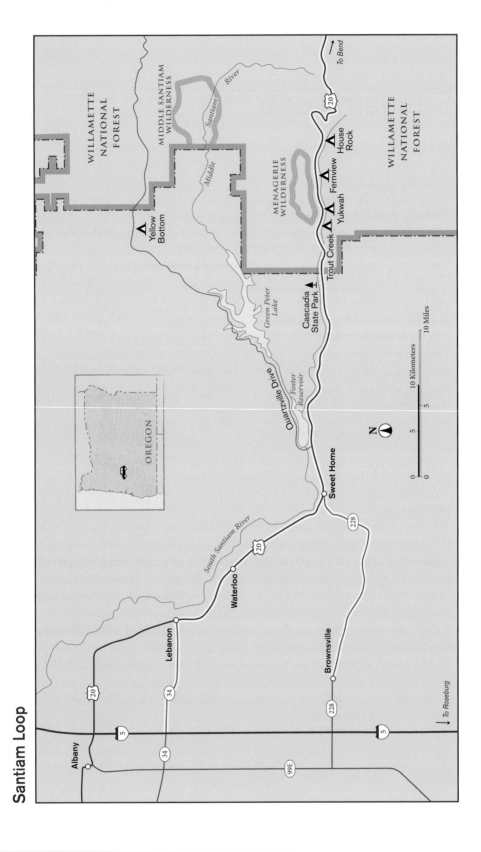

Albany

"Seems Like Old Times—Your Guide to Historic Albany," published by the Albany Visitors Association and available online, contains self-guided tours of the town's historic districts, which contain 350 homes that include every major architectural style popular in the US since 1850. Visitors can see the insides during an annual **Historic Interiors Tour** on the last Saturday in July or a **Christmas Home Tour** on the third Sunday in December.

The **Oregon Northwest Art and Air Festival** celebrates local art and aeronautics with morning hot-air balloon launches, evening night glows (when balloons are lit up by their burners), a juried art show, children's art, and concerts.

Monteith Riverpark, on the banks of the Willamette, is a pleasant spot to picnic and jog. It also hosts outdoor concerts featuring nationally known entertainers and is a departure point for river rafting and fishing. The Willamette River runs through the western edge, and the Calapooia River also crosses near town.

From **Albany** the drive begins by traveling 9 miles east through sheep and dairy lands to Crabtree Road, where it swings south. Crabtree Road (OR 226) is the access point for the 50-mile Linn County Covered Bridges Drive. If you decide to include it, it will add about 2.5 hours to your driving time.

Lebanon

Lebanon, 8 miles south of the junction, is a major producer of strawberries. Each year during an annual festival, 17,000 pieces of shortcake are given away. **Gill's Landing** at the Santiam River has a boat ramp, swimming, playgrounds, and overnight camping in 21 RV sites. **Ralston Square,** with a gazebo and rose garden, serves as an outdoor theater and a pleasant place to picnic by a canal.

South of Lebanon, trees intermingle with grasslands. East of the highway, **Waterloo County Park,** on the banks of the South Fork of the Santiam River, offers a boat ramp and covered picnicking along with short hiking and nature trails. **Waterloo Campground** is open year-round and has 100 electrical sites and 20 nonelectric sites. At **McDowell Creek Falls** a few miles farther, you can take a 3-mile hike to a small waterfall.

Sweet Home

Scenic tree-covered hills signal the approach to Sweet Home, 13 miles south of Lebanon. US 20 meets OR 228 at the western end of town. At the junction, sculptures of a miner and a logger hint at the collections inside the **East Linn Museum,** where you'll see firearms, china, Native American relics, and a large polished rock collection.

Sweet Home sits on the site of a prehistoric forest and has become a rock-hounding hot spot. Surrounding hills, streams, and lowlands have yielded everything from 70 kinds of petrified wood to arrowheads, crystal-lined geodes, and fish-eye agates. Though fossil leaves can be taken from a public dig, many sites are on private land, and you'll need the owners' permission before you dig.

Weddle Bridge (World Guide Number 37-22-05), downtown in Sankey Park, has been reconstructed as part of an exhibition of Northwest forest resources. When it was built in 1937, it straddled Thomas Creek near Scio. The park makes an ideal outing for small children, who can romp on playground equipment and fish for steelhead in **Ames Creek,** which flows under the bridge.

Within a couple of miles of the intersection as you continue east on US 20, you'll pass the chamber of commerce and the Willamette National Forest's **Sweet Home Ranger Station.** If you're planning on backcountry hiking, stop at the station for maps and recreation information.

Foster Lake

About 1 mile east, signboards at **Foster Reservoir Viewpoint** provide basic information on services, parks, and recreational opportunities along Foster and Green Peter Lakes. Both are Army Corps of Engineers projects. **Foster Lake,** which spreads along 3.5 miles of US 20, is a highly scenic reservoir encircled by a huge Douglas fir forest that starts at the water's edge. The scenery and languid waters have made it a favorite of boaters, photographers, and anglers, who take stocked rainbow trout and bluegills. It's also used for jet boat races and waterskiing.

Crossing **Foster Reservoir Dam,** the scenic North River Road takes you to a fish hatchery and 3 parks along the Santiam River, which is known for its salmon and steelhead. At the hatchery you can feed fish and see winter steelhead and summer salmon brood stock.

The Road to Quartzville & Green Peter Lake

To see **Green Peter Lake,** turn north on **Quartzville Drive** at the east end of Foster Lake. This magnificent drive on a two-lane paved road begins in a thick evergreen forest and follows the north shoreline of the 10-mile-long lake as it crosses several creeks en route to the Quartzville area at elevation 4,418 feet.

Quartzville was platted in 1865, and following the discovery of gold, lead, and silver, it grew to 1,000 people. By 1871 it was a ghost town. While nothing remains of the town, you can still try your luck at recreational gold panning in the region's creeks.

Commercial campgrounds along the 27-mile route are **Sunnyside,** on the edge of Foster Reservoir, with a three-lane boat ramp and 130 electrical and water and 35 no-hookup sites, and **Whitcomb Creek,** with a boat launch and 39 tent and RV hookups. The Bureau of Land Management's **Yellow Bottom Campground,** near the summit, has 22 sites, picnic areas, and fishing. Green Peter Lake is considered a good chinook salmon and bass fishery.

Cascadia State Park

East of Foster Lake the Willamette National Forest becomes so thick and dark, it virtually envelops US 20, and at times it almost seems as though you are driving through a tunnel. **Cascadia State Park,** 12 miles east of Sweet Home, is nestled in huge Douglas fir trees at the base of the mountains. In the secluded park, with 25 primitive campsites, you can pump mineral water from natural springs; walk through a mixed forest of fir, maple, oak, and alder down to the scenic river canyon; or take a 0.75-mile hike to a waterfall. **Short Covered Bridge** (World Guide Number 37-22-09), near the park, has been reconstructed several times since the original was built in 1845.

Camping Areas

Trout Creek Campground, the first of several Willamette National Forest camping areas along the highway, is about 8 miles east of the park. In addition to fishing and enjoying the fragrant pine-scented forest from 23 tent sites, you can hike to an adjacent elk refuge and into the Menagerie Wilderness Area. **Yukwah Campground,** 0.25 mile east of Trout Creek, has nature trails, fishing, and 19 sites suitable for RVs. **Fernview,** 3 miles east of Yukwah, contains 11 sites and a 2-mile trail to Rooster Rock viewpoint.

House Rock, 26 miles east of Sweet Home, features 15 sites. A 0.8-mile trail leads to 40-foot **House Rock Falls** through primeval forest and along the **Santiam Wagon Road,** where original ruts are still visible. It ends at House Rock, an overhanging boulder that once sheltered travelers from winter storms.

Crawfordsville

After returning to Sweet Home, as you travel west on OR 228, you'll pass **Crawfordsville Covered Bridge** (World Guide Number 37-22-15). It was built in 1932 but bypassed by a newer road. **McKircher Park,** 1 mile south of the bridge, offers an idyllic picnic spot overlooking a rushing cascade.

Some of the headstones in **Crawfordsville**'s cemetery, also along the highway, are more than 100 years old. As you continue west, roadside stands invite stopping to purchase fresh tomatoes, onions, squash, berries, and filberts when in season.

Brownsville

Brownsville, 7 miles west of Crawfordsville, is the third-oldest continuous settlement in Oregon. It began in 1846 and was named after one of its founders.

You'll see the aftermath of an 1880s building boom in a collection of buildings that represent styles from the 1850s through the 1920s. Greek revival "box" construction, Queen Anne Victorian, Italianate—you'll find all those and more on a self-guiding walking tour with maps available at the **Linn County Historical Museum.**

The **Moyer House** is Brownsville's pride and joy. The 1881 Victorian mansion was inspired by contemporary Italianate villa architecture. Interiors feature hand-painted landscapes, floral stenciling, and turn-of-the-20th-century furnishings. The Moyer House and many other buildings are listed on the National Register of Historic Places.

The railroad's heritage is represented in the Linn County Historical Museum, which is housed in a depot and several boxcars. Inside are artifacts brought over the Oregon Trail, Native American relics, and natural history exhibits. Replicas of a general store, bank, barber shop, and other buildings of the period are also displayed.

Other museums, within walking distance of one another, include the **Pioneer Picture Gallery,** which features large collections of historic photos that document the way people lived and the town used to look. **Living Rock Studios** is a good place to take children. The stone "castle" features a hollow tree made of petrified wood, pictures in translucent rock, and life-size wildlife paintings.

Brownsville's **Pioneer Park** has limited camping available during summer on a first come, first served basis. It's a pleasant setting for relaxing and enjoying the Calapooia River or attending an event in the 400-seat amphitheater.

Upon concluding your sightseeing, you can reach I-5 by traveling 4 miles west on OR 228.

22

Woodburn, Silver Falls, Salem Loop

General Description: A signed 35-mile drive on paved 2-lane roads through the eastern Willamette Valley's agricultural lands and forests to the Cascade foothills and Oregon's largest state park.

Special Attractions: Mount Angel Abbey, Silver Falls State Park with 10 waterfalls, Christmas tree farms, covered bridge, historic sites, horseback riding, hiking, camping.

Location: Eastern Willamette Valley between Silverton and Salem.

Drive Route Numbers: OR 214, OR 22.

Travel Season: All year.

Camping: 1 state park campground with electrical hookups.

Services: All services in Woodburn and Salem. Limited services in Mount Angel and Silverton.

Nearby Attractions: Oregon City historic attractions, 99 East–French Prairie Loop Drive, Albany historic districts, Linn County Covered Bridges Drive, North Santiam Canyon Scenic Drive, Table Rock Wilderness.

For More Information: Mount Angel Chamber of Commerce, (503) 845-9440, www.mtangel.org; Travel Salem, (503) 581-4325, (800) 874-7012, www.travelsalem .com; Silver Falls State Park, (503) 873-8681, www.oregonstateparks.org; Silverton Area Chamber of Commerce, (503) 873-5615, www.silvertonchamber.org; Stayton/ Sublimity Chamber of Commerce, (503) 769-3464, www.staytonsublimitychamber .org; Woodburn Area Chamber of Commerce, (503) 982-8221, www .woodburnchamber.org.

The Route

This signed scenic route begins in **Woodburn** at the junction of OR 214 and OR 99 East and travels southeast through hop yards and berry fields to **Mount Angel's Benedictine abbey.** It continues southeast through the quiet rural community of **Silverton,** climbs a ridge of foothills, and enters the dark forest of **Silver Falls State Park.** From the park it concludes through rolling hills to downtown **Salem.** The route can be joined from I-5 by taking exit 271 east to Woodburn or by driving the itinerary in reverse from exit 253 at Salem. Traffic is usually moderate.

Summer temperatures are usually in the low 80s. Winters range from daytime highs in the low 40s to the low 50s and near freezing on the slopes of the mountains. Days in the mid-60s are common during spring, and autumn temperatures range from the mid-60s to mid-70s.

From the busy intersection of OR 99 East and OR 214, the scenic drive quickly exits the congestion. After 2 blocks, you've left the businesses and

Woodburn, Silver Falls, Salem Loop

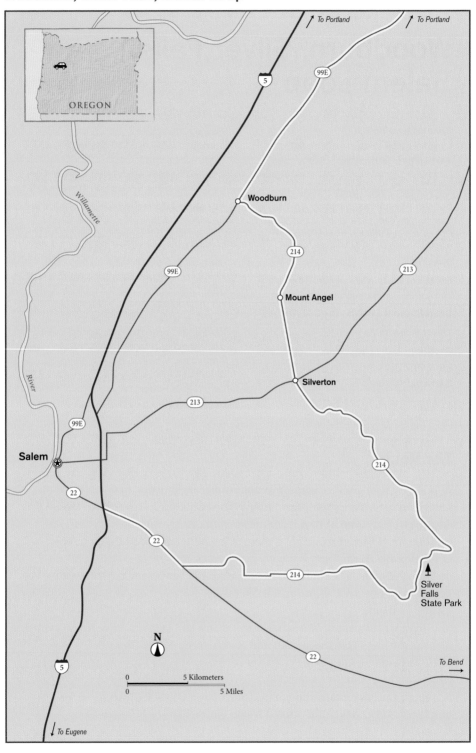

fruit-processing plants and are traveling through hop yards. The yards are intriguing, even in winter when the strings are bare and the 18-foot-high poles stand in stark relief. As the season unfolds they will be bustling with activity as mazes of strings are reconstructed and vines are hand wrapped around them. In the warmth of springtime, the vines grow up to 8 inches per day, and by late summer they form a lush golden-green canopy over the yard. Hops are natural preservatives that enhance the foam and quality of beer, and after the September harvest they are sold to brewers.

Mount Angel

During the 6 miles to **Mount Angel,** hop yards vie for attention with rustic barns and farmhouses, dairy herds, berry fields, and an occasional corridor of trees.

At Mount Angel a **Benedictine monastery** crowns a hill 1.5 miles east of the route. Along the entrance road you'll see a grotto and stations of the cross nestled in a quiet forest. A tiny cemetery chapel, near the entrance, was built in the 1880s and is the oldest building.

About 100 monks, who are members of **Mount Angel Abbey,** maintain the impeccable courtyard and elegant multistory brick buildings. A self-guiding walking brochure details the history and functions of the buildings and takes you along paths to viewpoints that encompass the Willamette Valley below, Mount Hood 50 miles north, and Washington's famed Mounts Rainier and St. Helens.

You may also wish to stop at the library. It is an architectural masterpiece designed by famed architect **Alvar Aalto.** A rare-book room exhibits ancient handwritten volumes that predate the printing press. The small museum displays Native American relics (not religious artifacts), miniature books, Civil War memorabilia, military medals, and a fine collection of stuffed birds and animals from the region.

Coming and going from the abbey on Church Street, you'll pass the cathedral-like **St. Mary's Church.** The neo-gothic brick building is a National Historic Site. It was built in 1910 in the form of a Latin cross, and its 22 stained-glass windows, paintings, and statues were designed as a religious picture story. Inside you'll find a brochure explaining the art.

Silverton

Silverton, 2.5 miles south, is an agricultural center where commercial crops range from strawberries and produce to flowers and Christmas trees. With many older homes perched on hillsides, you'll find Silverton quaint, charming, quiet, and beautiful. **Silver Creek** flows gently through town, and at **Silverton Reservoir,**

along the highway, you can fish for trout, salmon, and steelhead; enjoy an afternoon of boating; and relax with a picnic lunch on the peaceful shoreline. As in many Northwest towns, artists have painted larger-than-life murals on the sides of buildings. The murals display an eclectic mix of local sights, history, and other subjects. As you stroll through town with a downloadable mural map, you'll see local renditions of Norman Rockwell's "Four Freedoms," the Boston Red Sox, the Oregon Trail, Santa Claus, Silver Falls, and other subjects.

Silverton bills itself as Oregon's **Garden City,** and rightly so. The **Oregon Garden** was born of an idea of the Oregon Association of Nurserymen in the 1940s and flowered in 1997. With over 20 gardens it is larger than British Columbia's Buchart Gardens. It includes a children's garden and one of the few Frank Lloyd Wright–designed homes in the Pacific Northwest. This world-class public botanical garden offers concerts in an outdoor auditorium in summer and in an enclosed pavilion in winter.

Gallon House Bridge (World Guide Number 37-24-01), 1.5 miles northeast of Silverton via either Downs or Hobart Roads, spans Abiqua Creek near its confluence with the Pudding River. Built in 1917, the National Historic Site received its name during Prohibition, when whiskey sold for 10 cents a gallon, and it became a gathering place for illegal liquor sales.

To Silver Falls State Park

On the 14 miles south to **Silver Falls State Park,** the highway winds and climbs into the Cascade foothills. The hills are underlaid with basalt, which flowed down the Columbia River from eastern Oregon about 20 million years ago, and are covered with 10.8 million–year–old volcanic ash.

As the road clings to a cliff and becomes rough with patches, posted mileages drop to 25 and 30 miles per hour. You can also expect to meet farmers on tractors and heavy equipment as the road enters a belt of Christmas tree farms, where hillsides are covered with Nobel and Douglas fir seedlings. At the southern end an excellent all-weather road cuts into stately groves of Douglas fir, which form a virtual canopy over the highway as it approaches Silver Falls State Park.

Silver Falls, Oregon's largest state park, fills 8,700 acres of meadows and a ravine cut by Silver Creek and covered with second-growth Douglas fir, western hemlock, and a thick undergrowth of giant ferns, salmonberry, salal, and the state flower, Oregon grape. The quiet, cathedral-like forest is laced with a network of

At Silver Falls State Park, visitors can hike to several waterfalls, including South Falls. Licensed by Shutterstock.com.

paths that include 25 miles of hiking, 3 miles of jogging, 4 miles of biking, and 14 miles of horse trails.

The **Trail of Ten Falls** is the most popular and takes you through Silver Creek's canyons to 10 waterfalls. You can walk behind three of them, and you'll see others ranging from a 178-foot drop to 27-foot cascades. Some, like **Winter Falls,** are accessible by short walks from roadside turnouts. As you walk this 7-mile National Recreation Trail, watch for the state animal, the beaver, along with deer, rabbits, squirrels, and chipmunks. If you have a license, you can also fish Silver Creek.

In addition to 52 electrical and 45 tent sites, accommodations include 14 cabins, 6 horse camps, and 3 group camps, plus a conference center with 4 lodges, meeting rooms, and a dining hall. There are also 2 ranches with dormitory accommodations, activity fields, and picnic areas. The lodgelike visitor center's snack bar operates 7 days a week in summer and on winter weekends.

Because of its thick vegetation and its location in the Cascade foothills, Silver Falls is usually cool, even in the dog days of summer. Prepare for your visit by bringing at least a light jacket.

Continuing West

West of the park the highway winds through farmlands and rolling hillsides planted in commercial grass seed and Christmas trees ranging from seedlings to full size. **Silver Falls Winery,** in the community of Sublimity, offers pinot noir, pinot gris, and chardonnay tastings from 11 a.m. to 6 p.m., Friday through Sunday from March through December.

Twelve miles east of Salem, you turn onto OR 22 and follow it west to downtown, where it becomes Mission Street. Along Mission Street you'll find the **Bush Barn Art Center,** with 3 exhibition galleries and Northwest arts and crafts for sale. **Bush House,** on the grounds, was built in 1877–1878. The Victorian mansion houses original furnishings, gaslights, and 10 marble fireplaces. **Deepwood Estate** nearby displays an elegant Queen Anne home built in 1894, known for its elegant stained glass and magnificent staircase. It is surrounded by 6 acres of English-style gardens with a nature trail, an original carriage house, an English tea house, and a garden with a wrought-iron gazebo.

A gilt-covered 23-foot statue of a pioneer crowns **Oregon's State Capitol,** approximately 8 blocks north of Mission Street. The Vermont-marble building contains an exhibit area with extensive murals and a gift shop. At **Mission Mill Museum,** 3 blocks from the capitol, you can see 14 historic structures including three 1840s mission homes and an 1800s woolen mill with mill stream.

23

Robert Aufderheide Memorial Drive

General Description: A 70-mile National Forest Service Byway on a paved highway through a typical Cascade Mountain forest and along a Wild and Scenic River.

Special Attractions: Old-growth forest, Cougar Reservoir, Wild and Scenic North Fork of the Middle Fork of the Willamette River, Waldo Lake, French Pete and Three Sisters Wilderness Areas, wildflowers and autumn foliage, camping, horseback, riding, mountain hiking.

Location: West-central Oregon in the Willamette National Forest, between Blue River and Westfir, about 41 miles east of Eugene.

Drive Route Number: FR 19.

Travel Season: The byway opens and closes depending on snow, with the season usually starting in early June and closing at the end of October.

Camping: 9 national forest campgrounds with toilets, drinking water, picnic tables, and fire grates, plus numerous undeveloped sites.

Services: No services on the byway. All services in nearby Oakridge, Blue River, and McKenzie Bridge.

Nearby Attractions: McKenzie Pass–Santiam Pass Loop, Cascade Lakes Highway Loop, North Santiam Canyon.

For More Information: Willamette National Forest, Supervisor's Office, (541) 225-6300, www.fs.usda.gov/willamette; District Rangers: Middle Fork Ranger District, (541) 782-2283; McKenzie River Ranger District, (541) 882-7254; Oakridge/Westfir Chamber of Commerce, (541) 782-4146, www.oakridgechamber.com.

The Route

Robert Aufderheide was the Willamette National Forest supervisor from 1954 to 1959. The Memorial Drive starts midway between Blue River and McKenzie Bridge and extends north–south to Westfir along the South Fork of the McKenzie River and North Fork of the Middle Fork of the Willamette River. It is included as one-third of the West Cascades Scenic Byway. The other segments are Clackamas to Breitenbush and the McKenzie–Santiam Pass segment that is detailed as part of Route 20, North Santiam Canyon, and Route 24, McKenzie, Santiam Pass.

This is a popular bicycling route with elevations ranging from 1,052 to 3,728 feet. Since most of the drive is through a forested corridor that blocks views of rivers, cliffs, and hills, you will see some of the best scenery along the numerous hiking trails that start at the roadside. Mile-by-mile directional audiotapes of the drive are available free of charge at the McKenzie River and Middle Fork ranger stations. Birders are sometimes rewarded with sightings of eagles, kingfishers, ospreys, hawks, and lots of songbirds.

Robert Aufderheide Memorial Drive

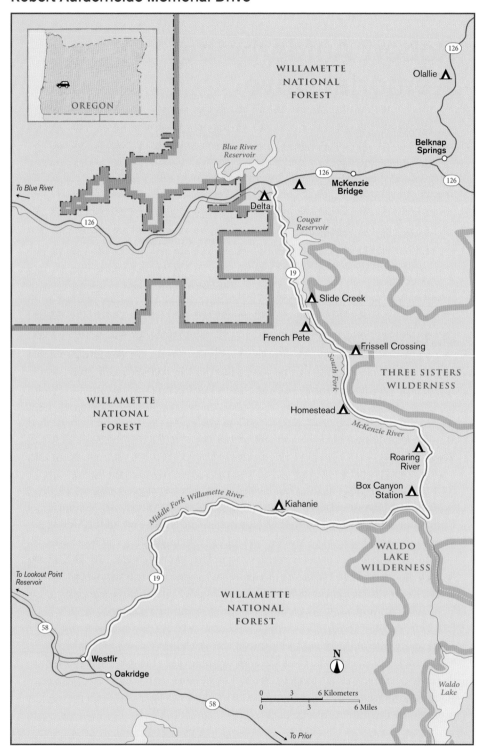

OREGON

WILLAMETTE
NATIONAL
FOREST

Olallie

Belknap
Springs

Blue River
Reservoir

To Blue River

McKenzie
Bridge

Delta

Cougar
Reservoir

Slide Creek

French Pete

Frissell Crossing

South Fork

THREE SISTERS
WILDERNESS

WILLAMETTE
NATIONAL
FOREST

Homestead

McKenzie River

Roaring
River

Box Canyon
Station

Middle Fork Willamette River

Kiahanie

WALDO
LAKE
WILDERNESS

To Lookout Point
Reservoir

WILLAMETTE
NATIONAL
FOREST

Waldo
Lake

Westfir

Oakridge

N

0   3   6 Kilometers
0   3   6 Miles

To Prior

Temperatures average 30 degrees in winter and 90 degrees in summer. Spring and fall temperatures peak at about 60 degrees. The area receives 71 inches of rain per year, with most of it falling between November and May and intermittently throughout the travel season. The forest service does not maintain the Aufderheide drive during winter, so snow blocks travel from late fall through early spring.

The **Blue River** region was settled in the 1860s. By 1892 it was a successful mining community with a general store, livery stable, mill, and hotel.

Delta Campground Nature Trail, at the Blue River entrance, provides a good introduction to the byway's plants and trees. The 0.5-mile wheelchair-accessible trail offers a refreshing walk through an old-growth forest of 200- to 500-year-old trees that tower over 38 campsites.

Cougar Reservoir

At the **Cougar Reservoir** powerhouse, 1 mile south of the campground, you may see beavers and other wildlife on a 0.5-mile trail along a side channel that feeds three small riparian ponds. The reservoir covers the site of a Molalla Indian summer camp and was named for cougars, which are seldom seen but still inhabit the area. The 452-foot dam is Oregon's tallest rock-filled structure, and when it's full, backwaters create a lake 6 miles long. During summer months the Army Corps of Engineers keeps it at a high level for scenic and recreational enjoyment, and in fall the surplus water is released to generate power. You'll find it an excellent lake for stocked rainbow trout fishing, waterskiing, and boating. Several boat launches and three US Forest Service campgrounds with 16 sites are situated on or near the shore.

Because of pedestrians, bicyclists, and sharp curves, speeds vary from 25 to 30 miles per hour along west-rim cliffs and shoreline. Rocks from the basalt cliffs were used to fill the dam structures and were sheared off in tiers to prevent rock from falling into the valley below. As you continue along the western rim, watch for osprey nests in tree snags. Northern bald eagles and western red-tailed hawks often soar across the lake.

From a viewpoint at milepost 5, you have a magnificent panorama of the lake, small islands, and the French Pete addition to the Three Sisters Wilderness. You can enter the wilderness by foot or horseback from several trailheads along the South Fork of the McKenzie River.

The only roadside waterfall plunges into a creek near milepost 7, where a pullout with parking provides a good view of the lake and a 0.3-mile trail up a steep embankment to Terwilliger Hot Springs. Six pools at the springs attract nudists and other bathers.

South Fork of the McKenzie River

After passing 2 miles of day-use area, you cross the South Fork of the **McKenzie River** and wind through its canyon lined with cottonwoods and willows. The McKenzie is free-flowing from its headwaters to the reservoir and offers outstanding scenery, fishing, wildlife viewing, and hiking opportunities.

During the next 12 miles, the river appears intermittently as a series of whitewater riffles surrounded by cliffs and forest. Occasionally you'll see seasonal cascades rushing through the lush growth on the east side of the highway. Groves of old-growth Douglas fir, hemlock, and moss-draped maple with a lush undergrowth of wildflowers, ferns, and late summer huckleberries create habitats for wildlife. You'll also pass trees sporting antique telephone insulators that provided communication with the fireguard station. There is also an old maple that was saved by building the highway in a curve around it, as well as timber standing at seemingly impossible angles on sloping ground.

This section is laced with campgrounds and hiking trails. **Slide Creek Campground** features 16 sites and a boat ramp. **French Pete Campground,** at milepost 11, includes 17 tent sites and a trail leading to the French Pete Wilderness. **Rebel Trailhead,** at milepost 13, was named for a Civil War sheepherder. The steep and strenuous 12-mile-loop trail rewards you with lush meadows and mountainsides filled with wildflowers.

At **Frissel Crossing** and **Olallie Campgrounds,** you'll find a total of 27 sites, horse camps, and trails to the Three Sisters Wilderness. **Roaring River Campground** is unique in that it is reserved for up to 50 people.

Roaring River & Box Canyon

At **Roaring River** the highway begins climbing to Box Canyon. The river is the major source of water for the South Fork of the McKenzie and is named for the sound it makes as it rushes over rocks and down the canyon in a series of whitewater cascades. Its constant temperature of 37 degrees makes it an excellent stream for fish reproduction. At a turnout you are within yards of the river and on the edge of its brush-filled canyon. Wild rhododendrons brighten the dark forest in May and June, and you may see deer and elk. They are attracted to the area by the lichens that hang like hair from trees.

The road reaches its highest point at **Box Canyon,** where elk sometimes graze in meadows beside a replica of the first fireguard station. An information station, built in 1933 by the Civilian Conservation Corps and used by the forest service as a fire station, is open during summer. The complex also contains a horse camp with 13 corrals and informational signs on the spotted owl and

Robert Aufderheide. There is water for horses but no drinking water. Several trails meander into the Three Sisters Wilderness and the Chucksney Mountain Roadless Area. The beautiful high vistas of the roadless area are habitats for bear, grouse, deer, elk, and bobcat.

Nearby, the arduous **Shale Ridge Trail** takes you along the river section that drops 2,400 feet in 3 miles and plunges over several waterfalls. As you hike through stands of Pacific yew and western hemlock, you'll pass the source of the McKenzie's North Fork and the forest's largest-in-diameter western red cedar.

Two miles south, **Fisher Creek** empties into the river. To access **Fisher Creek Trail,** take gravel FR 750 about 1.5 miles to the trailhead. The trail is over 6 miles long and crosses the smaller stream twice as it wanders through the Waldo Wilderness Area, then switchbacks up steep ridges to scenic Winchester Lake.

North Fork of the Middle Fork of the Willamette

The highway continues through a blowdown area, known for its spring and fall displays of dogwood and rhododendron. At milepost 38 you cross the **North Fork of the Middle Fork of the Willamette River,** which parallels the highway to Westfir. It has been designated a Wild and Scenic River because of its water quality, geology, scenery, hiking, kayaking, and other recreational opportunities.

Roadside maples form a natural tunnel over the highway en route to **Kiahanie Campground,** 1 mile south of the crossing. It offers 19 tent and trailer sites in a beautiful setting adjacent to a 3-mile-long deep canyon. The canyon has protected 400- to 500-year-old Douglas firs, allowing them to reach heights of 270 feet.

During the next 6 miles, several forest service roads branch off the main highway. They include FR 1934 to Blair Lake, 10 miles east, and FR 1928, which loops back 16 miles to Oakridge. It was built in the 1940s for a logging camp at milepost 45. While nothing remains of the camps, you'll see scars left by logging from the 1920s to the 1960s south to Westfir.

The drive concludes by following the Willamette River through a deep canyon with 1,000-foot-high walls. Rocks in the gorge were covered with lava 300 million years ago and are some of the oldest in the area. In spring this section is a favorite of river rafters and kayakers, anglers, and wildlife observers. It is restricted to fly fishing for chinook salmon and wild trout. The stands of alders and tall trees attract ospreys and beavers.

Office Covered Bridge at Westfir is perfect for beginning or ending the Aufderheide drive.

Westfir

Westfir, at milepost 57, is the drive's southern terminus. **Office Covered Bridge** (World Guide Number 37-20-39) stretches for 180 feet beside the highway and is Oregon's longest covered bridge. The town was founded in 1923 as a result of a timber sale that stipulated a stable community be established to encourage family life. Remains of the mill that operated into the 1980s and homes owned by the lumber company still stand. A forest service office and nursery are also located in Westfir. Several trailer parks are nearby.

From Westfir you can take OR 58 west to Eugene or east over Santiam Pass to US 97.

24

McKenzie, Santiam Pass

General Description: A 130-mile signed scenic loop through high mountain lava fields and past lakes and waterfalls. The loop portion from Sisters is a National Forest Service Scenic Byway.

Special Attractions: Outstanding views of 10 spectacular mountain peaks; McKenzie Lava Beds and Dee Wright Observatory; 2 national forests; headwaters of the Metolius River; llama, elk, and reindeer farms; several waterfalls; Pacific Crest Trail.

Location: West-central Oregon between Redmond and the western Cascade Mountains.

Drive Route Numbers: OR 126, OR 242, and OR 126 and US 20 and US 20/126.

Travel Season: All highways except OR 242 are open all year. OR 242 closes from November to late June or early July, depending on snowfall and snowmelt.

Camping: 17 forest service campgrounds with tables, fire rings, and toilets. Some have drinking water.

Services: All services in Redmond and Sisters. Limited services at McKenzie Bridge and Camp Sherman.

Nearby Attractions: Three Sisters Wilderness, Cove Palisades State Park, Robert Aufderheide Memorial Drive, Smith Rocks State Park, Crooked River National Grasslands.

For More Information: Central Oregon Visitors Association, (800) 800-8334, www.visitcentraloregon.com; Eugene, Cascades & Oregon Coast–Travel Lane County Oregon, (541) 484-5307, (800) 547-5445 (USA), www.travellanecounty.org; Metolius Recreation Association, (541) 595-6117, www.metoliusriver.org; Redmond Chamber of Commerce, (541) 923-5191, www.visitredmondoregon.com; Deschutes & Ochoco National Forests, (541) 383-5300, www.fs.usda.gov/centraloregon; Sisters Ranger District, (541) 549-7700; Sisters Area Chamber of Commerce, (541) 549-0251, (866) 549-0252, www.sisterscountry.com; Willamette National Forest, Supervisor's Office, (541) 225-6300, www.fs.usda.gov/willamette.

The Route

Several communities and organizations incorporate the **McKenzie–Santiam Loop** in their local drives. From Eugene it can be joined by taking OR 126 east 55 miles along the scenic McKenzie River to OR 242. It is also often included as an extension of the OR 22 North Santiam Canyon Scenic Drive. From Bend you can join by taking US 20 west to Sisters. The most direct access is OR 126 west from Redmond.

The central loop takes you to some spectacular high country and a variety of scenery, from magnificent snowcapped peaks to lava beds and graceful waterfalls. Since OR 242 is 16 feet wide, steep, and winding, it is not recommended for trailers, and vehicles over 50 feet long are prohibited.

McKenzie, Santiam Pass

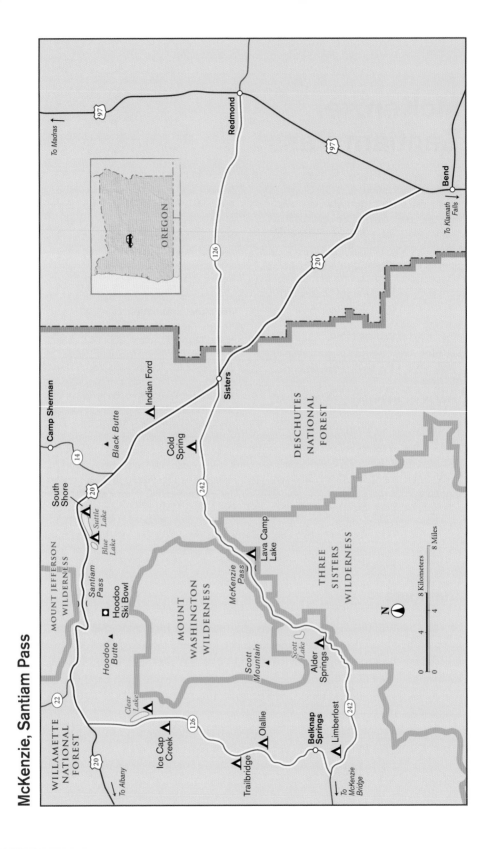

Elevations range from about 2,300 to 5,325 feet. Summer temperatures average between 70 and 90 at Redmond and 65 to 80 in the mountains. Winter days are usually in the 30s and 40s, with nights falling to the low 20s in the mountains. Spring and fall range from the 30s to the 50s.

Redmond's unique natural feature is **Dry Canyon.** It extends virtually the length of the town. A paved 4-mile path that bisects the gorge and a dirt trail along the western edge are popular with hikers, bikers, and walkers. The canyon's ends are largely undeveloped with groves of trees, grasses, and high sheer rim-rocks on the north and gently sloping walls on the south. A skate park, ball fields, tennis courts, and playgrounds fill the center.

Petersen's Rock Garden, south of town, displays an intricate network of miniature bridges, towers, and castles built of various rocks.

Sisters

The **Three Sisters** provide a magnificent backdrop as you travel west on OR 126. During the 19 miles to Sisters, you pass a reindeer ranch and may see llamas grazing near the roadside. **Cline Falls State Park,** on the Deschutes River bank, offers a picnic area shaded by juniper and willow trees. As you approach Sisters your panoramic view encompasses 9 major mountain peaks.

Sisters, named after the three mountain peaks, entices travelers to linger in its western false-front buildings and homey restaurants, and to enjoy a variety of outdoor recreation, arts, events, and festivals. The annual **Sisters Outdoor Quilt Show** is a month-long July event that attracts quilt makers and visitors from around the nation to see and display some 1,200 quilts strung around town. Mule deer sometimes wander into town and coyotes, bobcats, badgers, and other wildlife inhabit surrounding flatlands and mountains. Along the drive you may see blue grouse, pygmy and spotted owls, sandpipers, sapsuckers, red-tailed hawks, and other birds. The **Deschutes Ranger Station,** at the junction of OR 126 and OR 242 and US 20, is a must-stop for trail maps and backcountry, snow park, and wilderness permits.

In the first 5 miles, OR 242 passes an elk breeding ranch, enters the **Deschutes National Forest,** climbs through ponderosa pine, and reaches the drive's high of 5,325 feet at the **McKenzie Pass summit.** En route you'll pass **Cold Springs Campground,** with 23 sites, and the 7.6-mile round-trip **Black Crater summit trail.** It's a strenuous trek with steep climbs but rewards you with a spectacular 360-degree panorama of the Three Sisters Wilderness, McKenzie Pass lava flows, and on clear days far horizon views of the Cascade Range. Bring plenty of water and dress warmly, as it's often cold and windy at the summit even during summer. Portions of the roadway follow an 1860s wagon route, and the next 17 miles have been designated a historic highway.

McKenzie Pass

At **McKenzie Pass** you enter the edge of a 65-square-mile lava flow. **Dee Wright Observatory,** on the summit, is built of lava and named after a Civilian Conservation Corps foreman who helped build it. Viewing ports, cut into the lava walls, isolate Mount Hood, Mount Jefferson, Three Fingered Jack, Mount Washington, North Sister, and Middle Sister.

The lava flows originated about 2,600 years ago and are some of the nation's most recent and impressive examples of volcanic activity. Since it is extremely dangerous to walk on the piles of sharp, chunky rock, take the signed 0.5-mile **Lava River Trail Loop** through lava gutters, pressure ridges, levies, and crevasses.

After crossing the Pacific Crest Trail, a mile west of the observatory, you wind through a mixed forest of Douglas, white, and subalpine fir; scrub pine; and spruce. The descent starts with views of Belknap Crater, North and Middle Sister, Craig Lake, and several large roadside ponds. At **Scott Lake,** accessible from a north-side road, you can see the Three Sisters reflected in the mirror-smooth waters. **Obsidian Trailhead,** nearby, is one of the most popular routes into the 283,402-acre **Three Sisters Wilderness.** You can explore it on 433 miles of trail that lead across its many peaks and cones.

At **Deadhorse Grade,** about 9 miles west of the summit, the road drops from 4,749 to 3,566 feet in 0.2 mile. The grade received its name when a horse died of exhaustion trying to climb it.

Alder Springs Campground is near the base of the grade and is a Willamette National Forest Service site with 6 tent spots. Bring your own firewood. Nearby a trail leads to Linton Lake. Proxy Falls, a mile west and poorly marked, is accessible by a 1.25-mile loop trail. It takes you from the parking lot across several lava flows to 2 waterfalls that drops in two stages of 200 feet each.

The next 8 miles are a mixture of peaceful setting and sharp curves. A forested bowl frames the roadway as it meanders through a quiet glade of thick ferns and towering trees that shroud everything in perpetual shade.

OR 126 & Clear Lake

Crossing **White Branch Creek,** fed by Oregon's largest glacier, you pass **Limberlost Campground,** with 10 tent/trailer and 2 tent-only sites. Two miles west, OR

Several viewing ports cut into the rock walls of the Dee Wright Observatory at McKenzie Pass isolate individual mountain peaks, including Mount Hood, Mount Jefferson, and Three Fingered Jack.

242 reaches its junction with OR 126. Gas, food, and groceries are available at **McKenzie Bridge,** 6 miles west on OR 126.

About 2 miles north on OR 126, side roads lead to **Lost Creek** and **Belknap Hot Springs Resort,** where you can overnight in a lodge, cabins, or an RV campground, and bask in 2 mineral hot spring pools surrounded by acres of gardens. Crossing the McKenzie River, you continue north through a fir and alder corridor with a mountain of Douglas fir in front of you. At **Olallie Campground,** 2 miles north of the hot springs, you can camp at 17 sites on 2 levels by the banks of the river and Olallie Creek. A reservoir, a few miles north, offers boating and fishing from a jetty, trails around the small lake, and a connection to the McKenzie River National Recreation Trail, which follows the river upstream.

Five miles north, **Ice Cap Creek Campground** shares an access road with **Koosah Falls,** which is linked to **Sahalie Falls** by a 0.3-mile riverside hiking trail. The campground has 14 tent/trailer and 8 tent sites. Rocks at the precipice separate Koosah Falls into several graceful curtains. Sahalie, with a separate access, parking lot, and restrooms, thunders over a lava cliff. You can overnight in the quiet forest 1 mile north in 35 tent/trailer sites at **Cold Water Cove Campground.**

Clear Lake, east of the highway, is known for the exceptional clarity of its water. Fed by numerous springs, the lake is the headwaters of the McKenzie River and was created about 3,000 years ago when the stream was dammed by a lava flow. You can see a submerged forest at the bottom of the 195-foot-deep lake, which produces fair to good catches of brook trout, cutthroat, and stocked rainbows. A shoreline resort operates a store, restaurant, campground, and cabins.

Two miles north, another McKenzie River National Recreation trailhead leads to superlative mountain and river scenery and the last vestiges of the 1860s Santiam Wagon Road. **Fish Lake,** accessible by a dirt road near the trailhead, usually dries up by midsummer. A campground with 8 tent/trailer sites is situated near the basin.

US 20 & Hoodoo Ski Bowl

Two miles north, OR 126 joins US 20, and they continue east as a joint highway to Sisters. **Three Fingered Jack,** 7,841 feet elevation, fills the horizon in front of you as the road climbs toward Santiam Pass. The North Santiam Canyon Scenic Drive intersects your route as you enter the 15-mile-long **Metolius River Recreation Area** near Hoodoo Ski Bowl.

From the headwaters of the Metolius River, you see the essence of Oregon: verdant green forests, pristine streams, and snowcapped mountain peaks.

Hoodoo's 1,035-foot vertical rise is served by 5 lifts, including 3 quads. Facilities include 2 lodges, rental and repair shops, and a large day-care facility. Sixty percent of the ski runs are beginner or intermediate. It has 30 runs, approximately 12 miles of groomed trails, and the Autobahn tubing park. A campground with hookups can be reserved by the season, which usually runs from November through March.

Several side roads lead to snow-play and cross-country ski areas. **Big Lake,** 3 miles south on Hoodoo's access road, is shallow but yields good fishing for brook and cutthroat trout in spring and fall. In summer boaters, water-skiers, and sailboarders hold sway, and in winter the road becomes a cross-country ski and snowmobile trail. You can camp on the lakeside in the shadow of tall mountain peaks in 2 forest service campgrounds with 35 tent/trailer sites.

Shortly after Hoodoo you cross the Pacific Crest Trail and the Santiam Pass summit at 4,817 feet. As you continue east you will see some of the aftermath of the devastating forest fires that raged through this area in the summer of 2003. The burned forest attracts a variety of woodpeckers. A pullout offers a superb view of 7,794-foot Mount Washington and its 52,516-acre wilderness.

Suttle Lake Resort and Marina, 3 miles east, operates spring through autumn with an 11-room lodge, cabins, kayak rentals, gas, and a store. Deer, black bears, and bald eagles, not to mention boaters, water-skiers, sailboarders, and anglers, are attracted to its glacier-carved bowl and large brown and rainbow trout, kokanee, and whitefish.

At **Blue Lake,** 2 miles north, you'll find several forest service campgrounds, each with a few sites. Blue Lake offers a full-service resort with horse stables and pack service, horse and hiking trails, a restaurant and store, 12 cabins, and 40 campsites. Eleven feature water, electricity, sewerage, and television sets. In winter the trails become cross-country and snowmobile routes, and the lake turns into an ice-skating rink.

The picture-postcard lake sits in a small volcanic crater surrounded by a mixed forest of pines and firs. Hungry brook and brown trout, kokanee, whitefish, and monthly stockings of rainbow trout keep anglers returning. Because of its popularity, reservations are recommended, and there is a service fee for day-use areas.

Camp Sherman & Black Butte

One mile east, a trail leaves the main highway for the 111,177-acre **Mount Jefferson Wilderness.** A worthwhile side trip begins near the trailhead and includes the **Camp Sherman Resort area,** numerous forest service campgrounds, and a state fish hatchery with viewing ponds where you can see rainbow, brook, and cutthroat trout, Atlantic salmon, and other fish. The 10-mile round-trip will also take you to the headwaters of the **Metolius River,** where it emerges in full stream from underground springs at the base of Black Butte. An exceptionally scenic viewpoint overlooks the headwaters, lush meadows, and 10,497-foot Mount Jefferson. For the first 9 miles, the Metolius is a fly-fishing-only, catch-and-release stream for native rainbow, Dolly Varden, brown, and brook trout. It is heavily fished in summer with only fair results. The **Metolius River Fly Fishing and Bamboo Rod Fair,** at Camp Sherman, is a major event that attracts fly fishers, rod manufacturers, and instructors who probe the mystique of fly fishing and teach its basics to beginners.

With 6,436-foot **Black Butte** looming beside you, the main highway passes **Indian Ford Campground,** which has 25 tent/trailer sites. Hiking and biking trails fan out from the campground. A nearby trail gains 900 feet in elevation on its 3.8 miles to Black Butte's summit, where you're treated to sweeping views of the area's forests and flatlands, and Sisters township. Bring plenty of water if you hike it during summer.

The remaining 10 miles to Sisters are on a gentle downgrade through a ponderosa pine forest with a bitterbrush undergrowth. From Sisters you conclude the drive by retracing OR 126 back to Redmond.

25

Cascade Lakes Highway

General Description: An 87-mile signed highway through the Central Cascade Mountains, skirting 9 alpine lakes.

Special Attractions: Mount Bachelor Ski Area, 9 alpine lakes, 2 reservoirs, resorts, Three Sisters Wilderness, Deschutes River, camping, hiking, fishing, boating.

Location: Central Oregon between Bend and La Pine.

Drive Route Numbers: OR 46 and OR 42.

Travel Season: Open all year from Bend to Mount Bachelor. The remaining section closes because of snow but is usually open from early June to November.

Camping: 25 forest service campgrounds with tables, fire rings, and toilets; some have drinking water. Additional forest service and private campgrounds are situated near the route.

Services: All services in Bend, Sun River, and La Pine. Limited services along the route.

Nearby Attractions: Crooked River Gorge, Smith Rocks State Park, High Desert Museum, Newberry Crater National Monument, Three Sisters Wilderness, Cove Palisades State Park.

For More Information: Visit Bend, (866) 292-0141, www.visitbend.com; Central Oregon Visitors Association, (800) 800-8334, www.visitcentraloregon.com; Deschutes National Forest, (541) 383-5300, www.fs.usda.gov/centraloregon.com. La Pine Chamber of Commerce, (541) 536-9771, www.lapine.org; Sunriver Area Chamber of Commerce, (541) 593-8149, www.sunriver chamber.com.

The Route

From central Oregon's high desert, the drive climbs to about 6,000 feet at **Mount Bachelor.** As it moves south and east, the drive follows portions of Indian trails and wagon roads and crosses forested slopes explored by Nathaniel Wyeth, John C. Fremont, and Kit Carson. Although the route extends through a corridor of trees, lakes are easily accessible and usually within a mile of the main road. They are stocked frequently with rainbow trout and contain other species. Most of the route is straight and with gradual slopes, and traffic is light to moderate during the week. From US 97 the drive can be joined either in Bend, Sunriver, or La Pine.

While improvements have shortened the route, some signs and brochures still call it the **Century Drive,** in reference to its original 100-mile length. It is also called the **Cascade Lakes Tour.** Portions have been designated a National Forest Service Scenic Byway.

Summer temperatures average 60 to 80 degrees, and winter days generally fall between 20 and 40 degrees, with cold nights. Significant snowfall occurs in higher elevations. Spring days range from about 57 degrees to the high 60s, while fall

Cascade Lakes Highway

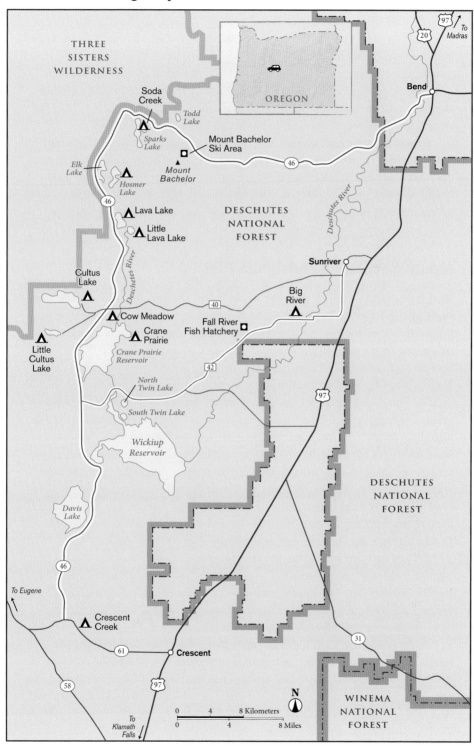

THREE SISTERS WILDERNESS

Soda Creek

Todd Lake

Sparks Lake

Mount Bachelor Ski Area

Elk Lake

Mount Bachelor

DESCHUTES NATIONAL FOREST

Hosmer Lake

Lava Lake

Little Lava Lake

Cultus Lake

Sunriver

Big River

Cow Meadow

Crane Prairie

Fall River Fish Hatchery

Little Cultus Lake

Crane Prairie Reservoir

North Twin Lake

South Twin Lake

Wickiup Reservoir

Davis Lake

To Eugene

Crescent Creek

Crescent

DESCHUTES NATIONAL FOREST

WINEMA NATIONAL FOREST

Bend

OREGON

To Madras

To Klamath Falls

Deschutes River

Deschetes River

N

0 4 8 Kilometers
0 4 8 Miles

temperatures are usually in the high 70s. The drive is closed beyond Mount Bachelor from November to Memorial Day.

Bend is the economic and recreational hub of central Oregon. In Bend the drive begins at US 97 and Franklin Avenue. **Drake Park,** on the route, stretches along 0.5 mile of the Deschutes River's eastern bank, offering in-town fishing for crappie and bass and 11 acres of lawns shaded by junipers and oaks.

As you drive west, you'll see the Cascade peaks on the horizon. After about 10 miles the scatterings of bitterbrush, sage, and ponderosa pine thicken as you enter the National Forest Service Scenic Byway. During the next few miles, the road climbs to 5,600 feet and passes the Deschutes River Recreation Area, several snow parks, and the Swampy Lakes region. Several hiking, bicycle, and snowmobile trails, 2 to 10 miles long, branch from the highway and into the mountains.

Mount Bachelor & Dutchman Flat

Mount Bachelor fills the horizon as it rises out of a valley covered with jack and sugar pine, ponderosa, Douglas fir, and western and Engelmann spruce. The mountain is a geologic infant and probably formed about 14,000 years ago when the earth's crust cracked and cooling lava created its symmetrical cone. Mount Bachelor is the Cascades' largest ski area, covering 3,700 acres spread over 360 degrees from the 9,065-foot summit in a vertical drop of 3,365 feet. It averages 370 inches of snow and sometimes receives over 500 inches per year. The ski season generally begins around Thanksgiving and ends in late May. A network of 11 lifts, including 7 with high-speed quads, serves 71 runs, and there are also approximately 35 miles of groomed cross-country tracks. Its alpine terrain is rated 15 percent novice, 25 percent intermediate, 35 percent advanced, and 25 percent expert. It also has 10 acres of groomed inner-tube runs and snowboard runs. At the resort you can relax in 6 day lodges and rent mountain bikes. Facilities include espresso bars, restaurants, retail shops, and 2 day-care centers. Summer services include a Deschutes National Forest Ranger Station with 7 interpretive guides.

For the best overview of the Cascades, take the chairlift to the 7,000-foot timberline or the 9,065-foot summit. The view from the top encompasses three states and the Three Sisters Wilderness, alpine lakes, cinder cones, volcanic domes, lava and pumice fields, chasms, and calderas. **Tumalo Mountain Trail,** which begins near the ski area, extends around the peak's rim.

In the next 3 miles, the highway enters **Dutchman Flat,** a pumice field of sparse vegetation with an outstanding view of **Broken Top Mountain,** and passes Todd Lake and Sparks Lake. Brook and stocked rainbow trout thrive in **Todd Lake,** which has a walk-in campground. A 0.4-mile walk from the parking area puts you on a trail encircling the beautiful lake, framed by a thick fir and spruce forest and

Broken Top's summit. Tiny wildflowers decorating the landscape include a proliferation of alpine star, columbine, elephanthead, and poison larkspur.

Sparks Lake, Green Lakes Trail Head & Springs

Sparks Lake is one of Oregon's most photographed scenic gems. The **Atkeson Memorial Trail,** near the boat ramp, honors Ray Atkeson, who as Oregon's premier scenic photographer often photographed it and helped make it famous. The easy loop trail includes a 0.25-mile paved section for wheelchairs. The lake has a 10-mile-per-hour speed limit and fly fishing limited to stocked rainbow trout. It covers about 250 acres, with a maximum depth of 8 feet. With no surface outlets, it is gradually turning into a marsh as it fills with sediment. Three trails of 2 to 4 miles each invite hiking through the pleasant forest and chunky lava to **Moser Lake** at the south end. You can also explore the terrain on mountain bike and horse trails.

Green Lakes Trailhead, near Sparks Lake Road, offers one of several entries into the 200,000-acre Three Sisters Wilderness. Numerous trails wind through the wilderness to 111 lakes, volcanic peaks, and Oregon's largest glacier.

Several springs surface at **Devil's Hill and Garden,** west of the trailhead, and feed a small meadow of thick marsh grass, lupine, and Indian paintbrush. Astronauts trained on the 2,000-year-old lava, and a rock from Devil's Hill was deposited on the moon. Archaeological finds indicate that Indians inhabited this region some 8,000 years ago, and several rocks still retain their pictographs.

As the route turns south, roadside evergreens shrink to the size of potted plants. **Devil's Lake,** crystal clear and emerald green, offers canoeing, fishing, horse and hiking trails, and camping in 6 sites at an elevation of 5,446 feet.

Elk, Hosmer & Lava Lakes

Elk Lake Recreation Area stretches for 4 miles along the roadway. The 390-acre lake is a scenic highlight, framed by Mount Bachelor and South Sister and ringed by lodgepole pine, fir, and hemlock. A resort with gas, a dining room, and a boat dock operates all year serving sailboarders, sailboaters, and skiers who follow cross-country trails to its shores in winter. Brook, brown, and rainbow trout make it attractive to anglers. You have a choice of staying in the resort's 10 cabins with kitchens or 100 sites in several shoreline campgrounds. The recreation area features horse camps and hiking trails.

Hosmer Lake, a mile south, is one of the few western lakes stocked with Atlantic salmon. Reserved for sportfishing, it is limited to 10-mile-per-hour speeds and fly fishing only with barbless hooks on a catch-and-release basis. In addition to campgrounds and hiking trails, a picnic area with 6 tables and fire grills has one of the route's few sandy beaches. While eating lunch, you have a superb view of Mount Bachelor and a forest that turns to varying shades of blue and green as it stretches from the water's edge to the distant mountains. The easy 3.5-mile **Elk Lake Trail** touches the shoreline of both lakes.

As the highway descends, trees gradually increase in height from 8 to 40 and 50 feet. **Lava Lake** and its resort are surrounded by lodgepole and Douglas fir. In addition to brook and rainbow trout fishing, you can rent boats and stay in 243 full-hookup campsites. Food, gas, and showers are available. **Little Lava Lake,** nearby, is the headwaters of the **Deschutes River,** which you will see briefly on the highway's east side as it flows south through lush meadows. **Little Lava Lake Campground** has a total of 16 sites.

During the next 11 miles—as you travel through an avenue of ponderosa pine, Douglas fir, white fir, white pine, lodgepole spruce, and mountain hemlock—watch for deer, elk, martens, marmots, porcupines, and ground squirrels. This section offers access to several trails and campgrounds, Cultus Corral Horse camp, and the Cow Meadow area with fishing and tent camping.

Cultus Lake Resort is 2 miles west of the highway and offers 23 cabins—some at lakeside—which you can use as a base for kayaking, Jet Skiing, swimming and fishing. Food, gas, and a campground with 51 tent/RV sites are also available. **Cultus Mountain** separates the resort from remote **Little Cultus Lake,** which has a 30-site campground and **Cultus Horse Camp**'s 11 tent/RV sites with no hookups.

Crane Prairie Reservoir

Osprey Point, on the west bank of 3,850-acre **Crane Prairie Reservoir,** is the drive's prime spot for wildlife viewing. A 440-yard trail takes you along a ponderosa-covered shoreline to a viewing area where migratory ospreys and Canada geese nest in tree snags and on artificial nesting poles. Over half of Oregon's ospreys nest here and can usually be seen between April and October.

Watching ospreys catch their dinner is a highlight. They soar into the sky, pause in midair, then power-dive into the water, catch their prey, and glide to a tree limb. Eagles sometimes steal their catches in midair. These magnificent birds share the habitat with great blue herons, deer, otters, and sandhill cranes. By taking the trail 170 yards north, you'll pass a historic tree and grave and end at the Quinn River's headwaters, which gush from a giant spring and over moss-covered rocks. Three western shore campgrounds provide 93 sites.

From the reservoir the Forest Service Scenic Byway continues south on OR 46 for 21 miles to a junction with OR 58. En route it passes **Davis Lake,** an old lava flow, and 3 campgrounds with over 60 sites and skirts the eastern foothills of 7,037-foot **Odell Butte.**

The Cascade Lakes Highway is a favorite of nature lovers, boaters, hikers, and everyone else who loves magnificent mountain and lake scenery.

The Cascade Lakes tour turns east onto OR 42. About 4 miles east of the junction, a short side road leads to **Crane Prairie Resort** on the reservoir's east bank. The resort area is an excellent place to see eagles, ospreys, deer, elk, geese, and a variety of ducks. **Crane Prairie Campground** has 145 tent/RV sites spread out in a pine forest, by lava flows, and near water. The resort offers a full-hookup RV park, marina, store, and restaurant.

Twin Lakes & Wickiup Reservoir

A mile east on OR 42, a side road takes you south to **Twin Lakes** and **Wickiup Reservoir. Twin Lakes Resort** opens with the fishing season and closes in October. It services lakes and reservoir users with a store, restaurant, several cabins, and 22 full-hookup campsites containing water, sewerage, electricity, and picnic tables. Four forest service campgrounds within a mile provide an additional 400 sites. The lakes are stocked several times a year with rainbow trout. Though powerboats are not allowed, you can swim, paddleboat, and kayak at Twin Lakes.

At **Wickiup** you can powerboat and water-ski and enjoy great fishing for heavily populated kokanee and brook and brown trout.

A few miles east, OR 42 meets OR 43, which leads 13 miles south to **La Pine.** If you begin or end the drive at La Pine, on OR 43, you'll pass **Pringle Falls** about

4 miles southeast of the junction. You can camp on both sides of the river and use it as a base for good fishing, canoeing, drifting, watching ospreys and deer, and exploring **Pringle Falls Experimental Forest.**

Northwest of La Pine, OR 43 begins and ends by crossing the **Little Deschutes River.** It meanders 120 miles north to empty into the main Deschutes near Sunriver. The Little Deschutes is a popular inner-tubing and drifting stream.

Fall River Fish Hatchery

OR 42 continues northeast through 7 miles of ponderosa pine corridor to the **Deschutes National Forest Guard Station.** Fall River's headwaters emerge from springs behind the station. **Fall River,** which is only 12 miles long, is known as an excellent fly-fishing stream. The 4 miles of the river between the station and **Fall River Fish Hatchery** are stocked with rainbow trout at least every other week during summer. This is also a scenic hiking and camping area with opportunities to see ospreys, eagles, and other wildlife.

Fall River Fish Hatchery, near the Deschutes National Forest boundary, offers a refreshing respite in a setting of ponderosa pines and beautiful lawns on the banks of the rippling stream. The hatchery releases 140,000 rainbow and 400,000 brook trout annually. In addition to feeding fish, you can picnic and fly fish the river from the hatchery grounds. Cross-country skiers use the area for staging winter trips.

To Sunriver

From the hatchery the road drops through waves of lodgepole pines. **Big River Campground,** with 13 sites and set in a forest overlooking the river, is a favorite departure point for rafting parties.

The drive concludes with farms, open fields, and a crossing of the Little Deschutes River. As you near Sunriver, Mount Bachelor and other peaks are a continuous presence on the western horizon.

Sunriver is a planned residential and resort community that lies along the eastern bank of the Deschutes River. Three of its golf courses have been awarded gold metal status by *Golf Magazine.* Canoeing, whitewater rafting, hiking, and biking on 30 miles of paved trails have also made it a popular destination. **Sunriver Nature Center and Observatory,** a private nonprofit educational and scientific organization, offers a last bit of sightseeing with hands-on activities for children, a botanical garden, an observatory, and a 0.4-mile nature trail through various habitats.

From Sunriver your options for other scenic drives include the Bend–Newberry Crater itinerary and the Oregon Outback Scenic Byway.

26

Sherman County Loop

General Description: A 110-mile loop through rolling hills of the Oregon wheat country, the Deschutes River Canyon, and into Washington state. Add about 20 miles for the Maupin Loop.

Special Attractions: Oregon Trail routes, waterfalls, Wild and Scenic Deschutes River, Columbia River Gorge, Stonehenge replica, Maryhill Museum of Art, fishing.

Location: North-central Oregon between The Dalles, Maupin, and Biggs.

Drive Route Numbers: US 197, OR 216, US 97.

Travel Season: All year.

Camping: 2 city park campgrounds; 1 state park campground with tables, fire rings, toilets, and boat ramp. 1 state park campground with primitive sites, about 4 miles off the loop; 2 Bureau of Land Management campgrounds with tables, fire rings, and toilets about 5 and 10 miles off the loop.

Services: All services at The Dalles, and Biggs. Limited services at Dufur, Maupin, Grass Valley, and Moro.

Nearby Attractions: Columbia River Gorge Historic Highway, Mount Hood, Warm Springs Indian Reservation, Hood River Sailpark, Goldendale Observatory.

For More Information: The Dalles Area Chamber of Commerce, (541) 296-2231, (800) 255-3385 (USA), www.thedalles chamber.com; Central Oregon Visitors Association, (800) 800-8334, www.visit centraloregon.com; Maupin Area Chamber of Commerce, (541) 993-1708, www .maupinoregon.com; Mount Hood National Forest, (503) 668-1700, www.fs.usda .gov/mthood; Barlow Ranger District, (541) 467-2291.

The Route

The Oregon Trail crosses the drive at several points as it begins in the **Columbia River Gorge National Scenic Area** at 175 feet elevation and climbs to about 3,000 feet. Distant Cascade peaks and forested foothills provide a magnificent contrast to the roadside scenery that is a succession of grasslands and wheat and barley fields. Depending on crop rotation and season, they form a colorful patchwork of bright greens, yellows, magentas, and sandy to chocolate browns. At Tygh Valley travelers have an option of taking a short route on OR 216 or adding 20 miles by motoring south to Maupin and returning by the Deschutes River Canyon.

Summer in the Columbia River Gorge usually brings highs averaging in the mid-80s while the southern portion reaches into the 90s. Winter days average 22 degrees in the southern section and have dropped to record lows of minus 39 degrees. In the gorge winter days in the 30s and 40s are common. Spring days range from 57 to 65 degrees, and fall brings temperatures between 63 and 74 degrees.

Sherman County Loop

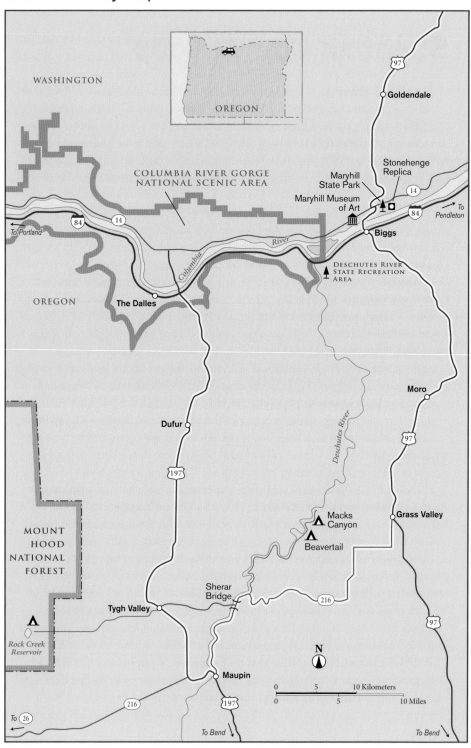

The drive starts at **US 197** near The Dalles Dam and climbs a dry grass hill overlooking a ravine of oak and poplar trees. The river's rock formations dictated a unique L-shape dam that connects separate spillways and powerhouse sections. You can learn about the area's cultural and natural environment and the Army Corps of Engineers at the visitor center.

At mile marker 2 the road passes **Bonneville Dam's Celilo Converter Station.** Brochures for a self-guided tour are available at the administration building. The station exhibits working examples of all stages of direct-current technology. The converter station is the terminus for converting direct content (dc) current and transmitting it through a high-voltage line 846 miles south to a station near Los Angeles.

Leaving the Columbia River Gorge National Scenic Area, you climb through rolling hills of wheat and grass, alternating with freshly plowed and unplowed ground. The land is mostly loess—wind-blown glacier silt that mixed with residual soil from underlying basalt and small layers of volcanic ash. It receives less than 12 inches of rain per year. To maximize production, crops are rotated and fields are planted every other year. In the off years they lie fallow. Sherman County, which you will see later, uses this method to produce 304,138 acres of wheat and barley, leaving 200,000 acres for beef pasture.

Dufur

As the road tops hills and dips into ravines, Mount Hood stands in bold relief on the western horizon. The landscape and vegetation changes to vibrant greens, golden wheat fields, and varying shades of earth. Except for poplars planted as windbreaks, trees are virtually nonexistent.

Dufur, 13 miles south, saw its first settler in 1863. Later it became part of the Barlow Road that ran down what is now its main street. The **Dufur Historical Society Living History Museum,** also known as the **log cabin museum, was** built as a family home in 1900 and used into the 1970s. It retains its original floor plan and logs. It contains Oregon Trail exhibits and collections of war memorabilia, padlocks, early-20th-century clothing, and household furnishings. The **Balch Hotel,** next door, dates to the early 1900s and has been renovated to provide a truly unique lodging experience. Each of the 19 rooms, plus a suite, has an individual style with antique furnishings and period decor. Rooms have wireless Internet connections but no telephones or TV.

Dufur City Park has 8 tent/trailer sites with showers, a picnic area, and swimming area. A commercial RV park offers 17 spaces with full hookups and a laundry. If you are planning to fish the area's streams and camp, stop at the Barlow Ranger Station of the Mount Hood National Forest in Dufur. Some streams are protected to increase steelhead runs.

Tygh Ridge & Valley

Eight miles south of Dufur, the route reaches its high point of 2,665 feet elevation at **Tygh Ridge,** then twists down through a rugged canyon. Unlike today's relaxing scenic drive, the rock walls and waves of ridges posed severe challenges for early wagon and automobile roads.

About 8 miles south of the summit, US 197 crosses a junction, seemingly in the middle of nowhere. The crossing is near the point where Oregon Trail wagons began the rugged ascent of Mount Hood's eastern slopes over the Barlow Road. The road opened in 1845–1846 and was the first route over the Cascade slopes, later becoming the final segment of the Oregon Trail.

OR 48 heads west through the settlement of **Tygh Valley,** known for its annual Native American rodeo, and parallels the Barlow Trail for about 14 miles to **Forest Creek Campground.** The pavement ends at the campground, which offers 8 tent/trailer sites. The remaining portions of the trail are on the National Register of Historic Places. It is a narrow, rough dirt road, and some parts are impassable. If you intend to explore it, check with the Barlow Ranger Station for road conditions and a self-guiding brochure. You'll also need a high-clearance vehicle suited to rugged conditions.

Tygh Valley or Maupin

From the junction you can either continue south on US 197 to Maupin or take OR 216 east. **Maupin** has a hotel that dates to the early 1900s and is a center for whitewater rafting, kayaking, and other outdoor recreation. A wheelchair-accessible fishing ramp is situated near the Deschutes River Road, which you will follow north to OR 216 near Sherar Bridge while enjoying the Deschutes River Canyon's rock formations and rapids. This portion of the Lower Deschutes is a National Wild and Scenic River and an Oregon State Scenic Waterway. En route you may see deer, bald eagles, Canada geese, antelope, wild turkey, and pheasants.

If you elect to take the shorter route and travel east on OR 216, after about 5 miles you'll come to **White River Falls State Park.** It offers a refreshing spot to enjoy river and canyon scenery from a picnic ground shaded by poplars and oaks. From the overlook you have a close-up view of **White River Falls,** which drops in two stages and several curtains of water. A short but rugged trail leads to the base of the falls. To the east, deep in the red rocks of the canyon, an abandoned power station sits on a seemingly impenetrable ledge. You can also fish the White River for trout and steelhead.

An abandoned power plant sits on a ledge in a deep canyon by Tygh Valley State Park.

Deschutes River Canyon

Two miles east, the road descends into the lava outcroppings, benches, and ridges of the **Deschutes River Canyon.** The river rushes and boils through **Sherar Bridge.** This section has been a traditional Native American fishery and was a campground for Oregon Trail wagon trains. They followed roughly the same route as the highway from Grass Valley, winding down steep basalt ridges and traveling west over the Barlow Road. A narrow wooden bridge that spanned the Deschutes became the gateway to central Oregon, despite the heavy tolls charged by its owner, Joseph Sherar.

Today Native Americans still stand on wooden platforms and dip for salmon or cast for trout and steelhead from the rocky shore. Pictographs, drawn centuries ago, are still visible on the west bank. Two Bureau of Land Management campgrounds, about 5 and 10 miles northeast, offer 38 sites in the rugged canyon.

The highway continues through several miles of rugged cliffs, then climbs the plateau to merge 22 miles east with US 97 at Grass Valley. If you're wondering about the names of the mountain peaks that frame the western horizon, a 10 peaks identifier at a viewpoint near the junction points out Mount Adams, Mount Washington, Mount Jefferson, the Three Sisters, Broken Top, Three Fingered Jack, and Mount Bachelor.

Grass Valley & Moro

Grass Valley, population 170, sits at an altitude of 2,350 feet. Its grain elevators, gas station, motel, restaurant, and RV park with full hookups are surrounded by wheat and barley fields and cattle ranches that stretch north to the Columbia River. Grass Valley's **Oregon Raceway Park** (93811 Blagg Ln., Grass Valley; 541-531-5695) is 2.3 miles long with 14 corners and follows the land's natural contours. It is the Pacific Northwest's only course offering both clockwise and counterclockwise driving. A small **Horses to Horsepower** museum exhibits farm machinery. Telephone (541) 333-2222 for hours and directions. According to legend, when the first settlers arrived, they found native grasses taller than a man's head, even when he was sitting atop a horse. Situated in Sherman County, Grass Valley became a division point on the pioneer stage line between The Dalles and Canyon City.

Moro, 9 miles north, also has an economy tied to agriculture. With 380 people, it may be among America's smallest county seats. The picturesque pioneer courthouse is a regional landmark. An agricultural experiment station has stood at the eastern edge of town on an original homestead since 1909, developing grains and testing them for diseases, winter hardiness, and yield. The **Sherman County Museum,** established in 1893, contains period rooms and 15,000 artifacts including a large collection of local cattle brands.

Three miles north on US 97, **De Moss Memorial Park** is on the National Register of Historic Places. The park was once a well-known local health resort, with streets named for musicians and avenues honoring poets. It was founded by a family of itinerant musicians who traveled from town to town entertaining cowboys and settlers. By 1893 they were famous and became the official songwriters for the Chicago World's Fair. The park has a few picnic tables and offers informal camping.

Ten miles north of Moro, side roads branch from US 97 east to Wasco and northwest to rugged Fulton Canyon. Nearby an Oregon Trail spur crossed a pioneer road linking the Columbia to the interior.

In Washington

Mount Hood, in Oregon, and Mount Adams, across the Columbia in Washington state, stand as two snowcapped cones as you enter another canyon 5 miles south of Biggs. Oregon Trail wagons descended to this point from the inland portion of the Columbia Plateau and headed north to the river. Small farms with aging barns and quaint windmills lie protected by the slopes of converging ridges. After a few miles the Columbia Gorge opens in front and you can see **Maryhill Museum** across the river in Washington.

Crossing the bridge at Biggs and entering Washington, you pass **Maryhill State Park,** which displays a steam locomotive and offers swimming, boating, picnicking, and 20 tent and 60 utility sites with power and water. The **Stonehenge replica,** a mile east of the park, is a full-size reproduction of England's Stonehenge and was America's first World War I memorial.

Maryhill Museum of Art, about 3 miles west on WA 14, sits isolated on a plain, literally in the middle of nowhere. Nothing prepares you for the imposing structure, and you are likely to come away somewhat overwhelmed by this curiosity and its fine art. It houses original bronzes, plasters, watercolors, and sketches by Auguste Rodin and extensive collections of chess sets, as well as 19th-century American, Dutch, and French paintings.

Returning to Oregon

You can conclude by returning to Oregon on US 97 to Biggs or by following WA 14 west and crossing the bridge to The Dalles. From Biggs your options are to return to The Dalles through the gorge on I-84 or take the Oregon Trail route along the rim and through 15 Mile Canyon. Deschutes River State Recreation Area, 4 miles west of Biggs, has 32 electrical and 25 primitive sites, along with a 17-mile hiking trail and an Oregon Trail exhibit.

27

Cove Palisades Loop

General Description: A 31-mile scenic drive through an agricultural plain to spectacular high desert canyons surrounding an artificial lake fed by 3 rivers.

Special Attractions: Round Butte Observatory, Lake Billy Chinook, Cove Palisades State Park, views of 10 Cascade Mountain peaks, fishing, camping.

Location: Central Oregon west of Culver and Madras.

Drive Route Names: Belmont Lane, Mountain View Drive, Frazier Drive, Fisch Lane, Feather Drive, Huber Lane.

Travel Season: All year. Park campgrounds and facilities close during winter.

Camping: 1 state park campground with 2 sections featuring full hookups and electricity.

Services: All services at Madras. Limited services at Lake Billy Chinook and Culver.

Nearby Attractions: Ogden Scenic Wayside, Smith Rock State Park, Crooked River National Grasslands, Crooked River Gorge, headwaters of the Metolius River, Pelton Dam and Park, Warm Springs Indian Reservation, Kah-Nee-Ta Resort.

For More Information: Central Oregon Visitors Association, (800) 800-8334, www.visitcentraloregon.com; Culver Visitor Information Center, (541) 546-6032; Maupin Area Chamber of Commerce, (541) 993-1708, www.maupinoregon.com; Madras–Jefferson County Chamber of Commerce, (541) 475-2350, (800) 967-3564, www.madraschamber.com; Oregon State Parks, (800) 551-6949, www.oregonstateparks.org.

The Route

Several Cascade peaks dominate the horizon as the drive extends west through flat farmland. Lake Billy Chinook and its canyons are hidden until you reach the gorge's edge, where the route follows the eastern rim to spectacular viewpoints and into the park and canyons. The drive concludes by traveling southwest through commercial field crops.

Summers in central Oregon average highs of 62 to 82 degrees, with occasional jumps into the 90s but rarely over 100. Winter highs generally fall between 35 and 41 degrees but seldom drop below zero, even though this is high desert country and the area does receive snow. Visitors can expect balmy spring days in the high 50s to mid-60s and autumns around 70 degrees.

Madras, with a population of 6,700 and an elevation of 2,245 feet, was founded in 1911. According to legend, it was named after a bolt of cloth.

Surrounding areas are frequented by rock hounds, who gather here every July Fourth for an annual convention and to mine landscapes for fossils, agates, and petrified wood. Several ranches offer digs for jasper, thunder eggs, and moss and rainbow agates.

Cove Palisades Loop

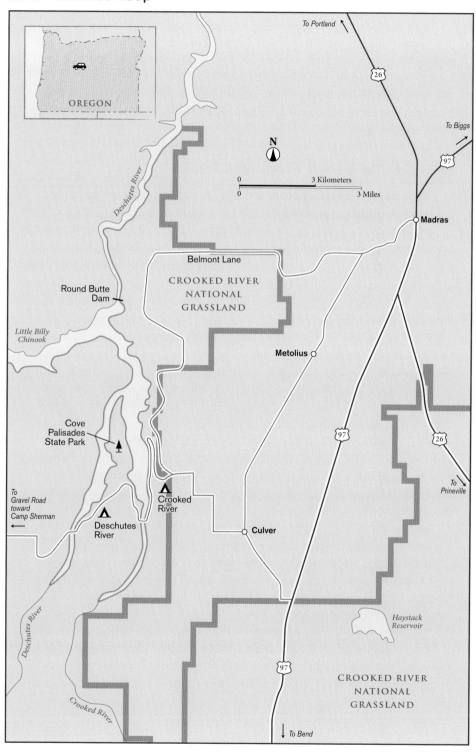

OREGON

To Portland

To Biggs

26

97

Madras

Deschutes River

N

0   3 Kilometers
0   3 Miles

Belmont Lane

CROOKED RIVER
NATIONAL
GRASSLAND

Round Butte
Dam

Metolius

Little Billy
Chinook

Cove
Palisades
State Park

97

26

To
Prineville

To
Gravel Road
toward
Camp Sherman

Crooked
River

Culver

Deschutes
River

Deschutes River

Haystack
Reservoir

97

Crooked River

CROOKED RIVER
NATIONAL
GRASSLAND

To Bend

Exiting Madras, you travel west through grasslands, farms, and low hills covered with sagebrush and isolated junipers. On clear days you may be able to see more than 100 miles of the Cascade Range and its most prominent peaks.

After 7.5 miles the drive turns south on Mountain View Road. Junipers have thickened into a forest and provide a cool corridor on the 1.7 miles to Round Butte Observatory.

Round Butte Dam & Prominent Peaks

The observation building, operated by Portland General Electric Company, overlooks **Round Butte Dam,** 400 feet below, and hints at the spectacular scenery to come as the vista encompasses Lake Billy Chinook, the Deschutes River, and sheer canyon walls. The rock-filled dam is one of the nation's largest earthen dams and holds back the Deschutes, Metolius, and Crooked Rivers. The Pelton–Round Butte project is owned by the Confederated Tribes of Warm Springs and Pacific Gas and Electric. As such, it is the nation's only hydroelectric facility jointly owned by a Native American tribe and a utility.

Information boards explain the geology, local history, and Round Butte and Pelton Dam projects and identify local fish and birds. The site has restrooms and drinking water. A 3-acre picnic area is a pleasant spot to savor the scenery.

You'll also find information on facilities at **Pelton Dam and Park,** situated 7 miles north of the observatory and also operated by the power company. Pelton Dam forms Lake Simtustus, which is also a center for water-based recreation surrounded by the high cliffs of a scenic canyon. Pelton Park features 69 campsites and a store with food, fishing supplies, boat rentals, and moorage space. **Pelton Wildlife Overlook,** north of the park, provides a good view of the regulating reservoir and the possibility of seeing great blue herons, eagles, and other birds that congregate here.

During the next 5 miles, four roadside pullouts on the rim of the gorge offer a variety of striking views. At the first viewpoint you can see the Deschutes River curve around the tall island butte, merge with the Crooked River, and continue as one stream north into a narrow canyon. A second viewpoint is directly across from the tip of the island, with Lake Billy Chinook below and the gorge walls seeming to converge to the north.

The third viewpoint is a prime spot for seeing the lake and canyon walls and 10 of the Cascades' most prominent peaks. They include Mount Adams in Washington state and Oregon's Mount Hood, Mount Jefferson, Three Fingered Jack, Mount Washington, Black Butte, the Three Sisters, Broken Top, and Mount Bachelor. From the last viewpoint you can look out at Mount Jefferson and the island between the rivers and see boaters and picnickers below.

Cove Palisades

Less than a mile south, the road enters **Cove Palisades State Park** and takes you down to Lake Billy Chinook's shoreline. It has 3 day-use areas and 2 campgrounds. **Crooked River Campground,** by the entrance, overlooks the lake several hundred feet below. It has 3 cabins near 91 sites with hookups for trailers and tents.

The near-vertical canyon walls were formed over millions of years. Between 10 million and 12 million years ago, the Deschutes and other rivers were rerouted by lava flows that formed the Cascade Mountains' base. As the foundation raised, land around Cove Palisades sank. Ancient rivers carried sediment from the mountains into the basin. Over an 8 million–year period, sediment, volcanic ash, cinders, and lava created a 1,000-foot-thick layer. Later, lava flows capped the rim-rock palisades and virtually filled the canyon, and rivers cut through the flow to their original depths.

Cove Palisades has been a favored fishing and recreation area since the late 1800s. Until the early 1960s, when Round Butte Dam was constructed, the state park was situated on the Crooked River's banks 900 feet below the canyon rim and 200 feet below the lake's present-day water level. In 1963 it was relocated to the peninsula that separates the river arms. It remains one of Oregon's most visited recreation areas. **Cove Palisades Resort and Marina** rents houseboats, fishing and ski boats, personal watercraft, and kayaks.

Lake Billy Chinook

Lake Billy Chinook, with 3 arms and 72 miles of shoreline, was named for a local Native American who helped guide Captain John C. Fremont through the region in 1843. In addition to waterskiing and other water sports, you have a good chance at landing a variety of fish, from kokanee, chinook salmon, Dolly Varden, and large- and smallmouth bass to rainbow and brown trout. The lake has produced record 20- and 23-pound bull trout. Its large size gives boaters and kayakers multiple opportunities to explore the many arms and inlets.

About 10 miles of paved road meander through the canyon and park. On the east rim the road ends at **Cove Marina,** 3 miles north of the park entrance. At the marina you can rent boats, motors, waterskiing equipment, and moorage space. The store carries groceries, ice, and fishing permits, and the restaurant opens at 6 a.m. for anglers and early risers.

Crooked River Day Use Area, 0.5 mile south of the marina, is a large lake-side picnic ground and a launching site for boaters and water-skiers. Russian olive, black locust, European beech, poplar, and other nonnative trees have been planted to shade day-use areas along the shorelines.

Several viewpoints along the rim of Lake Billy Chinook provide panoramic views of the lake and its arms, the desert, and distant mountains. Licensed by Shutterstock.com.

The road clings to a 30- to 50-foot ridge as it continues south 2 miles, crosses a bridge, and makes a moderately steep climb to the shallow gap that connects the peninsula to the mainland. On the west side the land opens into a flat plain.

At **Deschutes River Camp,** on the peninsula, you can sleep at the base of towering rock walls in 92 tent sites or 82 spots with hookups for water, sewerage, and electricity. Facilities include central restrooms, hot showers, and a fish-cleaning station. A nearby group camp has 3 areas, each capable of accommodating 25 people.

The **Crooked River Petroglyph,** a basalt boulder that was moved here, is situated between the two camps at the base of the often photographed "ship" formation. It is covered with symbols carved by prehistoric Indians.

Lower Deschutes Day-Use Area sits at the base of the island, and **Upper Deschutes Day-Use Area** is on the southwestern shore near the end of the pavement. Area hikes are rewarding, but watch for rattlesnakes. Hike the 6-mile **Tam-a-lau Trail** and you'll be rewarded with sweeping views of the Cascade Mountains as well as the Crooked and Deschutes Rivers' arms of the reservoir. In addition to rugged scenery, you may see mule deer, otters, ground squirrels, and raccoons. Bird life ranges from geese to magpies, red-tailed hawks, and meadowlarks.

Camp Sherman Side Trip & Back to Culver

A dirt forest service road connects to **Camp Sherman** and the headwaters of the Metolius, about 20 miles southwest. FR 1139, also unpaved, heads inland along the western rim to the forest service–operated **Perry South Campground** on the **Metolius River.** This is one of Oregon's most popular campgrounds, so arrive early on Friday if you're planning to spend the weekend here.

Irrigation has turned the high desert south of the rim into a productive agricultural area. As you leave the park, the Three Sisters provide a scenic backdrop on the 5 miles to **Culver** as you travel by fields planted for grass and carrot seed, potatoes, alfalfa, garlic, and a variety of grains. The area is particularly aromatic in late summer during the peppermint harvest.

If you are interested in country crafts, a stop at Culver's **Old Court House Mall** can be rewarding. From Culver your options for additional sightseeing include the Madras-Prineville Loop tour, the McKenzie–Santiam Pass Loop, and the Cascade Lakes Highway.

28

Madras-Prineville Loop

General Description: A 70-mile loop through rolling grass, sagebrush- and juniper-covered hills, and the Crooked River Gorge.

Special Attractions: Crooked River National Grassland, Crooked River Gorge, Smith Rock State Park, Ogden Scenic Wayside, 3 reservoir lakes, rock climbing, rockhounding, fishing.

Location: Central Oregon between Madras and Prineville.

Drive Route Numbers: US 26, US 126, OR 27, O'Neil Road, US 97.

Travel Season: All year.

Camping: 3 state park campgrounds, 1 with full hookups, 1 with primitive sites, and 1 with an informal walk-in bivouac area. 1 forest service campground and 1 Bureau of Land Management campground with tables, fire rings, vault or flush toilets, and drinking water.

Services: All services at Madras and Prineville.

Nearby Attractions: Cascades Lakes Highway, Three Sisters Wilderness, Pine Mountain Observatory, High Desert Museum, Lava Butte, Lava Cast Forest, Benham Falls, Sunriver Nature Center, Cove Palisades State Park, Lake Billy Chinook, McKenzie–Santiam Pass Loop, headwaters of the Metolius River, Pelton Dam, Warm Springs Indian Reservation, Kah-Nee-Ta Resort.

For More Information: Central Oregon Visitors Association, (800) 800-8334, www.visitcentraloregon.com; Crooked River Ranch–Terrebonne Chamber of Commerce, (541) 923-2679, www.crrchamber .com; Deschutes & Ochoco National Forest and Crooked River Grassland, (541) 475-9272 (Ochoco NF), (541) 416-6500 (CR Grassland), www.fs.usda.gov/centraloregon; Madras–Jefferson County Chamber of Commerce, (541) 475-2350, (800) 967-3564, www.madraschamber.com; Prineville–Crook County Chamber of Commerce, (541) 447-6304, www.visitprineville.com.

The Route

From **Madras** the route proceeds southeast across sagebrush and rolling hills through the **Crooked River National Grassland** to **Prineville** and the rugged **Crooked River Canyon.** Turning west, it extends through the sheer basalt cliffs of the rugged Crooked River Gorge to **Terrebonne.** As the route returns north on US 97, it is framed by the snowcapped peaks of the Cascades to the west and the high desert's low hills and prairie near the roadside. Traffic is usually moderate on US 26 and OR 126, light on OR 27 and O'Neil Road, and moderate to heavy on US 97.

Between 15 million and 20 million years ago, most of the area was covered by basalt lava to a depth of several hundred feet. Over time the Crooked River cut through the rock, creating the sheer-walled deep canyons, which you travel through on the southern section of the drive.

Madras–Prineville Loop

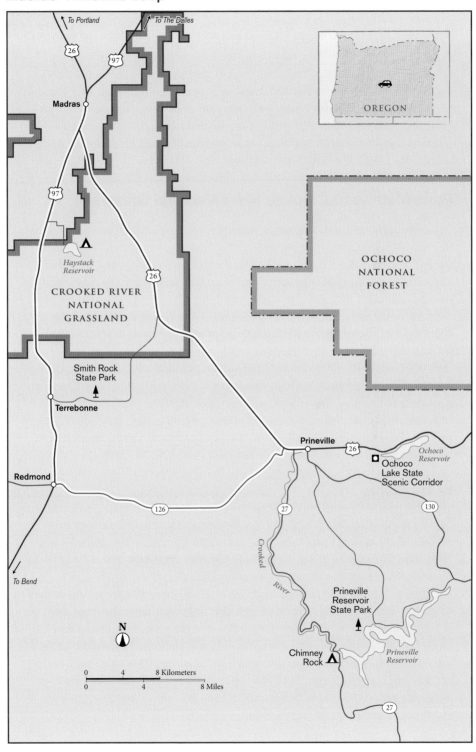

To Portland

To The Dalles

26

97

Madras

97

Haystack
Reservoir

CROOKED RIVER
NATIONAL
GRASSLAND

26

OCHOCO
NATIONAL
FOREST

OREGON

Smith Rock
State Park

Terrebonne

Prineville

26

Ochoco
Reservoir

Ochoco
Lake State
Scenic Corridor

Redmond

126

27

130

To Bend

Crooked

River

Prineville
Reservoir
State Park

Chimney
Rock

Prineville
Reservoir

27

N

0   4   8 Kilometers
0   4   8 Miles

Summers in central Oregon register from the 60s to the 80s and 90s, but rarely over 100 degrees. While the area does receive snow, temperatures seldom drop below zero and usually stay between 35 and 41 degrees. Spring days are usually in the high 50s to mid-60s, with autumn temperatures hovering around 70 degrees.

Madras, the Jefferson County seat, is the center of an agricultural area with cattle ranches and commercial crops of vegetable seeds, garlic, grain, potatoes, alfalfa, clover, and mint. It is also an outdoor recreation hub for fly fishers who come to the Deschutes and Metolius Rivers.

From Madras to Crooked River National Grassland

The drive begins in south **Madras,** where the route leaves US 97, and heads southeast on US 26. It starts by cutting through fields of hay, juniper, and sagebrush, framed by a low eastern ridge. After about 3 miles a wooden-framed structure, east of the highway, marks the site of one of central Oregon's many commercial cinnabar mines.

During the next 15 miles, you travel through the rolling rangeland of the 105,000-acre **Crooked River National Grassland,** which spreads into deep canyons and across scattered volcanic buttes. The grasslands are managed by the Ochoco National Forest to provide a habitat for antelope, wild horses, elk, and upland game. At **Rimrock Springs viewpoint,** 5 miles farther south, you can walk a nature trail to a grassy ridge with an observation platform overlooking a small reservoir. As you walk the 1.5-mile trail, watch for bald eagles, ducks, quail, chukars, and mule deer. The grasslands' wide-open spaces and terrain attract hikers, horseback riders, and off-road vehicle riders.

To Prineville

Leaving the grasslands, the highway tops **Grizzly Pass.** Hay fields and cattle ranches fill the valley between the summit and the 10 miles to **Prineville.** You'll enter town by traveling under the **Railway Express overpass.** The railroad is one of the few in the US that is owned by a municipality.

Prineville is the only incorporated city in Crook County. When it was settled in 1868, it became central Oregon's first town. Today it is an interesting mix of historic and modern buildings surrounded by rolling countryside and deep canyons. Native American artifacts, antiques, guns, and other regional relics are preserved in the **Bowman Museum,** which is housed in a 1910 stone bank building. The original teller cages, bank ledgers, and safe are still here. A second floor includes a period tack room, bedroom, store and post office, and vintage doctor and dentist equipment.

The surrounding hills, cliffs, and lowlands contain an abundance of thunder eggs, agates, fossils, petrified wood, and jaspers. Prineville is a focal point for rock hounds, who gather for annual conventions and digs. You can obtain lists and maps of digging sites from the chamber of commerce. While you can dig on public lands for free, some sites are on private land and charge a fee.

Six miles east of town alongside US 26, **Ochoco Reservoir** fills a wooded ravine between wooded hills. Situated on the centennial bike route and impounded by 125-foot **Ochoco Dam,** it is a favorite recreation area with year-round rainbow trout fishing, boating, and waterskiing. You can enjoy its peaceful setting from 22 primitive and hiker/biker campsites at nearby **Ochoco Lake State Scenic Corridor.**

Wild & Scenic Crooked River

The area's best scenery lies south of Prineville on OR 27. During the first few miles, you'll travel through the center of beautiful farms with impeccable buildings and white board fences, bordered by high ridges and lava outcroppings. After about 7 miles the **Crooked River** starts meandering along the roadside. It begins in the Ochoco Mountains and flows west 107 miles to empty into the Deschutes near Madras.

At about mile marker 12, the route enters the steep reddish brown basalt palisades of the **Lower Crooked River Canyon** and becomes a Bureau of Land Management National Scenic Byway. This section is also a National Wild and Scenic River and a popular canoe route. Riverside rattlesnakes temper local anglers' enthusiasm somewhat for runs of hungry brown and rainbow trout. Other wildlife to watch for are coyotes, deer, and raptors. You can enjoy a picnic lunch at several BLM picnic areas and overnight in 18 campsites at **Chimney Rock Recreation Area.** It is one of 9 BLM campgrounds, with a total of approximately 90 sites, between Prineville and Bowman Dam, and the only one with drinking water.

Prineville Reservoir

At mile marker 20, rolled-earth and rock-filled **Arthur R. Bowman Dam** rises 245 feet from a 1,100-foot-wide base, creating 12-mile-long **Prineville Reservoir.** Built for irrigation and flood control, it is a favorite of water-skiers and boaters during summer weekends. Scrappy largemouth and smallmouth bass, catfish, and native and stocked rainbow trout make it a year-round fishery.

The pavement ends at a boat launch on the western shoreline. If you elect to return to Prineville, you'll have a completely different view of the palisades. As you drive north the cliffs tower above you as a giant natural amphitheater. The

BLM byway continues south for 22 miles as a narrow, washboardy, all-weather gravel road with sharp turns through high desert sagebrush.

Prineville Reservoir State Park, on the eastern shore, has 22 full-hookup, 22 electrical, and 23 tent sites, a boat ramp, and a dock. It attracts boaters, water-skiers, and swimmers; rock collectors come to hunt for a variety of agates and pet-rified wood. Evening slide programs are presented in the campground's outdoor theater. The park is not accessible from OR 27 but can be reached on a separate side road that leads 17 miles south from Prineville.

Returning to Prineville, the loop drive continues by crossing the Crooked River on OR 126, makes a sharp turn north at the top of the first hill, and enters **Ochoco Wayside.** From the small park the sweeping view encompasses the valley, gorge, and surrounding area. Afterward, you continue west on O'Neil Road along the scenic **Crooked River rim.** A house across the valley at mile marker 11 became famous in a book titled *House Under the Rimrock* and was the home of former governor Tom McCall. O'Neil Road ends at a junction with US 97 near **Terre-bonne,** which is a French word meaning "good earth." Once a center of agricul-ture, the town is the gateway to Smith Rock State Park and Crooked River Ranch, which was once a working ranch but has been rezoned into a 12,000-acre subdivi-sion. The fifth hole of its golf course has been called the most spectacular golf hole in Oregon and has been awarded a four-star rating (out of 5 stars) by *Golf Digest.*

Smith Rock State Park

Smith Rock State Park, 4 miles east of Terrebonne, is one of Oregon's scenic icons and the drive's highlight. Junipers, ponderosa pines, and sagebrush stud its canyon floor. The Crooked River is a winding blue ribbon separating sheer talus rocks on the north and the rimrock plateau to the south.

A climbers' favorite since the 1940s, **Smith Rock** has acquired an interna-tional reputation as one of the nation's best rock-climbing areas. Three of its more than 600 routes have received the highest difficulty rating of 5.14, but the park offers excellent climbing for beginners and intermediates as well as experts. If you're not a climber, you can explore the 623 acres of scenic wonders on 7 miles of hiking trails. They range from easy riverside strolls to **Misery Ridge**'s 3.6-mile trek that gains almost 1,000 feet. Don't attempt it if you have heart or breathing problems. The spectacular view from the top encompasses the Cascade Mountain range on the far horizon and the Crooked River below. Coming down the trail is

Smith Rock is an Oregon scenic icon loved by climbers and photographers.

sometimes soft or littered with loose stones. You can also fish the river, picnic at a panoramic overlook, and camp beside the beauty in a walk-in bivouac or tent camping area that is open year-round.

As US 97 continues north, on clear days you'll see Mount Jefferson and several lesser peaks on the western horizon.

Crooked River Gorge

Ogden Scenic Wayside, 3 miles north of Terrebonne, offers a delightful rest stop and a close-up view of the sheer walls of 300-foot-deep **Crooked River Gorge.** The walls of the gorge expose basalt flows that buried 5 million– to 10 million–year–old blankets of volcanic ash and dust. The wayside honors Peter Skene Ogden, who led a Hudson's Bay Company trapping party on the first recorded journey into central Oregon in 1825. As he roamed the West, Ogden became an important figure in the early fur trade.

The route continues north through the grasslands and isolated junipers of the high desert, passing shallow ridges and swales. Six miles north, you pass a side road to Culver and the southern entrance to the **Cove Palisades Scenic Drive. Round Butte Dam** and **Cove Palisades Recreation Area,** about 10 miles west, offer boating, tent camping, fishing, and visitor information. The exit is in the middle of farmland and sagebrush/juniper grasslands with a good view of snow-capped mountains to the northwest.

Haystack Reservoir

A mile farther, Jericho Lane heads 5 miles east over juniper-covered hills to **Haystack Reservoir.** In early spring and late fall, it yields good catches of crappie, bass, catfish, kokanee, bullhead, and stocked rainbow trout. Speedboats and water-skiers take over during summer. A forest service campground provides 24 sites, a boat ramp, and a swimming area, and a KOA campground with 83 full hookups is situated on the access road, 0.5 mile east of US 97.

The drive concludes 7 miles north at the junction of US 97 and US 26. Access to the Cove Palisades Loop is 1.5 miles north off US 97 in Madras.

29

Bend, Newberry Crater

General Description: A 42.3-mile drive through pine forests and lava beds to the summit of Newberry Crater National Volcanic Monument.

Special Attractions: High Desert Museum, Lava Butte, Lava Cast Forest, Benham Falls, Sunriver Nature Center and Observatory, Lava River Cave, La Pine State Recreation Area, Deschutes National Forest, Newberry Crater National Volcanic Monument.

Location: Central Oregon between Bend and LaPine.

Drive Route Numbers: US 97, FR 21.

Travel Season: All year. Newberry Crater receives significant snow and is a center for cross-country skiing and winter recreation. East Lake Resort closes from mid-October to mid-May, and Lava River Cave closes in mid-September.

Camping: 8 forest service campgrounds with tables, fire rings, vault or flush toilet, and drinking water. 1 state park campground with full hookups. East Lake Resort Campground with full hookups.

Services: All services in Bend and Sunriver. Limited services at Newberry Crater National Monument.

Nearby Attractions: Cascade Lakes Highway, Smith Rock State Park, Crater Lake National Park, Three Sisters Wilderness, Pine Mountain Observatory, Fort Rock State Park, Hole-in-the-Ground.

For More Information: Central Oregon Visitors Association, (800) 800-8334, www .visitcentraloregon.com; Visit Bend (877) 245-8484 (toll free), (541) 382-8048, www.visitbend.com; Deschutes National Forest, (541) 383-5300, www.fs.usda .gov/centraloregon; La Pine Chamber of Commerce, (541) 536-9771, www.lapine .org; Sunriver Area Chamber of Commerce, (541) 593-8149, www.sunriverchamber .com.

The Route

Starting in **Bend,** the drive follows US 97 south, then turns east and climbs to over 6,000 feet elevation at the **Newberry Crater National Volcanic Monument.** The first 25 miles are a flat, tree-lined corridor, and the last 18 miles are a steep, mostly straight climb with views of forested mountains and valleys. As central Oregon's main north–south corridor, US 97 is generally busy, with traffic particularly heavy during the 8–9 a.m. and 5–6 p.m. rush hours. FR 21 to **Newberry Crater** is a signed Corridor 97 Association tour, whose traffic is usually light during the week but heavy on weekends.

Volcanism forged the landscape between Bend and Newberry Crater. The last volcanic activity occurred only 1,300 years ago. **Newberry Crater National Volcanic Monument** gained its monument status in 1990 and preserves 56,000 acres of lakes, lava flows, and other geological formations. Over 95 percent of the world's geologic features are visible here, including ash flows, cinder cones, pumice rings, and rhyolitic domes.

Bend, Newberry Crater

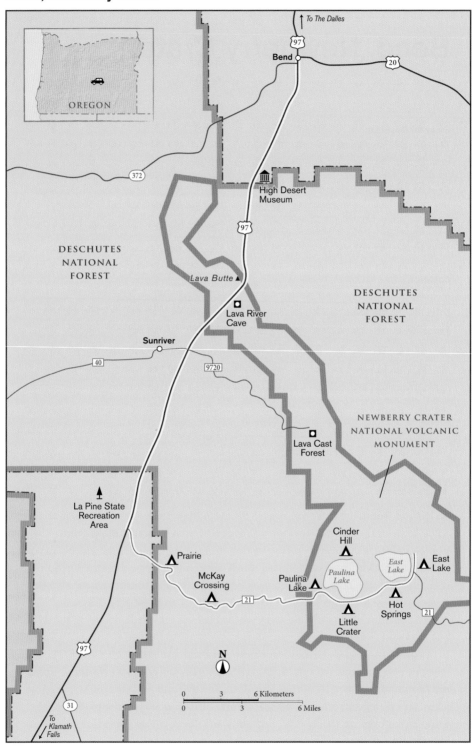

Summer temperatures average 73 to 82 degrees, while winter days generally fall between 20 and 40 degrees with cold nights. Although the area receives only about 12 inches of precipitation per year, significant snowfall occurs at Newberry Crater. Spring days average about 60 degrees, while fall days are slightly warmer at about 67 degrees.

Deschutes Historical Museum & High Desert Museum

Before leaving Bend, at 3,628 feet elevation, you may wish to visit the **Deschutes Historical Museum.** It is situated in a 1914 schoolhouse and exhibits artifacts from **Lava Island Rock Shelter.** Displays and period rooms interpret settlement of the Bend area from Native Americans, explorers, and fur trappers through farmers, ranchers, and railroaders. From Bend US 97 heads south in a straight line through a ponderosa pine forest. After about 7 miles you arrive at the **High Desert Museum.** The 150-acre complex is virtually a must for anyone interested in the high desert's history and wildlife. Many displays are interactive. You can trace the area's history from prehistoric to present times and step into a settler's cabin, a sheepherder's wagon, and the forestry learning center. A nature exhibit features burrowing owls, kangaroo rats, lizards, bats, rattlesnakes, and other desert animals that are seldom seen. You may see live eagles in a Birds of Prey center and porcupines, otters, and wild cats, including bobcats, in other exhibits.

Lava Butte

During the next 3 miles, the route enters the **Deschutes National Forest** and crosses the northwestern tip of panhandle-shaped Newberry Crater National Volcanic Monument. The panhandle section includes **Lava River Cave, Lava Cast Forest,** and **Lava Butte,** which can be seen west of the highway as you continue south 0.7 mile to **Lava Lands Visitor Center,** where interpretive displays provide an introduction to the area's volcanic landscape. Behind the center the short **Molten Land Trail** winds through a lava flow from Lava Butte, and the **Trail of the Whispering Pines** meanders into a ponderosa pine forest.

Shuttles operate from the center to Lava Butte's summit, 500 feet above the plain. At the summit you'll look down into a 150-foot crater. The outstanding view from a short paved rim trail encompasses Newberry Crater, the Three Sisters, Mount Bachelor, the high desert, Smith Rock, and a 6,100-acre lava field. Visitor center videos and displays interpret the area's geology and archaeology. You can also walk three short 0.25- to 0.5-mile interpretive trails around the crater.

At **Benham Falls,** 4 miles west of the visitor center, lava filled the channel of the Deschutes River for several miles to a depth of 50 feet and forced the stream over an ancient lava dome. A 0.5-mile trail through a stand of old-growth ponderosa connects the idyllic riverbank picnic area with the falls, which are really rapids. If they look familiar, it may be because you've seen them in *Rooster Cogburn, The Indian Fighter,* and other films.

Lava River Cave

Back on US 97, the drive continues south 1 mile to **Lava River Cave,** set in a ponderosa pine forest with a ground cover of bitterbrush, manzanita, and snowbrush. It is Oregon's longest known uncollapsed lava tube and has a main tunnel 5,200 feet long. You can rent lanterns and take a self-guided tour of its lava and ice stalactites and stalagmites, echo hall, and sand gardens. The 2.4-mile trail, including the walk to and from the parking lot, is relatively easy despite stairs and an uneven surface. Wear sturdy shoes and bring a jacket; the cave temperature is a constant 40 degrees.

Continuing south, you temporarily leave the national forest and monument. **Sunriver Nature Center and Observatory,** 2.5 miles south of the cave and 3.4 miles west of US 97, is located on sediments deposited by ancient lake beds that were created when lava flows dammed the Deschutes River. Many of the center's activities are geared toward children. There are natural history displays, exhibits of local ancient stone artifacts, a botanical garden, and an observatory.

Lava Cast Forest

From Sunriver a bumpy dirt road (FR 9720) heads east 9 miles to the **Lava Cast Forest.** Tree molds in this 5-square-mile area were created about 6,000 years ago when a Newberry Crater eruption spilled into the ponderosa, lodgepole, and white fir forest. As the lava cooled, the intense heat burned the wood and left the molds. You can see them on a paved 1-mile trail—some of which is too narrow and steep for wheelchairs—through lava logs, lava lakes, and a lava sea surrounding a forested island. The area is at its best in early summer, when purple penstemon and Indian paintbrush add a bit of color to the landscape.

US 97 exits the national monument and forest, passes the entrance to the Fall River/Cascade Lakes Highway, and continues south 7.5 miles to the **La Pine State Park.** At the park's entrance 4 miles west of the highway, a sign directs you to **Oregon's largest ponderosa pine.** It has a circumference of 326 inches and is 161 feet tall. From a lookout you have a commanding view of the Deschutes River and the devastation caused by the mountain pine beetle. It has infested many lodgepole pines and deprived them of nutrients. As they die the branches turn red.

A day-use area on the winding Deschutes River provides picnic tables, fireplaces, and drinking water. Though the river has a slight current, a bathhouse and swimming beach offer a welcome break from the summer heat. The campground, 1 mile west, provides 48 sites with electricity, tables, and water, and 80 sites with full hookups for water, sewerage, and electricity, plus a group meeting hall and 10 cabins.

Newberry Crater National Volcanic Monument

About 1 mile south the route leaves US 97 and turns east on FR 21 to climb the western slopes of **Newberry Volcano.** From the beginning at roughly 4,000 feet, the road rises dramatically during the 18 miles to 6,371 feet at **East Lake Prairie Campground,** with 16 sites, and **McKay Crossing,** with 10, are situated near the base in jack pine scrub forest on sandy soil. A group camp is also nearby. A 3-mile segment of the **Peter Skene Ogden Trail** starts near these campgrounds and can be hiked, biked, or ridden on horses.

As the road climbs through a lodgepole and ponderosa forest, several pullouts invite photographs of the forested slopes, cones, lava flows, the valley, and the Cascade Mountains to the west. After passing an area of dead timber devastated by beetles at mile marker 12, you reenter the national monument.

The **Newberry Crater National Volcanic Monument** you see today is the end result of millions of years of volcanism. Numerous ash and pumice avalanches swept down its sides, spreading a base 25 miles wide and covering 500 square miles. Named after J. S. Newberry, a scientist attached to an 1853 railroad surveying party, it is one of the largest volcanos in the US. During a series of major eruptions, the top collapsed into empty lava chambers, leaving a caldera of 17 square miles, 5 miles across. It is so vast that the rim appears to be a separate mountain range.

East Lake & Paulina Lake

The crater holds two scenic lakes, which were once a single body of water but were separated by lava and mud flows. **East Lake** is about 170 feet deep and covers 1,000 acres. **Paulina Lake** spans 1,500 acres and is about 248 feet deep. In the monument you can hike, horseback ride, snowmobile, or cross-country ski more than 100 miles of trails. Some are short, easy lakeside jaunts; others will take you on a 25-mile crater rim loop or along the 8.5-mile **Peter Skene Ogden National Recreation Trail,** which passes 20 waterfalls on Paulina Creek.

Most of the facilities and sites are situated near the monument entrance. A dirt side road to 7,984-foot **Paulina Peak,** the highest point on the volcano, is easily accessible by car and offers a view of the two lakes, the Cascade Mountains, central Oregon, Washington, and California. You can reach the **Paulina Creek**

Falls picnic area and the 100-foot falls on a short walk from the parking lot. At **Newberry Crater Wildlife Refuge,** also near the entrance, you may see bears, eagles, ducks, geese, badgers, bobcats, and occasionally elk.

Paulina Lake, behind the falls, is known for trophy-size brown, rainbow, and brook trout as well as kokanee salmon. You'll find it a pleasant and scenic setting for canoeing, powerboating, sailing, and waterskiing. A year-round resort on the lakeshore, housed in a 1929 log cabin, operates a restaurant, rents boats and 10 cabins, and sells groceries, tackle, and gas. Four forest service campgrounds on or near the lake provide 126 sites, a group camp, and stables for 12 horses. In winter the lodge is accessible via a Snowcat shuttle from a snow park. You can rent snowmobiles at the lodge and explore 150 miles of groomed trails or see the winter wonderland on cross-country skis.

From the entrance the road continues north to the obsidian flow. It occurred about 1,300 years ago and is the last known volcanic event at Newberry. When it reached the surface, the lava cooled quickly, creating a spectacular hill of black glass and volcanic foam. A 0.4-mile hike on an improved trail is moderately strenuous as it climbs to the top of the flow and overlooks tiny Lost Lake.

East Lake Resort

After passing three forest service campgrounds with 191 sites, the pavement ends at **East Lake Resort.** A dirt road, not recommended for passenger cars, continues around the mountain and back to Bend.

At East Lake you have an opportunity to sailboard in a volcano. Your efforts at still-fishing, trolling, and fly fishing are likely to be rewarded, thanks to planted Atlantic salmon and annual stockings of 225,000 ravenous rainbow trout, plus native brook and brown trout. East Lake Resort rents boats and 16 cabins and has an RV park with 40 full hookups. It operates a store, cafe, and boathouse. From the resort you have the best view of the pretty lake and the caldera, which are obscured by trees along the roadside.

On the return to the monument boundary, you have a much better view of Paulina Peak, which looms above the roadside, and a second opportunity to see interesting outcroppings and gravel slides you may have missed on the initial trip.

From Newberry Crater you can return to Sunriver or Bend and take the Cascade Lakes Highway, or travel south and drive the Oregon Outback Byway and/or Klamath County Loop.

Newberry Crater is so large that it contains two lakes, a mountain of obsidian, and graceful Paulina Falls.

30

Blue Mountain Scenic Byway

General Description: A 130-mile paved route from the Columbia River grasslands into the forested Blue Mountains.

Special Attractions: Oregon Trail site, lakes and reservoir, elk herds, forest views, Wild and Scenic North Fork John Day River, bird-watching, hunting, hiking.

Location: Northeastern Oregon, starting at I-84 exit 147, west of Boardman, and ending in the Blue Mountains, northwest of Sumpter.

Drive Route Numbers: OR 74, OR 207/74, FR 52, FR 51, and FR 73.

Travel Season: OR 74 to Heppner is open all year. Forest service roads are not plowed in winter but are used by snowmobilers and cross-country skiers. They are usually open June 15 to October 15.

Camping: 1 county park campground with full hookups. 1 state park campground

with primitive sites. 4 forest service campgrounds with picnic tables, vault toilets, and fire rings.

Services: All services in Heppner and Ukiah. Limited services in Ione, Lexington, and Granite.

Nearby Attractions: Columbia River Gorge, Elkhorn Scenic Byway, John Day Fossil Beds National Monument, Battle Mountain State Park, Strawberry Mountain Wilderness, I-84 Oregon Trail Route, Ritter Hot Springs.

For More Information: Eastern Oregon Visitors Association, (800) 332-1843, www .eova.com; Umatilla National Forest, (541) 278-3716, www.fs.usda.gov/umatilla; Heppner Ranger District, (541) 676-9187; North Fork John Day Ranger District, (541) 427-3231; Heppner Chamber of Commerce, (541) 676-5536, www.heppner chamber.com.

The Route

For the first 60 miles, you're likely to wonder why this route has been designated a Forest Service Scenic Byway. The only trees are stands of poplar planted as windbreaks, oaks by creek banks, and a few isolated junipers on distant hillsides. Meanwhile, you'll travel through wheat fields, grasslands, sagebrush, lava outcroppings, small cattle and sheep farms, and scattered settlements of a few hundred people. This segment is relatively flat and winding. A creek and railroad tracks meander a few feet from the road, which stays in a valley between rolling hills and distant mountains.

After **Heppner** the route starts climbing, eventually reaching an elevation of about 6,000 feet. Once it enters the **Umatilla National Forest,** it follows a ridgetop to **Ukiah,** then dips into a valley and climbs back into the mountains. Small meadows and firewood-cutting areas break into the tree-lined corridor.

Traffic is usually moderate between I-84 and Heppner. Forest service roads are less heavily traveled except during hunting season, when 20,000 hunters

Blue Mountain Scenic Byway

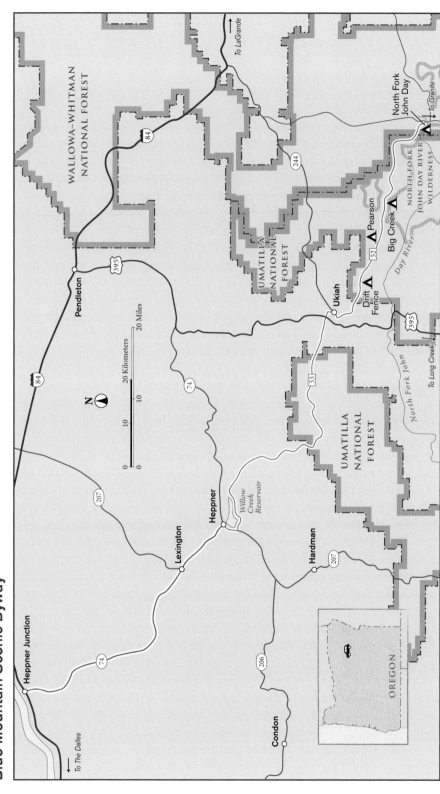

invade the area. As you travel the byway, keep your binoculars handy. The Umatilla National Forest supports 324 species of wildlife, and grasslands provide feed for deer and a variety of birds.

In the lowlands travelers can expect summer temperatures of 90 and sometimes 100 degrees. Winters plummet to the 20s and 30s, and at times to near zero. Spring averages about 65 degrees, while autumn days fall between 64 and 77 degrees.

A few homes stretch around a curve at the base of a ridge in **Cecil,** 14 miles south of exit 147. From 1849 to 1853 the Oregon Trail passed nearby. By traveling 14 miles east from the Oregon Trail sign on OR 74, you can see the actual trail ruts at **Wells Spring** along with an information center and kiosk.

At **Morgan,** 6 miles farther, a green valley and buckskin brown hills surround three water towers. Continuing south, you'll see a couple of grain elevators standing in the middle of nowhere and possibly cattle and sheep on the hillsides. At **Ione,** population 323, look for the picturesque country church and some turn-of-the-20th-century two-story buildings. A restaurant, lounge, several grain elevators, and another Oregon Trail sign line the highway. Eight miles southeast is **Lexington,** with 266 people. It sits in the middle of a large agricultural area.

Heppner

Heppner, the area's largest town, fills a small valley with 1,391 people and a few blocks of brick buildings. Settled in the 1800s, it suffered one of Oregon's worst natural disasters in 1903, when a cloudburst created a wall of water 200 yards wide that swept through town, killing 247 people. Today it is the **Morrow County seat** and is known as the **Gateway to the Blue Mountains.** It celebrates its Irish heritage with a 20-foot shamrock in the middle of town and a lively St. Patrick's Day weekend featuring sheepdog trials, a 5K run, the Iron Leprechaun bike ride, and a great green parade. The **Morrow County Museum** on the highway displays photo collections, local relics, and period rooms depicting a school and post office, while the **Morrow County Agricultural Museum** is devoted to farming, ranching, sheep and wool, and forestry with exhibits, demonstrations, and equipment. The stately courthouse, built in 1903, is on the National Register of Historic Places.

Willow Creek Dam, at the southern end of town, became the world's first roller-compacted concrete dam when it was built in 1981–1983 by the Army Corps of Engineers. From downtown you can take a short, easy walk to the 12-acre reservoir at the bottom of a wide expanse of hills with long gradual slopes that extend to the horizon. A day-use area, RV park, boat launch, and docking facilities are scattered around the rim, where people gather year-round to fish for bass and trout and enjoy summer boating and waterskiing.

For an interesting side trip, take OR 206/207 20 miles south to **Hardman.** During the late 1800s this semi–ghost town of a few homes, a community center,

The near ghost town of Hardman. LICENSED BY SHUTTERSTOCK.COM.

and 20 people was a stopover for freight wagons and stagecoaches. Several buildings still stand. The dance hall has been renovated to offer travelers some of the flavor of the lively past.

From Heppner the route follows Willow Creek Road and FR 53 as it climbs a ridge overlooking the reservoir. About midway you'll find a beautiful roadside picnic area facing the lake and mountains across a valley dotted with small farms and grasslands.

Umatilla National Forest

As it winds through hills and canyons, trees replace meadows, the road narrows, and long curves become hairpin turns. After about 17 miles you enter the **Umatilla National Forest,** and for the rest of the drive you'll travel through a corridor of mixed lodgepole pine, Douglas fir, western larch, ponderosa pine, and white fir. At higher elevations you'll also see subalpine fir.

The 1.4 million–acre national forest serves many purposes. As you continue east, watch for some of the 10,000 cattle and 8,000 sheep that graze on these lands. You can also expect to see woodcutters and pickup trucks stacked with firewood. Hikers, horseback riders, and mountain and dirt bikers depart from the highway to some of the 700 miles of trails.

Cutsforth Forest Park, near the entrance, has excellent equestrian trails and offers a pleasant break and the opportunity to overnight in the thick forest in a campground featuring campsites with 15 full-hookup and 7 tent sites with water.

Children can romp on playground equipment, explore a nature trail, and fish a creek or a wheelchair-accessible pond, both of which are stocked twice yearly with rainbow trout. You also can rent a pen for your horse and ride equestrian trails in the adjacent forest.

Lake Penland & Potamus Point

Lake Penland, 8 miles east and 5 miles south on a side road, offers swimming, trout fishing, and boating with electric motors. While most of the 70-acre lake's shoreline is privately owned, a day-use area and **Penland Lake Campground,** with a total of 7 sites that include 3 tent/trailer, 2 tent, and 2 group sites provides public access.

On the 7 miles between the Lake Penland and Potamus Point access roads, lines of spindly lodgepole pine and room-size Christmas trees are broken by small meadows, firewood-cutting areas, and snags of dead trees. Each year about 15,000 cords of firewood are cut throughout the forest, and more than 2,000 personal-use Christmas tree permits are issued.

From **Potamus Point,** 8 miles south of the main highway, your view overlooks several mountain lakes, rocky crags and outcroppings, and the Wild and Scenic North Fork John Day River drainage. In late fall and early spring, you may also glimpse herds of elk in distant meadows.

After several miles of traveling through subalpine fir and lodgepole and ponderosa pine, the forest disappears a few miles west of Ukiah, and you descend into a lake basin that was permanently emptied by an ancient earthquake. The area is particularly pretty in spring, when bright blue camas covers meadowlands.

Ukiah & Bridge Creek Wildlife Area

Ukiah, with about 250 people, has a restaurant, store, and gas. Check with the **John Day Ranger Station** if you need trail maps or wilderness permits or are exploring the backcountry. At **Ukiah-Dale Forest State Park,** 3 miles southwest of town on US 395, you can camp in 27 primitive sites on the North Fork John Day River banks.

Crossing Camus and Pine Creeks, the route quickly climbs back into mountains and forest. **Bridge Creek Wildlife Area,** about 4 miles east of Ukiah, was developed in the 1860s by miners who built pole bridges over area streams. Today it is a wintering habitat for one of the nation's largest herds of Rocky Mountain elk. In addition to approximately 16,500 elk, the forest is home to mule and white-tail deer, bighorn sheep, black bears, and mountain lions. During your drive you are likely to see bald eagles; peregrine falcons; barred, flammulated, and great gray owls; and pileated, black-backed, and three-toed woodpeckers.

The **North Fork John Day Overlook,** about 9 miles east, is a convenient pullout with an excellent view of the John Day Wilderness to the north and the Strawberry Mountains to the south. Bridge Creek elk herds can sometimes be seen from the viewpoint, along with logging operations on distant mountainsides.

The **Winom-Frazier Off-Highway Vehicle Complex,** a mile east of the overlook, has 140 miles of trails rated easy to most difficult for Class I and III ATVs in a scenic setting for enjoying fishing, hunting, and camping. **Winom Campground** provides 7 sites and 2 group shelters. At **Frazier Campground** you'll find 18 sites with tables.

Several trails begin near the highway between Bridge Creek and North Fork John Day Campground, 25 miles east of the overlook. They range from easy to difficult and from short hikes to extended treks through forested valleys, up mountain slopes, and into the John Day Wilderness. A sparse undergrowth invites short roadside explorations into the ponderosa pine forest. A dirt road leads north to 6,790-foot **Tower Mountain,** where the view includes the Elkhorn Range to the east, Malheur National Forest to the south, Washington state to the north, and the Cascades to the west. Big Creek, with 3 trailer/tent campsites, and Drift Fence, with 6 trailer/tent sites, are situated near the highway.

The Blue Mountain Byway ends at **North Fork John Day Campground,** where FR 52 and FR 51 meet. Twenty tent/trailer sites are frequented by hunters, hikers, and horseback riders. Anglers find the North Fork John Day River a rewarding stream for chinook salmon, steelhead, Dolly Varden, and rainbow trout.

Taking FR 51 and FR 73 south from the junction, the Blue Mountain and Elkhorn Scenic Byways overlap on the 10 miles south to Granite.

Old Chinese Walls & Fremont Powerhouse

A few miles south of the junction, the route passes the **Chinese Walls,** which were built by Asian miners more than 100 years ago. Gold was discovered at Granite on July 4, 1862. Several decades of varied mining activity produced more than $9 million in gold and a town with two hotels, three stores, five saloons, and many homes. The economy collapsed in 1942 when the War Labor Act made gold mining illegal. The population dwindled to 2 in 1960 but rebounded to 24 by 2000. Today only a few buildings and residents remain.

A nearby dirt road will take you 8 miles west to the remains of the **Fremont Powerhouse.** It was constructed in 1908 and used until 1967, and is listed on the National Register of Historic Places. Parts of the pipeline that provided water from **Olive Lake** are still visible along the road from the power plant to the lake. **Olive Lake Campground** has 21 trailer/tent and 2 group sites.

From Granite you can conclude your sightseeing either by traveling north 27 miles to Anthony Lakes and on to Haines or continuing southeast to Sumpter and Baker City.

31

Elkhorn Scenic Byway

General Description: A 106-mile paved loop through the desert valleys of the Baker and Powder Rivers and agricultural lands and into the Blue Mountains and Elkhorn Range.

Special Attractions: Oregon Trail route and interpretive center, lakes and reservoirs, historic gold-mining area, ski resort, forest views, Wild and Scenic North Fork John Day River, wildlife watching, recreational gold panning, hiking.

Location: Northeastern Oregon west of Baker and Haines.

Drive Route Numbers: OR 7, OR 410, FR 73, Baker County Road 1146, US 30.

Travel Season: From Baker City, roads to Granite and from Haines to Anthony Lakes are open all year. Between Granite and Anthony Lakes, routes are not plowed in winter and usually open around July 4.

Camping: 8 national forest campgrounds with picnic tables, fire grates, and flush or vault toilets. 1 has hookups.

Services: All services in Baker City. Limited services in Sumpter, Granite, and Haines.

Nearby Attractions: I-84 Oregon Trail Route, Blue Mountain Scenic Byway, John Day Fossil Beds National Monument, Strawberry Mountain Wilderness, Battle Mountain State Park, LaGrande–Ukiah–Weston Scenic Drive, Farewell Bend State Park.

For More Information: Baker County Chamber of Commerce and Visitor Bureau, (541) 523-5855, (888) 523-5855, www .visitbaker.com; Wallowa-Whitman National Forest, (541) 523-6391, www.fs.usda.gov/ wallowa-whitman; Umatilla National Forest, (541) 278-3716, www.fs.usda.gov/umatilla.

The Route

From **Baker City** the drive follows the Powder River west to **Sumpter,** where it climbs into the Blue Mountains. Passing the semi–ghost town of **Granite,** it continues through magnificent mountain scenery to **Elkhorn Pass** and the **Anthony Lakes Recreation Area.** The descent is through a steep canyon back to the Baker Valley, then it briefly crosses the original route of the Oregon Trail on the return to Baker City. Though the drive can be joined at Haines or Sumpter, or from the Blue Mountain Scenic Byway at North Fork John Day Campground, forest service route brochures start in Baker City.

Summer travelers can expect hot days with temperatures ranging from the 80s to over 100 degrees in the Baker Valley, 10 to 15 degrees cooler in the mountains. Winters are cold and snowy with temperatures dipping to below zero and the teens, 20s, and low 30s. Spring days are usually in the mid-60s, while fall ranges from 64 to 77 degrees.

Elkhorn Scenic Byway

Baker City & OR 7

In **Baker City** a walking/driving tour includes more than 100 elegant stone buildings and Victorian homes that are on the National Register of Historic Places. If you're in town on Saturday mornings the **Geiser Grand Hotel,** built in 1889, conducts tours showcasing its elegant mahogany woodwork, stained-glass ceiling, and crystal chandeliers. The downtown **Baker Heritage Museum** exhibits Oregon Trail artifacts and its rocks and mineral collection is among the state's largest. At the **National Historic Oregon Trail Interpretive Center,** 3 miles east of town, paths lead from the center atop **Flagstaff Hill** to the original wagon ruts. The outstanding view encompasses the Blue Mountains and Baker Valley.

Leaving Baker City on **OR 7,** the drive begins in dry grasslands; enters a canyon with rugged lava outcroppings, scattered juniper-covered hills, and creek-bottom willows; then crosses the **Powder River.** The Powder meanders for several miles along the roadside. After about 13 miles the route makes the first of several entrances into **Wallowa-Whitman National Forest.** As you travel through Sumpter to **Elkhorn Summit,** lodgepole pine is the forest's dominant species and is mixed with western larch, Douglas fir, and ponderosa pine. Douglas fir dominates east of Elkhorn Summit.

Near the forest boundary you'll see **Mason Dam** and **Phillips Lake** south of the highway. The 167-foot-high dam holds back a reservoir covering 5 miles and a surface area of 2,450 acres. The Powder River and Phillips Lake are fished for rainbow trout, coho salmon, and bass.

Union Creek Recreation Area

Union Creek Recreation Area offers camping in shady ponderosas beside the serene lake and is a launching pad for boating, waterskiing, and swimming. The campground's 78 sites include 20 with sewerage, water, and electrical hookups, and 18 with electricity and water.

Several habitats intermingle at nearby **Mowach Loop Picnic Area** and attract waterfowl, eagles, raptors, mule and white-tailed deer, elk, coyotes, and weasels. Ospreys nest on artificial snags. **Southwest Shore Campground** includes 16 tent/trailer sites on the lake. **Deer Creek Campground** has only 6 tent sites but offers the allure of recreational gold panning. Any gold you find is yours. Area campgrounds fill early during deer and elk season and are also staging areas for cross-country skiing.

Sumpter Valley Railroad Park

A short side road leads south to the **Sumpter Valley Railroad Park,** where you'll find a brightly painted depot, water tower, rolling stock, and short nature trails where you may see deer, cranes, and ducks. The restored train operates on summer weekends with a 10-mile round-trip pulled by an original 1915 steam-driven, wood-burning Heisler locomotive.

OR 7 turns south near the railroad access. You leave the national forest and continue west on OR 410 past fields of dredge tailings on the 3 miles into Sumpter.

Sumpter

With about 190 people, **Sumpter** is barely a shadow of its glory days when it had 3,000 people and 81 businesses and produced more than $10 million in gold ore. Today it mines most of its income from tourism, with two museums, 1 bed-and-breakfast, 1 RV park, several vacation rental cabins, galleries showcasing local artists, and antiques shops that have joined the gas station, general store, restaurant, and a few residences that straddle the highway. At the southern end of town, you can tour the five-story, 1,200-ton gold dredge that sits in its pond at the **Sumpter Valley Dredge State Heritage Area,** where millions of dollars' worth of gold were extracted. Sumpter has also gained a reputation for its Memorial Day, July 4th, and Labor Day flea markets.

Leaving Sumpter, the highway enters a thick forest, which will fill the roadside for most of the 16 miles to Granite. A side road heads north to **Bourne,** a picture-perfect ghost town The former town of 1,500 was at the center of hardrock mining, and a few privately owned claims are still producing. About 3 miles west you reenter the national forest at **McCully Forks Campground,** where you can camp in a pine forest with 7 tent sites.

Near the campground the road starts a dramatic climb, winding around ridges with distant forests and towering mountain peaks providing some of the drive's most striking scenery. The formations represent three distinct types of rocks from three time periods. Initially ancient sea sediments hardened into sandstone. Later, molten rock solidified into granite and was covered by more recent volcanic basalt flows. Glaciers, wind, and water have refined the mountains and valleys into the craggy peaks and steep slopes you see today.

Blue Springs Summit, at 5,864 feet, is a popular snowmobile area and signals the beginning of several miles of live, dead, downed, and logged trees that were victims of a mid-1970s Pine Mountain beetle infestation. **Boundary Guard Station,** north of the summit, was built during the Great Depression by the Civilian Conservation Corps and is worth a stop to see its many unique details.

Granite

Granite, a few miles farther north, is also nearly a ghost town with a booming past tied to gold. A store, a few residences, and abandoned buildings stand isolated among the evergreens.

For a venture into the deep woods, take FR 10 10.5 miles south to **Fremont Powerhouse.** Built in 1908 and used until 1967, it still contains massive turbines and other equipment. You'll see portions of the wood and steel pipeline that supplied water from **Olive Lake** along FR 10.

Granite represents the last fuel, lodging, and food for 57 miles. FR 73, which takes you north and east 26 miles to Anthony Lakes, starts with 8 miles of patchy, rough road through the Crane Creek area. Deer and elk are often seen along here in early mornings and evenings. The road also passes the **Chinese Walls**—large boulders and rock embankments that were worked by Asian miners more than 100 years ago.

The Elkhorn and Blue Mountain Scenic Byways meet at **North Fork John Day Campground.** With 20 tent/trailer sites, the John Day campground is a jumping-off point to the **John Day Wilderness,** plus area hiking and horseback riding trails. The river supports one of the largest spawning populations of wild spring chinook and summer steelhead. About 54 miles are set aside as a National Wild and Scenic River.

The Elkhorn loop continues east, passing alpine meadows and clear cuts with majestic peaks forming an amphitheater for smaller mountains and valleys, along with the aftermath of recent forest fires.

Elkhorn Mountain Summit, Grande Ronde & Anthony Lakes

After about 16 miles FR 73 crosses **Elkhorn Mountain Summit.** At 7,392 feet elevation, it is the highest point on the drive. A summit pullout overlooks the headwaters of the Grande Ronde River. **Grande Ronde Lake** sits nestled in a thick Douglas fir forest and is another prime spot for watching deer, and for use as a base camp for exploring the high country by hiking, biking, and horseback. Known for brown trout fishing, it is also popular with cross-country skiers. A lakeside campground has 8 sites but is not suitable for large trailers or motor homes.

At the Sumpter Valley Dredge State Heritage Area you can get up close to an historic gold dredge. Licensed by Shutterstock.com.

Anthony Lakes, a mile east of Grande Ronde Lake, receives an average annual snowfall of 300 inches and is famous for its powder snow. Its base elevation of 7,100 feet is the highest in Oregon. The ski area contains 21 downhill runs and serves as the hub for more than 400 miles of cross-country skiing and snowmobile trails. The season generally starts around Thanksgiving and lasts through mid-April. Facilities include a day lodge with food service, a deli bar, and a lounge, plus a ski school and Nordic center. If you want to see the backcountry there's a Cat-ski tour with guides to take you out and back via transfer vehicles pulled by caterpiller trackers.

A national forest recreation area surrounding the ski complex provides hiking and biking trails and camping and fishing at mountain lakes. **Mud Lake Campground** has 8 tent sites. **Anthony Lakes Campground** offers 10 tent and 21 tent/trailer sites in one of eastern Oregon's most picturesque settings. The lake, a 50-yard stroll from the ski lodge, is ringed by thick Douglas fir, tamarack, lodgepole, and white fir with a towering mountain behind it. Eleven- to 14-inch brook trout are common catches, along with brown and rainbow trout. From campsite, fishing area, or boat, you may see elk, deer, and other wildlife.

High Country Trails

The 22.5-mile **Elkhorn Crest National Recreation Trail** begins near the ski area. It is the Blue Mountains' highest trail and links with several shorter trails, taking you through valleys, by 6 remote lakes and spectacular peaks, and into the North Fork John Day Wilderness.

From Anthony Lakes the drive descends 8 miles of steep grade through a narrow, brushy canyon. A midway viewpoint overlooks the pastoral Baker Valley and the distant Wallowa Mountains near the Idaho border. **Dutch Creek Flat Trail,** 3 miles east, offers a final trek into the high country with an 11-mile walk through beautiful meadows by secluded **Dutch Flat Lake** and then joins the **Elkhorn Crest Trail.**

As the road straightens and enters the flat, open fields of the Baker Valley, you'll pass an entrance to **Pilcher Creek Reservoir,** where you can fish for rainbow trout. There are 12 campsites, a boat ramp, and a winter elk feeding station. The valley is a major livestock, hay, and grain producer; expect to see modern farms, meadows, and aging barns. Signs along the highway direct you to the Elkhorn Wildlife Area, a major winter feeding area for hundreds of mule deer and Rocky Mountain elk.

To Haines & Baker City

South to Haines and Baker City, your drive concludes with roadside pastures framed by the majestic peaks of the Blue Mountains, which rise abruptly from the plain and are often tinged with a purple haze.

Haines, population 395, has a quaint country church and general store. **Eastern Oregon Museum** preserves some of the region's rowdy past with brewery wagons, bootleggers' stills, a saloon bar, steam-powered threshing machines, and arrowheads.

At Haines the route joins US 30, which briefly parallels the Oregon Trail. You may wish to make a final stop at the **Wallowa-Whitman National Forest Ranger Station** on US 30 in Baker for information on Hells Canyon and other recreational opportunities in this vast forest. The station also issues backcountry permits, trail maps, and campground information.

32

LaGrande, Ukiah, Weston Loop

General Description: A 170-mile paved loop drive along the Grande Ronde River; through a wildlife test area, wheat fields, and farmlands; and into the Blue Mountains.

Special Attractions: Oregon Trail and Walla Walla Historic Trail routes, state parks and waysides, 2 national forests, elk habitat test area, mountain and valley scenery, Umatilla Indian Reservation, Spout Springs Ski Area.

Location: Northeastern Oregon between LaGrande, Ukiah, Pendleton, and Weston.

Drive Route Numbers: I-84, OR 244, US 395, OR 11, OR 204, Summerville Road.

Travel Season: All year. Snow and ice can create extremely dangerous driving conditions on US 395 at Battle Mountain State Park and on OR 204.

Camping: 6 forest service campgrounds with picnic tables, vault toilets, and fire rings; some with water. 2 state park campgrounds with primitive sites.

Services: All services in LaGrande and Pendleton. Limited services in Ukiah, Pilot Rock, Weston, and Tollgate.

Nearby Attractions: Oregon Trail route and interpretive center, Blue Mountain Scenic Byway, Elkhorn Scenic Byway, Whitman Mission National Historic Site, Farewell Bend State Park.

For More Information: Union County Chamber of Commerce, (541) 963-8588, (800) 848-9969, www.unioncounty chamber.org; Pendleton Chamber of Commerce (541) 276-7411, (800) 547-8911, www.pendletonchamber.com; Wallowa-Whitman National Forest, LaGrande Ranger District, (541) 963-7186, www.fs.usda.gov/ wallow-whitman; Umatilla National Forest, (541) 278-3716; North Fork John Day Ranger District, (541) 427-3231, www .fs.usda.gov/umatilla.

The Route

From **LaGrande** at 2,788 feet elevation, the drive crosses a variety of terrain and vegetation as it heads southwest through the Grande Ronde River bottomlands and plateaus to **Ukiah.** Turning north, it crosses **Battle Mountain** and descends to flat, rolling wheat fields and agricultural lands near Pendleton, where it parallels the historic **Walla Walla Trail** and the **Umatilla Indian Reservation** northeast to **Weston.** Taking OR 204 southeast, the drive climbs through the Umatilla National Forest to over 5,000 feet near **Spout Springs,** then returns through a steep canyon and farmlands.

At lower elevations summer travelers can expect temperatures in the high 80s, low 90s, and over 100 degrees. While winter days sometimes drop to near zero, the teens, and 20s, temperatures usually average between 39 and 49 degrees. Pendleton usually has a little milder weather. Spring days average about 65 degrees. Autumn temperatures range from 64 to 77 degrees.

LaGrande, Ukiah, Weston Loop

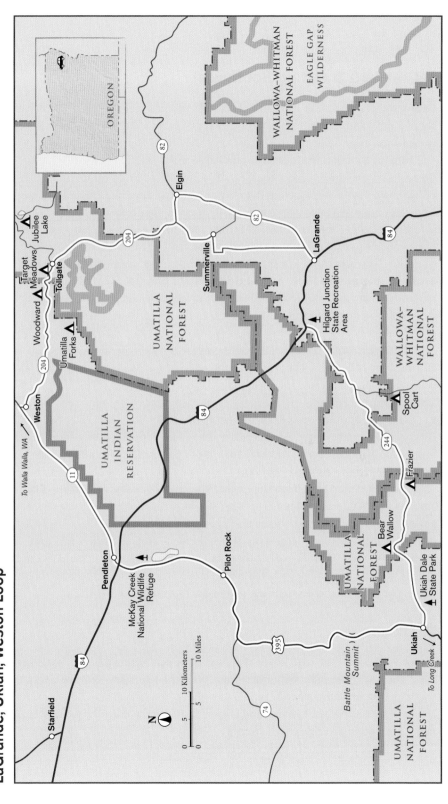

LaGrande & Traveling Southwest

LaGrande was named for its beautiful setting. As you travel north on I-84, drive about 1 mile, and take exit 252 southwest on OR 44, you are treated to an awesome landscape of steep mountains, isolated monoliths, deep valleys, and ravines.

Hilgard Junction State Recreation Area, at the junction of the two highways, sits on the north bank of the Grande Ronde River. From campground and picnic areas, you can look across the river and see the sheer bluffs where Oregon Trail wagons and livestock were lowered by ropes to the riverbank. The park is a departure point for river rafters and trout, salmon, and steelhead anglers. You can camp in the shadows of the high bluffs and on the riverbank in 17 primitive campsites. You also can see original Oregon Trail ruts at nearby **Blue Mountain Crossing Interpretive Park.** At **Red Bridge State Wayside,** 4 miles west, the shallow river invites wading and fishing. Paths meander under tall oaks and ponderosa pines along the north bank, and you can camp in 10 walk-in tent and 10 primitive sites.

During the next 10 miles, the road leaves the forested corridor of the canyon and cuts across flat hills. The river deepens, widens, and shares the landscape with lava outcroppings, isolated stands of pine, meadows laced with ravines, and occasional farms and corrals.

Near FR 51, which provides access to the Blue Mountain and Elkhorn Scenic Byways, the Grande Ronde River bends south through meadows to its headwaters in the Blue Mountains. You leave the hills as OR 244 enters 2.38-million-acre **Wallowa-Whitman National Forest.**

The thin ribbon of national forest that you cross contains the **Starkey Elk Habitat and Wilderness Area.** This one-of-a-kind test area encompasses 25,000 acres of forest and range where the effects of cattle, deer, and elk on managed forests are studied on a long-term basis. If you decide to stop and take a self-guided wildlife tour, you'll become part of the data for counters and cameras that record vehicle traffic. Information gathered from Starkey research has influenced forest, range, road, travel, and deer and elk management throughout the US.

To Ukiah

About 5 miles west the road leaves Wallowa-Whitman National Forest and enters 1.4-million-acre **Umatilla National Forest.** Near the boundary, short roads lead south to **Frazier Campground.** With 5 tent and 27 tent/trailer sites, Frazier serves as a base for trail bikers, hunters, and anglers. It is also the northern gateway to a maintained off-road vehicle trail system.

Nez Perce Indians once picked huckleberries in this area, and berry picking is still a popular activity, along with cross-country skiing, snowmobiling, hunting, hiking, swimming, and gathering mushrooms.

On the 16 miles to Ukiah, **Camas Creek** weaves in and away from the highway. It commands attention along a roadside of scrub brush, clear-cuts with graying stumps, and low, rolling dry grass hills. Two Umatilla National Forest campgrounds sit in a stand of ponderosa about 6 miles west of the hot springs. An interpretive trail at **Bear Wallow Creek,** which has 8 tent/trailer sites, explains the life cycle of salmon and their habitat requirements. **Adjacent Lane Creek Campground,** 1 mile west, has 6 tent/trailer sites and 1 group site.

Ukiah draws autumn deer and elk hunters, and local rivers are known for their exceptional early spring steelhead fishing. OR 244 meets US 395 west of town. **Ukiah-Dale Campground,** 3 miles south of the junction, is an Oregon state park with 27 primitive sites on the North Fork John Day River. The park is a base for fishing, camping, mountain biking, and snow sports.

Battle Mountain

North of Ukiah, US 395 splits the **Camas Prairie flatlands,** which are particularly scenic in spring when camas lily sunflowers and Indian paintbrush mix with sagebrush, grass, and juniper trees. After about 13 miles you begin weaving through yellow and white pine, tamarack, and western larch on the climb to **Battle Mountain**'s 4,270-foot summit. A general store with gas and groceries and a few residences are scattered among the trees on the south slopes.

Battle Mountain State Scenic Corridor, about 0.4 mile north of the summit, offers a refreshing break with picnic tables and lawns on a ridge shaded by Douglas fir, ponderosa, and planted spruce. The park commemorates the decisive engagement of the **Bannock War,** which was fought in the Battle Mountain foothills on July 8, 1878. It marked the last major Indian uprising in the Pacific Northwest. This was a Civilian Conservation Corps camp during the 1930s, and a stone fireplace built by the CCC is still in use.

As you leave the forest and continue north, the undulating line of the horizon is virtually unbroken, save for a lone grain elevator and a few horse corrals. Depending on the season and crop rotation, the fields are a blanket of fresh greens, golden wheat, and dark and light browns mixed with silver-blue sage and dark green bitterbrush.

About 12 miles north of Battle Mountain, US 395 intersects with OR 74 to Heppner, and the Blue Mountain Scenic Byway, and heads east through a ravine where ice and water have created a series of dark lava benches. Watch the marshland and fields south of the road, and you may see deer grazing or hawks swooping from rock to meadows. Two miles east, at **Pilot Rock,** US 395 separates grain elevators, log decks, gas stations, and a motel. Pilot Rock's **Bike Pit** is a nonprofit 32-acre public park built for motorcycle, ATV, and bicycle riders. Except for special events, it is open to the public at no charge.

McKay Creek National Wildlife Refuge & Traveling East

McKay Creek National Wildlife Refuge, 8 miles south of Pendleton, surrounds a reservoir that serves boaters and water-skiers. Warm-water game fish are plentiful, and the variety of crappie, smallmouth and largemouth bass, perch, catfish, and trout makes it a fishing hot spot. You may also see nesting osprey, bald and golden eagles, wintering Canada geese, and more than 33,000 ducks. It also draws pheasant and quail hunters.

At I-84 you turn east and after a couple of miles, take exit 213 onto OR 11. Traveling northeast through Pendleton, the highway follows the historic **Walla Walla Trail,** which was an Oregon Trail departure point for Washington-bound wagons that followed the spur to Whitman Mission.

Woolen mills and rodeos have brought Pendleton enduring fame. Its lively history is interpreted at the **Pendleton Round-Up Hall of Fame,** in brochures for walking/driving tours of Victorian homes, and through guided underground tours into tunnels constructed during the late 1800s by Chinese laborers. **Pendleton Woolen Mills** offers free tours and a salesroom Monday through Friday at the **Pendleton Blanket Mill** (1307 SE Court St., Pendleton; 541-276-6911). The woolen mills date to 1863 and are known worldwide for their quality blankets, men's woolen shirts, and other products. Local Indians brought the mills designs to be woven into blankets and thus became some of their first customers.

Umatilla Indian Reservation

In north Pendleton you cross the Umatilla River, which extends about 25 miles northeast through the **Umatilla Indian Reservation.** The reservation is home to a confederation of the Cayuse, Umatilla, and Walla Walla tribes, which have lived on the Columbia River plateau for over 10,000 years. At the **Tamastslikt Cultural Institute** you can learn about their cultures past and present, types of lodging from ancient times to the present, and watch tribe members practice traditional crafts, such as drying fish and weaving mats. At **Wildhorse Resort and Casino** you have the option of 98 hotel rooms, 100 RV sites with hookups, or camping and spending the night in a tepee. The complex includes a golf course and children's entertainment center.

To Weston

Twelve miles north, between Mission and Athena, the landscape becomes a geo-metric hodgepodge of squares, boxes, rectangles, and diamond-shaped green, brown, and yellow fields. **Athena's** Scotch heritage is celebrated in July's **Caledonian Days** with caber tossing, sheepdog trials, and a highland dance competition.

Weston dates to 1865. Its business district of mostly brick buildings is on the National Register of Historic Places. At Weston you turn southeast on OR 204, which starts with a gradual 6-mile, 3,500-foot climb up **Weston Hill.** At the top the commanding view includes the Blue Mountains, Walla Walla River, rugged Storm Canyon, Table Mountain, and a sea of wheat.

To Umatilla National Forest

As you continue climbing, the roadside is sprinkled with meadows, stands of ponderosa pine, scattered homes, picturesque barns, and Christmas tree farms. **Weston Lake** is at mile marker 10 and sits near a cluster of homes and cabins; it attracts local trout anglers. Clover, lupine, and other wildflowers add colorful touches and a fragrant aroma to springtime travel.

Reentering the **Umatilla National Forest,** the highway passes a winter recre-ation area. Several trails invite short hikes through a sparse ground cover and into a mixed forest of white fir, blue spruce, tamarack, ponderosa, and white pine.

North Fork Umatilla Trail begins near a roadside viewpoint and provides the nearest access to **North Fork Umatilla Wilderness,** a few miles west of the high-way. The wilderness, which you'll see from the overlook, is nestled in the North Fork Umatilla River's narrow valley. Despite some steep timbered cliffs, it is popu-lar with day hikers and horseback riders.

Nearby, the tiny community of **Tollgate** spreads along the highway and around small, private **Langdon Lake Woodward Campground**'s 15 tent/trailer sites serve as a base for trail bikers. Since Langdon Lake is private, campers cannot access it. **Target Meadows Campground,** 2 miles east of the highway, offers 18 tent/trailer and 2 tent sites.

Jubilee Lake & to Summerville

Jubilee Lake, 12 miles east of Tollgate via FR 6413, is a favorite of nonmotor-ized boaters, water-skiers, swimmers, and trout anglers. At **Jubilee Campground** you can overnight camp on one of the 48 tent/trailer or 5 tent sites at 4,800 feet. It is the largest and most popular campground in the Umatilla Forest and is surrounded by magnificent trees and mountain peaks. A 2.8-mile wheelchair-accessible trail circles the lake.

The 4 miles between Tollgate and Spout Springs Ski Area is a popular snowmobile route lined with blown-down trees, which were leveled by a rare windstorm several years ago. **Spout Springs** is one of Oregon's oldest continuously operating ski areas. Situated at 5,400 feet on **Tollgate Summit** of the Blue Mountains, it has 2 chairlifts and a T-bar. Most of Spout Springs' 14 ski runs serve beginning and intermediate skiers. There are also 11 miles of cross-country trails, which become hiking and mountain biking routes in summer. A chalet-style lodge with a cafe operates year-round.

A mile east of Spout Springs, the drive crosses the **Blue Mountains summit** at 5,158 feet. You can spend the night near the summit in 5 tent/trailer sites at **Woodland Campground.** From the summit you wind down the mountain on a steep grade through a deep, thickly forested canyon.

After about 12 miles you exit the Umatilla National Forest and turn west on Summerville Road. **Summerville,** 4 miles south, was an Indian and Oregon Trail campsite. Established in 1865, it enjoyed a rowdy history with numerous saloons, 24-hour poker games, and stagecoach holdups.

On the remaining 13 miles to LaGrande, field crops and low hills fill the eastern horizon. The forested slopes of the Blue Mountains rise from the valley floor to the west. If you are an ATVer, OHVer, or mountain biker you may want to conclude your sightseeing with a stop at **Mount Emily Recreation Area,** 2 miles north of LaGrande on Fox Hill Road. You can explore its 3,670 acres on 30 miles of easy to difficult trails for Class I, II, and III ATVs. There are also 12 miles of trails for horseback riders, mountain bikers, snowshoers, and cross-country skiers. It also has free dry camping, a day-use area, and a children's riding area. As you meander over the slopes, you're treated to changing views of the Grande Ronde Valley, the distant Eagle Cap Wilderness, spring wildflowers, and possible sightings of deer, bear, elk, and other wildlife.

33

Oregon Trail Route: I-84

General Description: A 190-mile drive on paved roads through desert and grasslands and over the Blue Mountains while following the route of the Oregon Trail.

Special Attractions: Oregon Trail ruts, campsites, and interpretive center; state parks; Blue Mountains; wildlife observation; historic sites; boating.

Location: Northeastern Oregon between Ontario and Echo.

Drive Route Numbers: I-84, US 30, OR 86, Echo Road.

Travel Season: All year. Deadman Pass can become extremely hazardous in winter due to snow, ice, and its steep grade.

Camping: 3 state park campgrounds, 1 with full hookups, 1 with electricity, and 1 with primitive sites. One Bureau of Land Management campground with tables, fire rings, vault or flush toilets, and drinking water.

Services: All services in Ontario, Baker City, LaGrande, and Pendleton. Limited services at Farewell Bend, Huntington, North Powder, and Echo.

Nearby Attractions: Lake Owyhee Scenic Drive, Eagle Cap Wilderness, Hells Canyon Scenic Byway, LaGrande–Ukiah–Weston Scenic Loop, Elkhorn Scenic Byway.

For More Information: Union County Chamber of Commerce, (541) 963-8588, (800) 848-9969, www.unioncounty chamber.org; Baker County Chamber of Commerce and Visitors Bureau, (541) 523-5855, (888) 523-5855, www.visitbaker .com; City of Echo, (541) 376-8411, www .echo-oregon.com; Ontario Chamber of Commerce/Visitor & Convention Bureau, (541) 889-8012, (866) 989-8012, www .ontariochamber.com; Pendleton Chamber of Commerce, (541) 276-7411, (800) 547-8911, www.pendletonchamber .com; Wallowa-Whitman National Forest, (541) 523-6391, www.fs.usda.gov/ wallowa-whitman.

The Route

From 1841 through 1884 the Oregon Trail was the major east–west route from the Idaho border to Portland. **I-84** parallels and overlaps portions of the trail between Farewell Bend State Recreation Area and Pendleton.

The original trail followed centuries-old Indian paths that had been used by early explorers and fur traders and wove over mountain passes, through valleys, and across rivers formed by more than 200 million years of geologic activity. The shape of the land has dictated routes of travel from the dawn of man to today.

From Ontario to Ladd Canyon, south of LaGrande, the highway crosses flat desert, wide valleys, rolling sand, gray and brown hills, and mountains. It is a land of little water, covered with sparse, pale grass sprinkled with juniper trees. Between LaGrande and Pendleton, the route climbs high into the Blue Mountains, then abruptly descends to flat fields.

Oregon Trail Route: I-84

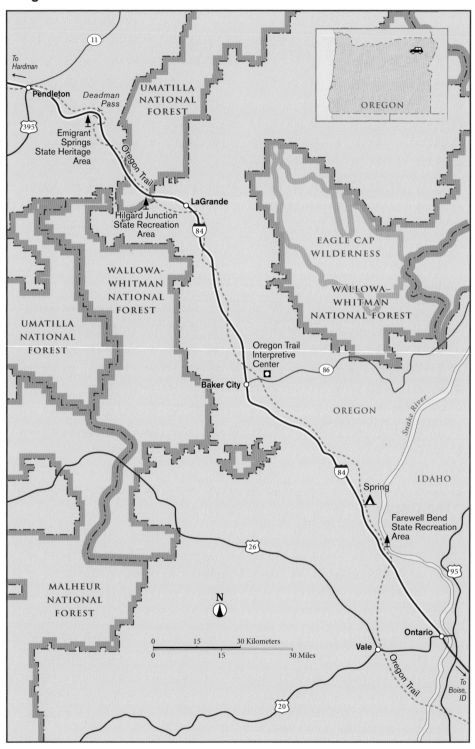

In summer temperatures jump to the high 80s and 90s, and over 100 degrees. Winter days can drop to zero but usually average between 39 and 49 degrees. Spring days average around 65 degrees, autumn about 70 degrees.

The Oregon Trail entered the state about 9 miles south of Ontario near Nyssa, meandered west, and extended north over rolling hills. About 23 miles north of Ontario, it entered Farewell Bend. Information boards at **Ontario State Recreation Site,** exit 374, highlight the history of migration and life on the trail. The park is on the west bank of the Snake River and offers a pleasant shaded spot for a picnic. Blue herons, otter, and other wildlife are sometimes seen along the river shoreline.

Seventeen miles north of Ontario, I-84 passes tilted and faulted formations of 15 million–year–old rocks. As you climb a long hill, the Snake River spreads in a gently curving bay to the east.

Farewell Bend

At **Farewell Bend,** exit 353, wagon trains saw the last of the Snake River, which they had followed for 320 miles. Here they rested and grazed livestock before attempting the mountainous terrain ahead.

The large lakelike river, with shaded picnic grounds and a campground with 101 electrical and 30 tent sites, hiker/biker camp, and 2 cabins, remains a popular spot for catfish and bass fishing, water-skiers, jet boaters, and swimmers. Hotels, restaurants, and gas stations are situated along the 1-mile entrance road.

From Farewell Bend the Oregon Trail headed northeast over a low divide and into the Burnt River drainage to Huntington, then meandered along eastern ridges 40 miles north to Flagstaff Hill. **Huntington,** a former frontier and cattle-shipping town, offers food, gas, and a BLM campground with 35 sites and drinking water. It boasts of being the catfish capital of Oregon. The Catfish Junction RV Park sells tackle, bait, and fishing licenses and provides a fish-cleaning station.

Burnt River Canyon

North of Farewell Bend, I-84 enters the Pacific and Mountain Time Zones (Pacific if traveling west and Mountain if traveling east) and cuts through the nearly 200 million–year–old sedimentary rocks of the **Lower Burnt River Canyon.** The rocks provided raw materials and jobs for 145 people at Lime's cement plant. About 5 miles north, on the highway's west side, you'll see the gray terraced hillsides and buildings left abandoned when the plant closed in 1980.

I-84 emerges from the **Burnt River Canyon** about 4 miles north. The canyon was a major obstacle for wagon trains, and it took pioneers five to six days to cross the 15 miles, which you will travel in a few minutes from Farewell Bend. The rigors of traveling this section are detailed at the **Weatherby Rest Area** at exit 335.

Farewell Bend State Recreation Area, today one of the most popular recreation sites in the state, was once a stopover for Oregon Trail wagon trains.

Hills, rocks, and flatlands of the **Conner Creek Fault,** near the exit, are fragments of 170 million– to 280 million–year–old ocean floors and islands that were broken, fused together, and moved here when tectonic plates shifted.

The sandstone is processed into cement at Durkee's Ash Grove plant. Between Durkee, exit 330, and Pleasant Valley, exit 315, the Oregon Trail and I-84 merge for about 15 miles. The banks of the Burnt River near Durkee often yield colorful fire opals. Pleasant Valley was settled by Oregon Trail farmers.

North Through Baker City

The highway weaves between **Iron Mountain,** an ancient volcanic neck, and **Elkhorn Ridge,** a fragment of a 200 million–year–old ocean floor. As you continue to Baker City and LaGrande, several western peaks dominate the horizon. From south to north they are: **Elkhorn,** 8,922 feet; **Rock Creek Butte,** 9,097 feet; **Hunt Mountain,** 8,232 feet; **Red Mountain,** 8,920 feet; and **Twin Mountains,** 8,920 feet.

North of Pleasant Valley you reach a 3,998-foot summit and continue on to **Baker City,** while the Oregon Trail skirts mountain slopes and heads north to Flagstaff Hill.

By taking exit 302 at Baker City, 7 miles east on OR 86, you can see original

Oregon Trail ruts at the base of 3,800-foot **Flagstaff Hill.** The **Oregon Trail Interpretive Center,** at the summit, features a gallery with life-size figures in scenes depicting trail life. Six major trail themes are interpreted through diary excerpts, photographs, and audiovisual displays. From the observation platform you have a magnificent view of the valley, mountains, and Baker City. The **Baker Heritage Museum** displays more Oregon Trail artifacts, along with one of the state's largest rock and mineral collections, and farming and ranching implements.

I-84 heads north from Baker City, flanked on the east by sagebrush flatlands and the distant white peaks of the Wallowa Mountains. By contrast, the glacier-carved Elkhorns rise behind green pasturelands to the west. The highway crosses the Oregon Trail at a rest area 14 miles north of Baker and stays on or near the route through Pendleton.

45th Parallel

Near the rest area, immigrants bartered with itinerant traders and found food and water for livestock. A few miles north, when you cross the **45th parallel,** you are halfway between the equator and the North Pole. At North Powder the trail passes through town along E Street. Three miles northeast on OR 237, a monument commemorates the first recorded birth on December 3, 1811, of a white child born west of the Rockies. From the North Powder exit, you can travel west to the Anthony Lakes Ski Area and US 30, which overlaps portions of the trail near Haines.

The red and yellow streaks that you'll see in I-84's embankments are layers of individual Columbia River basalt lava flows. Numerous eruptions between 6 million and 17 million years ago covered approximately 45,000 square miles of Oregon, Washington, and Idaho.

Ladd Canyon

The hills open into **Ladd Canyon,** which gave up its lush green grass to wagon-train livestock. Between 1843 and 1859 more than 350,000 settlers entered the Grande Ronde Valley near the **Charles H. Reynolds Rest Area,** at the canyon's southern edge. **Ladd Marsh Wildlife and Nature Trail** provides viewpoints to watch wildlife along a 1-mile path near one of the area's largest wetlands and a 1,200-acre elk habitat.

By taking exit 268 to Foothill Road and traveling east 2 miles, you can visit **Hot Lake,** another refreshment point on the trail. In the 1920s Hot Lake was a famous resort. After fire destroyed half of it, the building was abandoned and remained vacant for decades. Restoration began in 2003 and after seven years of rebuilding and refurbishing, it opened as a multi-complex with a bed-and-breakfast, history center featuring military and Native American artifacts, artists' studio, mineral springs, and spa. A commercial RV park nearby has 100 spaces, a store, and a seasonal pool/spa. The main brick building is listed on the National Register of Historic Places.

You can follow the general route of the Oregon Trail west on Foothill Road through the Ladd Management Wildlife Area, where you may see deer and migrating waterfowl, to a trail campsite at Bernie Park in southwest LaGrande. From the park the trail continued west on Avenue C to Fourth Street, then headed over forested hills to the south bank of the Grande Ronde River.

Hilgard Junction

Leaving LaGrande on I-84, you travel northwest about 2 miles through the rugged canyon of the Grande Ronde River to exit 252 and **Hilgard Junction State Recreation Area,** where Oregon Trail travelers took advantage of the abundant water supply before climbing the Blue Mountain slopes. Looking across the picnic area, campground, and Grande Ronde River, you can see cliffs where wagons, cattle, and horses were lowered by ropes to the meadows below. Information boards highlight the route of the Oregon Trail from Hilgard Junction to the summit of the Blue Mountains, about 15 miles northwest and 1,200 feet higher. The park contains 17 primitive campsites and is a popular rafting and trout-fishing spot.

Continuing northwest, you'll follow essentially the same route as the wagon trains by traveling on forested ridges overlooking the narrow, twisting river canyon. After 2 miles the highway crosses a small segment of 2.38-million–acre **Wallowa-Whitman National Forest.** During the next 10 miles as the elevation increases, trees become shorter and the trunks smaller. Alpine meadows break the forest's continuity.

Emigrant Springs

Reaching the Blue Mountains' summit at 4,193 feet, the route passes **Meacham,** where several emigrant graves are situated and you can see the deep ruts along short walking trails near the summit. At **Meacham Divide Nordic Ski Area,** off exit 243, you can enjoy the magnificent mountain and valley scenery on 18 miles of groomed trails.

At **Emigrant Springs,** exit 234, forest, springs, and meadows provided ready supplies of firewood, water, wild game, and grass for livestock. An Oregon Trail exhibit covers disasters and hazards, death and disease, and the importance of horses and oxen to pioneer travel. The state heritage area includes a stone Oregon Trail monument dedicated by Warren G. Harding in 1923, a group picnic area, and a meeting hall. Although the springs were destroyed by highway and pipeline construction, the park still offers camping at 8 full-hookup and 15 tent sites, and

8 cabins in a thick ponderosa, western larch, and Douglas fir forest. From **Squaw Creek Lookout** north of the campground, you have a good view of Squaw Creek Canyon.

Deadman Pass & Pendleton

About 4 miles west, you enter the southern section of the **Umatilla Indian Reservation,** which was established in 1856. Its facilities include a 98-room hotel, 100-space RV park, and scenic golf course. **Deadman Pass Rest Area,** at exit 228, straddles the highway in two sections. At the southern segment, accessible by a tunnel under I-84, you can see original Oregon Trail ruts by going through a gate and up a short trail. Information boards explain the trail's numerous side routes. The pass was named after four freighters who were killed near here by Indians in 1878.

At Deadman Pass the highway starts 6 miles of 6 percent downgrade. Slower speeds are recommended even in the best of weather; winter weather can make this stretch extremely dangerous. The winding road has a brake-check area and two runaway-truck ramps. From a viewpoint about 1.5 miles below the summit, the panoramic view includes the Cascade and Blue Mountains, rumpled hills covered with forest and hazy grasslands, and a checkerboard of green, yellow, and brown fields. At the mountain's base the route leaves the Umatilla Indian Reservation and passes the turnoff to the Walla Walla Trail, which leads north to Whitman Mission in Washington state.

Rodeos and woolen mills have made **Pendleton** famous. The rodeo's memorable moments are preserved at the **Pendleton Round-Up Hall of Fame,** and you can also tour the woolen mills and shop for bargains in its salesroom.

West of Pendleton the trail veers southwest across 20 miles of wheat and farmland to **Echo** (population 715). **Fort Henrietta** was established as a Umatilla Indian Agency, destroyed during the Indian Wars of 1855, and rebuilt as a military stockade. It was an Oregon Trail campsite and river crossing and has been designated a National Historic Trail Site by the National Park Service. The park includes covered wagon and antique firefighting equipment museums, the first Umatilla County jail, and a replica blockhouse. The adjacent Fort Henrietta RV park has 7 spaces with electrical, water, sewerage, and cable hookups.

Echo is a designated National Historic District, with 10 buildings on the National Register of Historic Places. They include the **Chinese House Railroad Museum,** dating to 1883, 3 historic cemeteries, and the 1920s Roman classical–style **Echo Bank Building and Historical Museum.** You can see them all with a self-guiding brochure that covers 23 historic buildings and sites. You can reach Echo either by exit 193 to Echo Road or by continuing about 12 miles west of Pendleton on I-84 and turning south at the Stanfield Rest Area.

34

Imnaha River, Hat Point Overlook

General Description: A 58-mile drive on paved and dirt roads through scenic canyons and into the mountains of the Hells Canyon National Recreation Area.

Special Attractions: Joseph, Wallowa Lake State Park, Wallowa-Whitman National Forest, Wild and Scenic Imnaha River, Hells Canyon National Recreation Area, Hat Point Overlook, North America's deepest gorge, Snake River.

Location: Northeastern Oregon between Enterprise and Hat Point.

Drive Route Numbers: OR 82, Imnaha Road, FR 4240.

Travel Season: FR 4240 to Hat Point is usually open from July through October. OR 82 and Imnaha Road remain open all year.

Camping: 1 state park campground with full hookups. 4 forest service campgrounds with tables, fire rings, and pit or vault toilets.

Services: All services in Enterprise and Joseph. Limited services in Imnaha.

Nearby Attractions: Hells Canyon Wilderness, Eagle Cap Wilderness, LaGrande–Wallowa–Hells Canyon–Baker Scenic Loop Drive.

For More Information: Wallowa County Chamber of Commerce, (541) 426-4622, (800) 585-4121, www.wallowacounty chamber.com; Wallowa-Whitman National Forest, (541) 523-6391; Eagle Cap Ranger District, (541) 426-5546, (541) 426-4978; Hells Canyon National Recreation Area, (541) 426-5546, www.fs.usda.gov/wallowa-whitman.

The Route

Beginning in **Enterprise** at 3,757 feet elevation, the drive travels the first 14 miles through level farm country framed by the magnificent Wallowa Mountains. After descending into a rugged canyon for 21 miles, the pavement ends at the tiny community of **Imnaha.** The final 24 miles to **Hat Point** climbs to 6,982 feet on a narrow, rough, and rocky dirt road. The scenery is spectacular as the road clings to cliffs, weaves through forest, and winds by deep gorges, sheer cliffs, hills, and mountains. For many this final segment has an irresistible, almost mystical allure. Be forewarned, however. The forest service recommends two and a half hours of travel time one-way, and that doesn't include sightseeing stops. If you value your vehicle's undercarriage, do not attempt this with a sports car or other low-clearance vehicles. Also, sharp turns and the one-lane road bed make it unsuitable for trailers and motor homes. Leave your boat trailer at home or in Imnaha, for there is no place to launch it along the way.

Summer temperatures reach the high 80s in lower elevations and are somewhat cooler at Hat Point. Winters bring significant amounts of snow, as temperatures range from the mid-20s to the low 40s. Spring days average between 61 and 71 degrees, and autumn temperatures range from 64 to 77 degrees.

Imnaha River, Hat Point Overlook

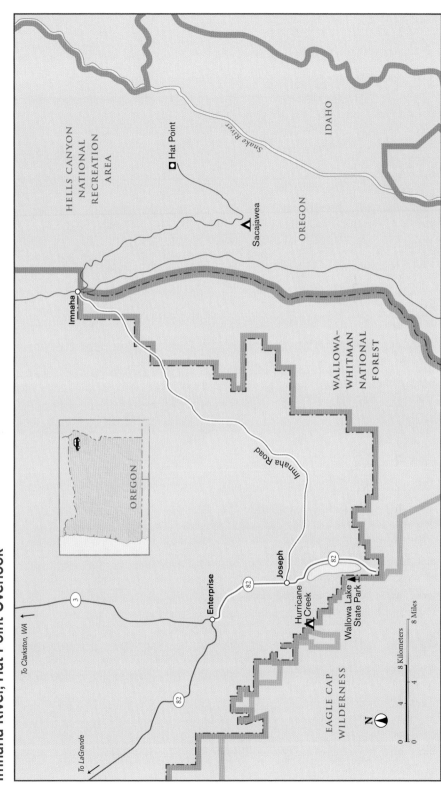

Before leaving Enterprise you may wish to stop at the **Wallowa-Whitman National Forest Visitor Center,** 1 mile west of town on OR 82. It offers displays on the Hells Canyon Recreation Area and the Wallowa Mountains, plus maps and camping information. If you plan to drive the Hat Point segment, check on road conditions. Cell tower coverage is limited.

Joseph

Joseph (population 967), 4 miles east, is a gateway to Hells Canyon and the Wallowa Mountains. During the 1980s the town became a mecca for artists. Many of the turn-of-the-20th-century buildings have been converted into shops, boutiques, and studios for sculptors, potters, painters, and photographers. A $3 million renovation created a cobblestone art walk with monument-size bronzes, museums, and a Nez Perce interpretive site.

Valley Bronze of Oregon has acquired a national reputation for its bronze, silver, sterling, and stainless steel sculptures. Its clients include the US Capitol Visitor Center and Washington, D.C.'s World War II Memorial. Several foundry tours show you the production process, from artists' clay models to the finished castings. They range from figurine-size to several-stories-high installations for public buildings and parks.

If you are camping, you can choose between 13 tent sites at the forest service's **Hurricane Creek Campground,** 6 miles southwest of Joseph on Hurricane Creek Road, or 121 full-hookup and 89 tent sites at **Wallowa Lake State Park,** 6 miles south of town on OR 82.

Wallowa Lake

Iwetemlaykin State Heritage Site is near Wallowa Lake's entrance and is adjacent to a Nez Perce National Historical Park Site that contains a cemetery with Old Chief Joseph's grave. He was the father of Chief Joseph. A short scenic trail leads through Iwetemlaykin, which is a Nez Perce word meaning "at the edge of the lake." **Wallowa Lake,** framed by the towering glacial peaks of the Wallowa Mountains and a mixed forest of white pine, ponderosa, and spruce, offers one of Oregon's most exquisite scenes. Easily accessible from OR 82, which hugs the northern and eastern shoreline, it is the hub for recreation that includes the state

From high atop Hat Point Overlook, the Snake River is over a mile below and appears as a thin ribbon of blue and green weaving its way through rugged mountains.

park, a resort, a mountain tramway, and hikes into the 349,987-acre **Eagle Cap Wilderness.** Anglers pull trophy-size rainbow trout, large catfish, kokanees, and mackinaws out of the water in summer and through winter ice. You can also water-ski, boat, swim, and enjoy the magnificent surroundings from rented rowboats, canoes, and paddleboats.

The region around the lake is often called the Little Switzerland of America. The **Wallowa Lake Tramway** has the steepest vertical lift for a four-passenger gondola in North America, and from lake level at 4,400 feet, it takes you on a spectacular 15-minute ride to the 8,200-foot summit of **Mount Howard.** At the top you can dine in Oregon's highest restaurant while enjoying the spectacular view encompassing the lake, the snowcapped mountains of the Eagle Cap Wilderness, forested foothills, and pastoral farmlands.

Imnaha Road

Taking **Imnaha Road** east from **Joseph,** you travel through lush pastures of grazing cattle, white board fences, and distant farm buildings situated at the base of the Wallowa Mountains that rise majestically in steep steps from the valley floor. **Ferguson Ridge Ski Area** (www.skifergi.com), 4 miles south of the highway, offers winter access to the mountains with a network of cross-country trails, alpine skiing, and snowboarding and a warming area. It has two 600-vertical-foot T-bar chairlifts to take you to a 5,200-foot summit. It has 7 runs with 35 percent rated easiest, 45 percent more difficult, and 20 percent most difficult. The longest run is 6,250 feet. Check in Joseph or call (541) 398-1167 or email Eagle Cap Ski Club through the website for operating times. NOTE: This is a community-owned and volunteer-operated ski area. It accepts cash and checks but no credit cards.

After 10 miles you weave down into a deep canyon with forested hills, past a few abandoned sheds, and along the side of the first of several creeks. Gradually the forest disappears, and the gorge narrows to steep basalt walls. Watch for cattle, sheep, and horses grazing on the greenery near the creek, for much of the wayside is not fenced.

Most of the twisted, massive rock walls you pass through came from volcanos that erupted on Pacific Ocean islands more than 300 million years ago. When the eruptions stopped, the region lowered into the ocean and sediment was deposited on the submerged platforms. Later geologic activity created basins that filled with sediments from surrounding streams and volcanic explosions of molten rock, which crystallized into granite. During and after these geologic processes, the rocks folded, faulted, and tilted. Wind, rain, and ice continue to deepen ravines that start on hillsides and converge by roadside creeks. With every twist and turn of the road, a new vista unfolds, and there are ample wide spots and turns to stop and photograph the surroundings. Due to rugged cliffs and steep embankments, opportunities for hiking and roadside treks are limited.

About 5 miles east of the canyon's entrance, the route begins riding the crest of low, dry grassland hills and weaves by more converging mountain ridges and through stands of ponderosa pine. In late spring the grass has an unusual moss-brown and green-velvet sheen. Near Imnaha you enter **Wallowa-Whitman National Forest** and the **Hells Canyon National Recreation Area.** At 2.38 million acres, Wallowa-Whitman is Oregon's largest national forest and stretches east into Idaho. The national recreation area includes the Hells Canyon Wilderness and the Rapid and Snake River segments of the National Wild and Scenic River System.

At **Imnaha,** 30 miles east of Joseph, the dirt road to Hat Point begins where the pavement ends at the community's sole restaurant-store. Look across the road and you can see the nationally designated Wild and Scenic Imnaha River flowing out of the wilderness. It was from along the Imnaha's banks that Chief Joseph gathered the Nez Perce tribe in May 1877 and began their famous fighting retreat to Canada, which ended in his defeat at Bear Paw Battlefield in Montana.

For overnighters the **Imnaha River Inn Bed and Breakfast** is a 7,000-square-foot log house with 7 themed rooms that include elk, bear, barn, Indian, antique, fishing hole, and cowboy bunkhouse. You may find yourself sharing a bathroom with anglers, hunters, skiers, rafters, hikers, and other outdoor enthusiasts who come to the Imnaha area to satisfy their pleasures.

The Road to Hat Point

In the first 5 miles from Imnaha, you'll climb 2,655 feet. At **Five Mile viewpoint** you have the first of many views of the Imnaha Canyon, Wallowa Mountains, and Sheep Creek Divide—a razor-sharp ridge that extends for miles.

The road then levels out and into ponderosa, lodgepole, and white pine. Watch the small meadows for Indian paintbrush, lupine, and several species of butterflies. You may hear the hoot of a horned owl and see mountain grouse and valley quail flutter from trees to rocks. Bobcats, cougars, and black bears also inhabit these woodlands but are rarely sighted.

At 9.7 miles you'll see several small rock cairns at **Monument Ridge,** which are thought to be boundary markers. Historians still debate whether they were built by Indians or sheepherders. About 1 mile farther, the road crosses a narrow ridge overlooking the walls of Imnaha and Horse Creek Canyons. At 17.1 miles a short loop leads 0.8 mile to **Granny Viewpoint,** where you can see the Imnaha River winding as a thin blue ribbon through pale yellow ridges 6,345 feet below. **Saddle Creek Viewpoint and Campground** at mile 18.8 overlooks Hells Canyon, which is accessible only by foot, pack string, or boat.

Several marked trails begin near Hat Point's summit. Most are 2 to 3 miles long and lead down off the ridge into the gorge. **Hat Point and Sacajawea Campgrounds,** 0.5 mile north of Hat Point, offer a total of 3 tent and 12 picnic sites. You'll need to bring all food and beverages, as there are no services or running water beyond Imnaha. Short side roads near the point lead to spectacular overlooks of deep valleys, natural amphitheaters, caves, and endless vistas of ridges, hills, and ravines.

Hat Point

From **Hat Point** you have the thrill of looking into North America's deepest gorge and seeing the Snake River more than 1 mile (6,982 feet) below you. Looking across the canyon into Idaho, you can see the craggy peaks of the Seven Devils Mountains. As you scan this land of serrated ridges, deep gorges, sweeping natural saddles, and plateaus, watch for elk in the valleys. Make sure to bring binoculars, for mountain goats may be seen on distant peaks and bighorn sheep on the high slopes.

For an even more encompassing view, you can climb a 100-foot-high forest service lookout tower that is manned during summer. A trail begins in the picnic area, meanders through wildflower meadows, and winds down the cliff to the canyon below.

On the return you have a second opportunity to view the spectacular scenery. Because of the rumpled topography and twisting road, much of it will look very different from what you saw driving to Hat Point.

35

Hells Canyon
Scenic Byway

General Description: A 270-mile scenic loop on paved roads through arid desert, lush farmlands, rugged canyons, and forested mountains.

Special Attractions: Historic sites, Joseph, Wallowa Lake State Park, Wallowa-Whitman National Forest, Wild and Scenic Rivers, Hells Canyon National Recreation Area, Oxbow Dam, Oregon Trail Interpretive Center, Eagle Cap Wilderness, wildlife observation, camping, fishing, hiking.

Location: Northeastern Oregon between LaGrande, Enterprise, Copperfield, and Baker City.

Drive Route Numbers: OR 82, Imnaha Road, FR 39, OR 86, I-84, OR 203.

Travel Season: With the exception of FR 39, all routes are open all year. FR 39 usually opens about mid-June and closes because of snow in late October or early November.

Camping: Three state park campgrounds, two with primitive sites and one with full hookups. Ten forest service campgrounds with tables, fire rings, and vault or flush toilets; some with drinking water.

Services: All services in LaGrande, Enterprise, Joseph, Richland, and Baker City. Limited services in Elgin, Wallowa, Halfway, and Copperfield.

Nearby Attractions: Hells Canyon Wilderness, Hat Point, LaGrande–Ukiah–Weston Scenic Loop, Elkhorn Scenic Byway, Farewell Bend State Park.

For More Information: Union County Chamber of Commerce, (541) 963-8588, (800) 848-9969; Baker County Chamber of Commerce & Visitors Bureau, (541) 523-5855, (800) 523-5855, www.visitbaker.com; Wallowa County Chamber of Commerce, (541) 426-4622, (800) 585-4121, www.wallowacountrychamber.com; Wallowa-Whitman National Forest, (541) 523-6391, www.fs.usda.gov/wallowa-whitman; Hells Canyon National Recreation Area, (541) 426-5546; Hells Canyon Scenic Byway, (541) 963-8588, (800) 848-9969, www.hellscanyonbyway.com.

The Route

The 225 miles from LaGrande to Baker City have been designated by the US Department of Transportation as **Hells Canyon Scenic Byway** and an All-American Road. From LaGrande to Joseph the route makes several crossings of the Wallowa and Grande Ronde Rivers as it winds through commercial croplands, dairy farms, and a scenic canyon. Turning south on FR 39, the drive extends through 54 miles of the Wallowa-Whitman National Forest and the Hells Canyon National Recreation Area. With the road climbing mountains, dipping into canyons, and swirling around ridges, you'll see the forest from a variety of vantage points. OR 86 also climbs mountains as it weaves west to Baker City through desert and arid grasslands along curves that are generally long and graceful and open onto spacious vistas. The final portion on OR 203 is divided between desert and forest.

Hells Canyon Scenic Byway

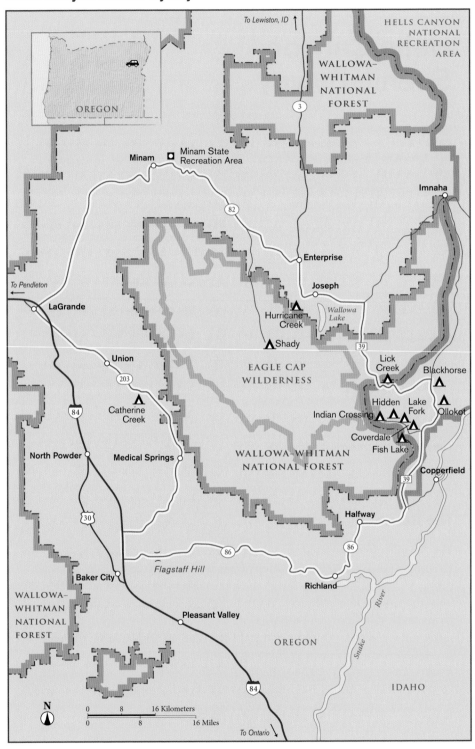

Because of the length, multiple attractions, and slow sections, plan a two-day trip with an overnight in either the Enterprise or Baker City areas. Traffic varies from light to heavy.

In the Oxbow, Baker City, and LaGrande areas, summer temperatures rise into the 80s, 90s, and over 100 degrees. At Enterprise and in the Hells Canyon Recreation Area, it will usually be 10 to 15 degrees cooler. Winters are cold and snowy, and temperatures may range from near zero to the mid-40s.

LaGrande, named for its beautiful setting, had its beginnings with a gold rush and today has many historic homes and brick business buildings. Stop by the **Eastern Oregon Fire Museum and Visitor Center** for a self-guiding walking brochure and to see several vintage fire engines. From LaGrande, OR 82 heads east through flat fields and small hamlets dominated by gray metal grain elevators. This area bills itself as the **Grass Seed Capital of the World** and also produces commercial crops of mint, wheat, and barley.

Elgin, about 20 miles east, was settled in 1882. The city hall and renovated opera house are listed on the National Register of Historic Places. The opera house is known for its excellent acoustics and also houses the **Elgin and Indian Valley Historical Museum.** The **Eagle Cap Excursion Train** departs from Elgin for a 39-mile 3.5-hour round-trip through deep canyons and along the Grande Ronde River and Wild and Scenic Wallowa River. Five miles east of town, look south from OR 82 and you'll see an old log barn. It served as an 1878 settlers' fort for anticipated attacks by Native Americans.

Minam Hill & Eastward

As the road climbs the 3,638-foot summit of **Minam Hill,** it affords continuing views of the valley sprinkled with farms, pastures, and dry grasslands and the forested mountains of the Eagle Cap Wilderness to the south. As you enter a canyon, steep walls rise in basalt benches, and a swatch of green oaks and willows, split by the Wild and Scenic Minam and Wallowa Rivers, fills slopes of low hills and ridges covered with fir and ponderosa pine. You can enjoy trout fishing, rafting, and camping from 12 primitive sites at **Minam State Park,** 2 miles north of the highway. Wallowa Wayside offers a scenic roadside picnicking and fishing spot.

Exiting the canyon, the road winds through foothills, then heads in a straight line across flatland dairy farms as it crosses the Wallowa and Lostine Rivers. En route it splits the settlements of Wallowa and Lostine. The **Wallowa Band Nez Perce Trail Interpretive Center,** in Wallowa, preserves the tribe's customs, traditions, and culture. **Boundary Campground,** 9 miles south of Wallowa on FR 8250, offers 8 tent sites and a trail into the Eagle Cap Wilderness. Four additional forest service campgrounds, 11 to 17 miles south of Lostine, are accessible by FR 8210.

They have a total of 36 tent sites and are situated in the Eagle Cap Wilderness and near the Wild and Scenic Lostine River.

East of Lostine, farms are set on vast meadows at the base of crumpled mountain slopes with silhouetted ridges of buff brown, mossy green, and light and dark blue. The **Wallowa-Whitman National Forest headquarters observation deck,** 1 mile west of Enterprise, offers the best view of the farms and rugged peaks. Exhibits highlight the forest's geology, wildlife, and multiple uses. At **Wallowa Hatchery,** nearby, you can take a 0.25-mile hike to a pond where waterfowl gather and geese nest during springtime.

At **Joseph,** 4 miles east, many early 20th-century buildings have been converted into artists' studios. At several foundries you can take a tour through the production process from artists' clay models to finished castings and see larger-than-life bronze sculptures on a town art walk.

Wallowa Lake

Campers can choose between 8 tent sites at the forest service's **Hurricane Creek Campground,** 4 miles southwest of Joseph on Hurricane Creek Road, or 121 full-hookup and 89 tent sites at **Wallowa Lake State Park,** 6 miles south on OR 82.

If you're interested in Nez Perce history, you'll want to stop at **Iwetemlaykin State Heritage Site** and a Nez Perce National Historical Park site near Wallowa Lake's entrance road. **Wallowa Lake,** at the base of the towering glacial peaks of the Wallowa Mountains, is one of Oregon's scenic jewels and the centerpiece for the state park, a resort, and a mountain tramway to the 8,200-foot summit of **Mount Howard.** Recreation includes fishing, waterskiing, boating, and swimming.

Last Gas for 69 Miles, FR 39

Before leaving Joseph make sure you have plenty of gas, for there are no services for the next 69 miles. Ten miles east, you turn south off Imnaha Road and onto FR 39. As you drive the 54 miles, weaving through the thick tree-lined corridor of tamarack, spruce, and Douglas, white, and red fir, watch for some of the 350 species of wildlife that inhabit the region. You may see deer, elk, several species of owls, hoary marmots, pileated woodpeckers, and golden eagles.

The drive starts with snowcapped peaks on the western horizon and quickly enters 2.38 million–acre **Wallowa-Whitman National Forest.** It stretches virtually unbroken as an ocean of tree-filled valleys, ridges, hills, and mountains from here to the junction of OR 86. At about 15 miles, after passing **Lick Creek Campground** with 7 tent and 5 RV/tent sites, you enter the Hells Canyon Recreation Area. Its 652,488 acres extend east across the Snake River into Idaho's Seven Devils Mountains.

Wallowa Lake is one of Oregon's scenic jewels and together with the mountains that surround it, is often called the little Switzerland of America.

Hells Canyon National Recreation Area

Following a steep downgrade through 11 miles of canyon highlighted with brilliant red rock outcroppings, the highway reaches a junction with FR 3955. It leads 28 miles northeast along the rugged Imnaha River. This segment of the river, which flows alongside your route for several miles, has been designated a Wild and Scenic River.

Logs in **Gumboat Creek,** near the junction, were victims of the spruce bark beetle. They provide a habitat for fish and other aquatic wildlife and protect a riparian zone from grazing cattle. **Blackhorse Campground,** with 16 tent/trailer sites, and **Ollokot Campground,** with 12, serve rainbow trout and steelhead anglers, whitewater rafters, and backpackers heading into the **Eagle Cap Wilderness and Recreation Area.** Four campgrounds, with a total of 50 sites, are also situated a few miles west on FR 3960.

For the easiest access to the Hells Canyon rim, take McGraw Lookout Road east about 5 miles. The gravel road, near Ollokot, leads to a 5,400-foot-high viewpoint overlooking the mile-deep gorge, the Snake River, and the Seven Devils mountains to the east.

As you drive along OR 86, you may still see ranchers moving cattle to and from summer grazing ranges.

Approximately 15 miles south, FR 39 levels and straightens as it passes a rest area with information boards and area maps. A National Recreation Trail starts nearby and follows Steep Creek into the mountains. About 5 miles south, you exit the recreation area near **Lake Fork Campground,** which has 10 tent/trailer units.

Copperfield & Oxbow Dam

Reaching OR 86, you can see more of Hells Canyon on a 7-mile side trip to **Copperfield** and **Oxbow Dam.** Watch for cattle running free on roadbeds and on the round, sandy foothills.

Oxbow Dam is one of three hydroelectric projects that have tamed the turbulent Snake River, leaving tranquil lakes with a surface area of 19,000 acres for boating, fishing, and water sports. The others are **Brownlee,** 12 miles south, and **Hells Canyon Dam,** 23 miles north of Oxbow. At **Oxbow** you'll find trailer and tent campgrounds with hookups and boat-launching facilities. Gas, groceries, and lodging are available at **Pine Creek,** 1 mile west on OR 86. By taking Snake River Road north from Oxbow, you can make a brief detour into Idaho while enjoying the rugged, steep walls and the Snake River. The road ends at Hells Canyon Dam, where a park overlooks the Wild and Scenic portion of the Snake and is a departure point for jet boat and float excursions. You'll find camping at 4 Idaho Power Company parks in the area: Copperfield with 62 sites; Hells Canyon Park on Oxbow Reservoir with 24 RV hookups; and near Browlee Reservoir, McCormick with 34 water and electric sites, and Woodhead with 124 water/electric sites.

Halfway & Richland

Returning west on OR 86, you'll find gas, food, and lodging at the farming community of **Halfway.** Halfway is the departure point for summer-based river and Eagle Cap Wilderness recreation as well as a network of trails for snowmobilers. **Pine Ranger Station,** west of town, dispenses national forest maps and campground information.

During the 13 miles to Richland, OR 86 climbs to 3,653 feet and overlooks vast expanses of flat fields, rolling hills, and distant rounded buff-colored mountain slopes dappled with sagebrush and junipers. **Richland** sits in flat, lush pastureland surrounded by buckskin mountains. At **Hewitt/Holcomb Park,** south of town, you can camp beside a small lake and enjoy the shade of larches and poplars while fishing for bass, perch, catfish, and bluegill. It has 47 RV hookups, 3 boat ramps, access to **Brownlee Reservoir,** a fish-cleaning station, and a children's play area.

A few miles west, the Powder River meanders along the road, through a shallow canyon, and by a collapsed mountain slope that blocked the stream and highway several years ago. In late summer the river is mirror smooth, but it can be a swift, rushing stream when full. About 14 miles east of I-84, the river bends north as the road tops a plateau and continues west through grazing land and hay fields.

Flagstaff Hill

The **Oregon Trail Interpretive Center,** at 3,800-foot **Flagstaff Hill,** marks the spot where pioneer wagon trains first saw the Baker Valley and Blue Mountains. Life on the trail is interpreted with a gallery of life-size figures, living-history performances, hands-on displays, and trails leading to original trail ruts. From the observation platform, the view encompasses the valley, mountains, Baker City 10 miles south, and paths leading to the original trail ruts.

The scenic byway and All-American Road segments end at Baker City. The city's many Victorian buildings are preserved as a National Historic District.

Seven miles west, the route turns north onto I-84 and travels 6 miles to exit 298 and OR 203. After a few acres of grassland, the road rides a series of ridges through a desert of sage and bitterbrush, crosses the Powder River, drops into an oasis-like valley of lush pasturelands, and arrives 18 miles northeast at Medical Springs. An abandoned outdoor pool, log cabin, and a former 40-room hotel stand next to each other as a reminder of the days when this was a health resort.

Toward LaGrande

The remainder of the drive from Medical Springs to LaGrande is part of the **Oregon State Grande Ronde Tour** that includes two loops through farmlands, sage-covered range, and forests in the surrounding area.

Medical Springs marks a transition from desert to forest. With the magnificent Blue Mountains ahead and the Eagle Cap Wilderness to the east, you top a 4,178-foot summit 4 miles north and briefly reenter Wallowa-Whitman National Forest.

A few miles farther, **Catherine Creek State Park** lies in a gorge with steep lava walls, its picnic grounds and 20 primitive campsites shaded by ponderosa pines and spruces. The shallow creek yields rainbow trout and is a great spot to take children inner-tubing, fishing, and picnicking.

About midway between the park and **Union,** 8 miles west, the forest ends at the edge of grassy farmlands. At Union on a short walk around town, you'll see a variety of Victorian architecture displayed in gothic, Renaissance revival, mansard, Queen Anne, foursquare, and T-shaped buildings. The highlight of a visit to the **Union County Museum** is the popular *Cowboys Then and Now* exhibit. It traces the history of cattle and cowboys from working on ranches to rodeos to motion pictures. The historic **Union Hotel** gives you the opportunity to stay overnight in 16 themed rooms.

Hot Lake, a few miles northeast, was set aside by Indians as neutral ground and became known as the **Valley of Peace.** Later its mineral waters rejuvenated Oregon Trail travelers and were the major attraction of a 1920s resort. You can see the 8-acre lake covered with lily pads and stay in the main brick building that has been restored as a bed-and-breakfast. It is listed on the National Register of Historic Places.

As you follow the route of the Oregon Trail north through the Ladd Management Wildlife Area, watch for deer and a variety of migratory birds. An RV park nearby has 100 spaces, a pool/spa, and a bird sanctuary. The drive concludes 12 miles north in LaGrande.

36

John Day Fossil Beds Loop

General Description: A 119-mile loop through the colorful gorge of the Sheep Rock Unit of John Day Fossil Beds National Monument and through northeastern Oregon orchards and mountains. Collecting fossils in the monument is strictly prohibited.

Special Attractions: Sheep Rock Unit of John Day Fossil Beds National Monument; Picture Gorge; Kam Wah Chung Museum; Malheur National Forest; North, South, and Main Forks of John Day River; colorful rock formations.

Location: Northeastern Oregon between John Day and Monument.

Drive Route Numbers: US 26, OR 19, CR 402, US 395.

Travel Season: Routes are open all year. The national forest campground closes from October 15 through May 30.

Camping: 1 state park campground with electricity and hiker/biker sites. 2 Bureau of Land Management campgrounds with primitive sites. 1 national forest service campground with tables, fire rings, and vault or pit toilets. Private RV parks in John Day, Dayville, Monument, and Long Creek.

Services: All services in John Day. Limited services in Mount Vernon, Dayville, Monument, and Long Creek.

Nearby Attractions: Strawberry Mountain Wilderness, Black Canyon Wilderness, John Day Fossil Beds Painted Hills Unit, Wild and Scenic John Day River, Monument Rock Wilderness, Ritter Hot Springs.

For More Information: Grant County Chamber of Commerce, (541) 575-0547, (800) 769-5664, www.gcoregonlive.com; John Day Fossil Beds National Monument, (541) 987-2333, www.nps.gov; Malheur National Forest, (541) 575-3000, www.fs.usda.gov/malheur.

The Route

Starting in the cattle country of John Day, the drive moves west, then switches to deep canyons of brilliant clay stone and lava as it heads north through the **John Day Fossil Beds.** Turning east at Kimberly, it follows a mountain ridge overlooking croplands and then returns south through the thick **Malheur National Forest.** The route crosses three branches of the John Day River several times, and the stream is a continuous presence during the first half of the drive. Although elevation ranges from 1,820 feet near Kimberly to 5,000 feet near Long Creek, grades are gradual with a minimum of curves. Traffic is usually moderate on US 26 and US 395 and light on OR 19 and CR 402.

The weather is characterized by cold winters and hot summers. Winter temperatures average 25 degrees to the low 30s and 40s. Summer days are usually in the 90- to 100-degree range. Travelers can expect temperatures in the mid-60s during spring and in the low 70s in fall.

John Day Fossil Beds Loop

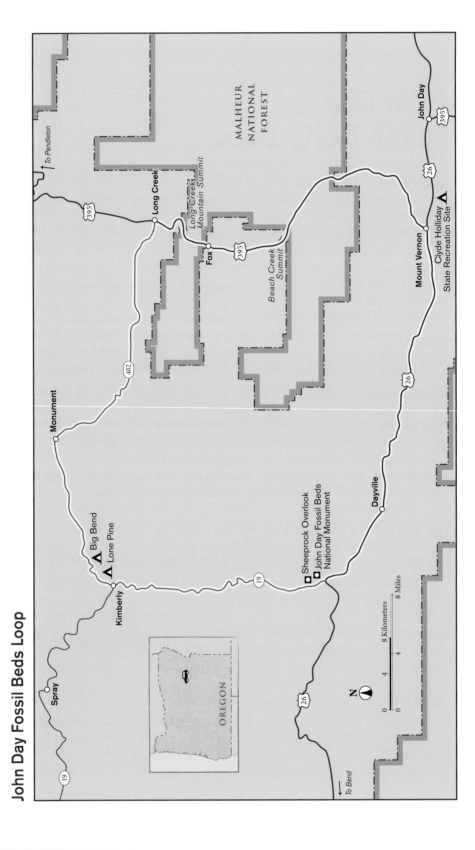

John Day

John Day, Grant County's largest town, was named for a Virginia explorer and trapper who came west in 1811 with the William Price Hunt expedition. After becoming separated from the main party near the Snake River, he endured tremendous hardship while wandering across Oregon for nearly a year before reaching Astoria. Although Day's major achievement seems to have been simply surviving, his name has been given to two rivers, a national monument, a region, and a dam.

The **Kam Wah Chung and Company Museum** in the city park offers a fascinating glimpse into local 1880s Chinese culture. Listed on the National Register of Historic Places, the two-story basalt building was constructed as a trading post in 1866–1867. It contains thousands of original relics from its days as a combination Chinese fort, general store, pharmacy, doctor's office, temple, and home.

The **Grant County Ranch and Rodeo Museum** in John Day interprets the best and worst of the cowboy lifestyle with photo exhibits, tools, and other artifacts.

A stop at the **Federal Building** (also called the Forest Service Building) in John Day provides an excellent orientation to the region and the monument, which comprises 14,000 acres in three separate units. Wall-size information panels describe the geologic history and environmental changes that have taken place during the past 65 million years.

US 26

The route follows US 26 west for 38 miles as it parallels the John Day River through a countryside of meadows filled with huge herds of beef and dairy cattle, picturesque barns, and farm buildings. Flat-topped, terraced, and rolling hills with a sparse covering of scattered junipers, sagebrush, and bunchgrass frame the valley. The hills and rimrocks were created by numerous volcanic eruptions that deposited more than 100 feet of ash and lava on the John Day Valley during a 10,000-year period.

Clyde Holliday State Park, 6 miles west of John Day, offers a hiker/biker camp, 31 electrical hookups, and fishing for trout and bass from a shaded riverside setting. The brick-red basalts and sandstone terraces across the valley were uplifted approximately 1,000 feet, forming a parallel step fault.

Cedar Grove Botanical Area

Just west of Mount Vernon, you can take a side trip from US 26 south to the **Cedar Grove Botanical Area** in the Malheur National Forest. It encloses a 26-acre grove of Alaska cedars that are unique to the area and the last remnants of a prehistoric forest. Parking is limited. A steep 1-mile National Recreation Trail climbs a ridge and passes through a dense forest and by large rock outcroppings. The round-trip drive to Cedar Grove and the hike will be about a two-hour side trip.

Dayville

The main and south forks of the John Day River meet at **Dayville,** where annual events include a cross-country horse race and a duck race. Five miles west of town, US 26 turns north and crosses Rattlesnake Creek, enters Picture Gorge and the Sheep Rock Unit of **John Day Fossil Beds National Monument,** and intersects OR 19. Fossils have been found in over 750 locations in the monument.

Picture Gorge's colorful basalt and sandstone cliffs rise over 1,000 feet from the river base. Buried in the steep clay-stone cliffs of the gorge and monument is one of the world's most complete fossil records. It spans over 40 million years of geologic time and is a continuous record of most of the Age of Mammals—the time between the extinction of the dinosaurs and the beginning of the ice age.

The record indicates that 250 million years ago, this region was an ocean floor. After being covered with lava flows, it was submerged again about 180 million years ago. For the past 60 million years, volcanism, mountain building, and erosion have reshaped the land and changed the climate. Some 50 million years ago, this was a near-tropical forest.

When the Cascade Mountains were born about 35 million years ago, eruptions showered the John Day country with ash. Fossils of more than 2,000 species of plants and animals, including 14 genera of horses, have been found in the beds and indicate that this was once home to saber-toothed cats, rhinoceroses, tapirs, dogs, horses, camels, sloths, peccaries, pronghorns, and ancestors of the elephant. The fossil record is the only indication of the existence of extinct oreodonts, beardogs, and gomphotheres.

At Mount Vernon in the John Day country, old barns and aged fences are a reminder that this is still cattle country and has been for over a century.

Sheep Rock Overlook

Sheep Rock Overlook, a mile north of the junction, affords an outstanding view of a graceful curve of the lazy John Day River and the banded brown, yellow, and russet layers of the towering gorge walls. Information boards interpret the landscape 25 million years ago and the importance of fossils as indicators of past environments, climate, and plant and animal life. Collecting and removing artifacts is prohibited.

The **Thomas Condon Paleontology Center,** 2 miles north of Picture Gorge on OR 19, is the monument's primary visitor center. Named in honor of a University of Oregon paleontologist, it is a world-class research laboratory for the study of fossils. Inside you'll find an extensive fossil museum, exhibits, theater and classroom, interpretive programs, and audiovisual presentations on fossils, geology and prehistoric life, and paleontology. It also has a bookstore and a viewing window that lets you look into the laboratory where paleontologists clean fossils and prepare exhibits. The center is open daily 8:30 a.m. to 4:30 p.m.

Sheep Rock's **James Cant Ranch House,** across the highway, was built in 1917 and along with 18 other structures is part of the 200-acre **James Cant Ranch Historic District.** The ranch house, named for a local sheep rancher and serving as the monument headquarters, is a cultural museum that traces the region's history from local American Indian tribes to the first settlers, cattle and sheep ranching, and the wool industry. Lawns, shaded by locusts, willows, cottonwoods, apple trees, and cherry trees, create a restful setting for picnicking and enjoying the scenic river and multicolored cliffs. A 45-minute guided walk details 20th-century ranch life and eastern Oregon's cultural history. A 0.3-mile asphalt trail is wheelchair accessible and takes you by several touchable exhibits.

North from the visitor center, the route continues through sheer cliffs banded with layers of mauve, pale greens, sulfur yellows, pinks, and reds. **Goose Rock,** named for the Canada geese that nest at its base, is about 110 million years old. It is impregnated with leaf imprints and pollen grains deposited when it was an undersea channel.

OR 19 Northward

At **Blue Basin,** a couple miles north, the easy 1-mile **Island of Time Trail** has interpretive plaques and fossil replicas and follows a creek into the blue-green canyons of the **John Day Formation.** For a longer, more strenuous hike, take the 3-mile **Overlook Trail.** It gains 600 feet on the way to **Blue Basin Rim,** where you have a spectacular view of the barren crumpled ridges of the valley badlands and an ancient 200 million–year–old landscape.

Cathedral Rock, a mile north, is a striking blend of greens, light and dark sand, and bright reds left by incandescent gas and volcanic debris. This giant bluff literally slid over a mile to its present position and forced the John Day River into a horseshoe bend at its base. A mile north, a hill topped with two prominent red and olive-drab ash layers marks the rock's original resting place.

The Foree area, nearby, offers a lovely picnic spot overlooking an eastern meadow, western limestone, green fossil beds, and riverbanks lined with junipers and sagebrush. The 1.4-mile **Flood of Fire Trail** gently ascends a ridge to a view of the John Day River Valley and surrounding basalt cliffs. The **Foree Loop Trail** is an easy 0.4-mile hike skirting a basin of blue-green clay stone that contains fossils of mammals who lived here 25 million to 30 million years ago.

Though the Foree area marks the monument's northern boundary, brilliant red, brown, and blue-green rocks frame the route as it weaves through nut orchards, dairy farms, silver sage-covered drylands, and tall terraced hills. Several volcanic dikes, formed when molten lava solidified in cracks, run through the cliffs as black, pink, and white bands.

Northeast from Kimberly

From Kimberly's general store the route follows the John Day River's North Fork 14 miles northeast to Monument. This segment is at its most colorful and fragrant in spring. After passing a large orchard of cherry, apricot, peach, and apple trees, the road opens into sweeping views of clover and mint fields, the river lined with cottonwoods, and tall, stark hills sprinkled with boulders, sagebrush, and juniper. You can spend the night in the midst of the pastoral scenery at BLM's Lone Pine Park with 8 sites and 4 sites at Big Bend Park, 1 and 3 miles east of Kimberly.

The North and Middle Forks of the John Day River meet near the small farming community of **Monument.** Usually this section has some of the best fishing in the river's system, and you stand a good chance of catching your limit of steelhead, rainbow trout, smallmouth bass, and catfish.

During the next 8 miles, you'll gradually climb and wind along a ridge overlooking a valley of sage and juniper, rolling hills punctuated by red rocks, and distant mountains with landslide fans spreading at their base. The most impressive is **Sunken Mountain,** where a steep valley wall was undercut by stream erosion. A parking area near the jumbled rocks that slid down from near the summit offers a fine view of the area.

Long Creek Mountain, 4.5 miles east, is an uplifted basalt block 1,400 to 1,500 feet thick. You'll see the base of the basalt as you approach the mountain and on the descent into Long Creek.

Malheur National Forest

At Long Creek the route turns south on US 395, enters **Malheur National Forest,** and climbs to its highest point of 5,101 feet. From a rest area near the summit, you have a good view of eastern long, rolling, buckskin-colored hills and narrow ravines.

The 1.46 million–acre forest features more than 200 miles of trails for hikers, horseback riders, cross-country skiers, and snowmobilers. It is a habitat for Rocky Mountain elk, mule deer, bighorn sheep, black bears, bobcats, coyotes, wintering bald eagles, and 235 species of birds. Forest streams contain northeast Oregon's largest wild runs of spring chinook salmon and summer steelhead.

After descending to Fox, a rustic mountain community where basalt flows converge from all sides to form a basin, the highway tops **Beach Creek Summit** at 4,708 feet.

Soon after, you leave the national forest. The drive continues through the tree-lined corridor for a few miles, descends into a canyon of converging hills, and concludes by coming full circle at Mount Vernon.

37

Umpqua Valley Wine Tour

General Description: A 109-mile loop through diverse agricultural lands, forests, canyons, and historic roads and communities.

Special Attractions: Winston Wildlife Safari, 21 wineries, historic buildings, North and South Umpqua Rivers.

Location: Southern Oregon west of Roseburg and Sutherlin.

Drive Route Numbers: OR 42, CR 5C (Reston Road), Coos Bay Wagon Road, Melrose Road, Garden Valley Road, OR 138.

Travel Season: All year. While many wineries along the route give tours and/or tastings, some may not. Wine tastings and tours vary with day, season, and individual winery. Some are by appointment only. Call in advance of visit.

Camping: No campgrounds on the route. Armacher County Park Campground at Winchester, midway between Roseburg and Sutherlin, has 30 tent/trailer sites, showers, toilets, and water.

Services: All services in Roseburg, Sutherlin, and Winston. Limited services in Tenmile.

Nearby Attractions: Umpqua-Rogue Scenic Byway, Douglas County Museum, Oakland Historic District.

For More Information: Roseburg Visitors and Convention Bureau, (541) 672-9731, (800) 444-9584 (USA), www.visitroseburg .com; Sutherlin Visitors Information Center, (541) 459-5829; Winston Visitor Information Center, (541) 679-0118, www.winston oregon.net.

The Route

Starting at I-5, the loop travels through a variety of terrain ranging from shallow canyons to rolling hills and flat, open farmlands. The drive passes 11 vineyards while offering a pleasant countryside of small crossroads communities, a historic wagon road, and the state's major wild animal park.

It begins and ends at I-5 and can be joined at exits 112, 119, 125, or 136. Traffic is usually moderate on OR 138 and OR 42 and light on county roads.

Umpqua River Valley

Protected by the Coast Range on the west and the Cascades to the east, the **Umpqua River Valley**'s moderate climate sustains a variety of crops and animals. The area's clay soil, cool morning fogs, and gentle breezes make it ideal for growing wine grapes. Oregon's first vinifera vineyard was established here in 1961, and the **Umpqua Valley Wine, Art, and Music Festival** in September is Oregon's oldest continuous festival of its kind. Over 20 local wineries and vineyards conduct

Umpqua Valley Wine Tour

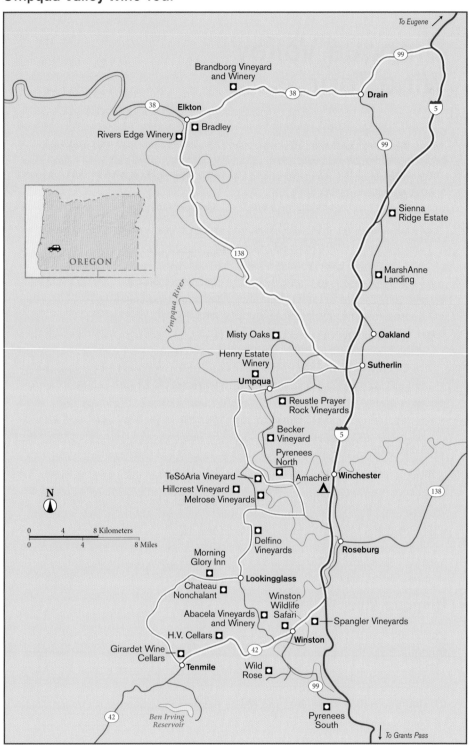

tours and hold wine tastings and special events. If you plan to stop for wine tastings and tours, call ahead, as dates, times, and hours vary. The Roseburg Visitors and Convention Bureau's Visitor Guide contains winery names, phone numbers and websites, and a tour map.

Travelers can expect foggy and frosty mornings in fall and winter. The Roseburg/Sutherlin area receives an average rainfall of 35 inches. Summer temperatures average from lows of 52 to highs of 84 and drop to between 34 and 48 degrees in winter. Spring temperatures range from 64 to 72 degrees, while autumns are usually between 69 and 83 degrees.

If you are beginning at Roseburg, you can start your sightseeing by driving north on I-5, taking exit 138, and traveling 1 mile east to the **Oakland Historic District.** Oregon's first organized historic district recognized by the National Register of Historic Places contains 136 properties and includes many 1890s brick buildings that are still in use. At **MarshAnne Landing,** situated on a former stagecoach stop off exit 142, you may sip Syrah, Grenache, and other wines in an art gallery–styled tasting room. **Sienna Ridge Estate,** off exit 148, has a tasting room built in 1906 and serves pinot noir, gwertzimeier, and chardonnay.

West to Elkton

At Yoncalla, exit 150, follow OR 99 north and west over rolling hills to **Elkton.** At **Brandborg Vineyard and Winery,** in Elkton, a variety of grapes cover 145 acres of rolling hills, and you may be able to sample Syrah, Riesling, and gewürztraminer along with a variety of cheeses and other specialties in a tasting room or on the patio. **Bradley Vineyards,** with views of the Coast Range mountains, has won awards for its Sugar N Spice desert wine, off-dry Riesling, Baco noir, and dry Riesling. South of town, **River's Edge Winery**'s 2,160-square-foot building has a tasting room that overlooks the picturesque Umpqua River.

Traveling south on OR 138, you begin with hills filled with old-growth and second- and third-generation forests. A patchwork of pastures, thoroughbred horse farms, and the open lands brought by a century of logging that started in the 1850s frame the route to a crossing of the Calapooya River. Turn west on Wilsox Road, then after 2 miles turn onto Cole Road loop to see and possibly sample **Misty Oaks Vineyard**'s blend of pinot blanc, cabernet Franc, and pinot noir, or maybe pinot gris or Malbec.

Continue west on the loop back onto Fort McKay Road and travel south. In the first 10 miles, you'll pass picturesque vintage barns, grasslands, herds of dairy cattle and sheep, a small reservoir, and filbert orchards. The Coast Range rises in front of you as a natural shallow bowl filled with oak trees.

Approaching **Henry Estate Winery,** the highway makes the first of the several crossings of the Umpqua River. A picnic area and a boat ramp, situated at the roadside, provide a pleasant spot to stop and enjoy the river that stretches from the Cascades to the Pacific Ocean and is famous for its native steelhead, spring chinook, and brown trout. During May and June whitewater rapids challenge rafters and kayakers. Henry Estate Winery, adjacent to the river, provides picnicking facilities and tastings of gewürztraminer, chardonnay, cabernet sauvignon, and pinot noir.

Backtracking to the Umpqua crossroads, the drive continues south on Garden Valley Road (CR 6) through 8.5 miles of fruit orchards, sheep ranches, a short corridor of overhanging trees, and the small scenic canyon of the Umpqua River. En route you'll pass several side roads in succession leading to **Reustle Prayer Rock Vineyards** on Cal Henry Road, where you can taste Syrah, Tempranillo, Grenache, and others; **Becker Vineyard,** on Klahowya Lane, a small family-owned boutique maker of Muller Thurgau and cabernet sauvignon; **Pyrenees Vineyard and Cellars North,** on Hess Lane, with a deck overlooking the Umpqua River where you can sip chenin blanc and classic Bordeaux; and **TeSóAria,** which was formerly Palotai, which hand-crafts award-winning pinot Syrah, Bulls Blood, Atila, and Bella Bianca.

River Forks Park

The North and South Umpqua Rivers merge at **River Forks Park,** near Hess Lane and Garden Valley Road. The park has 75 picnic sites, and you can enjoy a beach area, playground, and pavilion or use the boat ramp to launch your river explorations. **Singleton Park,** a few miles south on Garden Valley Road, also offers a pleasant picnic ground and a pavilion.

Continuing west on Melrose and then Doerner Road for about 10 miles to the community of **Melrose,** you'll see more fields of vegetables and seed crops, horse ranches, and Christmas tree farms. **Melrose Vineyards** is a place to picnic and sample wines in a beautifully restored barn surrounded by sweeping views of the vineyards. About 3.5 miles west of Melrose, you can visit **Hillcrest Vineyard** off Elgarose Loop Road. The 35 acres of Oregon's oldest vinifera vineyard yield grapes for Riesling, cabernet sauvignon, and pinot noir.

The loop continues south into the gently sloping hills and fields of the Lookingglass Valley on CR 52, passing **Delfino Vineyards.** The picturesque farm's multiple attractions are an antiques-filled cottage for overnight stays, hiking trails, a pond, a hot tub, a pool, and a vineyard with 14 varieties of grapes.

Lookingglass & Tenmile

At **Lookingglass** the general store is a gorgeous 19th-century two-story false front. From the store the loop heads west for 2 miles to the Coos Bay Wagon Road (CR 5B). Built in 1867, it was the first road to link Roseburg and Coos Bay on the Oregon coast. The **Morning Glory Inn** is an idyllic setting to enjoy a night in the heart of the Umpqua Valley wine country. A rustic octagonal barn, 4 uniquely decorated guest rooms, and a full breakfast included for overnighters add to the charming setting. **Chateau Nonchalant,** nearby, blends old world decor with new interpretations of pinot gris, Syrah, and pinot noir.

En route southwest to Reston Road, you'll pass several 1880s buildings and fragments of pioneer plum, apple, and pear orchards. The unique buildings include one of seven octagonal barns in Oregon and the Reston Stage Stop barn that still has the horse stalls in place.

Speed limits slow to 25 miles per hour as the road becomes a bit winding and descends a ridge into a picturesque canyon lined with basalt bluffs, oaks, and poplars. Acres of varietal and French cultivars spread over the hillsides around **Girardet Wine Cellars.** The vineyard produces blended wines in addition to Riesling, chardonnay, pinot noir, and cabernet sauvignon.

Tenmile, a mile south of the winery, has a general store, gas, and several homes. An access road 0.3 mile west on OR 42 leads to the 11,250-acre **Ben Irving Reservoir,** where you'll find 20 picnic sites, a large boat ramp, and a small dock. The lake is a favorite of trout and bass anglers and water-skiers. From Tenmile, which is roughly 10 miles west of I-5, OR 42 cuts east through a pastoral countryside of horse and sheep farms. **H.V. Cellars,** about 5 miles east of Tenmile, produces blackberry, cranberry, and pomegranate fruit wines.

At the junction of Lookingglass Road and OR 42 you have three options: A turn north on Lookingglass Road will take you to **Abacela Vineyards and Winery.** The sunny south-sloping hills produce premium Tempranillo, Syrah, Malbec, Grenache, and dolcetto grapes. The wines are aged underground in small oak casks.

Continue east and you'll see several buildings dating from 1887 to 1920 that exhibit bungalow, Queen Anne, and elements of classical revival architecture. The county-recognized historic district is situated south of the highway.

Winston Wildlife Safari

Winston Wildlife Safari, a mile east of town, is a prime example of the moderate climate's ability to sustain a variety of wildlife. More than 600 animals and birds, representing more than 100 species, roam free. The admission charge provides for

two drives through the park. En route you'll see Roosevelt elk and Damara zebras grazing side by side with hippopotamuses, Bengal tigers, cheetahs, Asian deer and sheep, Canada geese, and North American timber wolves. At Safari Village flamingos roam the grounds and children can pet Cameroon pygmy goats, four-horned sheep, and other exotic animals. You can also take an elephant ride, attend nature talks, browse in the gift shop, and dine in a restaurant overlooking the park.

East from Winston Wildlife Safari

If you continue east on OR 42, you'll cross the South Umpqua River and I-5 at exit 119. If you're an angler, the South Umpqua is a stream to try, for it contains most of the area's fall chinook salmon along with wild and hatchery winter steelhead, coho salmon, cutthroat trout, and smallmouth bass.

Spangler Vineyards, less than 0.5 miles west of the exit, produces 12 wines including cabernet sauvignon, cabernet Franc, sparkling wines, claret, and unoaked chardonnay. You can travel south from the Lookingglass/OR 42 junction approximately 5 miles to **Wild Rose Winery** on Porter Creek Road to try the pinot gris, pinot noir, and cabernet sauvignon. **Pyrenees South,** 5 miles south on Winery Lane, offers a perfect setting for beginning or concluding your tasting on a historic 30-acre estate with a deck overlooking the South Umpqua River and wines that include award-winning chardonnay, merlot, and Syrahs. Take exit 112 to I-5 and conclude your tour by traveling north to **Roseburg.**

You can add to your sightseeing by visiting Roseburg's **Douglas County Museum** and the **Mill-Pine Neighborhood Historic District.** Both can be reached by traveling north on I-5 and taking exit 123 east.

Outside the Douglas County Museum are displays of a steam donkey, turbines from a dam, a railroad depot, farm equipment, and a carriage. Inside you'll find four wings covering 8,000 years of Native American culture, natural history, and prehistoric animals. A spacious lot for parking RVs is adjacent to the museum.

The historic district was platted by the city's founder in 1887 and is on the National Register. This section is unique in that it is a neighborhood of lower-middle-class homes. Most of the 122 historic structures were built between 1887 and 1900.

In addition to having an ideal climate for growing wine grapes, the rolling hills of the Umpqua River Valley provide a habitat for rhinos, cranes, elk, elephants, zebras, and a host of other animals at Winston Wildlife Safari.

38

Grants Pass, Jacksonville Loop

General Description: A 78-mile loop drive through the Rogue River and Applegate Valleys.

Special Attractions: Riverside Park, Applegate River, Jacksonville National Historic Landmark, Table Rocks, House of Mystery, Rogue River, state parks.

Location: Southwestern Oregon between Grants Pass and Jacksonville.

Drive Route Numbers: OR 238, Table Rock Road, OR 234, I-5.

Travel Season: All year.

Camping: 1 state park campground with full hookups and electrical sites; 1 county park campground. 11 forest service campgrounds in vicinity of Applegate Lake, 15 miles south of loop, with tables, fire rings, and flush or vault toilets; some have water.

Services: All services at Grants Pass, Jacksonville, Central Point, and Rogue River. Limited services at Murphy, Applegate, and Gold Hill.

Nearby Attractions: Crater Lake National Park, Oregon Caves National Monument, Oregon Shakespearean Festival, Kalmiopsis Wilderness, Ashland–Howard Prairie–Hyatt Lake Loop, Wolf Creek Tavern.

For More Information: Grants Pass Tourism, (541) 476-7717, (800) 547-5927 (USA), www.visitgrantspass.org; Jacksonville Chamber of Commerce and Visitor Center, (541) 899-8118, www.jacksonvilleoregon .org; Rogue River Area Chamber of Commerce, (541) 582-0242, www.rogueriver chamber.com; Southern Oregon Visitors Association, (541) 522-0520, www.sova.org.

The Route

The loop begins at an elevation of 974 feet and remains relatively level as it heads southwest from Grants Pass to Murphy. Turning east, it moves through rolling hills and dips into small ravines as it passes through dairy farms and woodlands. From Jacksonville the route heads northwest through orchards at the base of flat-topped mesas and returns to Grants Pass along the Rogue River. Distant forests, mesas, and mountains command attention and provide a magnificent background for roadside farms, settlements, and tree-lined avenues.

The drive can be joined from I-5 at exit 32 at Jacksonville and Central Point, exit 40 at Gold Hill, exit 43 at Valley of the Rogue State Park, exit 45 at Rogue River, or exits 55 and 58 at Grants Pass. Traffic is usually light to moderate on the secondary roads and heavy on I-5.

Summertime travelers will find temperatures in the 80s and 90s with highs over 100 degrees. Evenings level off into the 60s and 70s. Winters usually range from the mid-40s to the low 50s. Sunny days are common throughout the year as spring temperatures average in the mid-60s and fall days are in the 69- to 83-degree range.

Grants Pass, Jacksonville Loop

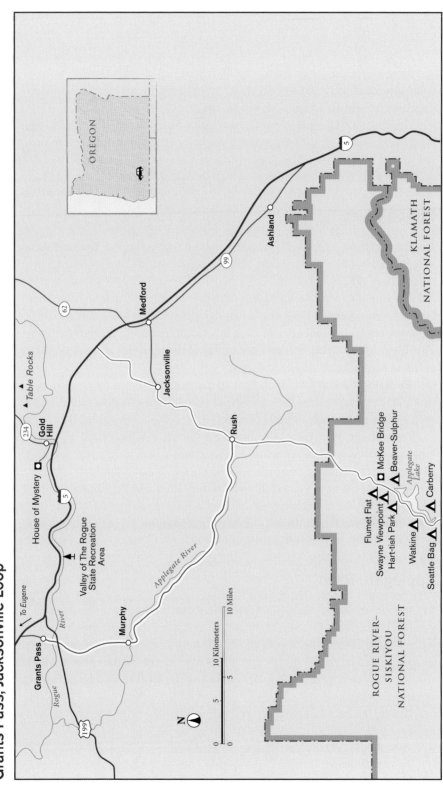

To start in Grants Pass from I-5, follow Sixth Street south through town. After approximately 3 miles you'll cross Caveman Bridge and the Rogue River. Continue straight ahead and follow signs to OR 238 and Jacksonville.

Grants Pass is the gateway to Oregon Caves National Monument and Rogue River recreation areas. Before departing you can tour 23 historic buildings on a self-guided walking tour. The downtown area has been designated a National Historic District and Caveman Bridge is on the National Register of Historic Places.

Rogue River

The **Rogue River,** a relatively placid stream as it moves through **Grants Pass,** lives up to its name with turbulent rapids, rugged canyons, and swift riffles as it flows from the foothills of the Cascades near Crater Lake and meanders 215 miles to empty into the Pacific Ocean near Brookings. A 32-mile segment west of Grants Pass was among the nation's first to be protected under the Wild and Scenic River Act and includes one of Oregon's most remote and rugged river courses. The Rogue has always been a premier steelhead stream and is also known for its excellent runs of coho salmon and trout.

Riverside Park, on the south bank of the Rogue and directly east of Caveman Bridge, offers shady picnic spots and departure points for boaters and jet boat excursions west through Hellgate Canyon.

From Grants Pass, OR 238 extends west through residences and small farms, broken by clumps of scrub pine and mixed stands of oak, laurel, madrone, and Douglas fir. The Siskiyou Mountains frame the western and southern horizons as the drive passes **Grants Pass Golf and Country Club and Fish Hatchery Park,** where you can picnic and fish from the banks of the Applegate River. Crossing the river and entering the lumbering community of **Murphy,** you'll see mills, a small marina, gas stations, and restaurants.

Applegate River

As the route turns southeast, the **Applegate River,** a tributary of the Rogue, parallels the highway for most of the way to Jacksonville. Too shallow for boating, it attracts river rafters and swimmers. Fishing for steelhead and trout is often sporadic in January and February but hot in March. The last Saturday in May signals the opening of generally good rainbow and cutthroat trout fishing that lasts through October.

During the next 7 miles, you travel through shaded tree-lined avenues and by modern farm buildings, meadows with grazing horses and cattle, stately stands of oak, dahlia and gladiolus nurseries, and a Hereford ranch. East of Provost Store, laurel trees—dark brown with broken patches of bark—alternate with fields of lush grass, giving way to thicker forests and foothills that eventually rise to meet the distant mountains.

At mile marker 19 you cross the Applegate River and enter the town named in honor of pioneers Jessie and Lindsey Applegate. Through various endeavors, including blazing a trail into southern Oregon, they were instrumental in attracting the first settlers to the region. The town today is a few residences and stores, an RV park, and a cafe.

Cantrall-Buckley Park, approximately 7 miles east and 2 miles south of the highway, provides 30 campsites, group reservation areas, interpretive displays, and fishing on the riverbank. **Valley View Vineyard,** a mile east of the park junction, offers daily wine tastings of merlot, chardonnay, cabernet sauvignon, Viognier, and Syrah.

Applegate Lake

From Rush, a small roadside community at milepost 28, a paved road leads south 15 miles to **Applegate Lake.** Perched on the Siskiyou's higher slopes, the lake is surrounded by some of southern Oregon's most striking scenery. The forested slopes and snowcapped peaks of the Siskiyou Mountains are often reflected in its mirror-smooth surface. Ten- to 14-inch trout, largemouth bass, and landlocked steelhead have made it a local anglers' favorite. Eleven forest service campgrounds with a total of 79 sites are situated around the lake.

McKee Covered Bridge (World Guide Number 37-15-06) is situated near the north end of Applegate Lake. Built in 1917, the 122-foot-long bridge served Oregon and California miners and loggers. It was closed to vehicles in 1956, repaired in 1965, and is open to pedestrians. A scenic park, adjacent to the bridge, was built in the l930s by the Civilian Conservation Corps and makes a nice picnic spot. The 0.75-mile **Gin Lin Mining Trail,** 9 miles south of Rush, offers an enjoyable lesson in hydraulic gold mining of the 1880s.

After Rush the vegetation thins into dry grass. Cottonwoods, poplars, and other bottomland trees line the roadside as the route dips into a ravine and approaches Jacksonville.

Jacksonville

Jacksonville is a picture of times past when streets were lit with gas lamps, churches were small and white, and wall-size hand-painted tobacco signs adorned sides of buildings. More than 80 buildings in the community of approximately 2,208 people date from the 1850s to the 1890s. The whole town is preserved as a National Historic Landmark and the National Trust for Historic Preservation named it one of its top 12 "distinctive destinations."

Jacksonville rose from an 1851 gold strike and 10 years later numbered more than 5,000 people. The decline came when the railroad bypassed the town in favor of Medford's flatlands, 5 miles east.

The former courthouse is one of the region's finest museums, with collections of minerals, pioneer artifacts, and Native American and Chinese exhibits. Next door a children's museum offers hands-on exhibits. Stores throughout the town also display pioneer artifacts, mining equipment, and 1800s merchandise. The **Peter Britt Music Festival** is a summer-long affair devoted to dance, classical music, bluegrass, and jazz.

Table Rocks

From Jacksonville the loop follows a former stagecoach route north to **Central Point,** then turns west on Table Rock Road. The **Crater Rock Museum,** in Central Point, interprets the area's natural history with gem and mineral exhibits, an extensive collection of Native American artifacts, geology seminars, and lapidary workshops.

The **Table Rocks** are two flat-topped mesas that dominate the horizon and stand in sharp contrast to the flatland orchards and rumpled mountain peaks. The rocks are remnants of ancient lava flows that covered the area 4.5 million years ago and have served as landmarks for pioneers, Indian battlegrounds, and treaty sites. Designated an area of environmental concern, they protect more than 80 rare and delicate plants. A species of dwarf meadow foam grows here and nowhere else. Brewer's rock cress, Henderson's fawn lily, and scarlet fritillaria mingle with common lupine, Indian paintbrush, honeysuckle, and three species of buttercup.

The Table Rocks are accessible from trailheads off OR 234 that you take south to Gold Hill. The 1.5-mile hikes up the 800-foot rocks are on maintained trails with informational panels that explain the topography. They are moderately strenuous due to grades that sometimes exceed 10 percent. In addition to sweeping views of cities, rivers, orchards, and mountains, you'll see a patterned ground of grassy mounds, temporary pools surrounded by wildflowers, and possibly deer, bald eagles, and ospreys. Watch for rattlesnakes in summer.

The Table Rock/OR 234 segment is particularly outstanding during March and April, when pear orchards bloom and add their special touches of pink and perfume. Table Rock Road also hosts **Tou Velle State Recreation Site,** where you can fish the Rogue River for trout, seasonal salmon, and steelhead; launch your boat; and picnic along the shoreline. **Danman Wildlife Area,** next to Tou Velle, is a prime place to spot local and migratory birds, as birds of prey, waterfowl, and upland birds congregate here. About 5 miles north of Gold Hill, the **Gold Nugget Recreation Area** provides another opportunity to picnic beside the river in a laurel- and oak-lined canyon.

House of Mystery

By following OR 234 west through Gold Hill and turning north on Sardine Creek Road, you can experience the unusual and seemingly improbable at the **Oregon Vortex,** which is also called the **House of Mystery.** The house is a former gold-mining company assay office in a 165-foot spherical force field, half above and half below ground. Inside the circle the majority of trees incline toward magnetic north, people appear shorter when facing south, perspective is altered, and physical facts are reversed.

Toward Valley of the Rogue State Recreation Area

As you follow I-5 from Gold Hill to Grants Pass, you'll overlook the Rogue River south of the highway and see steep forested hills and mountains on the north. The hills and rocks began as sea-floor sediments and volcanics some 200 million years ago. Later they were compressed by the moving ocean floor, covered by other rocks, and intruded by lava flows. The heat baked and transformed them into crystalline granite.

    Savage Rapids Park and Dam, at exit 45A, are popular spots for swimming and waterskiing. **Valley of the Rogue State Park,** off exit 45B, provides camping in 88 full-hookup, 59 electrical, and 21 tent sites in a shaded setting along with a boat ramp, riverside trails, and fishing. The city of Rogue River, accessible from exit 48, offers a local history display at the **Woodville Museum,** housed in a 1909 home. The annual **Rogue River Rooster Crowing Contest** has attracted national media attention and is held on the last Saturday in June.

    As you return to Grants Pass, the highway climbs a ridge. Below, the city is nestled on the valley floor and surrounded by dark blue mountains.

39

Ashland, Klamath Falls Loop

General Description: A 150-mile loop over the southern Oregon Cascade Mountains, along the western shore of Upper Klamath Lake, and through the Rogue River and Bear Creek Valleys.

Special Attractions: 2 national forests, Emigrant Lake, Cascade Siskiyou National Monument, Upper Klamath Lake, Lake of the Woods, Fish Lake, Sky Lakes Wilderness, Mountain Lakes Wilderness, hiking, camping, mountain biking, cross-country skiing, wildlife, historic highway, pioneer trails.

Location: Southern Oregon between Ashland, Klamath Falls, and Medford.

Drive Route Numbers: OR 66, OR 140, and OR 62.

Travel Season: All year, though portions of highways freeze and accumulate significant snow in winter, which, coupled with steep grades and sharp curves, create hazardous conditions.

Camping: 9 forest service and 4 Bureau of Land Management campgrounds with tables, fire rings, and flush or vault toilets. Some have drinking water. In addition, there are 3 county park campgrounds, 2 operated by Pacific Power and Light Company, and several commercial RV parks along the route.

Services: All services at Ashland, Medford, and Klamath Falls. Limited services at points along the route.

Nearby Attractions: Oregon Vortex, Crater Lake National Park, Grants Pass–Jacksonville Loop, Oregon Outback Scenic Byway and Klamath County Loop, Mount Ashland Ski Area, Lava Beds National Monument.

For More Information: Ashland Chamber of Commerce, (541) 482-3486, www.ashlandchamber.com; Medford Visitors Convention Bureau, (800) 469-6307, www.visitmedford.org; Discover Klamath (541) 882-1501, (800) 445-6728, www.travelklamath.com.

The Route

In the first 17 miles, the drive climbs from about 1,900 feet elevation near **Ashland** to more than 4,000 feet. Continuing east, OR 66 remains on a plateau as it extends through a forested corridor of Douglas fir, enters a transition zone, and climbs through ponderosa pine to 4,696 feet before descending through grasslands to **Klamath Falls.** OR 140 follows the shoreline of Upper Klamath Lake north, travels west through dense forest, and peaks at 5,105 feet before concluding in grass- and farmlands. Both highways are essentially tree-lined corridors with the best scenery sometimes hidden by forest.

Stands of ponderosa pine with sparse undergrowth invite easy hikes from the roadside along OR 66. On OR 140 dense forest, lush undergrowth, and lava flows necessitate using forest service trails. Traffic is usually moderate to heavy on both highways. If you are driving the route in reverse, start at exit 30 at Medford.

Ashland, Klamath Falls Loop

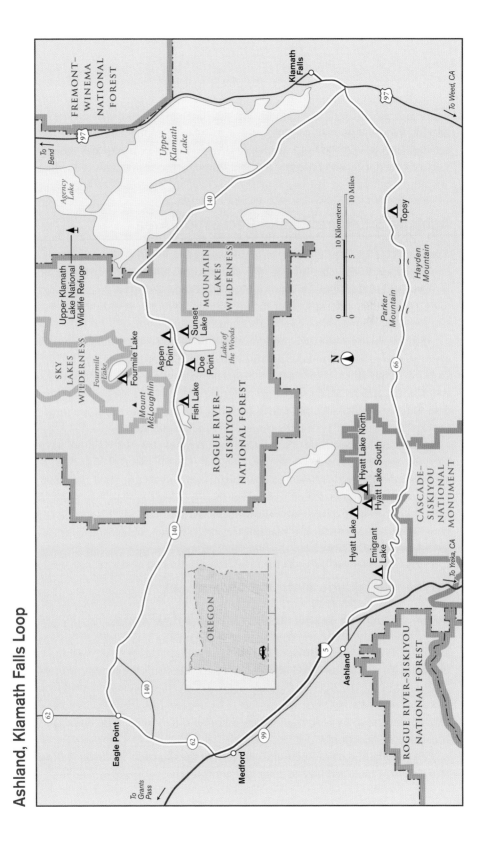

In the Ashland/Medford and Klamath Falls areas, travelers can expect summer temperatures averaging from the low 80s to the high 90s with peaks near 100 degrees. Winter lows average 32 degrees and highs, 52. In the mountains snow accumulates above 3,000 feet, with temperatures starting near zero and rising into the mid-30s. Spring and fall are warm and sunny, with temperatures in the high 60s and mid-70s.

Ashland & Emigrant Lake Recreation Area

Ashland is the home of the **Oregon Shakespearean Festival,** America's oldest Shakespearean festival. It began in 1935 and is recognized worldwide for its professional and innovative productions. **Mount Ashland Ski Area,** 18 miles south of town, offers a magnificent view of the surrounding mountains and valleys. Skiing usually starts around Thanksgiving and continues into April.

From Ashland take exit 14 and travel east on OR 66. Three miles east of the exit, you enter the Emigrant Lake Recreation Area. The man-made lake holds bass, trout, and other sportfish and is also a favorite of sailboarders, boaters, water-skiers, and Jet Skiers. Scrub oak and madrone shelter a 42-site campground with water and restrooms, and an RV park has 32 sites. A water slide and food concession operate 7 days a week from spring into September.

The route follows the lake's shoreline for 5.5 miles. The next 41 miles have been designated a state historic highway. Initially built between 1868 and 1873 as the Southern Oregon Wagon Road, it begins with an abrupt climb that takes you up more than 2,000 feet in 8 miles. As the road swirls around ridges and hugs cliffs, take advantage of several strategically placed turnouts, for this section contains OR 66's most spectacular roadside scenery. The view of the Bear Creek Valley below and deep canyons to the east becomes more awesome with each curve.

Cascade-Siskiyou National Monument

At the Green Springs summit, the highway enters a thick Douglas fir forest that will be your companion for the next 30 miles. Two miles east a paved side road leads north to **Hyatt and Howard Prairie Lakes.** Both feature resort facilities, fishing, water recreation, and lodging. On winter weekends the access road and lakes area are filled with cross-country skiers. Four campgrounds operated by the Jackson County Parks Department, with 117 sites, and 2 by the Bureau of Land Management, with 68 sites, overlook the lakes' shores. A lodge-style restaurant is situated at the junction.

Hyatt Lake and its campgrounds are part of the **Cascade-Siskiyou National Monument,** established June 9, 2000, and administered by the BLM. OR 66 crosses sections of the 52,947-acre monument, which is interspersed with a checkerboard of 32,000 acres of private land. If you are one of the many who camp, hike, climb, cycle, fish, hunt, ride horses, cross-country ski, or snowmobile in the monument, be sure to respect the boundaries of private landowners. Cascade–Siskiyou is the first national monument created in recognition of an area's biological diversity. It protects several wildernesses, natural research areas, and rare plant preserves.

Tub Springs State Wayside, at mile marker 19, offers a water fountain and picnicking in the cool forest by freshwater springs. In 1846 the springs were named by an exploration party led by Jessie Applegate. Between 1846 and 1860 the Applegate Trail, which the party blazed through the area, became an alternate to the Oregon Trail. It was used by immigrants traveling from Fort Hall in Idaho to the Rogue River and Willamette Valleys. You can see remnants of the Applegate Trail and two wagon roads built in 1862 and 1873 near the park's north entrance.

Applegate Trail

The route roughly parallels the **Applegate Trail** to the Klamath River. Continuing east, you'll have a definite feeling of traveling on a high, broad plateau as the road stays flat before dipping into a shallow swale near mile marker 22 and the **Pinehurst Inn.** The inn was a 1920s roadhouse and has been restored as a bed-and-breakfast and dinner restaurant. Its 5 rooms, including a suite, feature antique furniture and claw-foot bathtubs. **Green Springs Ranch,** 0.5 mile east, offers the opportunity to stay in cabins or trailers on a 1,000-acre working cattle ranch. With advance arrangements, you can tour the ranch and a small museum of Native American and pioneer artifacts.

The highway leaves a biological transition zone in which ponderosa, Douglas fir, and sugar pine mix, and it gradually climbs to **Parker Mountain**'s 4,356-foot summit. Nine miles east, you reach the road's highest point, 4,695-foot **Hayden Mountain.** After several curvy sections a gentle downgrade takes you into open farmland and dryland grassy hills.

Six miles east of the summit, the route crosses the Klamath River, which widens into **John Boyle Reservoir.** The reservoir and river are favorites of water-skiers and swimmers and offer good fishing for crappie, bass, and trout. You can camp near the reservoir in 2 Pacific Power and Light Company campgrounds or at the BLM's **Topsy Campground,** where you'll find 13 units plus a hiking trail and boat launch. This section has been a crossing point since the days of the Applegate Trail.

During the remaining 18 miles, you can experience fishing and picnicking on the Klamath River at **Sportsman's Park.** The 343-acre complex hosts a variety of shooting events, with ranges for archery, rifles, handguns, and sporting clays. You may also see motorcycles and ATVs, 4x4 obstacle and drag courses, a field for radio-controlled aircraft, and camping for self-contained RVs and tents.

Panoramic views of the river are available on a ridge near the settlement of Keno. You'll cross it one more time before entering the western city limits of Klamath Falls, where OR 66 and OR 140 meet.

Although Klamath County claims to have 300 days of sunshine per year, it is a major center for winter recreation. Its county lands attract snowmobilers, cross-country and downhill skiers, snowboarders, showshoers, ice skaters, ice fishers, and dogsledders.

The city of **Klamath Falls** was originally called Linksville. The name was changed to capitalize on a small falls, which has since been submerged by power dam backwaters.

Upper Klamath Lake & National Wildlife Refuge

OR 140 begins by climbing rolling hills as it extends north through a few miles of thick ponderosa pines broken by cattle and horse ranches. A few miles farther, it tops a ridge and descends to the western shoreline of Upper Klamath Lake's Howard Bay. Several pullouts and boat launches are situated along the shore.

Upper Klamath Lake, at 133 square miles and about 90,000 acres, is Oregon's largest body of freshwater. You're likely to see some of the 250 species of birds that are attracted to the lake and migrate along the Pacific Flyway. Canoe and kayak rentals are available to get closer to wildlife on marked water trails maintained by the forest service. Inside the Klamath Falls city limits you can walk the **Wing Watchers Trail** and the **Link River Trail** for possible sightings of the white pelicans, bald eagles, herons, and egrets that congregate here.

After climbing a rim overlooking the scenic lake, the road reaches the summit of 4,766-foot **Doak Mountain.** About 4 miles north, you enter the 2.3 million–acre **Fremont-Winema National Forest. Odessa Creek and Malone Springs Campgrounds,** near the forest boundary, have a total of 6 tent/RV sites.

OR 140 turns west in a few miles at a junction with West Side Road, which leads several miles north to small forest service campgrounds, several lakeside resorts, and the 14,000-acre **Upper Klamath Lake National Wildlife Refuge.** As you travel west through rows of quaking aspens and poplars, 9,495-foot Mount McLoughlin, southern Oregon's tallest mountain, stands behind an open meadow on the north. An endless forest fills the slopes of Brown Mountain south of the highway.

Mount McLoughlin, bathed in clouds, fills the horizon as you travel west on OR 140 from Klamath Falls to Medford.

Mount McLoughlin

Mount McLoughlin is a relatively young volcano that began forming less than one million years ago. It is composed of alternating layers of cinders, scoria, volcanic ash, and basalt. After the last eruptions, about 12,000 years ago, ice age glaciers ground it down, removing massive amounts of earth and rock. Both Mount McLoughlin and Brown Mountain are thought to be active volcanos. As you continue west to **Fish Lake,** watch for piles of rough blocks of lava along the roadside. Like Mount McLoughlin, they are products of recent eruptions.

Mount McLoughlin is part of the **Sky Lakes Wilderness,** which is accessible from **Cold Springs Trailhead,** 11 miles north of the highway. Near the access road you begin a long winding climb through a scenic pass where the highway meets Dead Indian Memorial Road. It skirts Lake of the Woods and heads 40 miles southwest to Howard Prairie and Ashland.

Lake of the Woods & Fourmile Lake

Lake of the Woods, a few miles south, is a popular recreation area offering stocked rainbow trout fishing and boating, as well as cross-country skiing and other winter sports. A resort, with 28 cabins and a marina, rents boats and has meeting rooms, a restaurant and lounge, and 26 RV sites. The forest service also operates Aspen Point and Sunset Campgrounds, with a total of 64 tent/trailer and 6 tent sites. Trailheads for several hikes begin at the campgrounds and lead into the Mountain Lakes Wilderness, where you'll find numerous small lakes inside a large craterlike basin surrounded by eight prominent mountain peaks.

Fourmile Lake Campground, with 29 sites, 10 of which accommodate horseback riders, is situated 6 miles north of OR 140 on FR 3661, and is also operated by the forest service. A difficult 10-mile round-trip hike to Mount McLoughlin's summit begins near this road. The **Pacific Crest Trail** meanders between the lake and Mount McLoughlin before crossing OR 140 a mile west of the visitor center. Fourmile Lake also enjoys heavy trout fishing and boating activity. In winter access roads serve cross-country skiers and snowmobilers. A few miles west, OR 140 reaches its high point of 5,105 feet. West of the summit, the forest thickens with Douglas firs, maples, and a dense ground cover. Lava, broken into large boulders and cracked by frost, provides a stark contrast to spring wild lilacs, lupines, trilliums, and tiger lilies.

Rogue River–Siskiyou National Forest

As you enter the **Rogue River–Siskiyou National Forest,** you'll see Fish Lake through the trees south of the road. At the lake you can fish for rainbow and brook trout in summer and try ice-fishing in January and February. Several trailheads start near the shore and range from a 0.5-mile hike to across-the-Cascades treks of several days. Several routes serve mountain bikers, horseback riders, snowmobilers, and cross-country skiers. They include a 27-mile groomed loop around Brown Mountain to Lake of the Woods.

Doe Point and Fish Lake Campgrounds, operated by Rogue River–Siskiyou National Forest, have 42 tent/trailer sites and 7 tent sites. **Fish Lake Resort** offers rustic cottages, lakefront cabins, 45 full-hookup RV sites, a cafe, a store, and boat rentals.

Nearby, FR 37 extends 13 miles north to Willow Lake and Butte Falls. Three forest service campgrounds on this road contain 29 tent and 36 tent/trailer sites. **Willow Prairie Campground** also has 10 sites with corrals for horses, a beaver swamp, and several ponds that attract sandhill cranes, Canada geese, ducks, elk, and deer.

As the highway continues west, it cuts across roadbeds of older volcanic and sedimentary rocks that were deposited on an ocean floor between 50 million and 75 million years ago. The purple and greenish shades of some volcanic rocks were caused by steam and hot water.

Eagle Point & Back to Medford

You exit the national forest on a 5 percent downgrade that stretches through 7 miles of Little Butte Creek's North Fork canyon, then follows a high plateau of meadows and farmlands west to **Eagle Point.** The **Eagle Point Museum** contains the second-largest history collection in Jackson County. At **Jackson County Sports Park,** near Eagle Point, you can watch drag and go-kart racing, shoot targets on 4 ranges, and fish for stocked trout in 4 ponds. The day-use area includes routes for all-terrain vehicles. Before turning south on OR 62 at Eagle Point, you may wish to visit **Butte Creek Mill,** built in 1872, and buy some of the flour it grinds in the gift shop. It is the West's last original water-powered gristmill, and is near **Antelope Covered Bridge** (World Guide Number 37-15-02), built in 1922.

Medford, 10 miles south, marks the conclusion of the drive. With approximately 50,000 people, it is southern Oregon's largest city and the leading business, commercial, and professional center. Medford's economy is based in timber, agriculture, and tourism.

40

Ashland, Howard Prairie, Hyatt Lake

General Description: A 48.8-mile loop past 3 man-made lakes into the southern Oregon Cascade Mountains and through the Bear Creek Valley.

Special Attractions: Howard Prairie and Hyatt Lake resorts, Emigrant Lake, Cacade-Siskiyou National Monument, rugged mountain and valley scenery, fishing, camping, cross-country skiing, wildlife observation, historic highway.

Location: Southern Oregon east of Ashland.

Drive Route Numbers: OR 66, Dead Indian Memorial Road, Howard Prairie–Hyatt Lake Road.

Travel Season: Usually all year, though Bureau of Land Management portions of highways around Howard Prairie and Hyatt Lakes sometimes close because of heavy snow. Portions of highways freeze,

which, coupled with steep grades and sharp curves, creates hazardous conditions.

Camping: 2 BLM campgrounds with tables, fire rings, flush or vault toilets, and drinking water. 4 Jackson County Park Department campgrounds with primitive sites. Several commercial campgrounds are also situated along the route.

Services: All services at Ashland. Limited services at points along the route.

Nearby Attractions: Rogue River, Oregon Vortex, Crater Lake National Park, Mountain Lakes Wilderness, Lake of the Woods, Fish Lake, Grants Pass–Jacksonville Scenic Loop, Ashland–Klamath Falls Scenic Loop, Applegate Lake, Mount Ashland Ski Area.

For More Information: Ashland Chamber of Commerce, (541) 482-3486, www .ashlandchamber.com.

The Route

As the drive leaves the Bear Creek Valley at about 1,900 feet elevation, it climbs through forested ridges to over 5,000 feet in 13 miles. Turning south, it continues through a forested highland prairie by two mountain lake resorts. The return is through a magnificent but steep canyon and along the shores of Emigrant Lake. Traffic is usually moderate on OR 66 and light on Dead Indian Memorial and Howard Prairie-Hyatt Lake Roads. Expect heavy traffic on weekends.

In Ashland travelers can expect summer temperatures averaging from the 80s to the high 90s with peaks near 100 degrees. Winters fall to lows averaging 32 degrees and highs of 52. In the mountains snow accumulates above 3,000 feet, with temperatures starting near zero and rising into the mid-30s. Spring and fall bring balmy days in the mid-60s and mid-70s.

Ashland, Howard Prairie, Hyatt Lake

To Grants Pass

OREGON

Dead Indian Memorial Road

Walker Creek

To 140

Howard Prairie–
Hyatt Lake Road

Howard
Prairie Lake

Howard Prairie
Lake

Hyatt Lake

Hyatt Lake North

Hyatt Lake South

Hyatt
Lake

Little
Hyatt
Lake

CASCADE–SISKIYOU
NATIONAL
MONUMENT

To Klamath Falls

66

66

66

Emigrant
Lake

Emigrant
Lake

To Yreka, CA

Ashland

99

66

5

N

3 Kilometers

3 Miles

0

0

Ashland

In its infancy **Ashland** consisted of a water-powered flour mill and sawmill and was named by early settlers with ties to Ashland County, Ohio, and Ashland, Kentucky.

The **Oregon Shakespearean Festival** has brought the town enduring fame. It began as a three-day event in 1935 and has grown to a season that starts in February and ends in October, as it interprets a rotating repertoire of 11 plays in 3 theaters. The **Shakespeare Exhibit Center,** open on performance days, displays costumes, set pieces, and props. In the Fantasy Gallery you can try on costumes and pose for pictures. The town has its share of Shakespeare-themed facilities, from *A Midsummer Night's Dream* and Anne Hathaway's Cottage bed-and-breakfasts to a Tudor-style ski lodge. **Lithia Park,** adjacent to the festival grounds, straddles 100 acres of creek banks and offers hiking, nature trails, tennis courts, and Japanese and formal rose gardens. At **Lithia Artisans Market,** held on weekends along the Ashland creek canal, you can have your portrait painted and purchase fine art, jewelry, metal and wood, art and hand-painted clothing from 35 to 40 artisans. If you have a scientific bent you may wish to visit the **Science Works Hands-On Museum.** It has over 100 indoor and outdoor interactive exhibits, a native plant garden, and a 44-foot geodesic-dome nursery. At 7,500 feet, **Mount Ashland Ski Area,** 18 miles south of town, is the **Siskiyou Mountains'** highest peak. It is known for its challenging terrain and offers 4 chairlifts, 23 runs, rental shops, a cafeteria, and daily snow grooming. Skiing usually starts around Thanksgiving and continues into April.

The drive begins by leaving Ashland and I-5 at exit 14, then briefly follows OR 66 east. After 0.5 mile you turn north onto **Dead Indian Memorial Road.** The road has been a main access for so long that the origin of its name is uncertain. According to one version, a band of Native Americans was killed and buried somewhere along the route.

At the beginning you'll travel through the center of flat, dry grasslands, low, rolling hills, a few steep bluffs, and rocky outcroppings. A creek, shrouded in alder and oak, parallels the south edge and adds color to the buff countryside. The flatlands are composed of sandstone that was deposited about 50 million years ago. It is a land of little water and is used mostly for cattle grazing.

Ashland's Lithia Park is an idyllic setting of shaded paths, formal gardens, spacious lawns, and woodland. Licensed by Shutterstock.com.

Soon the road snakes up and around ridges in a steep 13-mile climb through oak woodlands. Several turnouts afford opportunities to view the brushy, crumpled hills and ravines below. As you ascend, watch for cattle crossing the highway and bicyclists in the roadway, for this is a popular cycling route despite the steep grade. After 8 miles the alders disappear and aspens, laurels, Douglas and white firs, lodgepole pines, and other evergreens begin mixing with the oaks.

Near the summit the road straightens and flattens. Turning south at mile marker 17 onto Howard Prairie–Hyatt Lake Road, you begin traveling across a high-plateau prairie. It was named for local homesteaders who were among the first to settle in the area.

Cascade-Siskiyou National Monument

The recreation area is part of **Cascade-Siskiyou National Monument,** a checkerboard of 52,947 acres that extends east and south to the California border. It includes several wildernesses, rare plant habitats, and parts of the Pacific Crest Trail, which is accessible from the Hyatt Lake–Howard Prairie area. The **Hyatt Lake Recreation Site,** which is part of the national monument, is the hub for the **Table Mountain Snowplay Area** and cross-country ski trails. Cascade–Siskiyou and the Howard Prairie area also attract climbers, hikers, and hunters.

Small meadows hemmed in forests of Douglas fir, ponderosa, and black and white pine dot the roadsides, affording easy, short hikes into grassy fields. Watch for wildlife, for the woods are home to deer, elk, squirrels, raccoons, and black bears. Around the lakes you may see ospreys, bald eagles, pelicans, cormorants, and a variety of other waterfowl.

Plentiful game, a good water supply, easy access, and mild winters made this area a Native American trading center. Though it is illegal to collect them, you may find arrowheads and other artifacts along lakeshores, meadows, and trails.

Grizzly Campground, at mile marker 2, is a Jackson County Parks Department facility with 21 tent sites with fire pits, picnic tables, day-use areas, and boat access. A hiking trail begins at the campground and joins the Pacific Crest Trail east of the lakes. From 5,000 feet at the Dead Indian Memorial Road summit, you descend to 4,500 at **Howard Prairie Lake and Resort.**

Howard Prairie Lake

The 6-mile-long Howard Prairie Lake is dependent on snow for water and fluctuates dramatically from year to year. When it is full you can boat to several islands and take advantage of its reputation as an outstanding early-season wild and stocked rainbow trout fishery. By mid-June it becomes a recreation area for sailboating, swimming, and waterskiing, which is limited to the southern end. As a prime summer-sailing lake, it is the home base of a local yacht club.

The resort overlooks the lake, marina, swimming beaches, and boat ramp. In addition to groceries, gas, and a restaurant, it operates a large campground for tent and RV trailers with kitchens that serve as cabin rentals. Boat and Jet Ski rentals are also available. Three Jackson County Parks campgrounds offer 96 tent sites and 1 equestrian facility. They are available on a first come, first served basis.

Hyatt Lake

The highway climbs 300 feet in the 5 miles to Hyatt Lake. Along the way small meadows surrounded by stands of thick forest provide grass for deer and elk and serve as informal summer campsites and winter snow-play areas. This section, which also includes a small store with a cafe, sometimes closes due to heavy snow. East Hyatt Lake Road, about midway, loops around Hyatt Lake's eastern shore on 7 miles of winding paved blacktop and passes 2 BLM campgrounds with 68 sites, lakeside day-use areas, and a section of summer homes.

A short drive off the main road leads to **Hyatt Lake** and a small resort with a restaurant; boat, canoe, and cabin rentals; a campground with tent and full hook-ups; and a boat launch. Groceries, daily fishing licenses, bait, and tackle are available at the store, which is a drop-mailing site for hikers and equestrians using the Pacific Crest Trail. The resort operates 7 days a week beginning with the opening of fishing season in April and continuing through September, then serves cross-country skiers on winter weekends.

Nestled in a forest of tall ponderosa, Douglas fir, and lodgepole pine, Hyatt Lake is smaller and more secluded than Howard Prairie. Usually you will find excellent fishing for bass and stocked rainbow trout. Fish from 12 to 20 inches are often taken from the lake by trolling and still-fishing.

From Hyatt Lake you continue south through the thick roadside forest for 4 miles to OR 66. En route you'll pass a gravel side road to **Little Hyatt Lake,** which offers scenic camping and hiking, and the southern entrance to the Hyatt Lake Recreation Area loop road.

Oregon Historic Highway

A rustic restaurant is situated at the OR 66 junction. The section of OR 66, which you take west 18 miles to Ashland, has been designated an **Oregon Historic Highway.** It dates to the 1846 Applegate Trail, which was the major pioneer route into southwestern Oregon.

One mile west of the junction, you begin the descent from the **Green Springs Mountain summit,** elevation 4,551 feet. A trail near the summit extends through forest to sweeping views of the countryside.

During the next 8 miles, you'll descend more than 2,000 feet. With the road swirling around ridges and hugging cliffs, take advantage of several strategically placed turnouts, for this section offers superlative views of the **Bear Creek Valley** to the west and deep canyons to the east. In the morning and evening, deer are often seen along the highway. The dark gray basalt is only a few million years old and covers thin layers of light gray and greenish white volcanic ash.

Near the bottom you enter a canyon filled with willows, scrub oaks, and cedar. On the valley floor the road passes **Songer Wayside,** which offers a pleasant picnic spot overlooking Emigrant Lake.

Emigrant Lake Recreation Area

After following the lake's intermittent shoreline for 5.5 miles, you enter the **Emigrant Lake Recreation Area.** The man-made lake is a favorite local fishing spot for bass, trout, bluegill, crappie, and catfish. Midafternoon winds bring sailboarders, boaters, and water and jet skiers. In summer lake shores serve as outdoor theaters for music festivals, some of which feature name entertainers.

A 41-site campground with water and restrooms is sheltered in scrub oak and madrone. You can also enjoy a 280-foot twin-flume waterslide, group camps, day-use areas, and swimming beaches and rent jet boats. The **Point RV Park** offers 32 full hookups with electricity, water, restrooms, and showers.

The drive concludes at I-5 and exit 14, where nearby some 15 varietals cover the rolling hills of 120-acre **Ashland Vineyards and Winery.** Call ahead to taste merlots, cabernet sauvignon, and others. It also markets an upscale Shakespeare series of over 26 labels.

41

Upper Klamath Lake Loop

General Description: A 90-mile loop drive around Upper Klamath Lake and Wildlife Refuge, into the eastern Cascade foothills and Klamath basin farmlands.

Special Attractions: 3 museums, Upper Klamath Lake and Wildlife Refuge, fishing, canoe trails, historic sites, Winema National Forest, resorts, Collier Memorial State Park.

Location: South-central Oregon between Klamath Falls and Chiloquin.

Drive Route Numbers: US 97, OR 140, West Side Road, Seven Mile Road, Sun Mountain Road.

Travel Season: Route is open all year, with prime travel season from April through October.

Camping: 2 state park campgrounds, 1 with full hookups and 1 with primitive sites.

3 forest service campgrounds with tables, fire rings, and flush or vault toilets.

Services: All services in Klamath Falls, Fort Klamath, and Chiloquin.

Nearby Attractions: Crater Lake National Park, Lake of the Woods, Fish Lake, Lava Beds National Monument, Lower Klamath Lake National Wildlife Refuge, Klamath Marsh National Wildlife Refuge, Ashland–Klamath Falls Loop Scenic Drive, Oregon Outback Scenic Byway and Klamath County Loop.

For More Information: Discover Klamath, (541) 882-1501, (800) 445-6728, www.discoverklamath.com; Fremont-Winema National Forest, (541) 947-2151, www.fs.fed.us/r6/frewin.

The Route

The loop begins in **Klamath Falls,** at elevation 4,107 feet, and rises to 4,766 feet in the Cascade foothills. After traveling by three museums in downtown, it moves to Upper Klamath Lake's western shore, climbs through **Fremont-Winema National Forest** to a resort area, turns east, and levels off into farmlands. The return begins in a forest, then passes through open sagebrush country and onto the east shore of **Upper Klamath Lake.**

Klamath County's high, dry climate produces about 300 days of sunshine per year. In summer highs average 84 degrees and lows 52 degrees. Winter temperatures range from 21 to 38 degrees. Spring days span 64 to 72 degrees, and autumn falls between 69 and 83 degrees.

Klamath Falls

Native Americans inhabited the Klamath Basin for at least 5,000 years before the arrival of fur trappers in 1825. Kit Carson and John C. Fremont camped on Upper Klamath Lake in 1843 while searching for a pass through the Cascades. **Klamath**

Upper Klamath Lake Loop

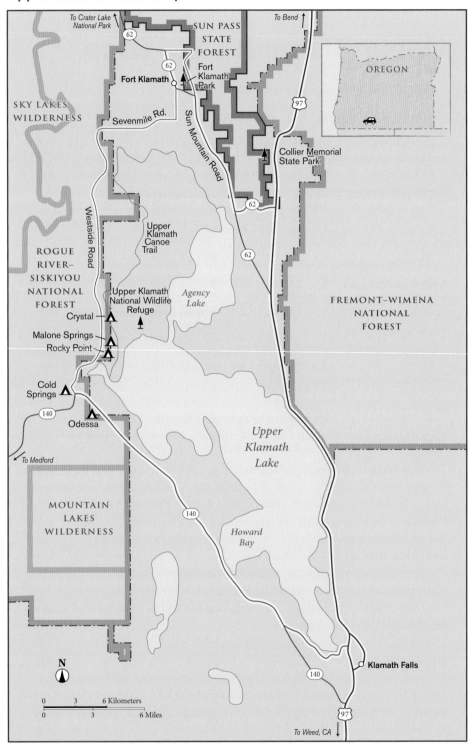

To Crater Lake National Park

SUN PASS STATE FOREST

To Bend

62

62

Fort Klamath

Fort Klamath Park

OREGON

Sevenmile Rd.

97

SKY LAKES WILDERNESS

Sun Mountain Road

Collier Memorial State Park

62

Westside Road

Upper Klamath Canoe Trail

62

ROGUE RIVER– SISKIYOU NATIONAL FOREST

Upper Klamath National Wildlife Refuge

Agency Lake

FREMONT–WIMENA NATIONAL FOREST

Crystal

Malone Springs

Rocky Point

Cold Springs

140

Odessa

To Medford

Upper Klamath Lake

MOUNTAIN LAKES WILDERNESS

140

Howard Bay

N

0   3   6 Kilometers

0   3   6 Miles

Klamath Falls

140

97

To Weed, CA

Falls began in 1867 as a ferry and bridge crossing on the Link River. Originally called Linksville, the name was changed to capitalize on a small falls, which has since been submerged by power dam backwaters.

The **Klamath County Museum,** housed in a former armory of classical revival design, offers an excellent introduction to Native American and pioneer history, wildlife, and regional geology. The town sits on an area of very young volcanic rocks and on top of natural steam and hot water.

After fire destroyed the original town in 1889, George Baldwin began rebuilding by constructing the hotel that bears his name. A state and national landmark, the four-story Baldwin Hotel Museum retains its original furnishings along with foundation stairs carved from solid rocks and bricks manufactured from Yreka, California, gold-mine tailings. Its 40 rooms are filled with artifacts.

The **Favell Museum,** situated 2 blocks west of the Baldwin Hotel on the banks of the Link River, features Indian artifacts from throughout the western US, British Columbia, and Mexico. Collections include 100,000 arrowheads, stone, bone, shell, quill work, pottery, miniature firearms, and extensive exhibits of western art, bronzes, and taxidermy. The **Link River Nature Trail** starts near the museum. On the easy walk along the riverbank, you may see white pelicans, great blue herons, and some of the other species of waterfowl that migrate in and out of the area.

An exit midway between the two museums takes you north on US 97 and west along Lakeshore Drive. The route passes marinas, a residential area, and small farms on or overlooking Upper Klamath Lake and then opens into fields as it reaches OR 140. At 435-acre **Moore Park,** you can picnic on the lakeshore with the Cascades as a backdrop and bike or hike on roads closed to automobiles into hills overlooking playgrounds, tennis courts, and a boat launch. Watch for snowy egret, green heron, hooded mergansers, and an assortment of warblers that stop here.

Upper Klamath Lake

Upper Klamath Lake, at 133 square miles and about 90,000 acres, is Oregon's largest body of freshwater. The lake fills a basin created sometime during the past million years when the earth's crust dropped along fault lines, which can be seen along both the east and west shorelines. Situated in the heart of the Pacific Flyway, it attracts more than 250 species of birds and an estimated 70 percent to 90 percent of the waterfowl that migrate along the route. Over one million birds fly through each year, including the largest concentration of Bald Eagles in the lower 48 states. If you're an angler, you stand a good chance of catching rainbow trout, catfish, yellow perch, and mullet. Several boat launches, rentals, and tackle shops

are situated along the shore. The lake serves as a natural reservoir for the Klamath Reclamation Project, logging operations, and Klamath River power plants. Its upper shores yield abundant algae, which is harvested commercially.

As you approach OR 140, watch for bald eagles, for they are present all year. At **Howard Bay,** a few miles north, you may see nesting pelicans, Canada honkers, blue herons, and snow geese. On clear days, as you drive north, you'll see the cylindrical cone of Mount McLoughlin on the western horizon. At 9,495 feet, it is southern Oregon's tallest mountain.

The **Running Y Ranch Resort,** nearby, sports Oregon's only golf course designed by the Arnold Palmer Company. *Golf Digest* ranked it number 66 among America's greatest public courses and number 4 in the nation for women. The resort is a base for horseback riding, canoeing, hiking, and bird-watching. Facilities include an 83-room lodge, a sports and fitness center, a full-service day spa, and a restaurant.

After climbing a rim overlooking the lake, the highway reaches the summit of 4,766-foot **Doak Mountain.** Two miles farther, a good dirt road leads 4 miles east to shoreline picnicking and tent camping in a ponderosa pine forest at **Eagle Ridge Park.** Four miles north of the turnoff, you enter the 2.3 million–acre **Fremont-Winema National Forest.** The 4.4-mile **Varney Creek Trail,** near the border, starts at 5,600 feet and is a moderately difficult hike to sweeping views of Upper Klamath Lake and wilderness peaks. **Odessa Creek and Malone Springs Campgrounds** contain a total of 6 sites. The first forest service timber sale took place at Odessa Point in 1905, and the event was immortalized by placing the site on the National Register of Historic Places.

Two miles north, OR 140 turns west, and the drive continues north on West Side Road to the lodge at **Rocky Point Resort.** It was originally a 1930s lumber camp. In addition to 4 cabins and 29 RV spaces, facilities include dock space for 28 boats, 4 tent sites, and 5 motel rooms.

Rocky Point Resort is a departure point for boaters who share Upper Klamath Lake with canoes and kayaks, bird watchers, and fishers.
LICENSED BY SHUTTERSTOCK.COM.

Upper Klamath National Wildlife Refuge

Four segments of a 9.5-mile canoe trail, through a portion of **Upper Klamath National Wildlife Refuge**'s 14,376 acres of marsh grass, bullrushes, cattails, and water lilies, begins at the resort and winds into two creeks and Pelican Bay. The routes, which can also be accessed from **Malone Springs Campground,** follow ancient Native American trails and are open from April through November. This section also produces trophy-size trout. Guide services for fly and drift fishing and duck hunting are available at the resort, along with boat and canoe rentals.

West Side Road continues north as a high mountain avenue lined with trees. From pullouts you can see the dark blue canoe trails meandering through the yellow and green marsh grass. **Cherry Creek Trail,** off FR 3450, provides a strenuous 5.3-mile trek through the **Cherry Creek Natural Research Area** and a mixed conifer forest into terrain carved by glacial action and the magnificent scenery of the **Sky Lakes Basin. Nanny Creek Trail,** accessible by turning west for 4.5 miles on FR 3438, rewards a difficult climb through 4.3 miles of rocky contours and heavily forested slopes of 6,917-foot **Lather Mountain** by weaving around the shorelines of several mountain lakes.

The road exits the forest through a corridor of willows, cottonwoods, dogwoods, alders, and ponderosa pines. Following Seven Mile Road east for approximately 7 miles, you travel by pastoral farms with picturesque older and modern barns and large herds of cattle grazing in meadows framed by the steel gray of the Cascade's eastern slopes. **Fort Klamath**'s quaint church, stores, motels, and restaurants line the highway as you travel north to Fort Dixon Road, turn east, and reenter the **Winema National Forest.** At **Jackson F. Kimball State Recreation Site,** north of the junction with Sun Mountain Road, you can camp in 10 primitive sites, hike in a ponderosa pine forest, fly fish and kayak the headwaters of the Wood River for trout, and watch for deer and other wildlife.

Fort Klamath

Sun Mountain Road offers several attractions as it heads south for 12 miles to join US 97. During summer **Fort Klamath Park and Museum** is open to the public. It was established in 1863 to protect settlers and wagon trains from Native American attacks. Prior to its abandonment in 1889, Fort Klamath's troops had been major participants in the Modoc War of 1872–1873. Artifacts on display date to the 1800s. At the park you can picnic in a gazebo built over the fort's original dance platform, see a replica of the guardhouse containing artifacts and exhibits on the fort's history, and visit the graves of the Modoc's leader, Captain Jack, and three other Native Americans.

Approximately 1.4 miles south, **Crater Lake Resort** is nestled among large ponderosa and scrub pines. It occupies 12 acres along Fort Creek and provides guests with free canoes during their stay and a choice of several cabins or full-hookup RV camping. **Klamath Fish Hatchery,** nearby, raises over three million rainbow, cutthroat, brook, and brown trout per year. It conducts guided tours, and ponds display hatchlings and trophy-size trout.

Next you drive by the original agency headquarters of the Klamath Indian tribe and the reservation's school, hospital, and administrative offices. By following a side road a few miles south, you can take a side trip to picturesque **Agency Lake,** relax in **Henzel Park,** and enjoy water-related activities at **Williamson River Recreation Area** while camping in one of 3 tent or 7 tent/RV sites.

Collier Memorial State Park & Back to Klamath Falls

A turn north on US 97 takes you through 5 miles of thick forest to **Collier Memorial State Park** at Chiloquin. It features a large collection of steam-driven logging equipment, a 50-unit full-hookup campground and 18 tent sites on the banks of the Williamson River, and good trout fishing on an adjacent creek.

During the 37-mile return to Klamath Falls, US 97 hugs the eastern shoreline of Upper Klamath Lake, while sagebrush, desert buttes, and bands of sedimentary rock provide the scenery on the east side of the highway. **Modoc Point** offers great east-side views of the lake with Mount McLoughlin visible across the Klamath Basin. En route you'll pass two forest service ranger stations and a junction to OR 62, which extends to Crater Lake National Park and the Fort Klamath Recreation Area. The Williamson River, which you also cross, is a major trout and mullet stream. **Hagelstein Park,** about midway to Klamath Falls, offers 10 tent/trailer sites and a final high vista view of the lake, basin, and mountains.

42

Rogue Umpqua Scenic Byway

General Description: A 180-mile drive on a National Forest Service Scenic Byway through the Rogue and Umpqua River Valleys, past lakes and waterfalls, into the southern Oregon Cascade Mountains.

Special Attractions: Wild and Scenic Umpqua and Rogue Rivers, waterfalls, mountain lakes, narrow rugged canyons, wilderness areas, Crater Lake National Park, state parks, historic inns, camping, fishing, winter recreation.

Location: Southern Oregon east of Roseburg and north of Gold Hill.

Drive Route Numbers: OR 138, OR 230, OR 62, and OR 234.

Travel Season: All year, though the Crater Lake North Entrance and rim drives close in winter.

Camping: 1 state park with electricity. 2 National Park Service, 5 Bureau of Land Management, and approximately 20 forest service campgrounds with tables, fire rings, and flush or vault toilets; some with drinking water. 2 county parks with hookups, plus several private RV parks.

Services: All services at Roseburg, Gold Hill, and Shady Cove. Limited services along the route.

Nearby Attractions: Umpqua Valley Wine Tour, Sky Lakes Wilderness, Oregon Vortex, Grants Pass–Jacksonville Loop, Ashland–Klamath Falls Loop, Applegate Lake, Mount Ashland Ski Area.

For More Information: Roseburg Visitors and Convention Bureau, (541) 672-9731, (800) 444-9584 (USA), www.visitroseburg .com; Umpqua National Forest, (541) 957-3200, www.fs.usda.gov/umpqua; Rogue River–Siskiyou National Forest, (541) 618-2200, www.fs.fed.us/r6/rogue-siskiyou.

The Route

From **Roseburg** the drive heads east through the **Umpqua River**'s spectacular narrow canyon, climbs into the Cascades, and reaches a high point of 5,820 feet. A side trip to **Crater Lake National Park** increases the elevation to 7,100 feet. The southern section descends through thick forest along the **Rogue River Gorge** and a reservoir lake and concludes in orchards and farmland. The drive can be joined from either exit 124 at Roseburg or exit 40 at Gold Hill. There are almost two dozen waterfalls along the route, which is often called the **Highway of the Waterfalls.**

In the Rogue and Umpqua Valleys, travelers can expect summer temperatures in the 80s and 90s with peaks near 100 degrees. Winters usually fall between 44 and 57 degrees. In the mountains summers bring sunny 70-degree days, while winters range from near zero to the mid-30s. At Crater Lake snow has fallen at least once on every day of the year. Spring days reach highs of 72 degrees and lows around 64, while autumn peaks at 83 and drops to 69 degrees.

Rogue Umpqua Scenic Byway

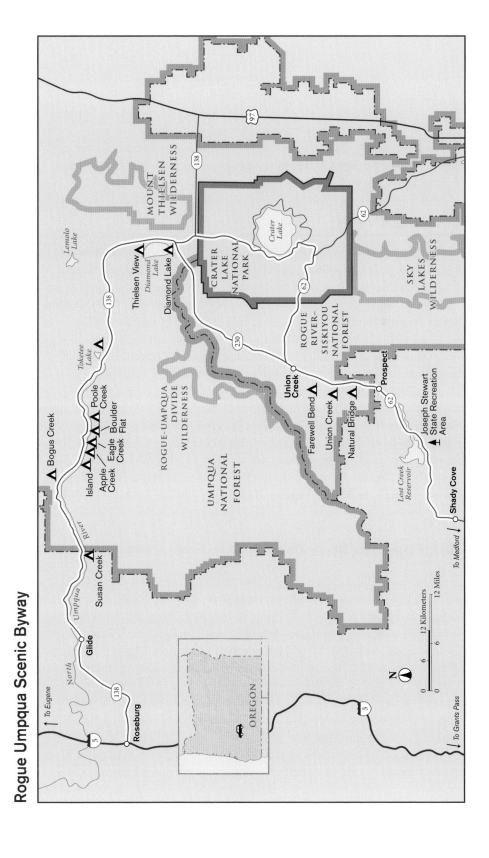

To help plan your sightseeing, contact the Roseburg Visitors and Convention Bureau for a detailed 20-page Rogue-Umpqua National Scenic Byway brochure created by the Bureau of Land Management and the US Forest Service.

From Roseburg, OR 138 starts east through 18 miles of grassy, flat-topped hills, broken by patches of scrub brush, oak, and pine. Whistler's Bend County Park, at mile marker 15, has 23 campsites.

Colliding Rivers

The **North Umpqua,** a designated Wild and Scenic River, and **Little River** collide at the community of **Glide,** and the rare phenomenon can be seen from a small park across the street from the North Umpqua Ranger Station. Part of the highway, as well as the building that houses the ranger station and the **Colliding Rivers Information Center,** was built during the 1930s by the Civilian Conservation Corps. Little River Road follows its namesake southeast for 24 miles to seven waterfalls and six campgrounds. **Cavitt Creek Covered Bridge** (World Guide Number 37-10-06) is also located near Little River Road.

The **Umpqua River,** which begins in the Cascade Mountains and empties into the Pacific Ocean, parallels the highway as you continue east through the **Umpqua National Forest.** A 30-mile section along the drive is limited to fly fishing. While summer steelhead fly fishing has made it famous, the Umpqua also attracts anglers for winter steelhead, spring and fall salmon, trout, smallmouth bass, shad, and striped bass. The 984,602-acre Umpqua National Forest spreads into three counties and includes the Mount Thielsen, Rogue-Umpqua Divide, and Boulder Creek Wildernesses.

North Umpqua River Canyon

Ten miles east of Glide, you leave open country and enter the towering basalt cliffs and thick forest of the **North Umpqua River Canyon.** The drive incorporates virtually every kind of scenery: waterfalls; forests that start at the road's edge and flow in waves up hills, ridges, and mountains; rock palisades; rushing rivers; quiet lakes; and—depending on the season—a variety of spring wildflowers or patches of brilliant fall foliage. The North Umpqua Wild and Scenic River and the North Umpqua Trail meet at the **Swiftwater Recreation Area.** A fly-fishing-only segment of the river extends 33 miles north from the recreation area. The **Rock Creek Fish Hatchery,** nearby, releases approximately one million salmon and steelhead annually into local lakes and streams and has an interpretive trail, an outdoor education center, and an aquarium filled with species of Umpqua River system fish.

Several waysides with viewpoints provide access to the river. At **Susan Creek Recreation Area,** you can enjoy the rugged scenery from 31 campsites or the picnic area and follow a winding 1-mile trail through a rain forest to 50-foot **Susan Creek Falls,** where piles of stones remain from a Native American spiritual site.

Waterfalls

If you are a whitewater rafter or a steelhead angler, you can launch into the river at **Bogus Creek Campground,** 6 miles east. The campground offers 15 sites with tables, 11 tent/auto/trailer sites, and 4 combination multifamily spaces. **Fall Creek Falls** and **Job's Garden Geological Area** are within 3 miles, and a segment of the North Umpqua National Recreation Trail is about 2 miles away.

A narrow 7.5-mile-long canyon of sheer tree-covered cliffs and a deep channel of surging rapids signals your arrival at **The Narrows,** which has been a popular salmon and steelhead fishing spot since the days of the Molalla Indians. **Swiftwater Park,** near the western end, marks the boundary for bait- and fly fishing.

Near The Narrows' eastern end, a side road leads to 100-foot **Canton Creek Falls,** set in steep canyon walls surrounded by large Douglas fir and western red cedar. Steamboat Creek Road takes you 6 miles east into a magnificent canyon to turbulent **Steamboat Falls,** which drops 20 to 30 feet. Campgrounds on the side roads or near the junction include Scared Man, Steamboat Falls, Island, and Canton Creek.

Wild & Scenic North Umpqua River

During the next 20 miles, the road bends southeast, passes three closely grouped falls at **Jack Falls,** parallels the Wild and Scenic portion of the North Umpqua River, and begins steadily climbing. The magnificent scenery continues with sheer cliffs marked by columnar basalt and thick forest as you pass Illahee and Boulder Flats. You can see rock paintings made hundreds of years ago by Native Americans by taking a 1-mile side trip on FR 4760. Your camping options in secluded forests include Apple Creek, Horseshoe Bend, Eagle Rock, and Boulder Flat Campgrounds.

In the **Toketee** area you can obtain hiking, snow-park, and wilderness permits at the ranger station, land small planes on the airstrip, and hike to beautiful **Toketee Falls** and 292-foot-high **Watson Falls Toketee Reservoir,** nearby, offers boating, a 33-site year-round campground, and fishing for brown, rainbow, and brook trout.

Approximately 10 miles east, you may savor the scent of pine from the viewpoint overlooking the 10- to 15-foot punch bowl of **Whitehorse Falls** or from its 5-site campground. **Clearwater Falls,** 3.5 miles east, is a beautiful 30-foot cascade that you can see on a short walk to an overlook or from its 12 campsites. This area is also a hotbed of cross-country skiing and hiking, with several routes starting at the highway.

Lemolo & Diamond Lakes

A few miles farther a side road takes you 5 miles north to **Lemolo Lake Recreation Area.** The lake is one of the few places in Oregon where you can catch wild trophy-size brown trout, along with rainbows, brook trout, and kokanee salmon. At 4,142 feet, it also offers frigid waterskiing, 3 boat launches, and 4 campgrounds around its rim. A resort with cabins and an RV park rents tackle and boats and has food, gas, and lodging.

Six miles east, you'll see **Diamond Lake** through the trees. Situated at 5,182 feet and bordered by 9,200-foot **Mount Thielsen** and 8,363-foot **Mount Bailey,** Diamond Lake is one of the Cascade's scenic jewels. During summer and fall you stand an excellent chance of catching some of the annual stock of 400,000 rainbow trout. Boating, canoeing, swimming, sailboarding, hiking, and hunting for deer, elk, and bear are popular pastimes. In winter, when ice usually covers the lake from January to mid-April, you can take snowmobile tours around its rim and to **Crater Lake National Park.** Sno-Cats will transport you to Mount Bailey for downhill skiing, and there are 300 miles of cross-country ski routes to explore.

Rustic **Diamond Lake Resort** rents 92 motel rooms and cabins with a capacity for 520 people. It has a grocery store, service station, full-service marina, and horse stables. You can also rent motorboats, canoes, paddleboats, mountain bikes, and horses. Three forest service campgrounds contain 450 tent and RV sites.

Crater Lake National Park

A few miles east, OR 138 leaves the Umpqua National Forest, offers access to the Mount Thielsen Wilderness, meets OR 230, and passes the north entrance to **Crater Lake National Park.** OR 230, part of the scenic byway, climbs to 5,320 feet. En route to a junction with OR 62 at Union Creek, it offers 24 miles of forested mountain scenery and access to the **Wild and Scenic Upper Rogue River, Mount Bailey trails,** and the **Rogue-Umpqua Divide Wilderness.** The **Upper Rogue River National Recreation Trail** is accessible on OR 230 and extends for 48 miles along the Upper Rogue River.

Crater Lake is Oregon's scenic icon, and virtually everything pales in comparison. The giant caldera was formed some 7,000 years ago when Mount

A side trip to Oregon's scenic icon Crater Lake National Park is just a few miles away on the Rogue Umpqua Scenic Byway.

Mazama collapsed in the aftermath of volcanic eruptions. The depth of 1,932 feet and the clarity of the water create its famous sapphire-blue color.

You can see the lake from viewpoints at **Rim Village.** A 9-mile western drive, a 23-mile drive along the eastern rim, and the north entrance road usually open by early July and close around mid-October. At 7,100 feet, they offer spectacular views of the lake and Cascade peaks. Trails branch off the loops to surrounding mountains and the Pacific Crest Trail. The Cleetwood Trail begins on the northeastern rim and concludes inside the caldera at the water's edge. Narrated 1-hour-and-45-minute boat cruises of the Lake start from the eastern drive. Rangers present amphitheater programs and special activities for children during summer.

The 183,180-acre park encompasses a historic lodge, **Rim Village Visitor Center** with a restaurant and gift shop, and an extensive network of trails to remote attractions such as sandstone pinnacles and the Wild and Scenic Rogue River headwaters. **Mazama Campground** features 198 sites, and **Lost Creek Campground** has 16. In winter you can cross-country ski and play in the snow on unplowed roads.

Rogue River-Siskiyou National Forest

Exiting Crater Lake by OR 62, you'll enter the 1.8 million–acre **Rogue River–Siskiyou National Forest.** This section of predominantly Douglas fir and ponderosa pine passes **Huckleberry Mountain** and a 25-site campground that bears its name. The area was a berry-picking site for the Klamath Indians.

The community of **Union Creek,** 22 miles west of Rim Village, was built in the 1930s by the Civilian Conservation Corps. It is on the National Register of Historic Places.

About 5 miles south, a turn west will take you to the brink of the **Rogue River Canyon and Natural Bridge,** where the river thunders through a deep, extremely narrow chasm in a spectacular display of whitewater. In summer it disappears into the Natural Bridge lava tube. During high water it overflows and buries the tube. A 2.5-mile hiking trail connects the gorge and bridge.

Several forest service campgrounds with a total of 202 sites, including 25 fifth-wheel sites, are situated along the 15 miles to Prospect junction. They include Farewell Bend, Union Creek, Abbott Creek, Natural Bridge, River Bridge, and Mill Creek.

Prospect & Lost Creek Reservoir

If you're traveling north, **Prospect** represents the last gas for 43 miles and signals the beginning of the tree-lined corridor that extends beyond Diamond Lake. The **Prospect Ranger Station** issues backcountry permits, maps, and trail information. **Mammoth Pines,** 5 miles north of town, offers a pleasant walk on a marked nature trail identifying trees and plants of the Rogue River–Siskiyou National Forest. To see more spectacular waterfalls surrounded by forest scenery and volcanic rock, take Mill Creek Drive to the Avenue of the Boulders, Mill Creek, and Barr Falls, which cascades 240 feet over several rock benches.

South of Prospect, with the highway paralleling the Rogue River and descending a high plateau, you leave the snow zone and pass by llama, horse, cattle, and sheep ranches. After about 6 miles triangular **Lost Creek Reservoir** fills a forested canyon that can be explored on 30 miles of biking and hiking trails. It is an idyllic spot for boating and trout and steelhead fishing. **Casey State Recreation Site**

Crater Lake was formed from the eruption of Mount Mazama 7,700 years ago and at 1,932 feet, it is the deepest lake in the US.

offers picnicking, boating, and lake fishing. At **Joseph P. Steward State Recreation Area,** you'll find 151 electrical and 50 tent sites, plus a restaurant, marina, and 6-mile bike trail. More than 5 miles of hiking paths include connections to the Pacific Crest Trail.

Cole M. Rivers Fish Hatchery, in nearby Trail, is Oregon's largest. It releases 3.7 million fish into the Rogue River each year. The **Spirit of the Rogue Nature Center** at **McGregor Park** interprets the area's natural and cultural history.

Shady Cove & OR 234

At **Shady Cove,** population 2,598, **Rogue Elk County Park** provides tent and trailer camping in 15 sites with RV hookups and is a popular departure point for river rafters, boaters, and anglers. It is also the home of several award-winning wineries.

South of town the drive concludes on **OR 234.** On the 18 miles to Gold Hill, you cross **Sams Valley** and pass near **Tou Velle State Park,** a day-use facility with fishing and a boat ramp on the banks of the Rogue River. At **Gold Nugget Waysides**—three Bureau of Land Management waysides—you can picnic, fish, and launch your raft or kayak. Short trails connect the middle and lower sections and lead to BLM-approved recreational gold-panning sites. During the last few miles, the flat-topped mesas of **Table Rocks** frame the western horizon.

43

Ontario, Lake Owyhee, Vale Loop

General Description: A 102-mile round-trip through a variety of agribusiness fields along an Oregon Trail route to a rugged canyon and scenic lake.

Special Attractions: Four Rivers Cultural Center; Nyssa Agricultural Museum; Vale Oregon Trail Murals; Oregon Trail route, ruts, and campsites; colorful rock formations; Lake Owyhee; rockhounding; water-skiing, boating, fishing,

Location: Eastern Oregon between Ontario, Lake Owyhee, and Vale.

Drive Route Numbers: OR 201, US 26/20, Lyle Boulevard.

Travel Season: Routes open all year.

Camping: 1 state park campground with full hookups and primitive sites.

Services: All services in Ontario. Limited services in Nyssa and Vale.

Nearby Attractions: Wild and Scenic Lake Owyhee River, Succor Creek Canyon, Leslie Gulch, Bully Creek Reservoir, Farewell Bend State Park.

For More Information: Ontario Chamber of Commerce/Visitor and Convention Bureau, (541) 889-8012, (866) 989-8012, www.ontariochamber.com; Nyssa Chamber of Commerce and Agriculture, (541) 372-3091, www.nyssachamber.com; Vale Chamber of Commerce, (541) 473-3800, www.valechamber.com.

The Route

Starting in **Ontario,** the drive begins by traveling through rich agricultural lands, then weaves through a rocky canyon and climbs a bit as it approaches **Lake Owyhee.** A rim drive around the lake's eastern shore offers spectacular views of the lake surrounded by steep, colorful cliffs. Returning through the canyon, the drive follows the route of the Oregon Trail north into dry, rolling hills described by a pioneer as "a barren, God forsaken country, fit for nothing but to receive the foot prints of the savage and his universal associate the coyote." From **Vale** back to Ontario, the route cuts through more of the 300,000 acres of desert that have been transformed by irrigation into fields producing 78 diversified crops.

Summer temperatures average from 74 to 84 degrees but can reach into the 100s. Winters range from the low teens to an average of between 37 and 47 degrees. Spring days are in the pleasant low 60s, and autumn averages between 62 and 74 degrees.

Ontario, Lake Owyhee, Vale Loop

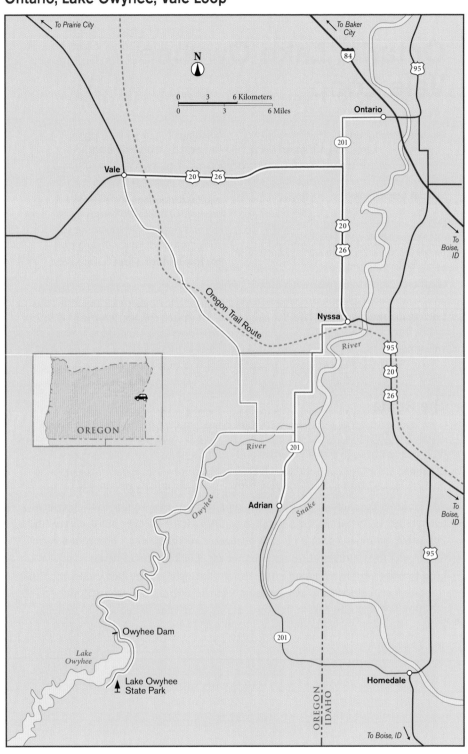

Ontario

Ontario is situated near the confluence of four rivers. All major highways entering Oregon from the east, north, and south converge in or near Ontario. An abundant water supply and strategic location have made it Oregon's second-largest agricultural area and an important transportation center.

The Malheur, Owyhee, Payette, and Snake Rivers flow through this region. The **Four Rivers Cultural Center and Museum** interprets the importance of the four rivers and five cultures (Northern Paiute, Basque, Hispanic, European, and Japanese American) that have been instrumental in developing the area. A 16,000-square-foot museum, North and South American artifacts from ancients to the Indian wars, a conference center, Japanese garden, and a performing arts theater are parts of the complex. Dioramas depict a Paiute river camp, reservation period, and removal; Japanese American World War II internment camp; and history of irrigation. Ontario celebrates the diversity of cultures each June with **America's Global Village Festival,** featuring exhibits, food, and dance from African, Basque, Dutch, German, Japanese, Mexican, and Scottish cultures.

Nyssa

OR 201 extends south from Ontario for about 3 miles, then becomes US 26/20. On the 7 miles to **Nyssa,** you'll receive a quick course in crop identification as roadside signs identify fields of wheat, sugar beets, onions, tomatoes, cabbage, sweet corn, potatoes, and bean seed. The varied crops attract wildlife, and you also have a good chance of seeing deer, pheasant, and other animals enjoying a quick snack.

Many of the underlying rocks in this area were laid down as sediments between 15 million and 20 million years ago when basalt flows dammed streams and created a large lake that extended as far east as Boise. The sediments make excellent soil for growing a variety of vegetables.

Nyssa is an agricultural community with a White Satin Sugar processing plant. The **Oregon Trail Agricultural Museum,** housed in a farmer's feed, seed, and mill built in the late 1930s, offers displays and demonstrations, farm and ranch equipment, and Oregon Trail history. Nearby, a blacksmith shop, saloon, and hotel are all on the National Register of Historic Places. From Nyssa you take OR 201 southwest through fields of clover seed, potatoes, onions, flax, and coreopsis flowers.

At mile marker 5 the route crosses the Oregon Trail. Look east from the historical marker and you will see the point where wagon trains forded the Snake River and entered Oregon. A grange hall, near the marker, sits on the trail, which parallels the highway for a few miles before angling northwest.

To Color Country

Nine miles west, the route leaves the flat farmlands and weaves between steep multihued cliffs and the narrow Owyhee River. Green poplars and cottonwoods and lush marsh grasses, sometimes frequented by geese, herons, and cranes, offer a pleasant, peaceful contrast to the brilliant reds and twisted, rolling hills and mountains.

During the next 10 miles, panoramas of rocks sitting precariously atop ridges, hills, and bluffs spread out in front of you and converge at the canyon's base. Small meadows of silvery sagebrush and dry washes fan out from cliff palisades and brush-covered buttes. Rocks and bluffs, pale yellow near the canyon's beginning, change to russet, bright red, chocolate brown, mauve, and pink.

The striking colors are a combination of volcanic basalts and sedimentary rocks. Though basalts are usually black, iron oxides released as the stone weathered and eroded have turned many in this area to rust and brown. The colors indicate to geologists that the climate was very hot and wet when the lava flowed into the area about 12 million years ago.

Lake Owyhee

A narrow rock tunnel opens into a wide field framed by red and pink cliffs. The highway climbs a grade overlooking the river, crosses **Owyhee Dam,** and hugs cliffs midway between the lake below and the ridgetops above.

The mountains, lake, river, and dam were named after two Hawaiians who were killed by Indians in 1819. An intricate system of tunnels, ditches, and pipes delivers water from the dam to more than 118,000 acres of crop, livestock, and dairy lands. When full, the 525-foot-high structure holds back 1.12 million acre-feet of water, forming a 53-mile-long lake with 310 miles of shoreline.

The lake is known for its largemouth and smallmouth bass, and you'll also find it a reliable fishery for crappie, perch, and catfish. With waters reaching 85 degrees in summer, this is a favorite spot for sunbathing, waterskiing, and boating.

The canyon surrounding the lake contains virtually every color of the rainbow. Along the shore are pinnacles and spires, steep cliffs, and alluvial fans

Coming to and going from Lake Owyhee, you'll pass through a tunnel carved out of solid rock that frames the magnificent redrock and sandstone formations.

coming down to the water's edge, outcroppings hundreds of feet high extending into the lake, and natural caves carved in cliff sides. While the steep, rocky terrain makes hiking difficult, rock hounds searching for thunder eggs and agates are often rewarded for their efforts.

Virtually all of the lake's 53 miles can be explored by boat. The Wild and Scenic section of the river, which feeds the lake, has a reputation for providing whitewater river-running thrills, and is a favorite of fly fishers. In fall this region is open to hunting for ducks, geese, chukar, quail, mule deer, antelope, and bighorn sheep. The pavement ends 5 miles south of the dam.

Lake Owyhee State Park, 2 miles from the entrance, features 31 sites with electricity and 8 tent sites. They are arranged on terraced levels, so every camper has an unobstructed view of the lake. The park sells fuel, ice, and food. **Indian Creek Campground,** also part of the park, has 26 electric and 9 primitive sites and sells food and fuel in summer.

From Lake Owyhee you retrace the last 24 miles through the magnificent canyon. Because of the jumbled landscape and winding road, the views traveling east are significantly different from what you saw coming into the canyon. You may wish to take advantage of numerous wide spots and pullouts for photographs.

Following the Oregon Trail to Vale

Turning north on Lyle Boulevard, the route follows the Oregon Trail 15 miles into Vale. Most of the rolling hills covered with brown grass, sage, and scrub brush are administered by the Bureau of Land Management and leased to local ranchers for grazing. Indian paintbrush, yellow Oregon sunshine, and penstemon brighten the landscape during May. About 6 miles south of town, you cross **Keeney Pass,** a gently rolling hill that did not pose a challenge even for wagon trains. BLM information boards highlight Indian conflicts along the trail, costs and amounts of clothing needed for the journey, types of wagons, and the role of mules and oxen. You can see the original trail ruts from the information center; a short trail leads to the ruts and over the hill. The grave site of one of the thousands who died on the trail is a couple miles north of Keeney Pass.

Vale, with about 1,880 people, is the Malheur County seat and an agribusiness center with fertilizer-blending plants, a grain elevator, several feedlots, and Oregon's top-volume livestock sales barn. Sites linked to the Oregon Trail include an emigrant grave and a marker on the courthouse lawn placed by Ezra Meeker, who led a wagon train west in 1845 and retraced the route in 1906. **The Rinehart Stone House** was built in 1872. It was the first permanent building in the area, and the community developed around it. It has been a private home, a way station, and a shelter during conflicts with Native Americans. On the National

Register of Historic Places, the house has been converted into a museum and displays period relics, Oregon Trail exhibits, and local crafts. Some 25 murals around town depict scenes from the Oregon Trail. Vale is also a favorite destination of pheasant hunters.

Malheur Crossing, situated on US 26/20 on the eastern edge of town, was a major Oregon Trail campsite. From the riverbanks on cool days, you can see steam rising as hot springs empty into the stream. Most wagon trains spent their first night in Oregon here and used the hot water for bathing and washing clothes.

The crossing was also the departure point for a famous lost wagon train and one of Oregon's most enduring legends. In 1845 a train of 200 people, led by Steven Meek, left the main trail and headed west through the Oregon desert to the Willamette Valley. Several died from lack of food and water when they became lost and wandered for several months through a maze of canyons, dry washes, and mountains. Surviving members claimed to have discovered a gold mine, which they named the Blue Bucket. Although the mine has never been found, the story precipitated a gold rush and the ultimate settling of Malheur County.

Malheur Butte

About 6 miles east of Vale, **Malheur Butte** rises above the mint and seed fields. A dirt side road extends from US 26/20 to its base; undeveloped trails lead to the summit. The butte is the neck of an extinct volcano and was used as a lookout by Native Americans who scouted wagon trains passing by to the west. The rich soils in surrounding fields were deposited as lake sediments between 3 million and 10 million years ago. In 1881 a ditch was dug by hand to irrigate these fields and is still a supply line from the **Malheur River.** You can read about the ditch and the area's agriculture, geography, and geology at a nearby wayside overlook. Fossil leaves found in underlying rocks include avocado and other plants that grow only in a very wet, humid climate, indications that this was once a tropical setting.

South of the highway, approximately 3 miles east of the butte, you'll see Oregon State University's **Malheur Experiment Station.** It is one of 10 substations operated by OSU and researches weed control, blights and diseases, alternative crops, and an assortment of locally produced vegetables to increase yields and improve crop strains. Though there is no formal tour program, visitors are welcome, and researchers explain their work.

After turning north on OR 201, the drive concludes back in Ontario.

Oregon Outback
Scenic Byway

General Description: A 325-mile signed loop through forested mountains, high desert, and rimrock hills.

Special Attractions: Klamath Marsh National Wildlife Refuge, Fort Rock, Summer Lake Wildlife Area, Abert Rim, reservoir lakes, 2 national forests, Collier Memorial State Park, winter recreation, fishing, hunting, hang gliding.

Location: Southeastern Oregon between La Pine, Chiloquin, and Lakeview.

Drive Route Numbers: US 97, Silver Lake Highway (CR 676), OR 31, US 395, OR 140, Sprague River Highway (CR 402).

Travel Season: Routes are open all year. Some side roads are not plowed in winter.

Camping: 1 state park campground with full hookups. 1 national forest service campground along route and several within 5 to 15 miles of route with tables, fire rings, and flush or vault toilets; some with drinking water. Several private RV parks along the route.

Services: All services in Chiloquin and Lakeview. Limited services in Silver Lake, Summer Lake, Paisley, Bly, Beatty, and Sprague River.

Nearby Attractions: Christmas Valley, Hole-in-the-Ground, Crack-in-the-Ground, Lost Forest, Warner Ski Area, Goose Lake Recreation Area, Gearhart Mountain Wilderness, Upper Klamath Lake, Crater Lake National Park.

For More Information: Central Oregon Visitors Association, (800) 800-8334, www.visitcentraloregon.com; Lake County Chamber of Commerce, (541) 947-6040, www.lakecountychamber.org; Fremont-Winema National Forest, (541) 947-2151, www.fs.fed.us/r6/frewin; Bly Ranger District, (541) 353-2427; Paisley Ranger District, (541) 943-3114; Silver Lake Ranger District, (541) 576-2107; Chiloquin District Ranger, (541) 783-4001.

The Route

The route between La Pine and the Oregon-California border at Goose Lake has been designated the **Oregon Outback National Scenic Byway.** You can also join the route at Valley Falls, Lakeview, Klamath Falls, and other points along US 97.

While elevations range from 4,000 to over 5,500 feet, most roads are flat and straight, with gradual climbs and long curves. From its beginnings on the **Silver Lake Highway,** the route travels through farmland and marshes, into forested mountains and by buttes, and then descends to sagebrush and grasslands near **Silver Lake.** Between Silver Lake and Valley Falls, it roughly follows John C. Fremont's route by staying on lowlands in the shadow of **Winter Rim** while traveling by desert, dead lakes, and huge corporate cattle ranches. The return west from **Lakeview** is through sparse forests in high mountain passes, pasturelands, and thick forest near **Chiloquin.**

Oregon Outback Scenic Byway

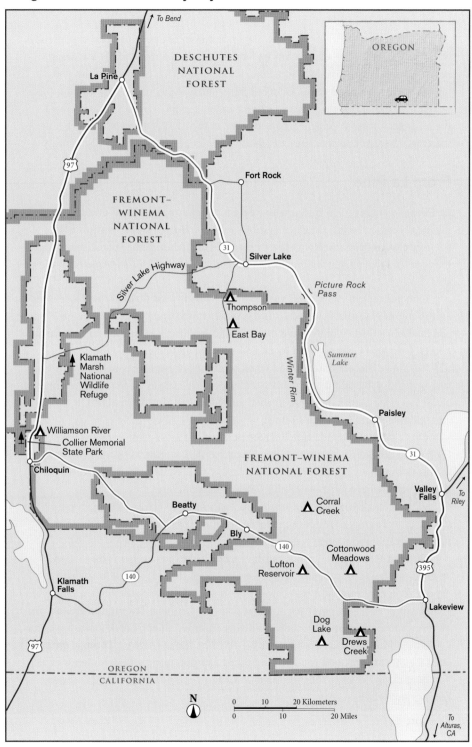

In 1843 John C. Fremont noted the extremes in temperature and topography when he wrote that his expedition was snowbound on a ridge while the desert below was bathed in summer sunshine. He named the ridge Winter Rim and the area below Summer Lake. Generally the high altitude brings warm but not unbearably hot summers, ranging from an average of 67 degrees in Lakeview to the mid-80s for the region. Winters average in the high 30s but often fall below freezing. Average temperatures are about 60 degrees in spring and 67 in autumn.

From La Pine

La Pine is a center for mountain and desert recreation, attracting hunters, anglers, hikers, bikers, campers, skiers, and snowmobilers. **Rosland Recreation Site,** 0.5 mile east on Rosland Road, is a Bureau of Land Management facility with 3.5 miles of trails in a beginner and advanced play area for ATVs and free camping on site.

One mile south of La Pine, you take OR 31 southeast through the Deschutes and Fremont National Forests. As forest gives way to grass, sage, and desert, you can take a brief side trip by leaving OR 31 and heading 8 miles east to Fort Rock and Hole-in-the-Ground. **Fort Rock** is the rim of an ancient volcano that rises 325 feet above the plain. It formed when molten rock burst through a prehistoric lake bed and solidified into a giant circular rim. Over time the south face eroded away, leaving a giant horseshoe-shaped amphitheater approximately 325 feet high and 0.3 mile wide. Trails lead into it.

Other sites nearby include **Fort Rock Cave,** an important archaeological site (excavated artifacts indicate this area was inhabited at least 9,000 years ago); **Hole-in-the-Ground,** a volcanic crater 1 mile across and 300 feet deep; and **Crack-in-the-Ground,** a narrow, 2-mile-long, 70-foot-deep chasm.

At Fort Rock you have the option of continuing to Silver Lake via a return to OR 31 or by taking 17 miles of gravel road south. The "lake" is a dry basin that fills with water about once every 30 years.

Duncan Reservoir, 5 miles south of Silver Lake, generally produces good stocked rainbow trout fishing. The no-wake lake is good for small boats and canoes. You can overnight in 4 campsites on the lake's west side or in a south-end group camp. April and May are the best fishing months at **Thompson Reservoir,** 18 miles south, as it usually runs dry during summer. Silver Creek flows out of the reservoir and is a redband wild trout fishery. The forest service's **Thompson and East Bay Campgrounds** total 36 single and 2 double sites with drinking water and boat ramps. Check with the Silver Lake Ranger Station for road conditions, fishing, and wildlife areas.

Picture Rock Pass

The 50 miles south to Paisley begins with vast expanses of sage and juniper desert framed by buttes and ridges. After 13 miles the road makes a gentle climb over **Picture Rock Pass.** At the 4,830-foot summit, a short trail takes you west from the pullout to a rock wall decorated with ancient Indian petroglyphs. The viewpoint affords a sweeping view of Ana Reservoir and Summer Lake in the desert below with the Winter Rim (also called Winter Ridge) fault block towering 3,000 feet above them. **Ana Reservoir,** fed by large freshwater springs, is one of the area's better rainbow trout lakes. White-striped hybrid bass grow fat feeding on tui chubs; the bass were introduced to control the chubs. Though there are no formal camping areas, camping is permitted around the perimeter.

Summer Lake

Summer Lake, with a store, cafe, RV park, cabin rentals, and a bed-and-breakfast, sits between its namesake and Winter Rim. A wayside with restrooms commemorates the Fremont expedition, which camped here on December 16, 1843, and included Kit Carson and Tom Fitzpatrick as scouts and guides. Their reports encouraged others to migrate to the Oregon country.

At **Summer Lake Wildlife Area,** near the wayside, 18,000 acres of marsh, potholes, and dry brushland provide breeding and resting areas for Pacific Flyway birds. Over 250 species of birds congregate here. You may see Lewis woodpeckers, larks, black terns, Franklin gulls, trumpeter swans, owls, kingfishers, tundra swans, curlews, and cranes. In autumn parts of the refuge open for duck and geese hunting. The 8.3-mile tour route through the area closes during hunting season.

The road continues south between Winter Rim and 20-mile-long **Summer Lake.** With a high alkali content and a depth of 4 to 5 feet, Summer Lake is too shallow for boating, contains no fish, and sometimes dries up completely during summer. A picturesque, classic one-room schoolhouse, built in 1890, is situated west of the highway about 4 miles south of town. **Slide Mountain Geologic Area,** at Winter Rim's southern end, is a remnant of a dome-shaped volcano. Thousands of years ago the entire north face collapsed, exposing the interior and leaving a huge pile of debris at its base.

Summer Lake Hot Springs, 5.7 miles north of Paisley, overlooks the lake and caters to campers with a 15-by-30-foot enclosed pool fed by 106- to 118-degree hot springs. Accommodations include tent sites, full-hookup RV sites, a three-bedroom ranch house, and a two-bedroom house.

Paisley

At **Paisley** the route makes the first of several crossings of the rainbow trout–stocked **Chewaucan River.** The community includes a trailer park, a motel, a state-owned private-plane airstrip with a 4,400-foot paved runway, and public shooting range. Ten buildings in the Paisley Ranger Station compound were built by the Civilian Conservation Corps in 1938–1939 and are on the National Register of Historic Places.

Continuing southeast, you'll cross land owned or leased by the **ZX Ranch.** It is the Northwest's largest ranch and includes more than 1.4 million acres of private and government permit land. Three other ranches in the area have been owned by the same families for over 100 years. On the 22 miles to Valley Falls, the highway cuts through sagebrush-covered rolling hills and mesas that change during the day from browns to a variety of blues and dark yellows.

Valley Falls

OR 31 ends at **Valley Falls,** where you'll find a general store and RV park. Looking east from the store, you can see **Abert Rim,** named by Fremont for one of his party. The 30-mile-long fault escarpment rises 2,000 feet above the desert floor and is topped with a sheer 800-foot lava cover. Forest service and Bureau of Land Management personnel have installed facilities at the southern end to accommodate the increasing numbers of hang gliders who use it for launchings.

Taking US 395 south, the route passes **Chandler Station Ranch,** which is preserved with turn-of-the-20th-century furnishings. Nearby, **Chandler Wayside State Park** provides a refreshing break with picnic tables by a small stream.

Reaching a junction with OR 140, which heads east to **Warner Mountain Ski Area** and **Hart Mountain National Antelope Refuge,** US 395 merges with OR 140 West. They remain a joint route for the 6 miles to Lakeview.

Warner Ski Area, 10 miles east of Lakeview, is owned by Lake County and operated by a nonprofit ski club. It is one of Oregon's oldest ski areas and is known for its light and dry snow. There are 22 runs and over 200 acres of terrain.

Lakeview

Oregon's only geyser sits along the highway 1 mile north of town and across the road from **Fremont National Forest Ranger Station.** Part of a resort complex with a motel and two hot spring–fed pools, **Old Perpetual** traditionally shot 60 feet into the air every 90 seconds. By the 1990s watchers were sometimes waiting more than half an hour, as droughts and drilling had altered the schedule.

At 4,800 feet, **Lakeview** bills itself as Oregon's tallest town and the hang-gliding capital of the West. The buttes, mountains, and faults surrounding flat-lands and often-perfect wind conditions attract hang gliders from throughout the nation.

Goose Lake State Recreation Site, 14 miles south of Lakeview, straddles the Oregon-California border. At the lake you can camp in 47 electrical sites and watch a variety of wildlife. The Oregon Scenic Byway portion ends here at Goose Lake State Recreation Area.

Mountains & Valleys

As OR 140 leaves Lakeview by climbing **Oregon Tunnel Hill summit** at 4,863 feet, side roads lead 5 and 18 miles south to Little Cottonwood and Drews Reservoirs. **Cottonwood** is home to a variety of fish, including brook and rainbow trout. Two forest service campgrounds offer 21 sites near hiking trails and boat ramps. Cast your line in **Drews Reservoir** and the rewards are uncertain. You may land a bullhead, crappie, trout, or 10-pound channel catfish. **Drews Creek Campground** features 5 family units and 2 group sites.

During the next 20 miles, the drive dips into the **Drews Valley,** reenters Fremont National Forest, climbs **Drews Gap** at 5,306 feet, then reaches its highest point of 5,504 feet at **Quartz Mountain Pass.** A network of cross-country ski and snowmobile trails that range from 3 to 21 miles in length start near the summit. Other popular snowmobile routes begin at **Cottonwood Meadows,** 24 miles west of Lakeview, and end in Drews Valley. Cottonwood Meadows, 8 miles north of OR 140 via FR 3870, includes a 21-unit family campground, boating facilities, fishing for stocked rainbows, and 3 trailheads into the surrounding area.

Lofton Reservoir Recreation Area

Other side roads head south 9 miles to the **Lofton Reservoir Recreation Area** and north 17 miles to Corral Creek Campground and the Gearhart Mountain Wilderness.

In addition to a 26-unit forest service campground in a scenic lake and woodland setting, Lofton features fishing for stocked rainbow trout, electric motorboating, and a good chance of seeing deer, elk, muskrats, and bald eagles. As the name implies, horses are allowed at **Corral Creek,** where you camp in 6 tent/trailer sites. Fishing the **Sprague River,** photographing deer and elk, and hiking into the 22,823-acre **Gearhart Mountain Wilderness** are camp-based activities.

The wilderness centerpiece is **Gearhart Mountain,** a broad sloping network of ridges, glaciers, and streams topped by craggy cliffs. Elevations range from

5,900 feet at Corral Creek to 8,364 feet at the summit. The Chewaucan and North and South Forks of the Sprague River originate in the wilderness.

After **Quartz Mountain** the scenery opens to plateau meadows, ringed with ponderosa and lodgepole pines, isolated islands of trees, and distant high, round, dry-grass-covered mountains. **Fremont Forest Sprague River Picnic Area,** 8 miles west, provides a perfect spot for enjoying the scenery while swimming and fishing the Sprague River for brown and rainbow trout.

Bly

Bly Ranger Station, 4 miles west, exhibits Civilian Conservation Corps stone-work and rustic architecture. Eight structures, built between 1936 and 1942, are on the National Register of Historic Places. During World War II the Japanese dropped a balloon bomb near Bly, killing six people, and causing the war's only known civilian casualties in the continental US. The **Mitchell Monument Shrapnel Tree,** a ponderosa pine located approximately 9 miles east of Bly on FR 34, marks the spot where the bomb hit. The monument honors Reverend Archie Mitchell and his wife, who had taken five children from his Sunday school on a picnic and fishing outing here. Apparently the bomb was small and did not detonate on impact. One of the children picked the bomb up and it exploded killing all five plus Mrs. Mitchell.

West of **Bly,** the drive continues on top of the plateau as it follows the Sprague River 13 miles to Beatty. Turning northwest onto Sprague River Road, the scene changes from sparse forest with a sagebrush and dry-grass ground cover to 9 miles of farmlands with grazing cattle ringed by distant low mountain slopes. After the community of Sprague River, the route follows the river through a picturesque gorge and reenters the **Fremont-Winema National Forest.** At Chiloquin, it turns north onto US 97.

Collier Memorial State Park

Five miles north, **Collier Memorial State Park** straddles the highway. A campground with 50 full-hookup and 18 tent sites, plus a 4-corral primitive horse camp, sits on the bank of the **Williamson River.** The west-side day-use area in a tall ponderosa forest offers relocated pioneer cabins with artifacts and an extensive collection of historic logging equipment ranging from high-wheel skidders to locomotives. A 0.5-mile nature trail winds through the village and along rippling Spring Creek, which is known for its trout fishing.

Watch for deer as US 97 heads north through the thick forest to the Silver Lake Highway.

Klamath Marsh

Klamath Marsh National Wildlife Refuge, a few miles east of US 97 on the Silver Lake Highway, is an important nesting, feeding, and resting area for geese, sandhill cranes, yellow rails, and a variety of waterfowl, shorebirds, and raptors. The refuge was established when land was bought in 1958 from the Klamath Indians. Later expansions brought the total area to 40,626 acres and a name change from Klamath Forest National Wildlife Refuge to Klamath Marsh.

From **Klamath Marsh** you have several options. The 41-mile Silver Lake Highway continues east, climbing into the mountains and the 2.3 million–acre Fremont-Winema National Forest while passing cider pits, buttes, and meadows, and completing the loop back at the community of Silver Lake.

Unpaved forest service roads branch off the main highway for access to fishing, mountain hiking, and snowmobiling. **Jackson Creek Campground,** 15 miles east of the refuge and 5 miles southeast on FR 49, offers 12 tent/trailer sites in a secluded forested setting at 4,500 feet. Watch for antelope, elk, and mule deer as the highway continues through the national forest and descends from high ridges to Bear Meadows and Antelope Meadows.

Other options are to return to US 97 and continue north through the Deschutes National Forest to complete the loop back at La Pine, or to head west to Crater Lake National Park via several access roads from the main highway.

Malheur Wildlife Refuge, Diamond Craters

General Description: A 161-mile loop through the Malheur Wildlife Refuge and the Diamond Craters Outstanding Natural Area.

Special Attractions: Malheur National Wildlife Refuge, Diamond Craters Outstanding Natural Area, Frenchglen Hotel, Peter French P Ranch and Round Barns, Harney Lake, Malheur Lake, wildlife, rock formations, historic sites.

Location: Eastern Oregon between Burns and Frenchglen.

Drive Route Numbers: OR 78, OR 205, Center Patrol Road, Harney County Roads.

Travel Season: Routes are open all year. Flooding often necessitates detours and gravel road route changes. Check with refuge headquarters on road conditions. While there is wildlife at Malheur all year, migrations are greatest in late March, September, and October.

Camping: No campgrounds on the route. The Bureau of Land Management maintains 3 campgrounds from 4 to 18 miles southeast of Frenchglen on the Steens Mountain access road.

Services: All services in Burns. Limited services at Malheur Field Station, Frenchglen, Diamond, Princeton, Crane, and Lawen.

Nearby Attractions: Steens Mountain, Kiger Gorge, Wild and Scenic Donner und Blitzen River, Alvord Desert.

For More Information: Harney County Chamber of Commerce, (541) 573-2636, www.harneycounty.com; Malheur National Wildlife Refuge, (541) 493-2612, www .fws.gov/malheur; Malheur Field Station, (541) 493-2629, www.malheurfieldstation. org; Frenchglen Hotel State Heritage Site, (541) 493-2825, (800) 551-6949, www .oregonstateparks.org; Bureau of Land Management (Burns District), (541) 573-4400, www.blm.gov/or/districts/burns.

The Route

Malheur National Wildlife Refuge is situated in southeastern Oregon's high desert country. Although the elevation is 4,100 feet, the roads are flat and straight. Throughout the drive the scenery is a mixture of alkali flats, rimrocks, and sagebrush-covered hills, with the distant Steens Mountain on the southern horizon. Along the roadside you'll see extensive marshes, meadows, and riparian areas. While OR 205, OR 78, and Diamond Lane are paved, prime wildlife viewing areas are on long stretches of gravel; side roads into **Diamond Craters** are dirt.

Be prepared for extremes in temperatures. Freezing is common September through May. Summers zoom into the 90s and over 100 degrees. If you visit during summer, bring mosquito repellent and drinking water. In autumn temperatures average about 67 degrees.

Malheur Wildlife Refuge, Diamond Craters

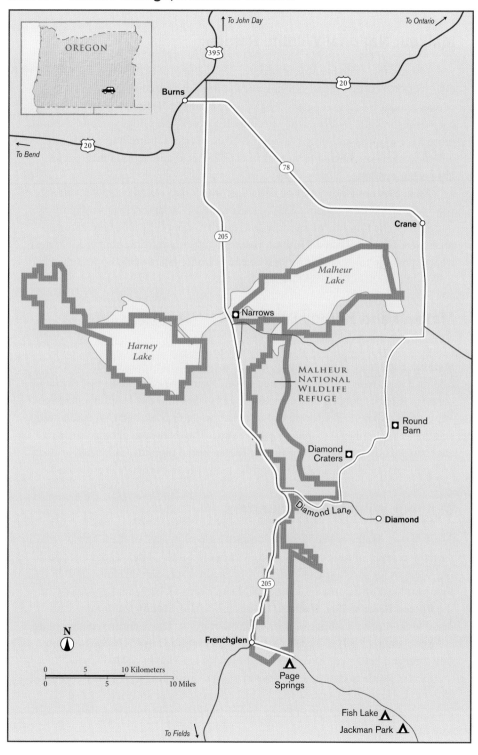

Malheur National Wildlife Refuge

From **Burns** the route heads southeast for 2 miles on OR 8, then turns south on OR 205. After cutting through 9 miles of flat hay fields, it climbs a ridge rimmed with columnar basalt and enters 185,000-acre **Malheur National Wildlife Refuge.** Established in 1908 by President Theodore Roosevelt, the refuge extends south for more than 40 miles and preserves several lakes, marshes, numerous ponds, and hills as a migratory bird sanctuary. A total of 287 bird and 58 mammal species have been seen here.

From a summit viewpoint on the ridge, which fans out like a tilted table top, your panoramic view encompasses vast expanses of flat desert sagebrush and bunchgrass, the thin line of highway, and gently rolling hills. The land and rim-rocks were formed about 2.9 million years ago, when a volcanic vent erupted near what is now the town of Burns. Pumice and volcanic ash covered approximately 7,000 square miles in a layer 30 to 130 feet thick.

Malheur and Harney Lakes

About 12 miles south you cross **The Narrows,** a thin strip of land that separates **Malheur Lake,** east of the highway, and Harney and Mud Lakes on the west. A side road leads west 7 miles to **Harney Lake.** During the early 1980s three years of heavy snowpacks flooded the basin, turning the lakes into one huge inland sea covering 180,000 acres and creating Oregon's largest natural lake. Dry years followed, and the waters returned to their original basins. The rising and ebbing waters created new islands and uncovered ancient Indian burial grounds, campsites, artifacts and gem-quality agates. Collecting organic materials and artifacts is prohibited.

Malheur Wildlife Headquarters

A side trip to **Malheur Wildlife Headquarters,** 6 miles east of the highway on a partially paved and rough gravel road, is virtually a must. The refuge issues birding hot-spot tip sheets and checklists. A museum displays approximately 200 mounted local birds, and a 0.4-mile trail to an overlook presents a good view of the **Blitzen River Valley, Malheur Lake,** and distant **Steens Mountain.** Various trees and shrubs attract warblers and other birds. The headquarters buildings were constructed in 1933 by the Civilian Conservation Corps. The visitor center, museum, and restrooms have been upgraded for wheelchair accessibility.

If you decide to continue on paved OR 205, during the next 15 miles you will climb more low ridges—some framed by columnar basalt and rimrocks—pass cattle grazing areas, and possibly see cranes, ducks, and scattered wildlife in roadside marshes.

Center Patrol Road

Graveled **Center Patrol Road,** which begins at the midpoint of the headquarters' access road and parallels OR 205 and the **Donner und Blitzen River,** offers a slower pace and a better chance of seeing wildlife. The river was named by an 1864 cavalry company. After enduring a thunderstorm here, they named one channel Dunder and the other Blitzen, German for "thunder" and "lightning." Later the name was Anglicized to Donner. The river is often simply called Blitzen.

Center Patrol Road starts with **Malheur Field Station,** which provides hostel and dormitory facilities to individuals and educational groups, and **Wright's Pond,** a Canada geese and redhead duck nesting area. Topping a low hill, the road continues south through hay fields and marshlands. Beaver dams, which sometimes interfere with water flow and must be removed, may be seen near stands of riverbank willows. **Rattlesnake Butte,** a lava-shaped cinder cone east of the highway, was a major Native American campsite. The area south of it was homesteaded in the 1880s. You may see deer and ducks feeding on hay and seeds in this area.

Buena Vista Ponds & Krumbo Reservoir

Buena Vista Ponds, accessible by a connecting road to OR 205, are spring and summer nesting areas for trumpeter swans; a summer stop for white pelicans, great blue herons, and egrets; and a staging site for mid-November migrating waterfowl. A dike separates the ponds and divides the area into nesting and feeding sections for cranes, ducks, geese, blackbirds, and other birds that also use the ponds. A viewpoint on a lichen-covered steep bluff offers an overview of the ponds with Steens Mountain in the background.

Rejoining OR 205, the route passes through grazing land with horse corrals, juniper- and sage-covered hills, and a canyon with striking columnar basalt walls. At roadside pullouts take time to scan the columns slowly. You may see mud swallow nests, wood rats, and the threatened prairie falcon. Golden eagles and bobcats, which usually prowl under cover of darkness, also inhabit the rimrocks.

On the 4 miles of dirt road east to **Krumbo Reservoir,** take time to search out fading Indian petroglyphs, or rock carvings, made centuries ago. At the lake, surrounded by juniper-covered hills, you can fish from boat or shore for trout, warmwater bass, and crappie.

At **Benson Pond,** a mile south of Krumbo's access road, cottonwood trees shade mirror-smooth water. The area offers a good chance of seeing mule deer, coyotes, great-horned owls, orioles, and an assortment of ducks.

Frenchglen & Steens Mountain

Frenchglen, 10 miles south, has gas, a general store, and a private campground. The **Frenchglen Hotel,** built in 1914, is an Oregon State Heritage site. Operated by a concessionaire, it offers 8 rooms, and meals. **Steens Mountain Resort** offers year-round camping in 37 full-hookup and 39 water and electrical sites.

From Frenchglen a rough dirt road heads east up and around Steens Mountain, a rugged 30-mile-long fault block with glacier-carved hanging valleys, spectacular gorges, and alpine lakes. It should not be attempted with long trailers or low-clearance vehicles. Heavy-duty four-wheel drives are best for this route.

The first 3 miles to BLM's **Page Springs Campground** are easily passable by any vehicle. The campground has 36 sites with water and pit toilets near the Wild and Scenic Donner und Blitzen River. It has been upgraded to provide accessible restrooms, water lines, and fixtures. **P Ranch Barn,** 2 miles east of Frenchglen on this road, represents the last remnants of the cattle empire of Peter French. Before he was killed by a competitor in 1897, French's land totaled 132,000 acres and included most of the wildlife refuge. The site contains the chimney of his ranch house, several willow fences, and the barn, which was built in 1876. Sandhill cranes, Canada geese, red-tailed hawks, and roosting wild turkeys are often seen here.

From the ranch at the refuge's southern boundary, you can return by a gravel road along the Donner und Blitzen Canal and several ponds or retrace OR 205 north 17 miles to Diamond Lane.

Diamond Lane (CR 409) crosses the Blitzen River and meanders east to Diamond Junction through 6 miles of hay fields, alkali flats, and sage-covered flatlands sandwiched between graceful sloping buttes. The community of **Diamond,** 6 miles east on a dirt loop road, dates to the 1870s and at its peak had a population of about 50 people. Services include a store and a hotel, built in 1898. Three rooms have private baths; five share two baths.

Diamond Craters Outstanding Natural Area

Turning north on CR 404 (Lava Beds Road), the route enters the **Diamond Craters Outstanding Natural Area.** The black craters were formed sometime during the past 25,000 years when molten basalt surfaced through cracks in the earth and spread in a thin layer over a dry lake bed. Before the first layer cooled, more

Take care and proceed with caution if you decide to explore and hike the rough terrain of Diamond Craters Outstanding Natural Area. Licensed by Shutterstock.com.

molten rock was interjected beneath the hardening but pliable surface, forcing the crust upward and creating six structural domes. The area, 4,150 to 4,700 feet above sea level, has been described by geologists as "a museum of basaltic volcanism" containing the "best and most diverse basaltic volcanic features in the US."

During the next 15 miles as the route passes through lava flows, you'll see pressure ridges, shield volcanos, lava tubes, trenches, collapsed craters and calderas, natural bridges, spatter cones, ramparts and ridges, driblet spires, small box-shaped grabens, and volcanic maars, which have filled with water and become small ponds and lakes. If you decide to hike into the lava fields, proceed carefully, for the rock texture varies from smooth to wrinkled, ropy, and billowy. Rocks, from pebbles to room-size boulders that were hurled into the air during eruptions, are everywhere. Park your vehicle only on hard-packed road surfaces, or you may become stuck in loose cinder, volcanic ash, and clay.

Three miles north of Diamond Craters, **Peter French's Round Barn** sits in grand isolation on a flat plain of sagebrush. It was built around 1880 and used for breaking and exercising horses in winter. The conical roof is supported by juniper center posts, braces, and poles. It encloses a stone corral 60 feet in diameter and a track between the corral and outside wall. The barn has become the hub for a visitor center, gift shop, and family museum featuring doll and miniature collections, and local area tours.

Back to Burns

The 50-mile return to **Burns** passes through farmlands covered with hay and roadside marshes where you can sometimes see deer foraging in the tall grass. After exiting the wildlife refuge, the route takes OR 78 through **Princeton, Crane, and Lawen**—small communities, each with a store, gas, and a few residences. **Crystal Crane Hot Springs,** about midway, is a health resort with hot tubs, a naturally heated outdoor swimming pool, 5 rustic cabins, a tent camping area, and RV sites.

Low hills on distant horizons frame the flat fields leading northwest to Burns. The town of about 3,000 residents was named by an early Scottish settler for the poet Robert Burns, who is honored with an annual event featuring a roast beef dinner and Scottish dances. You can learn more about local history by visiting the **Harney County Museum,** which is built on a site that has been occupied by a brewery, laundry, and wrecking yard.

APPENDIX A:
FOR MORE INFORMATION

Convention & Visitor Bureaus & Information Centers

Albany Visitors Association
250 Broadalbin SW, #110
PO Box 965
Albany, OR 97321
(541) 928-0911, (800) 526-2256
www.albanyvisitors.com

Baker County Chamber of Commerce & Visitors Bureau
490 Campbell St.
Baker, OR 97814
(541) 523-5855, (800) 523-5855
www.visitbaker.com

Visit Bend
750 Lava Rd., Suite 160
Bend, OR 97701
(877) 245-8484
www.visitbend.org

Charleston Information Center
Boat Basin Drive and Cape Arago
Highway
PO Box 5735
Charleston, OR 97420
(541) 888-2311 (May–Sept), (800) 824-8486

Eugene, Cascades & Oregon Coast–Travel Lane County
3312 Gateway St.
Springfield, OR 97477
754 Olive St.
Eugene, OR 97401
(541) 484-5307, (800) 547-5445
www.visitlanecounty.org

Washington Country Visitor Association
11000 SW Stratus St., Suite 170
Beaverton, OR 97008
(503) 644-5555
www.visitwashingtoncountyoregon
.com

Coos Bay–North Bend Visitors & Convention Bureau
50 Central Ave.
PO Box 457
Coos Bay, OR 97420
(541) 269-0215, (800) 824-8486
www.oregonsadventurecoast.com

Corvallis Tourism
553 NW Harrison Blvd.
Corvallis, OR 97330
(541) 757-1544, (800) 334-8118
www.visitcorvallis.com

Culver Visitor Information Center
411 First Ave.
Culver, OR 97734
(541) 546-6032

Grants Pass Tourism
1995 NW Vine St.
PO Box 970
Grants Pass, OR 97526
(541) 476-7717
www.visitgrantspass.org

Gresham Area Visitors Association
701 NE Hood St.
Gresham, OR 97030
(503) 665-1131
www.greshamchamber.org

Illinois River Valley Visitor Center
201 Caves Hwy.
PO Box 312
Cave Junction, OR 97523
(541) 592-2631
www.cavejunction.com

Discover Klamath
205 Riverside Dr., Suite B
Klamath Falls, OR 97601
(541) 882-1501, (800) 445-6728
www.discoverklamath.com

Lebanon Area Chamber of Commerce & Visitors Center
1040 Park St.
Lebanon, OR 97355
(541) 258-7164
www.lebanonchamber.org

Lincoln City Visitor and Convention Bureau
801 SW Highway 101, Suite 401
Lincoln City, OR 97367
(541) 996-1274, (800) 452-2151
www.oregoncoast.org

Medford Visitors Information Center
1314 Center Dr.
Medford, OR 97501
(800) 469-6307
www.visitmedford.org

North Bend Information Center
1380 Sherman Ave.
North Bend, OR 97459
(541) 756-4613, (800) 472-9716

Travel Portland Administrative Offices
1000 SW Broadway, Suite 2300
Portland, OR 97205
(503) 275-9750, (800) 962-3700
www.travelportland.com

Travel Visitor Information Center
Pioneer Courthouse Square
701 SW Sixth Ave. at Morrison Street
Portland, OR 97204
(503) 275-8355, (877) 678-5263

Roseburg Visitors Center and Convention Bureau
410 SE Spruce St.
PO Box 1262
Roseburg, OR 97470
(541) 672-9731, (800) 444-9584
www.visitroseburg.com

Travel Salem
181 High St. Northeast
Salem, OR 97301
(503) 581-4325, (800) 874-7012
www.travelsalem.com

Seaside Visitors Bureau
7 N. Roosevelt
Seaside, OR 97138
(503) 738-3097, (888) 306-2326
www.seasideor.com

National Forests

USDA Forest Service
Pacific Northwest Region
333 SW First Ave.
Portland, OR 97204-3440
Reservations: (877) 444-6777
www.fs.fed.us/r6/rec.htm

National Monuments

Cascade-Siskiyou
National Monument
Medford District BLM
3040 Biddle Rd.
Medford, OR 97504
(541) 618-2200
www.blm.gov/or/medford

John Day Fossil Beds
National Monument
32651 Highway 19
Kimberly, OR 97848
(541) 987-2333
www.nps.gov/joda

Newberry Crater
National Monument
Deschutes National Forest
1001 SW Emkay Dr.
Bend, OR 97702
(541) 383-5300
www.fs.usda.gov/goto/ centraloregon/
nnvm

National Recreation & Scenic Areas

Columbia River Gorge
National Scenic Area
902 Wasco St., Suite 200
Hood River, OR 97031
(541) 308-1700
www.fs.usda.gov/crgnsa

Hells Canyon
National Recreation Area
201 E. Second St.
PO Box 905
Joseph, OR 97846
(541) 426-5546, (541) 426-4978
www.fs.fed.us/hellscanyon

National Wildlife Refuges

Klamath Basin
National Wildlife Refuges
4009 Hill Rd.
Tule Lake, CA 96134
(530) 667-2231
www.fws.gov/klamathbasinrefuges

Lewis and Clark
National Wildlife Refuge
46 Steamboat Slough Road
Cathlamet, WA 98612
(360) 795-3915
www.fws.gov/lc

Malheur National Wildlife Refuge
36391 Sodhouse Ln.
Princeton, OR 97721
(541) 493-2612
www.fws.gov/malheur

McKay Creek
National Wildlife Refuge
c/o Mid-Columbia National Wildlife
Refuges
64 Maple St.
Burbank, WA 99323
(509) 546-8303
www.fws.gov/mckaycreek

Oregon Coast
National Wildlife Refuge Complex
2127 Marine Science Dr.
Newport, OR 97365
(541) 867-4550
www.fws.gov/oregoncoast

William L. Finley
National Wildlife Refuge
26208 Finley Refuge Rd.
Corvallis, OR 97333
(541) 757-7236
www.fws.gov/willamettevalley/finley

Oregon State Tourism

Travel Oregon
670 Hawthorne Ave. Southeast,
Suite 240
Salem, OR 97301
(800) 547-7842 (travel information)
www.traveloregon.com

Oregon State Forests & Parks

Oregon Department of Forestry
2600 State St.
Salem, OR 97310
(503) 945-7200 www.oregon.gov/ODF

Oregon State Parks
725 Summer St. Northeast, Suite C
Salem, OR 97301
Information: (800) 551-6949
Reservations: (800) 452-5687
www.oregonstateparks.org

Bureau of Land Management
Oregon State Office
333 SW First Ave.
Portland, OR 97204
(503) 808-6002
www.or.blm.gov

INDEX

INSIDERS' GUIDE®

The acclaimed travel series that has sold more than 2 million copies!

Discover: Your Travel Destination.
Your Home. Your Home-to-Be.

Albuquerque

Anchorage & Southcentral Alaska

Atlanta

Austin

Baltimore

Baton Rouge

Boulder & Rocky Mountain National Park

Branson & the Ozark Mountains

California's Wine Country

Cape Cod & the Islands

Charleston

Charlotte

Chicago

Cincinnati

Civil War Sites in the Eastern Theater

Civil War Sites in the South

Colorado's Mountains

Dallas & Fort Worth

Denver

El Paso

Florida Keys & Key West

Gettysburg

Glacier National Park

Great Smoky Mountains

Greater Fort Lauderdale

Greater Tampa Bay Area

Hampton Roads

Houston

Hudson River Valley

Indianapolis

Jacksonville

Kansas City

Long Island

Louisville

Madison

Maine Coast

Memphis

Myrtle Beach & the Grand Strand

Nashville

New Orleans

New York City

North Carolina's Mountains

North Carolina's Outer Banks

North Carolina's Piedmont Triad

Oklahoma City

Orange County, CA

Oregon Coast

Palm Beach County

Palm Springs

Philadelphia & Pennsylvania Dutch Country

Phoenix

Portland, Maine

Portland, Oregon

Raleigh, Durham & Chapel Hill

Richmond, VA

Reno and Lake Tahoe

St. Louis

San Antonio

Santa Fe

Savannah & Hilton Head

Seattle

Shreveport

South Dakota's Black Hills Badlands

Southwest Florida

Tucson

Tulsa

Twin Cities

Washington, D.C.

Williamsburg & Virginia's Historic Triangle

Yellowstone & Grand Teton

Yosemite

**To order call 800-243-0495
or visit www.Insiders.com**

Regional Travel at Its Best

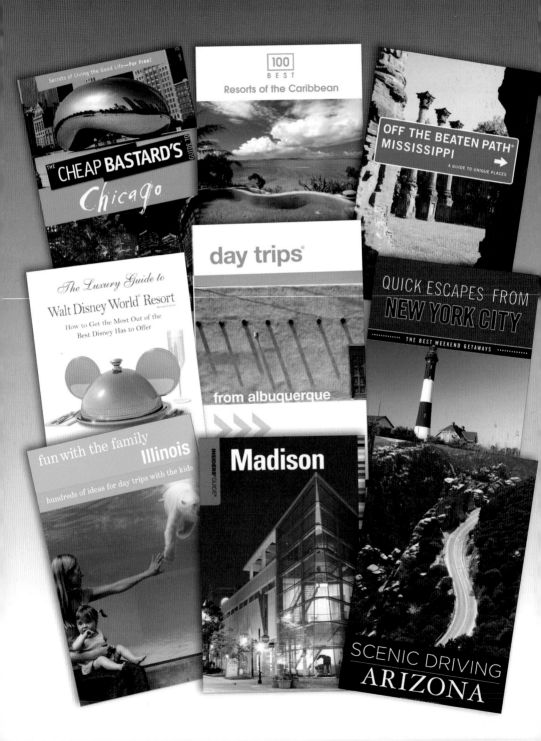